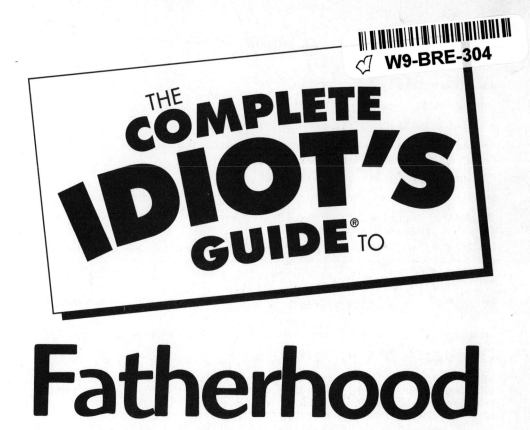

THE COMPLETE IDIOT'S GUIDE TO

Fatherhood

by Kevin Osborn

ALPHA

A member of Penguin Group (USA) Inc.

To Casey, Molly, Ian, and Megan: this father's best teachers.

ALPHA BOOKS

Published by the Penguin Group

Penguin Group (USA) Inc., 375 Hudson Street, New York, New York 10014, USA

Penguin Group (Canada), 90 Eglinton Avenue East, Suite 700, Toronto, Ontario M4P 2Y3, Canada (a division of Pearson Penguin Canada Inc.)

Penguin Books Ltd., 80 Strand, London WC2R 0RL, England

Penguin Ireland, 25 St. Stephen's Green, Dublin 2, Ireland (a division of Penguin Books Ltd.)

Penguin Group (Australia), 250 Camberwell Road, Camberwell, Victoria 3124, Australia (a division of Pearson Australia Group Pty. Ltd.)

Penguin Books India Pvt. Ltd., 11 Community Centre, Panchsheel Park, New Delhi—110 017, India

Penguin Group (NZ), 67 Apollo Drive, Rosedale, North Shore, Auckland 1311, New Zealand (a division of Pearson New Zealand Ltd.)

Penguin Books (South Africa) (Pty.) Ltd., 24 Sturdee Avenue, Rosebank, Johannesburg 2196, South Africa

Penguin Books Ltd., Registered Offices: 80 Strand, London WC2R 0RL, England

Copyright © 2000 by Kevin Osborn

International Standard Book Number: 978-0-02-863189-9
Library of Congress Catalog Card Number: 99-067562

10 09 08   10 9 8

Interpretation of the printing code: The rightmost number of the first series of numbers is the year of the book's printing; the rightmost number of the second series of numbers is the number of the book's printing. For example, a printing code of 00-1 shows that the first printing occurred in 2000.

Printed in the United States of America

Note: This publication contains the opinions and ideas of its author. It is intended to provide helpful and informative material on the subject matter covered. It is sold with the understanding that the author and publisher are not engaged in rendering professional services in the book. If the reader requires personal assistance or advice, a competent professional should be consulted.

The author and publisher specifically disclaim any responsibility for any liability, loss, or risk, personal or otherwise, which is incurred as a consequence, directly or indirectly, of the use and application of any of the contents of this book.

Most Alpha books are available at special quantity discounts for bulk purchases for sales promotions, premiums, fund-raising, or educational use. Special books, or book excerpts, can also be created to fit specific needs.

For details, write: Special Markets, Alpha Books, 375 Hudson Street, New York, NY 10014.

Alpha Development Team

Publisher
Marie Butler-Knight

Associate Managing Editor
Cari Shaw Fischer

Acquisitions Editors
Randy Ladenheim-Gil
Amy Gordon

Development Editors
Phil Kitchel
Amy Zavatto

Assistant Editor
Georgette Blau

Production Team

Development Editor
Jennifer Williams

Production Editor
Mark Enochs

Copy Editors
John Sleeva
Cliff Shubs

Cover Designer
Mike Freeland

Photo Editor
Richard H. Fox

Illustrator
Brian Mac Moyer

Book Designers
Scott Cook and Amy Adams of DesignLab

Indexer
Lisa Lawrence

Layout/Proofreading
Angela Calvert
Terri Edwards

Contents at a Glance

Part 1: The Seeds of Fatherhood: Pregnancy and Childbirth **1**

1 What's Going On in There? 3
What you may be feeling, and what you may fear, upon hearing the news that you're about to become a father.

2 Okay, Where Do I Fit In? 15
Getting involved in your partner's pregnancy and making it real for you.

3 Your Wife Has the Stomach for Labor and Delivery, Do You? 25
Making an informed choice whether to participate in labor and delivery. (Yes, you do have a choice.)

4 Hey, What About Me? 35
Adjusting to your new role as the invisible man—and making sure to take care of your needs.

5 Get Ready, 'Cause Here I Come 47
What to do in the final months of pregnancy—from gassing up the car to planning paternity leave.

6 Choose Your Own Adventure: What Kind of Father Do You Want to Be? 61
Exploring fathering options—from the Family Breadwinner to Mr. Mom.

Part 2: Your Rookie Year: Fathering Infants **77**

7 After Care: Post-Partum Recovery 79
Taking care of yourself, your partner, and your baby as you adjust to new fatherhood.

8 Crying Out for Contact: Soothing and Handling Your Baby 91
Interpreting your baby's cries and taking care of her needs.

9 In One End and Out the Other: Feeding and Cleaning Your Baby 101
Fun with bottle-feeding, spoon-feeding, changing diapers, and bath time.

10 Daddy Doctor 117
Preparing for accidents and medical emergencies, and dealing with everyday illnesses.

11 Making Time for Baby 131
Building a bond with your baby: It just takes time and playfulness.

12 Baby in the Bedroom: Is There Sex After Childbirth? 145
What may stop you from having sex after your partner gives birth—and how you can get started again.

Part 3: Mapping Out Strategies for a Long-Term Parenting Partnership   159

   13 Getting on the Same Page: Parents as Partners   161
       Working together to define goals, identify priorities, resolve conflicts, and help each other be the best parents you can be.

   14 How Much Is This Kid Gonna Cost, Anyway?   175
       What few fathers realize before they have kids: Just how expensive child-rearing can be.

Part 4: Nuts and Bolts: Fathering Toddlers and Preschoolers   193

   15 Helpful Handyman: Childproofing Your Home   195
       Preventive and educational steps you can take to keep your child safe in and around your home.

   16 Beating the Bedtime Blues   211
       Making the transition from wide awake to fast asleep as trouble free as possible.

   17 A Shift in the Balance of Power: The Arrival of Siblings   229
       Preparing for—and dealing with—the arrival of a sibling.

   18 The Serious Business of Child's Play   245
       Why play, toys, games, and even television are important to your child's education—and how to make the most of your playtime together.

Part 5: The Wonder Years: Fathering Older Children   267

   19 Love, Death, and Other Topics of Conversation   269
       Opening the lines of communication with a young child— and keeping them open throughout childhood—on potentially uncomfortable subjects such as sex and death.

   20 Just Wait 'Til Your Father Gets Home   283
       Disciplining your children—and helping them develop self-discipline and a conscience—from twos to teens and in between.

   21 Fun for the Whole Family?   305
       Making the most of weekends, outings, and family vacations.

   22 School Days   317
       Introducing your child to school, sports, and safety with strangers.

   23 Teenage Wasteland   335
       Driving, drinking, drugs, and college applications: No wonder parents and teenagers stop talking to each other.

Appendices

   A Paterniterms: Words You May Need to Know   357

   B Paternal Resources   361

      Index   369

Contents

Part 1: The Seeds of Fatherhood: Pregnancy and Childbirth   **1**

1 What's Going On in There?   **3**

Second That Emotion 4
  Accidents Can Happen 4
  Can You Relate? 5
  How Fat Is Your Wallet? 6
  What Are You Like? 6
What Are You Afraid Of? 7
  What's Wrong with the Baby? 7
  I Can't Handle This Alone! 8
  I Ain't Got No Money, Honey 9
  Ready or Not, Here I Come 10
  I Don't Wanna Share! 11
  I Don't Wanna Die! 11
Spare Some Change? 12
  So What Have You Got to Lose? 12
  Good Grief! 13

2 Okay, Where Do I Fit In?   **15**

Mother's Little Helper 16
  Open Hands and Open Ears 17
  Mop-Up Detail: The First Trimester 18
  Glory Days: The Second Trimester 19
  The Final Stretch and Stretch and Stretch: The Third Trimester 20
Get Real 21
  Overcoming Sensory Deprivation 21
  Getting Your Kicks 22

3 Your Wife Has the Stomach for Labor and Delivery, Do You? 25

To Be or Not to Be in the Delivery Room 25
  Why Should I? 26
  Why Shouldn't I? 27
  Decision Time 29
What Am I Supposed to Do? 30
Go to the Head of the Class 30
  *Women Have Been Giving Birth for Thousands of Years—
  So Why Do We Need a Class?* 31
  It's All in the Timing 32

4 Hey, What About Me?   **35**

The Invisible Man 36
  The Pregnancy No Body Knows 36
  What Happened to That Old Gang of Mine? 36
  Something's Coming Between Us 38
What's Happening to My Body? 39
  Monkey See, Monkey Do 39
  The Shape of Things to Come 40

How the Heck Did Your Partner Get Pregnant Anyway? 41
Navigating a Sexual Obstacle Course 42
You've Lost That Loving Feeling 43
Pregnancy: Turn-Off ...? 43
... Or Turn-On? 44
Let's Get It On 45

5 Get Ready, 'Cause Here I Come   47

It May Not Take a Village, But You Will Need Help 48
Time Off for Good Behavior 48
Help! I Need Somebody 49
What's the Plan? 50
You Need Professional Help! 50
Buy, Buy, Baby 51
All You Need Is Love? 51
What Else Could You Possibly Want? 53
Packed and Ready to Go 54
You Can't Have a Baby without Paperwork 55
What Did You Forget? 55
Lights, Camera, Action? 56
Is There Gas in the Car? 57
So Where's the Baby? 58
The Waiting Game 58
Last Rest Stop for Miles and Miles 59

**6 Choose Your Own Adventure: What Kind of Father
Do You Want to Be?   61**

Typecasting: Filling the Role of Father 62
Rewriting the Roles 64
The Full-Time Breadwinner 65
The Children's Hour 65
The Split Personality 66
Not Enough Hours in the Day 67
Mr. Mom 68
Is Anybody Out There? 69
Maintaining a Balanced Load 70
Wanted: Role Models 70
Memories of Childhood 71
From the Ridiculous to the Sublime: TV Dads 73
Cine-Ma? What About Cine-Pa? 74
On Your Own 76

Part 2: Your Rookie Year: Fathering Infants   77

7 After Care: Post–Partum Recovery   79

I Want to Go Home! 80
Leave It to the Professionals 80
No Sleep for the Weary 81
Getting Your Partner Back on Her Feet 82
Where Are You Taking My Baby? 82

Homeward Bound 83
   Where Does It Hurt? 83
   No Heavy Lifting 84
The Baby Blues 85
   Oh, Mama! 85
   Mother's Little Helper 87
   She's Not the Only One 88
   Getting Away from It All 89

8 Crying Out for Contact: Soothing and Handling Your Baby   **91**

The Crying Game 91
   Okay, So It Loses a Little in Translation 92
   Stop Your Sobbing: Tricks of the Trade 93
   It's Crying Time Again: Colic 97
Handle with Care 98
   No Sudden Movements 98
   Heads Up! 98
   The Neck Bone's Connected to the Head Bone 99

9 In One End and Out the Other: Feeding and Cleaning Your Baby   **101**

What's for Dinner? 101
   The Wonder Dad: Offering Style, Support, and Comfort 102
   It's 3 A.M. Do You Know Where Your Baby Is? 103
   Pass the Bottle This Way, Pal 103
   A Formula for Success 104
   Spoon-Feeding 105
Cleanliness Is Next to Impossible 107
   It's a Dirty Job, But Somebody's Got to Do It 108
   Get Ready, Get Set … 109
   … Go! 109
   All Red in the Cheeks 110
   Call in the Toxic Waste Crew 110
   We're Having Some Fun Now, Aren't We? 111
Super Soakers: Bath Time 111
   Little by Little: Sponge Baths 111
   Sink or Swim 113
   Tubby Time Is Fun Time 114

10 Daddy Doctor   **117**

Daddy, I Don't Feel So Good 118
   Is There a Doctor in the House? 118
   Patience! Patients! 119
   Calling for Reinforcements 119
   Tell Me Where It Hurts 121
Playing Doctor 122
   The Daddy-Doctor Motto: Be Prepared 122
   Home Remedies 124
   A Spoonful of Sugar 125

In Case of Emergency 126
   Ready for Anything? 126
   Are Your Papers in Order? 127
   The ABCs of CPR 127

11 Making Time for Baby   **131**

Take Your Time, 007 133
   The Stranger Among Us 133
   What's the Rush? 134
   Bonding for Beginners 134
That's Entertainment! 135
   A Feast for the Eyes (and Ears) 136
   Toy Story 137
   Power Trip 139
   Play Nice 140
   By the Book 143

12 Baby in the Bedroom: Is There Sex After Childbirth?   **145**

Ready or Not, Here I Come? 146
   Cleared for Takeoff 146
   Okay, Okay, Don't Rush Me! 147
So What Are You Afraid Of? 148
   You're Such a Pain 149
   Deja Vu? 150
   Three's a Crowd 151
   Everything's Changed 152
In the Mood? 153
   Take Your Time 154
   It's a Date! 154
   Relax, It's Only Sex 155
   Warm-Up Acts 156
   Talk Dirty to Me 157
   Hey, I've Got an Idea! 157
   We Have the Technology 157
   Help! 158

Part 3: Mapping Out Strategies for a Long-Term Parenting Partnership   **159**

13 Getting on the Same Page: Parents as Partners   **161**

Goal Tending 162
   What Do You Want Anyway? 162
   When Worlds Collide: Conflicting Goals 163
   What Do You Think? 163
   Doing the Right Thing 164
Crunch Time: Resolving Conflict 164
   The Art of Persuasion 165
   Mutual Compromise 165
   Deferential Treatment 166
   Lord of the Manor 166

Domestic Goddess 167
Spheres of Influence 167
Okay, Let's Try It Your Way 168
Calling It in the Air 168
Asking an Expert 169
Breaking Up the Mommy Monopoly 170
Cornering the Market 170
On-the-Job Training 171
Learning to Share 172
Play Nice 172

14 How Much Is This Kid Gonna Cost, Anyway? **175**

The *Real* Money Pit 175
Children: A Cost-Benefit Analysis 177
Where's All the Money Going? 177
What You Get for Your Money 179
If You Die, What Will You Do Then? 180
Where There's a Will, There's a Way 181
That's Life Insurance 183
College Bound 185
The High Cost of Higher Learning 185
A Diller, a Dollar, a Quarter-Million-Dollar Scholar 186
Where's All This Money Coming From? 187
Investing Wisely in Education 188

Part 4: Nuts and Bolts: Fathering Toddlers and Preschoolers **193**

15 Helpful Handyman: Childproofing Your Home **195**

Is This Really Necessary? 195
Mini-Magellans and Newtons in the Nursery 196
Right Here, Right Now 196
Staying Out of Touch 197
Locked Up Tight 197
Do Not Enter 199
Keep Away 200
Hazardous Waste 201
Short Falls 202
What Goes Up Must Come Down 202
Avoiding Window Pains 203
Refinishing the Furniture 204
The Heat Is On 205
Don't Get Burned 205
Shock Treatments 206
Where There's Smoke … 206
Something's Out There! 207
Safety First 207
Teach Your Children Well 208
In Case of Emergency… 208
Start All Over Again 209

16 Beating the Bedtime Blues   **211**

Sleeping Like a Baby 212
 Rites of Passage 213
 The Calm Before the Snore 214
Breaking Up Is Hard to Do 215
 *Does Your Child Need You to Stay—Or Merely Want You
  to Stay?* 216
 Making Hard Choices: Which Is the Lesser Evil 216
 Independence Night 218
Things That Go Bump in the Night 219
 Midnight Snackers 219
 Hey! I'm Awake Here! 220
 Exercise Some Restraint (You, Not Your Child) 221
 Little Runaway 222
 Is Three a Crowd in Bed? 223
 Nightmare on Your Street 224
 The All-Night Horror Show 224
 Accidents Happen 225
 Sleep Deprivation 226

17 A Shift in the Balance of Power: The Arrival of Siblings   **229**

The New Math: Two Times One Is Greater Than Two 230
 Juggling and No-Look Passes 230
 Age Differences 231
Is Everybody Ready? 232
 Is Ignorance Really Bliss? 232
 Let's Talk Baby Talk 233
 Accepting the Inevitable 234
 You're Part of This, Too 234
The Final Stretch 235
 Having a Baby Doesn't Change Everything 235
 I Thought You Were Calling the Sitter 236
 Hey, Kid! Want to See Something Really Gross? 237
Take That Thing Back! 237
 Visiting Hours 238
 Coming Home 238
 Will the Real Baby Please Stand Up? 239
 Father's Little Helper 240
Which One of Us Do You Love More? 240
 The New Rival 241
 No Fighting, No Biting 241
 Growing Up Together 242

18 The Serious Business of Child's Play   **245**

Class Is in Session 245
 Setting the Curriculum 246
 Evaluating the Faculty 246
Tips on Toys 247
 His and Her Toys? 248
 Everything Old Is New Again 248

Game Hunting 249
Point-Shaving Scandals 249
Rules of Play 250
It's Only a Game 250
Playing the Part of Playmate 252
Social Play 253
Imagine That! 253
Art for Art's Sake 253
The Wonderful World of Make-Believe 254
Why Do You Think They Call Them Monitors? 255
Welcome to TV Land 256
Too Much TV 256
... Or Too Much Bad TV? 258
Everybody's a Critic 259
Welcome to the Computer Age 260
Screening Software 261
Breeding Readers 262
Learning How to Read to a Child 262
Who Needs Pictures When You've Got a Thousand Words? 263
Tale Spinning 264

Part 5: The Wonder Years: Fathering Older Children   267

19 Love, Death, and Other Topics of Conversation   269

Unspeakable Silence 270
Who Are You Really Protecting? 271
Shhh! If We Don't Say Anything, Maybe It Will Go Away 272
Everything You Know About Sex (But Were Afraid Your
  Child Would Ask) 272
The Body Shop 272
Hint: It Ain't the Stork! 273
Just the Facts, Ma'am 275
Caught in the Act: Handling Embarrassing Situations 275
The Moral of the Story 277
The Talk 278
The Mask of Death 279
Death Is All Around Us 279
Bringing It Home 280
Good Grief 281

20 Just Wait 'Til Your Father Gets Home   283

Sizing Up Your Authority 284
Size Isn't Everything 284
The King Is Dead, Long Live the King 284
Setting Limits: Where It All Begins 285
Ain't Misbehavin' 285
Spare the Rod 286
Tricks of the Trade 287
The Nays Have It 287

Setting the Ground Rules 288
   I Can't Control Myself, So There: Why Your Toddler Misbehaves .. 289
   You Are the Rules 291
   Polite Society 291
   How Would You Feel If …? 292
   Share and Share Alike 293
Finding Punishments That Fit the Crimes 294
   The Hot Seat: Time Out 295
   Might Makes Right? 296
   Making Up Is Hard To Do 296
   Profound Losses 297
The Not-So-Stern Disciplinarian 297
   Whoa, Boy! Controlling Your Own Anger 298
   My Mistake 298
   Listen to Reason 298
What It's All About: Doing the Right Thing 299
   Soaking It All Up 300
   Back-Up Systems in Place 301
Educational Values 302
   Liar, Liar, Pants on Fire 302
   Upping the Ante: Encouraging Responsibility 303

21 Fun for the Whole Family?   **305**

Staying Close to Home 306
   Avoiding Lost Weekends 306
   Outing the Entire Family 307
   Ladies and Gentlemen, and Children of All Ages 308
Vacation, Everybody Wants One 310
   Ah, That's the Spot 310
   Reservations About Lodgings 311
   Adventures Abroad 312
In-Flight Turbulence 312
   Having Reservations Already? 312
   The Terror of Flight 606 314
   Mapping Out a Flight Plan 315
On the Road Again 315

22 School Days   **317**

Off to School 319
   You Have Nothing to Fear but Fear Itself 319
   Rallying the Team 320
   Crisis Management 322
   Have You Done Your Homework? 324
Smart Kids, Safe Kids 326
   A Stupid Rule 327
   Two Smart Rules 328
   No Means No! 328
Soccer Dads 329
   The Only Game in Town 330
   Those Who Can't Play, Coach 331

23 Teenage Wasteland   **335**

How to Talk to a Teenager 336
Turning Down the Heat *337*
Mastering the Approach Shot *337*
Keeping It Going *338*
Driver's Education 340
Easing into the Fast Lane *341*
Your Car, Your Rules *342*
A Model Driver *343*
Volunteering to Be the Designated Driver *343*
Accidents Happen *344*
Dangerous Habits 345
An Ounce (or a Gram) of Prevention *345*
The Rap on Drugs *346*
But Dad, You Drink and Smoke *347*
You're Drunk! *347*
You're Smoking! *348*
You're Stoned! *349*
Give It That Old College Try 349
On the Record *350*
Off the Record *351*
This Is Only a Test. Had This Been a Real Emergency *352*
Narrowing the Field *352*
Apply Yourself *354*

Appendices

A Paterniterms: Words You May Need to Know   **357**

B Paternal Resources   **361**

   Index   **369**

Foreword

The only thing that made me wince in deciding to write the foreword to *The Complete Idiot's Guide to Fatherhood* is the book's title. This is a wonderful book loaded with practical and easy-to-digest information for the expectant and veteran father. Any man choosing to read this book in preparation for fatherhood or to develop his fatherhood skills is surely no idiot. Neither is Kevin Osborn: He has covered it all here from the anxious and exciting period of awaiting a first child through the important developmental periods that follow from birth through the teen years.

I remember participating as actively as I could as I prepared to become a father nine years ago. While my wife was very open to my full participation, I found that the wide range of popular and professional literature, health professionals' attitudes, and other important cultural phenomena were heavily skewed to the mother's experience. While we recognize that women are the ones doing the heavy lifting in giving birth, we must also recognize that fathers are a necessity, not a luxury. We are reawakening to the crucial role that fathers must play if we are to raise caring, strong and healthy children. This pearl of wisdom is thousands of years old but somehow got lost in modern America. While social theorists today debate whether fatherhood is a biological or social construct—whether we fathers are necessary at all—millions of American children are suffering from the lack of a consistent, caring, and loving father in their lives.

This guide to fatherhood will help today's fathers find their way to an active and involved role in the lives of their children. Single fathers, married fathers, and divorced fathers need to know there's no such thing as too much love, caring, and guidance they can give their children. And here's another truism: Fathers are not male mothers. Fathers will find that as they spend time with their children, they'll develop their own unique ways of loving and parenting their children. We relate to our children differently. We help them develop different sets of skills and the ability to cope with a wider range of people and problems if we get involved and stay involved as parents.

The father who reads and applies this book is giving himself, his children and society a gift, making a statement about who and what is important in his life. Like anything worthwhile, fatherhood can be difficult, test our limits and is short on easy answers. Fatherhood is also the most rewarding activity a man can undertake in his life. So get ready to enjoy this book in the service of our noblest and most important role as adults: fatherhood.

—Michael Horowitz, Ph.D.

Michael Horowitz, Ph.D., is the father of Eli, age 9, and Maya, age 6, and the husband of Jeannie Gutierrez, Ph.D. He received his doctorate in Clinical Psychology from Northwestern University and certificate in Psychoanalysis from the Chicago Center for Psychoanalysis. He is Dean and Professor of Clinical Psychology at the Arizona School of Professional Psychology. His teaching and scholarly interests include Adult Development and Parenthood. Dr. Horowitz is the former director of the *Fatherhood Project*, a study of the role of fatherhood in men's lives.

Introduction

"There is no good father, that's the rule. Don't lay the blame on men, but on the bond of paternity, which is rotten. To beget children, nothing better; to have them, what iniquity"

—Jean-Paul Sartre

Cheer up, Jean-Paul, it's not so bad. (Well, what do you expect from an existentialist?) Actually, as you've already found out (or soon will find out), having a child is both a burden and a blessing. No one would deny that, in becoming a father, you have taken on an enormous and important responsibility—and that the weight of this responsibility may sometimes seem crushing. At the same time, however, fatherhood offers unique delights and an unending stream of rewards:

➤ Your baby's beaming smile upon seeing you—a smile so broad it lifts his entire face

➤ The way your toddler shouts "Daddy!" as she runs to greet you

➤ The countless new tricks that your preschooler proudly shows you, and the pride you feel in these demonstrations of incredible intelligence and agility

➤ Your child's happy wave from the stage as she stars in her elementary school's holiday extravaganza

➤ The innumerably humorous ways you can embarrass your preteen, who will seem mortified at the thought of having any father, much less you

➤ The way your adolescent, no matter how hostile he becomes, still knows he can turn to you for help, advice, and support in a pinch

So congratulations on becoming a father (or expecting a child)! It ain't always easy, but it's always worth it.

Any Idiot Can Do It

Almost any idiot can conceive a child; both you and I are proof of that. But actually being a father, that's not nearly as easy. Once you've got a child, what do you do? Sure, you'll love and protect her and hopefully teach her a thing or two, but how will you make the most of the time you and your child have to share?

You may feel some degree of confidence in your ability as a father, but what do you really know about fatherhood? Chances are, you have no experience as a baby-sitter, except perhaps for a younger sibling or two (and even they were probably only a couple of years younger than you). Have you ever held a baby? Have you ever had to figure out why a toddler was crying? Have you had the surreal experience of trying to converse with a four-year-old child?

You may have seldom even thought about what the role of father might mean to you. When you played make-believe as a child, you probably played at being a cop, a robber, a cowboy, an Indian, a Jedi warrior, or a home-run slugger about ten thousand times. But how many times did you pretend to be a daddy? As you got older and imagined what you might do when you grew up, you may have envisioned yourself in any number of different professions. But how many times did you think of yourself as a future father?

Whether you feel totally unprepared for fatherhood or supremely confident, I can predict one thing with certainty: You're in for some surprises in the years to come. You may be surprised that some aspects of fathering come easily, or you may be surprised at how hard some of the "simplest" of parenting tasks seem, but one thing's for certain: The life of a father—and the life of his child—is full of surprises.

On-the-Job Training

You don't need to go through years of school or months of training to be a father. Oh, sure, a training program is essential to prepare someone to be a stockbroker, airline pilot, surgeon, switchboard operator, or fast-food clerk. But fatherhood? We don't offer training for that.

Instead, fatherhood is an intense and never-ending course of on-the-job training. You'll find yourself thrown into situations with little or no preparation and be expected to handle them like an expert in no time at all. Fortunately, if you throw yourself into the role of fatherhood and have as much fun with it as you possibly can, you really can become an expert fairly quickly.

You might not feel like an expert—indeed, you might often feel ill-at-ease—but you will master much more than you give yourself credit for. You will know what your baby wants or needs when she cries (most of the time). You will be able to change a diaper without getting drenched (or worse). You will be able to interpret your child's unique way of expressing himself better than anyone else (with the possible exception of your partner). You will grow accustomed to your child's likes and dislikes.

Who will provide you with your on-the-job training? How will you learn all these fathering skills? If you pay attention, your baby will teach you more than anyone else, and, though sometimes impatient, she will almost always forgive your mistakes along the way. Your wife, who will undergo her own on-the-job training program at the same time, will no doubt share her knowledge with you. (You may be able to teach her a thing or two, as well.) And, hopefully, you can pick up some fathering skills by reading *The Complete Idiot's Guide to Fatherhood*.

This book, which you can think of as an owner's and operator's manual for fathers, offers you essential information and advice that will come in handy as you tackle the many challenges of fatherhood.

In *The Complete Idiot's Guide to Fatherhood*, you will find tips on safely negotiating the challenges of pregnancy, infancy, and childhood from the toddler years to the teenage years. You will discover suggestions on how to handle everything from bottle-feeding to teenage driving, cautions about dangers you'll want to avoid, and advance warnings about common problems you're likely to face. You will also find discussions of the most troubling issues that fathers must confront: from setting and enforcing limits to talking about sex and drugs (and rock and roll), from defining your role as a father to getting your child to sleep on his own.

The Complete Idiot's Guide to Fatherhood will do much more than help you become a confident and competent father. Throughout the book you will find hundreds of practical tips and easy-to-use strategies to help you become the best father you can be. You will discover not only how to help your child learn, but also how you might learn something at the same time. As your child comes into her own, *The Complete Idiot's Guide to Fatherhood* will help you come into your own as a father, too.

The Complete Idiot's Guide to Fatherhood provides hundreds of guidelines, suggestions, and bits of advice. No book, however—no, not even this one—can tell you precisely how to father your child. You have your own style, your own personality, your own way of doing things, no doubt well-established over the last 20, 30, or even 40 years. Your child also will have his or her own unique personality, likes and dislikes, talents and interests. Being a father (and being a child) means developing a relationship, with each of you talking and behaving toward each other in your own unique ways.

With that in mind, if you find any suggestions here that you don't like, feel free to ignore them. Although I would encourage you to try new parenting practices, ideas, or techniques (no matter how foreign they seem) just to see if they work, if you cannot picture yourself doing something, then don't torture yourself with guilt or feelings of inadequacy because you can't do it. The suggestions offered here have worked for me and the many other fathers with whom I've spoken while writing this book. But not everything offered here is guaranteed to work for you and your children. In fact, since every child is an individual, even if something works with one of your children, it might not work for all of them. So if something you find here doesn't work for you and your children, don't do it.

Fathering is an evolving relationship between an adult and a child, not a dogmatic set of rules. So just keep working on that relationship, and you'll become an expert father to your child.

How This Book Is Organized

The Complete Idiot's Guide to Fatherhood aims to make your experience of fatherhood as fun, easy, and gratifying as possible for both you and your child. The book is divided into five parts. Four of the parts address concerns that will come up at particular stages of fatherhood, from your partner's pregnancy to your child's school years. In each of these four parts, you will find information on your child's physical, mental, and emotional development; on health and safety concerns; and on making the most of your time with your child.

Each of the four parts also has special chapters that address the challenges most often faced by fathers during that particular stage of parenthood. Because no child sticks to a rigid schedule of development, however, some of the material in one part may overlap slightly with the concerns of other stages. The suggestions on first aid, for example, though included in the discussion on infancy (Part 2), are no less relevant during the preschool years (Part 4). Similarly, some of the tips on talking to your child about thorny issues such as sex and death, though situated with the material on the school years (Part 5), can be used even before your child turns five or six.

In addition to the four parts that roughly anticipate your child's chronology, Part 3, which is centrally located due to the importance of the issues it covers, addresses issues of special concern for all fathers, no matter how old their children are. This part features information and advice on how to work productively with your partner and how to plan for the high cost of rearing a child.

Part 1, "The Seeds of Fatherhood: Pregnancy and Childbirth," focuses on *your* experience during the nine months leading up to the birth of your baby. You will learn to navigate the transition from being part of a couple to being a father, strengthen your relationship with your partner before the onslaught of early parenthood, help your partner through the more difficult periods of pregnancy, and attend to some of your own needs. (If you don't, no one else will.) You will also find a discussion of what to consider as you decide whether, and how much, to participate in labor and delivery, and some last-minute tips on preparing for the arrival of your baby.

Part 2, "Your Rookie Year: Fathering Infants," covers the basics of baby care: bottle- and spoon-feeding your infant, changing her diaper, bathing her, and keeping her healthy. You will also find advice on how to calm your crying baby and how to remain calm if your baby turns colicky. Finally, you will find tips on how to play with your infant during her first year.

Part 3, "Mapping Out Strategies for a Long-Term Parenting Partnership," offers advice on some problems that will recur time and again throughout your life as a father. It features pointers on how to work effectively with your partner in setting goals, establishing priorities, and resolving conflicts. In addition, Part 3 provides astounding information on how much it costs to rear a child today, and financial guidance to help you cover most of the expenses.

Part 4, "Nuts and Bolts: Fathering Toddlers and Preschoolers," provides guidance that will help you through your child's years of rapid development—from his first steps to his first day at school. You will find pointers on making your home safe for your increasingly mobile toddler. This part offers guidelines on how to play with a young child, as well as suggestions on how to smooth the transition from only child to big brother or sister. In addition, it provides much-needed advice on the issue that plagues all parents of young children: how to get your child to go to sleep by himself—and then sleep through the night.

Part 5, "The Wonder Years: Fathering Older Children," brings up the challenges most often faced during the years from kindergarten to high school graduation. You will find advice on disciplining your child and helping her to develop a conscience. You will find tips on how to open a lifelong conversation on topics such as sex and death. This part also provides guidance on how to make the most of weekends and vacations with your child. Finally, it covers the major issues likely to crop up during your child's elementary and high school years—from working with your child's teachers and coaching her sports teams to coping with teenage rebellion and applying to colleges.

Extras

The Complete Idiot's Guide to Fatherhood not only offers clear, concise information on child development and safety concerns, it offers practical guidance regarding the more difficult challenges that will arise in the course of day-to-day parenting. Throughout the book, you will find a generous supply of fathering tips, words of wit or wisdom, surprising statistics, and odd facts about fatherhood. You can browse through these extras with ease by looking for the following icons:

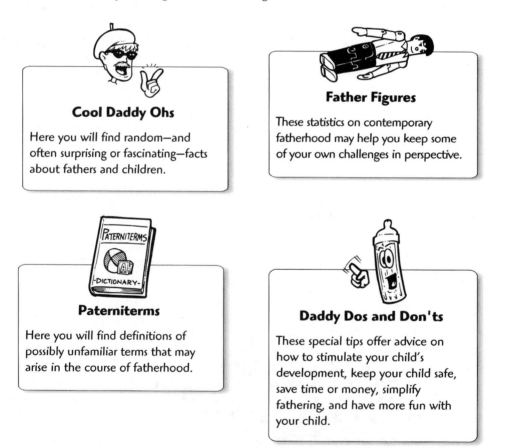

Cool Daddy Ohs

Here you will find random—and often surprising or fascinating—facts about fathers and children.

Father Figures

These statistics on contemporary fatherhood may help you keep some of your own challenges in perspective.

Paterniterms

Here you will find definitions of possibly unfamiliar terms that may arise in the course of fatherhood.

Daddy Dos and Don'ts

These special tips offer advice on how to stimulate your child's development, keep your child safe, save time or money, simplify fathering, and have more fun with your child.

Father Knows Best

These wise and witty observations by fathers (and some mothers) about children and about fatherhood will entertain and enlighten you.

Acknowledgments

I am deeply grateful to a number of people who made substantial contributions to the conception, birth, and fathering of this book. As always, Richard Parks looked out for my best interests throughout this project. Jessica Faust and Bob Schumann had a hand in its development. Tim Kiley of Rainey, Kiley & Associates provided me with a crash course in insurance and financial planning. Keith Boyd, M.D., Director of the Pediatrics and Medicine Residency Program at the Rush-Presbyterian-St. Luke's Medical Center, offered valuable guidance on medical issues. Jennifer Williams offered great patience and much-appreciated editorial advice and guidance. Thank you all.

I'd also like to thank all the fathers who have shared their wisdom and experience with me over the years. You know who you are guys. You've helped me become a better father—and this become a better book.

Finally, I'd like to offer my undying love and appreciation to Susan Kiley, who has taught me more about good parenting than anyone, and to our children, Megan, Ian, Molly, and Casey, for allowing me to practice parenting on them, for better or for worse. They've taught me more than I can say.

Trademarks

All terms mentioned in this book that are known to be or are suspected of being trademarks or service marks have been appropriately capitalized. Alpha Books and Penguin Group (USA) Inc. cannot attest to the accuracy of this information. Use of a term in this book should not be regarded as affecting the validity of any trademark or service mark.

Part 1

The Seeds of Fatherhood: Pregnancy and Childbirth

Hey, great, your wife is pregnant! No doubt by now she has that pregnancy "glow" that comes from puking her guts out night and day, sleeping fitfully, and sweating up a storm.

So how are you *feeling? (I just thought I'd ask, since God knows no one else will.) If you feel unprepared or overwhelmed, join the club. Pregnancy demands a tremendous emotional and psychological adjustment—and not just for mothers.*

Besides getting used to the idea of becoming a father—whatever that means—you need to help your partner cope with her discomfort and volatile emotions. What's more, you need to prepare yourself and your home for the imminent arrival of your new baby.

Look on the bright side, though: Pregnancy lasts only nine months. What follows, fatherhood, lasts a lifetime.

Chapter 1

What's Going On in There?

In This Chapter

➤ Common—and often ambivalent—feelings of expectant fathers

➤ The different factors—from the strength of your relationship with your partner to your financial security—that might influence your feelings about fatherhood

➤ The fears of expectant fathers—and what you can (and can't) do about them

➤ Preparing emotionally for the big changes to come

➤ Celebrating the gains and mourning the losses brought on by pregnancy and upcoming paternity

---

Congratulations! You're going to have a baby! That's great! You must be thrilled. I'll bet you can't wait to see the new life you and your partner have created. By the way, how's your wife feeling? Not too bad yet? That's good. Wow, a baby! That's terrific. Again, congratulations. Your life will never be the same again.

If you've recently learned you're about to become a father (and if you're reading this chapter, you no doubt are) and have shared the news with friends, family members, or colleagues, you've probably heard most of the preceding sentiments. Everyone you tell about your partner's pregnancy will take it for granted that you're thrilled at the prospect of starting a family.

And it's true, you probably are excited. After all, you and your partner have created what will soon be a living, breathing child—a creation that almost everyone regards as miraculous.

But having a baby—especially a first baby—is a monumental event. Your life really will never be the same again. So though you may truly feel joy, awe, and excitement about the pregnancy, in all likelihood, you feel much more ambivalent about your upcoming fatherhood.

So in addition to offering congratulations, let me be the first—and perhaps the only—person to ask: How do *you* feel about the pregnancy?

Second That Emotion

The immediate circumstances of your life cannot help but influence your feelings about becoming a father. So how you feel overall about your partner's pregnancy (and your own status as the father-to-be) is probably not a simple thing. Some of the major factors that may have an impact on how you feel about the pregnancy include:

➤ How your partner became pregnant

➤ The nature of your relationship with your partner

➤ Your current financial state

➤ Your personality and personal history

Although other elements may also influence your feelings about the pregnancy, these major factors deserve a closer look. If you've seldom taken the time to analyze or pin down your emotions, your partner's pregnancy provides you with an ideal opportunity. Not only is the news of upcoming fatherhood likely to release a flood of emotions (many of them conflicting), but you have a full nine months to examine and deal with these feelings before the actual event arrives. So as you read the next sections, think how they might apply to what you are feeling.

Father Knows Best

"Most of us become parents long before we have stopped being children."

—Mignon McLaughlin

Accidents Can Happen

The way in which your partner got pregnant has an enormous influence on the way you're likely to feel about fatherhood. If you and your wife planned this pregnancy, think how differently you would feel if it were an accident. If you and your partner have been planning the timing of this pregnancy for years, for instance, or if you've been trying to get pregnant for many, many months, you probably feel some combination of joy, relief, self-satisfaction, pride, excitement, and great love for your wife. That's not all you're likely to be feeling; other factors certainly come into play, too. But you will no doubt share at least some of these emotions.

Father Knows Best

"The new father … feels that his mere impregnation of his mate, done every day by otters and apes, is Olympic gold medal stuff."

—Bill Cosby

By contrast, if this pregnancy began as an accident—a ripped condom, a cracked diaphragm, a poorly timed sexual adventure without contraceptives, or some other birth control failure—you most likely still feel some degree of shock, fear, anger, and ambivalence. To make matters worse, you probably feel guilty about having these emotions.

You may even mistrust your partner, wondering whether she became pregnant "accidentally on purpose." You and your partner may have had to decide whether to keep the baby at all. Worst of all, if your partner decided to go ahead with the pregnancy despite your wishes, you can add a sense of betrayal and resentment to your anger and fear.

Can You Relate?

The strength of your relationship with your partner will also influence your feelings about pregnancy and fatherhood. Some couples, for example, decide to have a baby in a last-ditch attempt to fix a failing marriage (or relationship). This kind of pregnancy may prompt feelings of hopeful anticipation, renewed closeness, anxiety, or uncertainty.

Other couples decide to get pregnant at a time when their relationship has never been better, when each feels a powerful and unshakable love for the other. In this case, the pregnancy is likely to spark eagerness and even deeper love. At the same time, however, it may give rise to fears that having a baby will interfere with or diminish your love for each other, that the baby will disturb the idyllic life the two of you have carved out for each other. (See Chapters 12 and 13, for tips on how to rebuild or maintain a strong relationship with your partner despite the onslaught of children.)

How Fat Is Your Wallet?

Since most new and soon-to-be fathers become the sole wage earners in the family, at least for a while, the state of your family finances will have an impact on how you feel about pregnancy and fatherhood, too. If you're already stressed out trying to make ends meet with two incomes and no kids, a pregnancy will only add to your anxiety.

Even if you've managed to sock away some money in anticipation of this joyous event, the costs that child-rearing entails should give you some cause for anxiety. Direct costs include

➤ Furniture and decorations to outfit your nursery

➤ Baby equipment, such as car seats, strollers, playpens, and high chairs

➤ Clothes that get used for just one season before your child outgrows them

➤ Skyrocketing medical bills

➤ Toys that remain "age appropriate" for only a year or two

➤ An ever-expanding amount of food

➤ First daycare, and then schools

Indirect costs may include such big-ticket items as a bigger house, a bigger car, and life insurance (which may never have seemed necessary before). So if new money worries are starting to give you heartburn, it's no wonder. (See Chapter 14 for a "cost-benefit analysis" on rearing children.)

What Are You Like?

Your personality, of course, influences your emotional response to any situation. And it certainly has an impact on how you feel about pregnancy and fatherhood. No matter what you are like, pregnancy is likely to magnify your strongest personality traits.

An optimist will find dozens of things to eagerly anticipate. A pessimist will find just as many things to dread. A "putterer" will find dozens of baby-related projects to start working on. A worrier will find dozens of new concerns during pregnancy. Pregnancy—and fatherhood—offers a little something for everyone.

Curiously, however, you might find that pregnancy either subtly or radically alters certain aspects of your personality. You may have been totally laid back before the pregnancy but now find yourself tense and anxious. Conversely, you may have lived every aspect of your life (including baby planning) according to a strict schedule, but during the pregnancy, you suddenly find yourself unable to get started fixing up that spare room as a nursery. Such personality changes, not at all uncommon among expectant fathers, often indicate the presence of deeply ambivalent feelings about pregnancy and fatherhood.

What Are You Afraid Of?

No matter how thrilled you are about your partner's pregnancy, you no doubt feel at least a little anxious about the pregnancy, labor and delivery, and your upcoming fatherhood. For both expectant parents, pregnancy commonly gives birth to a number of fears.

Though some of these fears have a reasonable basis, they may become exaggerated well out of proportion. Although rational arguments might not dispel your fears surrounding the pregnancy and fatherhood, it may help to know that other men have felt these same fears before, yet only rarely have their fears come to pass.

Father Knows Best

"Despite my fears of fatherhood, I had strong nurturing urges. These I sublimated for years with a succession of pussycats upon whom I doted to a sometimes embarrassing degree."

—Dan Greenburg

What's Wrong with the Baby?

Your most concrete worry probably centers on the health and safety of your unborn child. Could something be wrong with the baby? Could the baby be physically deformed or mentally impaired?

It's natural to wonder about such things. After all, you can't see what's going on "in there."

Meeting with your partner's obstetrician should allay some of your fears. The doctor will no doubt reassure you that regular obstetrical check-ups, supplemented with appropriate testing, are aimed at catching many of the things that might go wrong. Such tests include an *AFP test* and often (but not always) a *sonogram*.

If your wife is older than 35 or has already given birth to a baby with defective chromosomes, her obstetrician might suggest another test,

Paterniterms

An **AFP test** is a blood test that measures the levels of alpha-fetoprotein—a protein secreted in large amounts by a fetus with a malformed brain or spinal column. Abnormally high levels of AFP may indicate problems in the formation of the fetal brain and spinal cord, but may also result from a multiple pregnancy or a miscalculated due date (since levels normally increase as a pregnancy progresses).

amniocentesis. This test does carry some risk; about half of one percent of women who take the test develop problems in pregnancy, including an increased chance of miscarriage, due to the test itself. Obstetricians will not recommend it unless a woman's age or medical history warrant it. Even then, you and your wife have the right to refuse this test (or any other medical test or procedure, for that matter).

Despite the increasing sophistication of genetic testing and ultrasound technology, no one can offer you a guarantee of a perfectly healthy baby. Some birth defects *do* go undetected. They are becoming increasingly rare, however.

Paterniterms

A **sonogram** produces an image on a computer screen by bouncing ultrasound waves off the fetus. The technician checks the size, development, and condition of vital organs, such as the heart and kidneys. A sonogram can also determine the gender of the baby, though not with absolute certainty.

Paterniterms

In an **amniocentesis,** a small amount of amniotic fluid is removed from the womb through a needle inserted in the belly of the mother-to-be. Testing of this fluid can reveal certain chromosomal defects (more common among older women) as well as the baby's gender.

Nevertheless, you cannot know for sure how your baby is developing until she arrives and you can count her fingers and toes to make sure for yourself. So until the birth of your child, you cannot avoid living with a degree of uncertainty, however small.

In the face of this uncertainty, you have a choice—one that's not entirely in your control but more so than you might think at first. You can either torture yourself relentlessly with worry about something that's out of your control, or you can try to let go of your fears and push them out of your mind, resigning yourself to fate or God's providence, or the sheer impossibility of knowing the unknown, whichever you prefer. If you can manage to move past your fears, since you can't do anything about them anyway, you will make much better use of the nine months of pregnancy—and enjoy it more, too.

I Can't Handle This Alone!

Perhaps even more devastating than worries about your baby are concerns about your partner's health. You may become preoccupied wondering whether something might be wrong with your wife and whether she will survive the trauma of childbirth. If she suffers from severe *morning sickness*, you may worry that she'll become dehydrated. If she puts on too little weight during the pregnancy (or if she puts on too much), you may worry about that. And if hormonal changes make her an entirely different person emotionally, you may question her sanity.

Try not to worry too much about whether your partner will survive. This fear lingers on from a long-past era in which women often did lose their lives during labor and delivery.

Every pregnancy—and its physical and emotional impact on the mother-to-be—is unique. Try to have faith that if anything is really wrong, your partner's obstetrician or midwife will recognize it and take steps to correct it. If anxiety about your wife's health persists, however, go to her next check-up with her. Talk to the doctor, nurse, or midwife, who can probably quickly allay your particular concerns.

I Ain't Got No Money, Honey

The days of the DINKs (Double Income, No Kids) are ending, at least for you. Like many couples today, both you and your partner have most likely been working hard to make a living. But even if your partner continues to work full-time (or part-time) throughout the pregnancy, the time will soon come when she will take at least some time away from her job or career. She may take an extended leave of absence or even quit her job entirely. (It's not uncommon for a woman to plan to go back to work after, say, two or three months, but then end up staying home with the baby for a year or longer.)

The loss of your partner's income will leave the financial burden for your entire growing family squarely on your shoulders. You will be solely responsible for the welfare of three (or more) people. So if you feel a bit anxious—or terrified—wondering where you're going to come up with the money you need to support a family, welcome to the club. Most fathers worry about money—even before their babies are born.

If the flow of money concerns you, start saving now. If necessary, take out a loan to cover the costs of childbirth and the period afterward when your wife will be staying home. At the same time, try not to dig yourself too deep a hole. If you have health insurance or belong to an HMO, find out now what the cost of childbirth and hospitalization will be. And if after all that you have a few dollars left over, start that college fund now. (See Chapter 14 for more information on the costs involved in bringing up your child and what you can do to plan your financial future.)

Father Figures

Birth defects occur in about eight percent of American births. Now, odds of 11 to 1 in your favor are pretty good. And the odds that your baby will survive childbirth are even better. The infant mortality rate in the United States is 1.51 percent, which means that your baby has a 66 to 1 chance of living.

Paterniterms

The hormonal changes brought on by a new pregnancy often cause **morning sickness**—persistent nausea, often accompanied by vomiting. Despite the name, the symptoms of morning sickness can waylay a pregnant woman any time during the day—or only in response to the smell or sight of particular foods.

Father Figures

In the 1920s, childbirth was the leading cause of death among women of child-bearing age. In the United States today, however, only 1 in 7,000 pregnant women die during childbirth.

Ready or Not, Here I Come

Throughout the pregnancy, you may be plagued with doubts about whether you're ready to be a father. You may fear that you will prove incompetent in holding, feeding, and generally taking care of a newborn. You may question your ability to offer both emotional and physical support to your wife. You may even have second thoughts about whether you really want a child at all. You may begin to ask yourself questions like

➤ Am I ready to give up the life I know and love for the sake of a baby?

➤ How will I measure up? Will I be a good father?

➤ Will I accidentally hurt the baby?

➤ Will I do something wrong to my child that will take years of psychotherapy to fix?

➤ Am I grown up enough to be a father? Do I have to be?

➤ Will I even like being a father?

➤ Do I really want to be a father at all?

Father Knows Best

"Who of us is mature enough for offspring before the offspring themselves arrive? The value of marriage is not that adults produce children but that children produce adults."

—Peter de Vries

Try not to let concerns about your competence or readiness for fatherhood (or about your partner's maternal instincts and skills) weigh too heavily on you. This kind of performance anxiety is common among expectant fathers wary of the extra responsibility they will soon face. After all, every father is a rookie father to start. But with a little on-the-job training you'll handle fatherhood like a pro.

If you lack confidence in your fathering skills, you can take steps to prepare yourself. Use the nine months of pregnancy to gather as much practical information and fathering philosophy as you can. Read books (like this one, for example). Spend some time with nieces and nephews or friends of yours who have young kids. Although being an uncle or a parent's friend is hardly the same as being a father, it will give you a taste of what it's like to have kids around, and you can learn a lot by observing how your friends and relatives behave with their children. Talk to other men whom you consider good fathers. Ask them any questions you have about specific areas of parenting. By doing a little research, you'll be more than ready when your baby's birthday finally arrives.

Father Knows Best

"Parentage is a very important profession, but no test of fitness for it is ever imposed in the interest of the children."

—George Bernard Shaw

I Don't Wanna Share!

Many expectant fathers also fear being replaced by the baby in the affections of their wives. During the pregnancy, you may have noticed your partner becoming increasingly focused on the baby growing inside her. Understandably, you may wonder whether she will have any time, energy, love, or attention left for you after your baby is born.

In addition, you may worry about the changes that pregnancy—and later parenthood—will impose on your sexual relationship with your partner. The fear of being replaced or abandoned, coupled with a changing sexual relationship, may go a long way toward explaining why some expectant fathers become involved in extra-marital affairs during the later stages of pregnancy. Guard against this destructive possibility by talking about your fears, feelings, and sex life with your wife (or with someone else close to you). (See Chapter 4 for more information and suggestions on sex during pregnancy.)

I Don't Wanna Die!

Like many expectant fathers, you may become anxious not just about the possibility that your wife might miscarry or that she or the baby might die in childbirth, but about your own mortality as well. With the anticipation and arrival of a baby—the next generation in the flesh—many new fathers (and new mothers) feel pushed one step closer to the grave. A new consciousness of your own mortality may gradually dawn on you during the pregnancy or rush in like a tidal wave. Fear for your own life may become even stronger when you realize just how much your wife and your child-to-be will depend on you.

Unfortunately, there's no practical solution to the fear of your own mortality. Some men begin taking fewer risks—giving up dangerous physical activities, for example—during their partner's pregnancy. But you can't avoid every risk; what kind of life would that be?

Daddy Dos and Don'ts

Talk to your partner about your feelings and fears. Many fathers-to-be maintain a stoic silence because they don't want to add to their wives' burden. Your partner may be suffering from some of the same fears and concerns, however. By opening up and talking about your own worries, you may invite your wife to do the same, which will only enhance the intimacy between you. Far from adding to the burden of her pregnancy, you may give your partner an opportunity to unload some of it.

As for the feeling of being pushed toward the grave by your new baby, get used to it. Every major event in our lives leads us closer to the grave; that's the inexorable direction of life. But most of us have plenty of life left. So why not make the most of whatever time we're here on earth instead of worrying too much about when we'll be leaving?

Some of the emotions and fears highlighted here may seem ridiculous or even childish to you, but most expectant fathers feel at least some of them. Examine your own feelings and find someone with whom you can share them.

Spare Some Change?

The nine months of pregnancy have long been recognized as a transition period for women. Some have even suggested that pregnancy lasts nine months to give the mother plenty of time to get used to the idea of change, to prepare for it physically, mentally, and emotionally. Throughout her pregnancy, your wife's rapidly transforming body will provide very concrete—and often uncomfortable—cues that both signal and guide her through the physical and emotional changes of pregnancy:

➤ Hormonal changes may cause morning sickness, which served as an important indicator of pregnancy long before the invention of home pregnancy tests.

➤ Contractions may begin as early as the fourth month of pregnancy, hinting at the labor contractions that will come five long months later.

➤ Her breasts will begin growing larger early in the pregnancy and may even begin producing a sticky "pre-milk" long before the baby arrives.

The adaptation of your partner's body to the baby growing inside her can thus provide a physical counterpart to the emotional transition she's going through in anticipating the arrival of your baby.

So What Have You Got to Lose?

For fathers-to-be, pregnancy also serves as a time of profound transition: nine months of mental, emotional, material, perhaps physical, and almost certainly financial preparation to become a father. The next nine months will be full of anticipation, sometimes joyful and excited, other times fearful and anxious.

By the time your child is born (especially if you're having your first child), you will have undergone a transition as profound as—and perhaps even more transforming than—the one you experienced when you got married (or, if you never married, when you gave up the single life to live together as a couple).

In celebrating the joy of becoming pregnant and preparing to welcome your child into the world—and into your hearts—don't forget to acknowledge your losses along with your gain. Everyone takes for granted that having a baby is a terrific thing for you and your partner, that you joyfully welcome every aspect of the event (aside from your wife's discomfort during pregnancy). And so you should—in an ideal and carefree world.

But what everyone says upon hearing of your partner's pregnancy is true: *Your life really will never be the same again.* And if you've enjoyed your adult life up until now, the monumental changes introduced by pregnancy and parenthood will involve at least some degree of loss.

Good Grief!

In recent years, a number of engaged couples have prepared for the celebration and joy of embracing a life partner and declaring undying love at their wedding by first undergoing a kind of "grief counseling" or "grief therapy." Grief counselors help marrying couples to acknowledge and mourn the losses and sacrifices that marriage necessitates. In getting married, for instance, both spouses agree to give up the perks of single life, the ability to do what each wants without considering the other, and a great deal of their privacy. These are concrete losses that mark the end of single life and the beginning of married life.

Presumably, since you've gone on to have a child, you agree that the benefits of becoming a couple (whether married or not) far outweighed any sacrifices you needed to make. The things you gave up to gain your life's partner were well worth it. That doesn't mean they should go unrecognized, however!

And so it is with having a baby. Of course, you are filled with joy and eager anticipation at the prospect of your baby's arrival. That's a given. But in gaining a child, you will also lose or sacrifice a great deal. In transforming you and your partner from a couple into a family, from lovers into parents, you will probably need to give up the following (at least to some degree):

➤ Spontaneity

➤ The freedom to do what you want whenever you want

➤ A carefree attitude about finances

➤ Sleep, sleep, sleep

➤ Privacy

➤ Your sex life

➤ Night life

In addition to these sacrifices commonly offered up by new parents, you will probably also have to make additional sacrifices unique to you (or your partner). So feel free to fill in the blanks with your own sacrifices below:

➤ _____

➤ _____

➤ _____

You'll no doubt discover that these sacrifices, like those you had to make in choosing each other as lifetime lovers, will be well worth it. Yet taking the time now to acknowledge these sacrifices and mourn these losses can help eliminate a good deal of the ambivalence you may feel about becoming a father.

The Least You Need to Know

➤ Ambivalent feelings about impending fatherhood will not make you a bad father. Nearly every man has some ambivalence about fatherhood.

➤ Don't feel guilty about how you feel about fatherhood. Recognize your emotions and deal with them (with help, if necessary).

➤ The odds that you, your wife, and your baby will survive childbirth are strongly in your favor. Your baby will most likely be healthy and whole.

➤ Talk about your feelings and fears about pregnancy with your partner. She may be looking for a chance to share her own feelings, too.

➤ In celebrating the joys of pregnancy and upcoming fatherhood, don't forget to mourn the losses, too. The rewards of fatherhood are worth the sacrifices you'll need to make.

Chapter 2

Okay, Where Do I Fit In?

In This Chapter

➤ How to become more involved in your partner's pregnancy

➤ Finding the best ways to help and support your partner during her pregnancy

➤ What your partner might appreciate most at various stages of the pregnancy

➤ The importance of foot and back massages late in the pregnancy

➤ Ways to make the pregnancy more real for *you*

Okay, so your wife's pregnant. Your inner life is perhaps in turmoil as you struggle to reconcile yourself with what impending fatherhood means to you. You've filled a number of roles in your life up to now, including son, student, wage-earner, friend, lover, and husband or long-term boyfriend. You also may have played other roles as varied as brother, athlete, addict, hobbyist, collector, gardener, gambler, class president, juvenile delinquent, or musician, just to name a few. But now you're taking on a role unlike any in the past: father.

Fatherhood, or at least preparing for the role, begins during pregnancy. As your partner's pregnancy progresses, you will no doubt feel encouragement—and even pressure—from your partner, family, and friends to make yourself fully part of the pregnancy. Yet you probably know next to nothing about pregnancy and childbirth.

What's more, you can never truly share the sensations and emotions that your wife is feeling. You will never know the serene pleasure of having a living being grow inside you. You will never know the discomfort of having an ever-growing fetus kick against your bladder. You will never go through the horrendous pain of childbirth.

If you can't feel what she's feeling, how can you participate fully in your partner's pregnancy? Sure, you want to be involved in your wife's pregnancy, but how?

Mother's Little Helper

Okay, so you can't carry the fetus and bear the child yourself. Although you might not be able literally to lighten your partner's load, you can do so figuratively by offering her all the physical, emotional, and moral support you can.

Actively supporting your wife during the pregnancy will not only help her a great deal, it will help you, too. For one thing, the more help you offer, the more involved you'll feel in the pregnancy, which can help to stave off any feelings of isolation or separateness. Actively preparing for the baby to come can also take your mind off the fears that can sometimes beset expectant fathers. (See Chapter 1 for a discussion of the most common of these fears.)

In general, the best way to make yourself useful is to ask your wife what she needs and wants in the way of help and support. Be solicitous (though not so overly solicitous that she begins to feel like an invalid, if only in your eyes). Simply ask questions such as

➤ How do you feel?

➤ What can I do to help?

➤ Would you like me to do that for you?

➤ Is there anything I can do to make you feel better?

Asking these questions on a regular (though not necessarily daily) basis not only keeps the lines of communication open, but also allows you to steer your supportive efforts in the direction most useful to your partner. In this way, you will prevent the pregnancy—and your inability to share directly in its physical manifestations—from becoming a wedge between you. Indeed, using your communications skills to share in the pregnancy can actually bring you and your partner closer together.

Father Knows Best

"Make sure that she sits in comfortable chairs; and then help her out of the chair when it's time to leave, or else you'll find yourself in the street without her because she'll still be in the chair, flapping her arms and trying to get airborne."

—Bill Cosby

Open Hands and Open Ears

Throughout the pregnancy, your wife will be grateful for whatever you can do to help around the house. Because individual women react differently to pregnancy, what you do to help depends on what her pregnancy has made most difficult for her. If driving makes her sick, it may mean doing the shopping; if heavy lifting has become too taxing, it may mean doing the laundry.

If your partner did most of the household chores before the pregnancy, offer to relieve her of the most taxing ones. If, on the other hand, you already divide the various household chores, consider which of them is most difficult for her and assume responsibility for it. (Her condition will change during the course of nine months, of course, so you'll need to remain somewhat flexible.) If you don't have time to take on another household chore, offer to trade one of your less strenuous but more time-consuming responsibilities for one she finds most unbearable during the pregnancy.

In general, your help and support will prove especially useful during the first and third *trimesters* of the pregnancy. That's because during the first trimester your wife may not feel like doing anything but puking, while during the third it will become increasingly difficult for her to maneuver. At this point, anything that involves heavy lifting or prolonged stooping will be very difficult for her.

As with offering general support, it may make the most sense to ask your partner what would be most helpful, to find out what normal household activities tax her the most. Make a list of everyday tasks that you could do to make her life easier. Scrubbing the bathtub, for example, is next to impossible for most women in their third trimester. For one thing, getting up after kneeling down is a chore in itself. For another, the enlarged belly of late pregnancy makes it very hard to lean over a bathtub.

If you own a cat, one job you should definitely take over throughout your wife's pregnancy is cleaning the cat's litter box. Cat feces can contain organisms that cause *toxoplasmosis*.

In addition to physical support, your wife will also depend on you throughout the pregnancy for emotional support. Encourage her to talk about what she's feeling: her physical symptoms, her emotions, her hopes and fears, her dreams and nightmares.

Paterniterms

A **trimester** is one-third of a pregnancy, a three-month period. Typically (but by no means always), the first trimester features morning sickness; the second, a feeling of general well-being as the pregnancy becomes more obviously apparent; and the third, a dramatic increase in the size of her belly accompanied by backache and general discomfort.

Paterniterms

Toxoplasmosis is an infection that may cause few or no symptoms in a pregnant woman. Although it may go unnoticed in the mother, if passed on to the fetus in the womb, it may cause grave consequences ranging from blindness to stillbirth.

17

When asking how your partner is doing, allow her to complain all she wants about her physical ailments but try not to feel obligated to fix them or make them disappear. This isn't always possible. If you can do anything to relieve some of her physical discomfort, by all means do it. But when you can't fix her problems, do the best you can; offer her your sympathy and understanding.

Mop-Up Detail: The First Trimester

The first three months of pregnancy, as noted earlier, are marked primarily by morning sickness, which is the body's response to radical hormonal changes. The symptoms of morning sickness range from mild nausea to vomiting so frequent that hospitalization is required. Although rare, if your wife vomits frequently for many successive days, she may need to be hospitalized to have fluids and nutrients supplied intravenously. (Vomiting during morning sickness rarely gets this bad.)

Unfortunately, morning sickness is often a misnomer, since many pregnant women suffer from nausea and vomiting not only in the morning but throughout the day and night as well. Others feel sick only in the evening, and many experience their most severe nausea only in response to the smell or sight of particular foods.

Father Knows Best

"Why do pregnant women become nauseous? Because the first time you realize there's something alive in there ... you puke."

—Mel Brooks (as the 2,000-Year-Old Man)

The severity of morning sickness varies not just with the individual woman, but with the particular pregnancy. It's not at all uncommon for a woman who experienced horrendous morning sickness during her first pregnancy to breeze through a second pregnancy without vomiting once, or vice versa.

In addition to nausea, your wife might suffer from profound fatigue during the first trimester. If she throws up repeatedly, her body will become depleted of fluids. Even if she never actually vomits, however, the hormonal changes of pregnancy and her body's attempts to adjust to them will likely leave her exhausted. She may want to do nothing more than lie in bed all day. And if she's working outside the home, don't expect her to rush back to cook dinner. She'll want to collapse on the bed or sofa as soon as she walks in the door.

Sadly, there's not too much you can do to help your wife through morning sickness except to demonstrate sympathy and a sense of humor about it. In addition, you might want to set her up with a glass of water and a sealed plastic bag with a couple of crackers in it on the bedside table at night. Some women find that eating a small, easily digestible snack before they get out of bed in the morning helps ease morning sickness.

You might also try to reassure your partner that morning sickness does (usually) end. By around the fourth or fifth month, both her nausea and vomiting should subside. Of course, there are no guarantees. Some women feel nauseous and vomit at least occasionally throughout the nine months of pregnancy. But more commonly, the body adjusts to hormonal changes around the beginning of the second trimester.

Glory Days: The Second Trimester

Most pregnant women come into their glory during the second trimester. During these three months, your partner may develop the "glow" of pregnancy that people always mention. Hopefully, any morning sickness she has experienced will fade away. And though she will begin to "show"—that is, her belly will begin to grow visibly larger— she will not carry nearly so large and uncomfortable a burden as she will during the final three months of her pregnancy.

Because (with any luck) she'll be feeling so much better, your partner will probably need little help during the second trimester. Keep in mind that pregnancy is neither a disease nor a disability. Your wife is neither fragile nor an invalid just because she happens to be pregnant. She's carrying your child, so of course you should pay attention to her needs. But she has no need—and probably no desire—to have you patronize her or become overprotective of her or your baby.

Your partner can still do almost any physical activity that she has done in the past, including, for example, skiing, playing tennis, and having sex. (For more on sex during pregnancy, see Chapter 4.) Regular exercise and sexual activity actually does your partner a great deal of good and does not pose any danger to either her or the baby. (The fluid-filled amniotic sac protects the baby from almost any routine bouncing or shock.) So take her for a walk, play a set or two of tennis, or swim a half-mile in the pool with her. Have some fun engaging in vigorous physical activity while you still can.

Daddy Dos and Don'ts

Before your pregnant partner engages in any strenuous activity, make sure she checks with her doctor first. Your partner will probably receive medical clearance to continue any exercise program she has followed prior to the pregnancy. If she seldom exercised before pregnancy, however, her doctor will caution your partner to start any new exercise program slowly. In either case, it won't hurt to ask her doctor's advice.

The Final Stretch and Stretch and Stretch: The Third Trimester

The final trimester of pregnancy gives you the greatest opportunity to support, comfort, and assist your partner. Now she's getting BIG. And the bigger her uterus and belly become, the more she needs your help—not just in picking up some of the slack in everyday chores, but also in relieving some of her physical ailments.

Since your partner is no doubt avoiding most medications—and indeed shouldn't take any drug without first consulting her obstetrician—you may be called upon to help alleviate some of her aches and pains. In general, massage and the warmth of your touch will help soothe, if not necessarily eliminate, many of the aches typical among pregnant women.

Nowhere will your gentle touch be appreciated more than your wife's lower back. The uterus is attached to a pregnant woman's lower back—and nowhere else. As your baby grows inside her, the weight of the uterus pulls more and more on this sole point of attachment, fatiguing the muscles and making them sore. A gentle massage of the lower back—especially applying consistent pressure by rubbing the small of her back with the base of your palm—will be greatly appreciated during the final trimester of pregnancy.

Most pregnant women also gratefully welcome foot massages during the final trimester. If your partner is still working and/or spends much of the day on her feet, the extra weight of pregnancy puts an unaccustomed burden on the muscles of her feet. A good foot massage may be just what the doctor ordered. (If you've never given your wife a foot massage, be prepared for a positive response. She may moan with ecstasy and profess her undying love for you. In fact, she may grow to love foot massages even more than sex.)

During the third trimester, your partner also may suffer from severe leg cramps, which often happen in bed, once she's taken the weight off her legs. If leg cramping occurs, avoid massaging the calf, which may in fact create more pain than relief. Instead, ask her to lie down (if she isn't already lying down) and gently but firmly bend her foot at the ankle up toward her face. Then hold her foot gently but firmly in place, perhaps wrapping your other hand around her calf, but without squeezing.

Insomnia may become a problem in the third trimester as well. Impending labor, delivery, and the baby care to come make it essential that your partner (and you) get as much rest as possible in the final months of pregnancy. Yet physical discomfort—hammered home by

Daddy Dos and Don'ts

Your partner will appreciate back and foot massages even more if you use warm lotion or oil. Warm your own hands in advance, too. Nothing defeats the relaxing effects of massage more than ice-cold hands, which adds to your partner's tension instead of relieving it.

fetal gymnastics—may make it hard for her to get to sleep or stay asleep. Anxiety about labor, delivery, and her own parenting skills may make your partner's insomnia even worse.

Finally, your partner may be more high strung, moody, or sensitive than you've ever known her to be. This moodiness may stem not only from hormonal changes, but also from genuine concerns and anxiety regarding the living creature growing inside her. (An increasing absent-mindedness is also common during the third trimester of pregnancy, as women focus more and more on thoughts of the baby.)

Daddy Dos and Don'ts

Place pillows under your partner's back and knees to help her find a comfortable sleeping position. A back rub in bed may help calm her to sleep, too. You might also want to try some relaxation and breathing exercises, perhaps practicing those learned in a childbirth class. This, too, can help soothe her to sleep.

So try to be understanding, sensitive, and patient. Invite her to talk about her feelings, doubts, and worries. And if she ever blows up at you, stop to evaluate each potentially explosive situation before responding in kind. Ask yourself, "Is this worth taking a stand on?" Even if your answer is "yes," ask yourself, "Do I have to do it right now, or can I wait for a calmer moment?"

Get Real

In addition to supporting, comforting, and helping your wife, you can become more involved in the pregnancy by trying to get closer to your child. The baby growing inside your wife may seem entirely abstract and somewhat unreal to you. In your wife's case, any sense of abstraction becomes concrete fairly soon; she can begin feeling the baby move around inside her during the fourth month of pregnancy, and has felt other effects of the baby's presence even earlier on than that.

For you, however, it's another story; the baby remains abstract much longer. You can't feel it growing and moving inside of you. To make this baby real, you need more sensory data.

Overcoming Sensory Deprivation

One way to make the baby seem more real is to attend a prenatal checkup with your wife. Make it a point to meet with your wife's obstetrician at least once—or more, if your schedule allows—during the pregnancy. This will give you the opportunity to ask any questions you might have about the pregnancy, fetal development, labor, and delivery. Many men find a doctor's authority very persuasive.

Even more convincing is the evidence of your own ears. Before the doctor comes in, a nurse will probably check the fetal heartbeat by pressing an electronic monitor against your partner's belly. The electronic beats come very fast, averaging about 140 beats per minute (though a healthy fetal heart rate can range from as low as 100 to as high as 200). Many men point to this sound as the first thing that made the reality of the pregnancy sink in. Since it probably won't sound like any heartbeat you've ever heard, however, the fetal heartbeat may still be too abstract to make your baby more real for you.

You'll reap even greater rewards by attending a sonogram with your wife. Although not every pregnancy calls for them, sonograms are often used to pinpoint the age of the fetus, based on its size, and to determine a due date with a greater degree of accuracy. If your partner has a sonogram, standing by her side will provide your first opportunity to see your baby (in a manner of speaking).

Father Knows Best

"We look in awe at the screen. We have absolutely no idea what we are looking at. The technician points out the fetus's head, buttocks, arms, and legs, and after awhile we can pretty much identify the various parts ourselves.

'There's the head!' I say excitedly.

'Well, uh, no, that's the buttocks,' says the technician."

—Dan Greenburg

Again, many men mark the first sight of the fetus through a sonogram as a turning point in accepting the reality of the baby growing inside their partners. But then again, the images are often so shadowy and difficult to read that you may have no real concept of what you're seeing. You may need even more evidence than sight (a sonogram) and sound (a fetal heartbeat) can provide. You may need something more tactile.

Getting Your Kicks

Around the fifth month (or sometimes as early as the fourth month), you will get some tactile evidence that you really are going to have a baby. You will be able to feel kicking inside your partner as the baby begins exercising her muscles. Some babies content themselves with low-impact stretches, occasionally allowing you to see—and feel—an elbow- or foot-shaped hill travel across your partner's belly. Other babies, however, go through what seem to be full-scale workouts: jumping jacks, running in place, leg lifts, and high-impact aerobics. If your baby is this active, your wife's belly will look (and, to her, feel) like a sack of gigantic jumping beans or something out of the movie *Alien*.

Feeling the movement of your baby inside your wife's belly will probably intensify the sense of reality for you. The changes in your wife's body (morning sickness, fatigue, enlarged breasts, a swollen belly) may have served as evidence enough for her. But even if you have heard the electronically distorted fetal heartbeat and have seen the hazy sonogram images of the fetus, you have had little if any concrete evidence of what's developing inside her. (Just as some die-hard skeptics suspected that the video footage of the moon landings was nothing more than trick photography, you might—if only for an instant in the darkest recesses of your mind—have questioned whether the sonogram you saw and the fetal heartbeat you heard were fake.) A baby's kicks, however, offer solid, tactile proof and confirm fetal development for the father-to-be.

By the beginning of the fifth month, your baby will have already developed functioning sensory organs. The fetus, for example, can feel the pressure of a hand against the womb and may kick back in response. (Your wife also can feel this pressure, of course, so be gentle!) Playing gentle games of "tag" can help you feel closer to your baby even before she is born. Just remember to ask your partner's permission first; after all, she's the playing field.

Your baby can also hear sounds. For the most part, the fetus hears sounds that resonate inside your wife's body: her voice, heartbeat, and digestion, for example. But even from within the womb, your baby can also hear some external stimuli. (Just ask your wife how the baby reacts to any loud noise within range of her belly.)

Your baby's developing sense of hearing gives you another opportunity for interaction. Now you have the chance to talk to your baby.

Some experts have suggested that if you talk to the fetus, your newborn baby may later recognize your voice, which can facilitate the bonding process between the two of you. Considering the layers of skin and muscle your voice needs to travel through, not to mention the muffling effect of the amniotic fluid, your baby's ability to recognize a particular voice may seem somewhat far-fetched, but tests have shown that when their parents speak, even newborns turn their heads toward them (while not doing the same when other adults speak).

Whether or not it helps your baby to bond more easily with you after birth, however, talking to the fetus inside the womb may help *you* to bond with your baby. It can also provide valuable practice, preparing you to speak to your baby in soothing, gentle tones when she finally does arrive.

Daddy Dos and Don'ts

Music—classical, folk, or children's—can have a soothing effect on the fetus. Although some expectant parents play foreign-language tapes or other "educational" material in an attempt to give their child a "head start," this, it seems to me, is getting off on the wrong foot with your baby. Even before she arrives in the world, you're putting pressure on your child to excel. Lighten up a little.

If you feel silly or uncomfortable talking to your wife's belly, then don't do it. After all, communicating with the fetus still inside the womb is not nearly as important as communicating with your child after she is born.

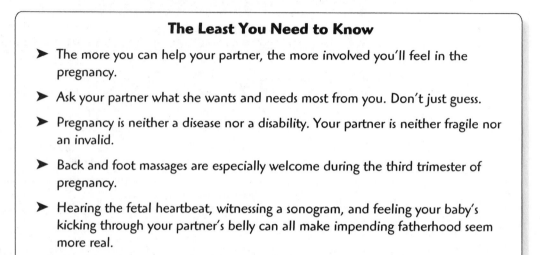

The Least You Need to Know

➤ The more you can help your partner, the more involved you'll feel in the pregnancy.

➤ Ask your partner what she wants and needs most from you. Don't just guess.

➤ Pregnancy is neither a disease nor a disability. Your partner is neither fragile nor an invalid.

➤ Back and foot massages are especially welcome during the third trimester of pregnancy.

➤ Hearing the fetal heartbeat, witnessing a sonogram, and feeling your baby's kicking through your partner's belly can all make impending fatherhood seem more real.

Chapter 3

Your Wife Has the Stomach for Labor and Delivery, Do You?

In This Chapter

➤ Deciding whether or not to participate in childbirth

➤ Reasons to take part in childbirth—for your own sake as well as your partner's

➤ Why you might feel reluctant to serve as your partner's labor coach

➤ What you'll be expected to do as a labor coach

➤ How to find a childbirth class and what you can expect to learn there

It seems hard to believe that men—not only husbands but doctors, too—were once considered intruders in delivery rooms. In the 1950s, it was extremely rare for a father-to-be to join his wife in the delivery room. Social custom has changed dramatically, however. Today, as many as 90 percent of fathers participate in the birth of their babies.

Indeed, most pregnant women today have come to expect that their partners, by social convention, will be at their sides as they undergo the painful, laborious process of delivering a child. In all likelihood, your partner has no doubt that you will be her coach throughout the birth of your child. Believe it or not, however, despite social convention, you still have a choice in the matter.

To Be or Not to Be in the Delivery Room

Most people today will take it for granted that you not only will be in the delivery room with your wife, but that you want to be there. If you have any doubts, reluctance, concerns, fears, or ambivalent feelings about being present at the birth of your child, however, you owe it to yourself and your partner to discuss them with her. Try to articulate how you feel about the prospect of being with your partner as she delivers your child. And then listen to what she has to say; find out how she feels about your being there.

Why Should I?

Most women today want their husbands with them in the delivery room. If your partner wants you by her side during labor and delivery, she may offer any of the following reasons:

➤ Only you, who knows and loves her best, can provide the loving support—both physical and emotional—that she needs. Your encouragement, love, and support can make an enormous difference in her experience of labor.

➤ She wants you to share the pleasure of your baby's first few moments of life. Like all moments in your child's life, these won't ever be repeated.

➤ In the wake of childbirth, many couples feel an exquisite closeness and renewed intimacy toward each other.

➤ The first moments of your newborn's life are a special time for both of you to bond with the baby (and each other). You and your wife will be relieved, excited, and overjoyed to see your new baby. And a brand new baby is usually alert, with eyes wide open, for only a short time before sinking into a long slumber. It may be an entire day before you see your baby displaying any alertness again.

Cool Daddy Ohs

In an earlier era, even male doctors were barred from labor and delivery rooms. In the early 1500s, a curious German doctor disguised himself as a woman and, posing as a midwife, sneaked into a room where a woman was about to give birth. Caught, he was burned at the stake for his "voyeurism."

Father Knows Best

"Even though it has come to be a sort of routine for me, I am stirred and moved and filled with happiness every time."

—Leo Tolstoy, after participating in the birth of his ninth child

Most fathers today do choose to participate as their partner's labor coaches. Men do so not only for the sake of their wives, who depend on them for support and almost always benefit both emotionally and physically from the presence of their loving coaches, but for their own sakes. A sense of adventure drives most expectant fathers to embrace this unique experience. In its wake, most men report an intense high, an awe at the miracle of creation, an absolutely unforgettable moment.

Why Shouldn't I?

Nonetheless, the minority of expectant fathers who do bow out of the labor room have good reasons for not participating—concerns often shared by fathers who do choose to take part. So even if you know you want to remain with your wife during labor and delivery, don't skip over this section. You may recognize some fears and concerns that you've been reluctant to voice.

The following are some of the reasons fathers-to-be give for not participating in labor and delivery (or for their apprehension of the experience):

➤ **Queasiness.** Expectant fathers often fear becoming squeamish at the sight of blood. You may fear fainting—not an unreasonable concern given the bloodiness of delivery and the uncomfortable warmth of most hospital rooms.

Most men who decide to take part in childbirth, however, discover that the excitement of the moment and the responsibilities they have for soothing, supporting, and helping their partners leave little or no time for queasiness. If you coach your wife through labor and delivery, you will probably be too busy, too curious, and too fascinated to feel nauseous or faint.

➤ **Witnessing pain.** You may feel ill-equipped or unable to bear the sight of your wife's pain in labor. Childbirth is truly a traumatic event for both mother and child. You, also, may fear that it's too traumatic to witness. Worst of all, you may fear your own helplessness to do anything to ease her pain.

Father Knows Best

"If you want to know how childbirth feels, just take your bottom lip and pull it over your head."

—Carol Burnett

27

Yet a well-taught, well-rehearsed coach (who does not necessarily have to be you, of course) can actually ease the pain of a laboring mother—or at least help her to get through it. You may feel untrained or unqualified to take part in this kind of "medical" procedure, lacking confidence in your ability to do anything helpful. Again, practice and good training, which you can get by taking a childbirth class, can overcome both ignorance and lack of confidence.

➤ **Fear of being a fifth wheel.** You may be uncertain about your role in the labor and delivery. Perhaps you envision yourself positioned between your partner's knees, ready with a catcher's mitt. You may fear that, far from helping, you'll only make things worse. This fear can be especially strong if you are also preoccupied with the possibility of complications, ranging from a birth defect all the way to the death of your wife or child. You may fear that if anything goes wrong, you'll just be in the way.

Again, a little education will help to alleviate your fears. A good childbirth class will clarify your role in labor and delivery and reassure you that your presence can be helpful. You will also learn how rare complications in childbirth have become today. Finally, rest assured that if serious complications arise, the medical staff will not allow you to get in the way. You either will be instructed to sit quietly at your wife's side or escorted out of the room.

➤ **Privacy.** You may see childbirth as an intimately female activity—a "woman thing"—and your wife may very well feel the same way. Although some couples cannot wait to share this experience, your partner may not regard childbirth as a romantic thing at all. She might be very modest and find it embarrassing to be seen half-naked and in pain.

Cool Daddy Ohs

In many nonindustrialized countries, childbirth is still a private, female affair. Fathers—and medicine men—are barred from participating in labor and delivery. Instead, women in labor are attended to by other females: mothers, older sisters, aunts, and neighbors.

Furthermore, some couples adhere to religious beliefs that see childbirth as unclean or impure, and believe that the process should remain confined to women. According to such religions, the mother—and sometimes the child as well—requires cleansing or purification after childbirth. Orthodox Jews, Hindus, and some African religions uphold a taboo on male participation in childbirth.

If your own or your wife's religious beliefs forbid you from participating in childbirth, no one should try to persuade you otherwise. It would be disrespectful to argue against your religious beliefs.

Furthermore, if both you and your wife regard childbirth as a private affair appropriate only for women, then that belief—whether based on religious credos or not—also deserves to be respected. If your wife regards the presence of anyone who doesn't absolutely have to be there as an intrusion on her privacy, or if her embarrassment at the immodesty of childbirth inhibits her, your presence could actually make for a longer, more difficult labor and delivery.

> ➤ **Discomfort with gender role reversal.** Husband-coached childbirth requires a reversal of the traditional gender roles that still prevail in our society. In child-birth, the laboring woman amply demonstrates her courage, competence, strength, grit, and fortitude. By contrast, the man who acts as labor coach must offer emotional support, soothing words, encouragement, and as much comfort as he can provide. In short, the woman acts as the quarterback (or, more prop-erly, the center); the man serves as the cheerleader.

If you and your partner have established a very traditional relationship, you may feel uncomfortable trading gender roles. If these feelings are entrenched, your attendance could make childbirth more difficult for your wife.

If you participate in childbirth, however, the temporary switching of gender roles can actually deepen your relationship with your partner. Most women whose partners coach them through childbirth develop a new appreciation for their husbands' tender-ness and compassion. Similarly, most men who act as labor coaches develop a new or renewed respect for their partner's strength and courage.

Decision Time

No matter how you feel about the possibility of participating in the birth of your child, you should discuss it with your partner before reaching a final decision. If both of you agree on the extent (or lack) of your participation, there's no problem. If you disagree, however, you'll need to come to some sort of compromise (or perhaps one of you will persuade—or give in to—the other). If, for instance, she wants a coach but you don't want to do it, ask a reliable relative or friend to attend childbirth classes with her and be her labor coach.

If you do choose to be among the 10 to 20 percent of expectant fathers who don't participate in labor and delivery, you'll have little to do but pace the waiting room, hoping that everything works out for the best but not really knowing what's going on.

No matter what anyone might say, if you decide that shared childbirth isn't for you, don't beat yourself up about it. Your ultimate success as a father depends much less on the fact that you were or weren't present at your child's birth than on the fact that you will be present for the many years to come.

Daddy Dos and Don'ts

Once you've learned some relax-ation and breathing exercises (in a prenatal class), you might find it helpful to practice them in bed at night, just before falling asleep. These exercises can help soothe your partner into as good a night's sleep as she can get with a growing baby doing somersaults inside her.

What Am I Supposed to Do?

If you choose to be among the 80 to 90 percent of fathers-to-be who serve as a labor coach for their partners, you'll be kept very busy. Don't expect just to stand around watching. Your wife will depend on your active participation in labor and delivery. It will be your job to

➤ Time your partner's contractions as they increase in frequency, duration, and intensity. In the latter stages of labor, when contractions come regularly, you can coach your partner to begin breathing and relaxation exercises just before the next contraction hits. This will make it easier for her to maintain her breathing throughout the pain of a contraction.

➤ Rehearse the breathing exercises that you learned in prenatal classes, and then coach her to use them during labor. This can make the pain of labor and delivery more manageable for her.

➤ Massage the base of her spine to relieve, if only a little, the intense *back labor* of delivery.

➤ Recognize signs that your partner is tensing up and then take action (massage, soothing words, or putting on her favorite relaxing music, for example) or coach her to relax.

➤ Serve as your partner's chief advocate and spokesman. You know your wife better than anyone else in the birthing room. Who better to make sure she gets everything she needs during labor and delivery?

➤ Feed her ice chips.

➤ Comfort, reassure, soothe, placate, and encourage your partner.

➤ Hold her hand.

Sounds like a lot of responsibility, doesn't it? It is, but fortunately, you can learn how to handle it in a good childbirth class.

Go to the Head of the Class

Childbirth can be a nerve-wracking, anxiety-provoking experience for both the father and the mother. You'll

Paterniterms

Back labor, an intense backache during labor, occurs most commonly when the baby faces up toward the front of the mother's pelvis, rather than face down. This makes it more difficult for the head to flex and move through the birth canal. Unfortunately, you can't turn the baby around at this stage, so there's nothing you can do about it but apply counterpressure on the mother's lower back.

Daddy Dos and Don'ts

If a doctor, nurse, anesthesiologist, or anyone else asks you to leave the room so that they can perform a certain examination or procedure, find out what they plan to do, and then ask your partner whether you can stay. If she wants you to keep holding her hand or stand by her side, don't budge unless there's a medical emergency.

both be better able to keep your cool if you know something about the experience—and how you can cope with it—beforehand.

That's the whole idea behind childbirth classes. By making you knowledgeable about labor and delivery, a good childbirth class can demystify the experience, replacing the mystique surrounding childbirth with practical knowledge. In turn, this knowledge can relieve some of your anxiety (if you have any) about the upcoming event. By diminishing your sense of helplessness, the knowledge you get from your childbirth class can make you much more confident as you enter the birthing room.

Women Have Been Giving Birth for Thousands of Years—So Why Do We Need a Class?

Most fathers today who participate in labor and delivery, at least for the birth of their first child, take prenatal or childbirth classes with their partners. If you're planning on helping your partner through labor and delivery, you should probably take one, too. Even the best instruction provided by books pales compared to what you and other pregnant couples can learn and practice in a good childbirth class.

Typically, childbirth instructors teach expectant parents through a combination of lectures, group discussions, demonstrations of relaxation and breathing exercises, practice "labor" sessions, and films. In addition to learning what to expect during labor and delivery, you'll also learn about the following:

➤ Relaxation, breathing, and massage techniques to ease your partner's labor pains.

➤ Fetal development.

➤ Why, when, and how a *Cesarean section* (C-section) might be performed.

➤ Infant care, including, for example breastfeeding pointers for your partner and tips on diapering, bathing, and bottle-feeding for both of you.

Most childbirth classes also show films that demonstrate vaginal births, C-sections, and breastfeeding techniques.

Most childbirth classes given in hospitals or birthing centers also include a tour of the obstetrical ward or birthing rooms. Don't skip this tour. When the time comes, you'll be glad you've familiarized yourself with the area.

Many hospitals now offer state-of-the-art birthing rooms, which allow labor, delivery, and recovery to take place in the same room. (You may notice, however, that not all birthing rooms have comfortable chairs for the labor coaches.) You'll probably also be shown the obstetrical operating room, in case a C-section becomes necessary.

Paterniterms

A **Cesarean section** is a surgical birth rather than a vaginal birth. An obstetrical surgeon makes incisions in the abdominal wall and uterus in order to remove the baby and the placenta. As with any major surgery, a C-section requires a lengthy recuperation period.

Father Knows Best

"The films of the births, with moms pushing out baby after baby with hardly more than a brow beaded with perspiration, were a complete lie. The unruffled women of the films were either numb below the waist or had vaginas the circumference of the Holland Tunnel."

—Dan Greenburg

The final advantage offered by childbirth classes is that they give both you and your partner a chance to meet other expectant couples. This affords you the opportunity to discuss concerns or emotions common among mothers- and fathers-to-be as they await the birth of their children.

Daddy Dos and Don'ts

Take advantage of the tour to find out, among other things, the location of the nearest vending machines, cafeteria, and men's room. (Not all birthing rooms have private bathrooms.) Labor and delivery can take a long time; you'll probably need a bite to eat or a chance to relieve yourself.

One word of advice about childbirth classes: Don't make the mistake of thinking that they are for your wife, not you. You don't deserve a pat on the back simply for being a good sport and escorting her to the classes. Childbirth classes are as much for you as for your partner—if not more. She will give birth, one way or another, with or without classes. You, however, will not be an effective coach if you don't know what you're doing.

Indeed, the breadth of subjects covered by most childbirth classes—fetal development, early childcare, and so on—makes them useful not only for fathers-to-be who plan to coach their wives through childbirth, but also for those who plan *not* to do so. If you fall in the latter category, however, be forewarned: The "PC police"—represented by the teacher or students in the class—may try to pressure you to change your mind and become your wife's labor coach.

It's All in the Timing

You should start looking for a childbirth class during the second trimester. Ideally, your childbirth class should begin early in the seventh month of pregnancy. Of course, you'll be very busy during the final trimester, but classes rarely demand too taxing a time commitment. Generally, courses range from six to eight sessions, each running from 90 minutes to three hours.

Timing your course to begin in the seventh month will allow you to complete a six- to eight-week course before the birth, but not so much in advance that you'll forget everything you've learned in the excitement. A class in the seventh and eighth months will also reassure both you and your partner that your child will arrive soon—welcome news after what seems like an eternity of pregnancy.

To find a childbirth class, begin by asking your partner's midwife or obstetrician. Though not all obstetricians make such recommendations, those who do generally steer their patients toward classes that match their own philosophy of childbirth.

Other good sources of information on childbirth classes include

> ➤ Your local hospital.
> ➤ Your local American Red Cross chapter.
> ➤ New parents in your neighborhood.
> ➤ The American Academy of Husband-Coached Childbirth.
> ➤ The International Childbirth Education Association.
> ➤ The American Society for *Psychoprophylaxis* in Obstetrics.

(See Appendix B for addresses, telephone numbers, and web sites of organizations that help fathers through pregnancy, childhood, and beyond.)

By taking advantage of these resources, you should find a good childbirth class that fits your schedule. Make sure you can attend most—preferably all—of the classes before you sign up. If you will miss more than one session, look for another class that better suits your schedule. Both you and your partner will be glad you did.

Daddy Dos and Don'ts

If you can't find a childbirth course that begins early in the seventh month of your partner's pregnancy, try to get into an earlier class rather than a later one. Babies have been known to come early on occasion. If yours does, it's better to risk forgetting some of what you've learned than not to have all the knowledge you need.

Paterniterms

Psychoprophylaxis is the fancy name for the Lamaze method of childbirth, a series of breathing and relaxation techniques developed in the 1950s by Fernand Lamaze, a pioneering French obstetrician. Lamaze claimed his techniques helped women in labor work with their contractions rather than fight against them.

The Least You Need to Know

➤ Despite all the social pressures, you still have a choice whether to participate in childbirth. Talk it over with your partner, even if you're sure you want to be her labor coach.

➤ Men who choose not to be present at the birth of their child cite a variety of reasons: fear of queasiness, fear of witnessing a partner in pain, fear of getting in the way, religion, concerns about privacy, and discomfort with the supportive role of coach.

➤ Most men who have served as labor coaches for their partners are glad they did. They use words like "unforgettable," "incredibly intimate," "awe-inspiring," and "miraculous" to describe the experience.

➤ As a labor coach, you will have many responsibilities: timing contractions, offering massages, coaching relaxation and breathing techniques, and calming, supporting, protecting, and cheering on your partner.

➤ Childbirth classes are just as worthwhile—if not more so—for you as for your partner.

HEY!...

Chapter 4

Hey, What About Me?

In This Chapter

➤ The invisibility of the expectant father

➤ Whether men's bodies also change during pregnancy

➤ Taking care of your body during pregnancy

➤ How pregnancy can affect your sex life

➤ Whether pregnancy is a turn-on or a turn-off

Everyone acknowledges that women go through a monumental transformation during pregnancy. You can't ignore it. Throughout pregnancy, your partner's belly and breasts—and often her ankles and cheeks—may seem to grow larger with each passing day. After a few months, she begins to glow and you can actually feel—and, startlingly, often see—the baby moving around in her belly, poking her in the abdomen, ribs, and bladder, and generally making life uncomfortable for her.

So let's take it as a given that pregnancy changes a woman. After all, who could argue with a belly like that?

Unfortunately, few people acknowledge that pregnancy also changes a man. As outlined in Chapter 1, however, pregnancy often does transform an expectant father. Pregnancy marks the end of life as a couple and the beginning of life as a family. With the birth of the child (and even before) comes the birth of a father. For this reason, pregnancy brings all sorts of raw feelings and fears to the surface—for both women and men.

What may make all this upheaval even harder to handle is that no one else seems to notice it, comment on it, or ask questions about it. During a time of monumental change in your life, you seem to be the only one who can see it. You're all alone out there.

The Invisible Man

Face it: You're the invisible man in the story of your partner's pregnancy. Most people—including the most well-meaning and sensitive of your friends and relatives—don't realize that pregnancy is a time of transition for both the mother- and the father-to-be. Friends and family members may offer all the support they can to your partner, asking how she's feeling and perhaps volunteering to help her. Few, if any, of these generous and caring people, however, will ask about *your* feelings, thoughts, and fears.

The Pregnancy No Body Knows

If you are like most men, you will undergo a transformation during your partner's pregnancy. Unlike your partner, however, you are "pregnant" in a vacuum. Unless you suffer from "sympathetic" pregnancy symptoms, the dramatic changes you're going through are all internal—emotional and psychological—rather than external. True, many expectant fathers put on a little weight during their partners' pregnancy, while others grow—or shave—a beard or mustache. But your body will not experience anything close to the radical and involuntary changes that your wife's body is undergoing.

Since you lack physical cues—such as morning sickness, a growing belly, swelling breasts, and random contractions—you may feel ignored or left out of the pregnancy. (Don't get me wrong; it's really not a bad deal. After all, how many expectant fathers would trade their invisibility for their partner's physical discomforts? On the other hand, if your wife could make that trade, she'd no doubt jump at the offer.)

What Happened to that Old Gang of Mine?

As the progress of your partner's pregnancy renders you more and more invisible, you may find yourself feeling particularly isolated from other men, both friends and co-workers. Fatherhood tends to leave much less time for hanging out with buddies—even less time than after you got married or became the other half of a couple. Most of the men you know who have become fathers have probably dropped out of circulation. And in all likelihood, most of the men whom you've been seeing outside of work have been childless. After all, they're the ones with the most free time.

Of course, just because most of your friends don't have kids doesn't mean that you can't talk to them about your experience of pregnancy (and, later, fatherhood). But childless friends, simply by virtue of not having been through it themselves, will find it harder to understand and empathize with your situation. You may sense—rightly or wrongly—that your friends and co-workers are getting tired of hearing you talk about the pregnancy. You may begin censoring yourself. You may begin reining in not only your anxieties, worries, and negative feelings about pregnancy and fatherhood, but also your excitement and enthusiasm. Even your most joyful feelings in the anticipation of fatherhood may remain yours alone.

Unfortunately, you may find it difficult to talk about your impending fatherhood and the flood of emotions it stirs up even to your friends and colleagues who *have* had children. Men seldom talk about fatherhood, either during pregnancy or after a child is born. Most of us don't seem to know how to start the conversation and lack a common language to continue it.

If you take the time and initiative to share your experiences, thoughts, and feelings regarding pregnancy and fatherhood with other fathers and fathers-to-be, you will probably discover that they are not at all uncommon. You will find that nearly every expectant father has:

➤ Worried about his partner's health and whether his child will be "normal."

➤ Entertained, either briefly or at length, an impulse to flee.

➤ Wondered what his baby will look like.

➤ Felt intrigued, thrilled, and disconcerted by the movement of the fetus inside his partner's belly.

➤ Felt simultaneously impatient and apprehensive about the upcoming birth.

Similarly, after your child is born, your feelings (most of which have been experienced by millions of fathers before you) will cover a wide spectrum, including:

➤ Joy at your baby's first smile, first rollover, first crawl, first steps, first words, and other famous firsts.

➤ Anger so great that you could "murder that kid."

➤ Pride regarding your partner's way with the baby, your baby's many accomplishments and obvious superiority to all other infants, and your own shining moments as a father.

➤ Anxiety about your child's health and safety.

➤ Feelings of being ganged up on (or left out) by your wife and child.

➤ An occasional urge to get the hell out.

Nearly all fathers have felt the same way at times. Yet because we rarely talk about them, we may fail to recognize the universality of our own experiences and feelings as fathers and fathers-to-be.

Feeling alone with your emotions, relegated to the margins of the pregnancy, and perhaps feeling slighted or ignored by your friends and relatives, you may find yourself becoming increasingly isolated during your partner's pregnancy.

Something's Coming Between Us

So with whom do you discuss your feelings? In an ideal world, you would talk to the person who has made a commitment to share your most intimate moments, feelings, and gestures: your wife. Unfortunately, it's not at all uncommon for fathers-to-be to feel more and more isolated from their partners as the pregnancy progresses.

A number of factors can come into play in increasing the distance you feel between you and your partner. You may feel somewhat alienated by the creature growing inside her and by your inability to share directly in your wife's experience. You may also feel left out as your family and friends focus their attention on your wife and soon-to-be-born child. As the invisible man, you might even begin to resent your partner. After all, you have feelings, needs, and concerns, too.

Finally, you may have altruistic motives for remaining silent about your fears and feelings. You may censor yourself, keeping your anxieties and emotions to yourself in a misguided attempt to protect your partner. As long as she's in what was once called a "delicate condition," you may feel reluctant to burden her with your worries, thoughts, or fears.

If you keep all of your feelings and fears locked up, however, they will only become worse and create even more distance between you and your partner. They will eat away at you from the inside, leaving you not only invisible, but hollow as well.

So, talk to your partner about how you feel, your anticipation, emotions, and anxieties. As mentioned in Chapter 1, she may have concerns of her own that she wants to share with you. You can provide her with that opportunity. Talking to each other about your emotions and concerns about the pregnancy is one way the two of you can truly share in the experience and, thus, enhance your intimacy.

Remember, pregnancy is neither a disease nor a disability; despite any appearances to the contrary, your partner's condition is not all that delicate. Your openness about your fears and feelings will not endanger the pregnancy in any way. Both your partner and your baby are made of stronger stuff than that, as you will soon see during labor and delivery.

Your wife is probably not the only one willing to listen to your concerns. Other fathers you know might also welcome this kind of dialogue.

Daddy Dos and Don'ts

If, for some reason, you find it impossible to share your feelings and fears with your partner, find a good friend or a therapist who can give you the time you need to air your concerns.

You must know at least one or two men who have already been through all this. Perhaps you have a brother, cousin, or other relative who has a child. One relative certainly has: your own father. Maybe you should call him and ask him to reminisce. Or think of the men who dropped out of your after-hours get-togethers when they became dads. You could give one of them a call, too.

If you contact some of the fathers you know, you will find that they are some of the greatest untapped sources of wisdom in the world. Every man who is or has been a father has picked up some valuable lessons about pregnancy, children, and fatherhood itself. Unfortunately, most fathers seldom get the opportunity to share their hard-won knowledge.

What's Happening to My Body?

Obviously, fathers-to-be do not undergo any physical changes as a direct result of pregnancy. Your hormone levels won't go wild to facilitate the development of the fetus in your womb; your breasts won't become larger to prepare your body to produce milk for nursing your baby; and your belly won't expand to make room for your rapidly growing fetus. The calories and nutrients you consume won't be diverted to your womb. And your back, legs, and feet won't ache with the extra burden of the baby you're carrying (at least not until after your baby is born).

That your body won't demand attention in the same way your partner's will doesn't mean that you should ignore your physical health and well-being. Some men become so preoccupied with their partners' health during pregnancy that they unwittingly neglect their own. Don't let this happen to you.

Pregnancy offers both you and your partner nine months of transition time. Making the most of this time means not just preparing yourself mentally, emotionally, and materially for the arrival of the baby, but preparing yourself physically as well. You need to get in shape—or stay in good shape—for your baby.

Monkey See, Monkey Do

You may be surprised to discover that you may develop some of the same physical symptoms of pregnancy as your partner. It is not uncommon for expectant fathers to develop certain symptoms that mimic their partners' physical changes. You may feel somewhat nauseous or physically drained during the first trimester. You may gain weight in the second and third trimester. Throughout the pregnancy, you may suffer from restlessness or insomnia, and lose as much sleep as your wife.

Anthropologists first observed these kinds of "sympathetic" symptoms, which they called *couvade syndrome,* among fathers-to-be in non-industrialized countries. Later studies, however, suggested that couvade syndrome afflicts some—though certainly not all—fathers in industrialized cultures as well.

Paterniterms

The term **couvade syndrome** is derived from the French word for "hatching" or "brooding." Its symptoms include the following: nausea, sleeplessness, loss of appetite, weight gain, exhaustion, and vomiting. No definitive study has yet determined the prevalence of couvade syndrome among expectant fathers.

The physical symptoms you may experience do not arise as a direct consequence of hormonal changes or pregnancy itself, of course. Nonetheless, if you notice physical changes, they are probably related, if indirectly, to the pregnancy.

Psychiatrists might suggest that sympathetic symptoms during pregnancy result from extreme empathy for your partner, or represent the indirect expression of intense emotions you have suppressed during pregnancy. The symptoms might also satisfy a need for attention or to be involved in the pregnancy. These are good theories, of course, but it seems just as likely that symptoms of couvade syndrome result more directly from the unique situation of living with a pregnant woman.

If, for instance, you feel nauseous or lose your appetite early in your wife's pregnancy, it might have something to do with the fact that your wife is constantly throwing up. After all, it's not easy to see someone you love vomiting again and again and again without feeling somewhat sick yourself. It's no wonder that you don't feel too hungry when your wife is suffering from morning sickness.

Similarly, if you gain weight in the second and third trimesters, it may be that you're just trying to keep up with your wife's ravenous appetite. You may be accustomed to eating whenever she does.

Finally, your sleeplessness—and the exhaustion that follows—may be caused by your wife's restless struggles to find a comfortable sleeping position or her desire to talk when the baby's gymnastics wake her up in the middle of the night.

The Shape of Things to Come

To best serve yourself, your partner, and your baby-to-be, take advantage of the nine months of pregnancy to get, or stay, in shape. You'll do a better job of taking care of your wife and child if you've taken care of yourself.

In the months remaining before the birth of your baby, try to accomplish the following goals:

➤ **Maintain or lose weight.** Perhaps the most common physical problem among expectant fathers is weight gain. Try to eat sensible and nutritious meals. Keep in mind that just because your partner is "eating for two" doesn't mean that you have to eat more, too. As the growing baby leaves less and less room for her stomach, your partner may need to eat six or seven small meals and snacks a day. Avoid the temptation to join her for all of these meals.

➤ **Exercise regularly.** Yes, your time with your partner is becoming increasingly precious, and you want to do all you can to make the pregnancy easier on her. But save one hour a day at least three times a week to exercise. Regular exercise has not only physical, but mental and emotional benefits as well. It offers you the opportunity for both physical and emotional release.

➤ **Get rest.** Once your baby arrives, you can count on going months without a good night's sleep. Newborns tend to wake up several times a night for "midnight feedings," and chances are that when your baby wakes, so will you. So get plenty of rest now, while you still have a chance. (Exercise may help in this regard, too; exercising during the day improves your sleep at night.)

➤ **Quit smoking.** If you smoke, quit now. You'll find it much more difficult to quit smoking when you're feeling the stress of caring for a newborn. If your partner smoked, she has almost certainly stopped during the pregnancy. If she hasn't, strongly encourage her to do so; smoking has been linked with low birth weight and other complications of pregnancy. Support her decision to quit by quitting yourself.

Even if your partner weren't pregnant, your best strategy to maintain good health should involve controlling your weight, eating sensibly, exercising regularly, getting enough rest, and not smoking. These steps make even more sense when you're preparing to become a father. Unfortunately, common sense sometimes goes out the window when pregnancy comes in the door. So consider this a reminder to use your common sense and stay healthy during your partner's pregnancy.

Daddy Dos and Don'ts

If you can't—or won't—quit smoking, at least be a courteous smoker. Do everything you can to provide your partner (and later your baby) with a smoke-free environment. Step outside every time you want to light up. And avoid smoking in the car when driving anywhere with your partner (or child).

How the Heck Did Your Partner Get Pregnant Anyway?

Now comes the question you've been waiting for: Is there sex after conception?

The simple (and reassuring) answer: Of course there is.

Despite your wife's morning sickness, expanding belly, and the fact that a fetus is developing inside her, there is absolutely no medical reason why your partner's pregnancy should interfere with your sex life. Sexual intercourse during pregnancy will harm neither your wife nor your baby.

But let's face it, you need more than medical permission to maintain a sexual relationship. Whether justified medically or not, pregnancy will almost definitely affect your sex life with your partner.

Daddy Dos and Don'ts

The exceptions to the rule: If your partner has a high risk of miscarriage, her doctor may (or may not) advise her to abstain from intercourse for some or all of the pregnancy. In addition, if your partner has had vaginal bleeding problems, her cervix has begun to dilate, or her water has broken, you should abstain from any sexual relations that involve vaginal penetration. Of course, sex does not always have to include penetration.

Navigating a Sexual Obstacle Course

A variety of factors—both physical and emotional—can influence your sex life during the course of your partner's pregnancy. (As Yogi Berra might have said, 90 percent of sex is half mental. The other half is physical.)

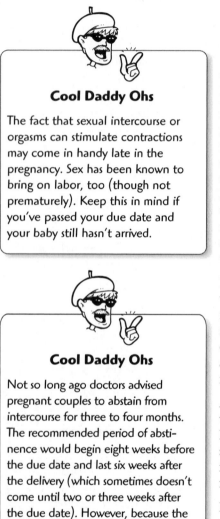

Cool Daddy Ohs

The fact that sexual intercourse or orgasms can stimulate contractions may come in handy late in the pregnancy. Sex has been known to bring on labor, too (though not prematurely). Keep this in mind if you've passed your due date and your baby still hasn't arrived.

Cool Daddy Ohs

Not so long ago doctors advised pregnant couples to abstain from intercourse for three to four months. The recommended period of abstinence would begin eight weeks before the due date and last six weeks after the delivery (which sometimes doesn't come until two or three weeks after the due date). However, because the subject was rarely discussed—and then often with some discomfort—the doctor's advice went unquestioned. Although the temporary ban on sex after childbirth does have a medical basis, the third trimester ban has no medical justification.

During the first trimester, for example, your wife may suffer from severe morning sickness. If she does, chances are that sex is one of the furthest things from her mind. (It was, after all, sexual intercourse that brought all this on her in the first place.)

Even if your partner doesn't suffer from morning sickness, hormonal changes will make her fatigued—again, not the ideal condition for love-making. In addition, if you've been trying for many months (or longer) to conceive a child, you may be especially fearful that sexual intercourse—or even your partner's orgasm—may harm the baby or cause a miscarriage. No reliable studies confirm this fear. If your wife has already had one or more miscarriages, however, her obstetrician will likely advise abstinence, at least during the first trimester, just to play it safe.

During the second trimester, your wife's hormone levels will stabilize and her morning sickness will probably fade. Your fears for the baby's safety will probably subside somewhat as well when you see your wife's belly expanding (and perhaps see a sonogram of the fetus). As a result, both of you will probably relax, and your sexual needs and desires will increase.

As your partner's belly becomes increasingly large, though, she will find it more and more uncomfortable to lie on her back. This may require the exploration of new sexual positions, but it need not mean the end of sexual intercourse. Indeed, you may have a lot of fun finding new ways to stimulate each other.

During the third trimester, fears for the baby's health and safety may resurface as you re-embrace the myth of the "delicate condition." Sexual logistics may also become a problem late in the pregnancy, when your wife's belly may grow so large that you find it an obstacle to intercourse in almost any position. What's worse for your partner is that intercourse or orgasm can stimulate contractions—sometimes painfully intense ones. In fact, contractions can begin as early as the second trimester.

Even though sexual intercourse is almost always medically permissible, even during the final weeks of pregnancy, many couples choose to refrain. Every couple has valid reasons, but their motivation (or lack of motivation) often springs from one or more of the following:

➤ Concerns about the welfare of the baby.

➤ Fatigue from preparing for the baby's arrival.

➤ The fear that sex will initiate labor prematurely.

Any of these can decrease your sex drive significantly.

You've Lost That Loving Feeling

Most couples have sex less frequently during pregnancy than they did before, especially if they've been diligently trying to conceive for months. (Hey, it's hard work, but somebody's got to do it.) In addition to having less energy, emotion, and motivation for sex, some couples actually seem to lose their taste for it.

If you or your partner have lost your appetite for sex, it may be due to the following:

➤ **You're afraid you'll hurt the baby.** This won't happen, so try not to worry about it. The amniotic fluid in your partner's womb will cushion any sexual pounding. And don't flatter yourself. No matter how big your penis is, it's not big enough to reach—much less puncture—the uterus.

➤ **You feel it's getting awfully crowded in your bed.** The baby may literally be coming between you as you try to make love. You may feel the baby's presence—a third party in your bed—as an insurmountable obstacle. Don't worry; your baby can't see your penis coming—and doesn't think it's the attack of a Cyclops.

➤ **You have too many "pregnancy worries" to focus on sex.** The anxieties about finances, the impending responsibilities of parenthood, and the freedom you'll soon lose—crystallized by the sight of your wife's swelling belly—may inhibit your sexual drive or interfere with your ability to get an erection. (The same worries can inhibit your wife's arousal, too.)

Pregnancy: Turn-Off ...?

Another obstacle that can get in the way of your sex life during pregnancy is that you may not find

Cool Daddy Ohs

The notion that pregnant women cannot be objects of sexual attraction may be traced to the traditional stereotyping of women as either madonnas or whores, but never both (at least not at the same time). An over-idealization of motherhood, coupled with a view of sex as "dirty," transforms pregnancy into something too pure to despoil with something sexual.

pregnant women—even your own wife—sexually attractive. And she might feel exactly the same way, seeing herself as fat or bloated or otherwise unattractive.

... Or Turn-On?

On the other hand, you may find your pregnant wife very sexy. Pregnant women really do develop a glow (although your partner may dismiss it as nothing more than sweat due to her extra load). And many men find the roundness of their partner's belly a sensual turn-on. Far from seeing her as fat, you may see your pregnant wife as

➤ The woman who loves you so much she wants to carry your baby.

➤ Living proof of your own virility.

➤ A goddess of fertility.

Everything about your partner's body becomes fuller, rounder, and more sensual during pregnancy. Your partner's breasts, for instance, become increasingly large throughout the pregnancy—a change that many women and, of course, men—welcome. Couple this with the sensual air of fertility that pregnant women undeniably possess, and you have someone who's very sexy.

Paterniterms

Engorgement of tissue means that blood rushes to it and fills it to maximum capacity. When your penis becomes engorged, you get an erection. Similarly, when your partner's vaginal tissue becomes engorged, she becomes aroused.

Father Knows Best

"It is as if somebody is steadily blowing her breasts full of air like beach balls. I worry that they will explode."

—Dan Greenburg

Your partner also may be turned on by her own pregnancy, embracing the whole "fertile earth mother" image. Some women find that their own pregnancy—and the emotions it engenders—makes them feel very sexy.

In addition, many women find that pregnancy *engorges* the tissue around the vagina, making them more sensitive and more readily stimulated sexually. Vaginal lubrication often increases during pregnancy, as well.

Let's Get It On

Whatever you're feeling about sex with your partner, talk to her about it. Don't let her wonder whether you still find her attractive or still love her. You may not find pregnancy itself all that attractive. If not, talking about it may help to unearth underlying fears, preconceptions, or anxieties. Even if it doesn't, your partner may need to know that it's not her, but the condition of pregnancy, that you find unattractive. She needs to know that you still love her.

On the other hand, if you find her pregnancy sexually arousing, she needs to hear this, too. If she feels particularly unattractive because of her changing body, the fact that you find her attractive will be especially welcome news. Even better, if the pregnancy has increased her sexual arousal as well as yours, you can both take advantage of each other's heightened sensuality.

So don't keep silent about your sexual feelings during pregnancy. After all, sex is an important part of your intimate relationship with your partner. Sexual relations can provide a great deal of pleasure, as well as feelings of warmth, love, and security.

Daddy Dos and Don'ts

Your partner's increased vaginal sensitivity will likely require a gentler touch on your part. Your partner's breasts may also become increasingly tender, demanding greater gentleness when fondling, kissing, and caressing.

Continued sexual intimacy may provide a great deal of reassurance to both of you, especially during pregnancy. Your wife may find it comforting to know that you still find her sexy, attractive, and cherished. And you might find it reassuring to know that your wife remains devoted to you and has not forgotten you in her attention to the baby growing inside her. As your partner's pregnancy progresses, you may discover (shockingly) that it has actually enhanced your sex life together.

Nonetheless, you and your partner may decide, for whatever reason, that you would rather refrain from sexual intercourse and other types of overtly sexual activity during pregnancy. If so, don't let that decision stop you from expressing affection in other ways, whether through holding hands, giving massages, fondling, or just talking.

The Least You Need to Know

➤ Pregnancy is a time of transition not only for mothers-to-be, but for fathers-to-be, too. Unfortunately, few people will acknowledge or even recognize the changes you're going through.

➤ If you seek them out, other fathers (or expectant fathers) can offer understanding and valuable insights. They've been there, too.

➤ Getting—or staying—in shape during pregnancy will better prepare you for fatherhood.

➤ Unless your partner has a high risk of miscarriage, problems with vaginal bleeding, her cervix has dilated, or her water has broken, there's no medical reason to abstain from sex during pregnancy.

➤ Whatever you decide to do about your sex life during pregnancy, decide it together with your partner. And don't forget to show your love for each other in other ways.

Chapter 5

Get Ready, 'Cause Here I Come

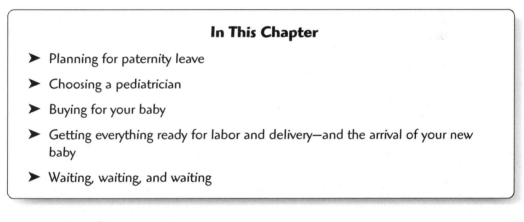

In This Chapter

➤ Planning for paternity leave

➤ Choosing a pediatrician

➤ Buying for your baby

➤ Getting everything ready for labor and delivery—and the arrival of your new baby

➤ Waiting, waiting, and waiting

The final month of pregnancy often seems to take a year to pass. You and your partner may be so eager to welcome your child into the world that in the weeks leading up to the due date—and perhaps beyond—time may seem to come to a standstill. Years from now, think back to this time when your child pipes up from the back seat during a long car trip, endlessly repeating the question, "How many more miles?" You'll know exactly how your child feels.

Unfortunately, the answer—as my father always told me when I asked that question—is that you'll get there when you get there.

Unlike a child on a long journey, however, you can do more than just sit and wait until you get there. You can make productive use of the final weeks by making last-minute preparations for the arrival of your baby. Here are some tips on how to make the final month's journey bearable.

It May Not Take a Village, But You Will Need Help

To make life easier on yourself and your partner in the weeks following childbirth, you will do well to prepare for your baby's homecoming in advance. And it would be nice if you and your partner could count on some help when you get home.

Time Off for Good Behavior

One question you'll need to resolve is whether you'll be taking a paternity leave from your job—and if so, when and how much. Unless you are living at or below the poverty level, you should seriously consider taking some time off from your job. Whether your partner is recovering from the trauma of vaginal birth or from a C-section (which is major surgery), she will be hard pressed to handle baby care on her own for at least the first week (and perhaps as long as six weeks if she's had surgery).

Relatively few men have taken advantage of the Family and Medical Leave Act since it became law in 1993. If you can afford it, however, you should buck the trend and take advantage of your right to take a paternity leave. Barring complications, you probably don't need to take the full 12 weeks. But taking at least some time off will not only allow you to gain precious time to get to know your baby, it will give you the chance to help your wife when she needs you the most.

If job commitments or dire financial straits make a lengthy leave of absence impossible, then take as much time as you possibly can afford. Remember, however, that the less time you have to take for a paternity leave, the more important the timing that leave becomes.

Of course, you'll want to use a personal day for your baby's birthday. If you'll be coaching during childbirth, you'll probably have no choice but to take the day off. You'd probably be wise to take off work the next day, too, when you'll most likely be simultaneously exhausted and exhilarated by the arrival of your child.

If you plan to take a limited paternity leave after those first two days, consider when you might be most useful to your family. For instance, if your wife and child remain hospitalized after childbirth for more than a day, it might be more helpful to go back to work during their hospitalization. Instead, save your personal days, vacation time, and leave days for when they come home. After all, your partner will need your help much

Cool Daddy Ohs

Did you know that you have the legal right to take up to 12 weeks of unpaid leave every year for family reasons? As long as you work for a company that employs 50 or more people, the 1993 Family and Medical Leave Act gives you that right. In theory (and according to the law), taking such a leave of absence should neither endanger your job status nor negatively affect your standing with your employer.

Daddy Dos and Don'ts

Ask your obstetrician what the local laws are regarding hospital discharges following childbirth. Laws governing hospital stays after childbirth vary from state to state, but many call for 48 hours after a vaginal delivery and three to four days following a C-section.

more when she gets home than she will when she's still under the watchful eyes of the maternity nurses (especially if she's recovering from a Cesarean section). Besides, you'll have much more time and opportunity to get to know your new baby at home than you will in the hospital.

Help! I Need Somebody

You and your partner will welcome all the help you can get in the first weeks after your baby's arrival. Infant care provides a new and exhausting challenge. In the wake of childbirth, your wife will not feel up to much of anything—especially if your baby is delivered surgically.

So do whatever you can to line up a few helpers for the initial weeks at home with your baby. First, do everything you can do on your own to help. But also ask for—or, if you can afford it, hire—the help you need to do the things you can't do.

The people who are the most willing to offer help—often before you even ask—will probably be your siblings, parents, and in-laws. If they offer to assist, seriously consider taking them up on it. If they don't, ask them directly.

You know your relatives better than I do, of course. You have a good idea how much help each relative can actually provide, and you know which ones are likely to drive you crazy. Yet despite any tension between you and your relatives or in-laws, you will probably welcome any help they can provide as you adjust to life with your new baby.

If one of your relatives or in-laws can do a little grocery shopping, help clean your baby's spit-up, or tackle the endless stream of laundry, you will be grateful—no matter how irritating you might find them under other circumstances.

Try to get your priorities straight, particularly if you're hiring someone to help out. For instance, you might consider hiring someone to watch the baby so that you or your wife can mow the lawn, wash the car, do the laundry, go grocery shopping, or clean the house. These things do need to get done to keep a household running smoothly, and you're probably used to doing them yourselves. For now, however, think about hiring (or asking) someone else to do these chores so that you and your wife and child can spend more time together. After all, it won't be long before you or your wife (or both) will have to return to work. So take advantage of the time you've set aside to be together as a family.

Daddy Dos and Don'ts

Don't rely on just one plan. Have one or two contingency plans lined up in case your first choice of helpers becomes unavailable, incapacitated, or otherwise unable to come through for you. People get sick, get called away on family emergencies of their own, or get delayed by bad weather or an airline strike. So it's a good idea to have at least one—and preferably more—backup plan.

What's the Plan?

When arranging for the help you'll need after the baby arrives, try to maintain as flexible a schedule as possible. For example, you probably won't need your mother-in-law to arrive on the baby's due date. Since many babies arrive late, having helpers arrive on the due date makes little sense. If the baby is late, you don't need an extra houseguest. Your relatives, friends, or hired help will have much more to do after your baby comes home than during the days—or even weeks—before her arrival.

You Need Professional Help!

Before your child arrives, you'll also want to consider lining up a pediatrician. You may not have thought much about this yet, but aside from a day-care provider or babysitter, a pediatrician will be the most important helper you'll choose over the next few years. So take some time to make the right choice. Here's what to do:

➤ **Get recommendations.** Ask your friends who have children, your partner's obstetrician or midwife, and relatives for suggestions. (Of course, if you belong to an HMO or preferred-provider plan, you'll need to check any recommended pediatricians against the list of doctors who belong to your health insurance plan.)

➤ **Arrange interviews.** Once you've weeded your list down to two or three doctors, meet with each one. Some will charge you for their time (or do so only if you choose another pediatrician); others won't charge at all.

➤ **Check on board certification.** Contact your state or local medical society—or see if your local library has a copy of the Directory of Medical Specialists to find out if the pediatricians you're considering are *board certified.* Certification guarantees a level of experience and expertise in treating children.

➤ **Ask questions.** To find out if the pediatrician's child-rearing philosophy matches your own, ask his or her opinion on breast-feeding versus bottle-feeding, feeding on demand, thumb-sucking or the use of pacifiers, when (or if) parents should return to work, the use of antibiotics, and how to handle sleep disturbances. Your discussion will establish how comfortable you feel talking with the pediatrician and whether the doctor's answers are consistent with your own beliefs.

Paterniterms

Board certification means that a doctor has trained for at least three years in an approved pediatrics residency training program and then passed a qualifying exam. Pediatricians who have been board certified have gained experience not only in well-baby care, but in treating a variety of more complicated childhood ailments.

By taking the time to do some homework before your baby arrives, you can avoid getting stuck with a pediatrician with whom you never quite feel comfortable or in whom you have little confidence. No prenatal interview can take the place of seeing how your pediatrician interacts with your child, however. If you decide to switch pediatricians after your baby is born because the doctor you've chosen seems insensitive to the needs and feelings of your baby or is brusque and inattentive to your infant as an individual, you can always repeat these steps.

Buy, Buy, Baby

Welcome to the baby consumer market! Even before your baby arrives, you will probably find yourself wandering with glazed eyes through one of those baby warehouses that stock nearly every baby product under the sun.

Most baby products will be immediately recognizable to you. Some, however, will be so unfamiliar that you may have no idea what they are or what they do. Don't get discouraged or think your ignorance about a certain baby product is a sign you're not ready to have a baby. Instead, try adopting this rule as a consumer: If it takes too long to figure out what it is, you probably don't need it.

Cool Daddy Ohs

Orthodox Jews and adherents of other conservative religions will not buy any baby products—or open baby-shower gifts—until after their children are born. These believers consider counting your chickens before they are hatched to be disrespectful of the miraculous gift God has given us—an act of arrogance that courts disaster.

All You Need Is Love?

You don't need to buy everything in the baby store. After all, you and your partner really won't need that much to take care of a newborn. Babies have very limited needs: food, sleep, bathing, clothing, and love. If your wife plans to breast-feed, the food and love are free. So all you absolutely need to buy for your baby are clothes, bath supplies, and a place to sleep.

Here's what you'll absolutely need:

➤ **Cloth or disposable diapers.** Expect to go through an incredible 80–100 diapers a week! Cloth diapers are also handy for mopping up the endless stream of spit-up your baby will produce. Stock up with at least 100 diapers before the birth. You'll also want a diaper pail with a secure lid and some diaper cream for treating diaper rash. (See Chapter 9 for tips on changing diapers.)

➤ **Clothing.** Babies go through almost as many outfits a day as they do diapers. Unless you want to do non-stop laundry, you'll need at least 8–10 T-shirts, a dozen or more outfits (one-piece coveralls that snap down the legs are most convenient), and almost as many one-piece pajamas. For cold—or even just cool—weather, a few sweaters and hats will be essential, too.

Father Knows Best

"Any baby clothes with flop-eared bunnies on them reduce me to a gibbering idiot. We end up buying lots of baby clothes featuring flop-eared bunnies."

—Dan Greenburg

Paterniterms

A **bassinet** is not a little hound dog; it's a cozy basket—sometimes portable and sometimes attached to a stand—just big enough to hold a sleeping baby.

Daddy Dos and Don'ts

Newborns don't seem to know what to do with all the freedom of movement outside the womb. In fact, most prefer to be wrapped tightly in a blanket, with only their head free (especially at sleep time).

➤ **Bassinet or crib.** Although you will almost certainly want a crib for your baby down the line, you don't need one for a newborn. If your wife has a surgical delivery, it will be more convenient and less painful for her not to have to lean over a crib railing to put the baby down. A *bassinet* can come in handy during the first months if you don't want to take the baby into bed with you.

➤ **Sheets and blankets.** A few fitted crib sheets and at least two waterproof mattress pads are essential. You'll also need at least half a dozen blankets for the crib, for the stroller, and just for wrapping around your baby.

➤ **Feeding supplies.** If your partner is going to breast feed the baby and doesn't plan to go out alone for more than an hour or so, you won't need anything but her breasts. If you plan to bottle feed on occasion (to give your partner a break) or bottle feed full-time, however, you'll need at least half a dozen bottles, newborn nipples, and formula (which comes ready-made, in liquid concentrate, or in powdered form).

➤ **Child-safety car seat.** If you own a car, you *must* buy an infant safety seat. You should strap your baby in securely whenever you go anywhere in the car together. And if you don't buy the car seat before the birth, how will you get your baby home from the hospital or birthing center?

➤ **First-aid supplies.** To care for your baby if he gets sick or some other medical emergency arises, you'll need the essential medical supplies: a rectal thermometer for taking your baby's temperature, acetaminophen drops to help reduce fever, and syrup of ipecac to cause vomiting if your baby swallows something he shouldn't. (See Chapter 10 for a complete list of items you'll need in your first-aid cabinet.)

➤ **Bath supplies.** Because they're not yet mobile, newborns really don't get all that dirty (except in their diapers). To clean your newborn, all you'll need are a dozen soft washcloths, water, some towels, and perhaps a box of baby wipes. In most cases, you won't even need soap! You can also buy a baby tub, which will come in handy later, but you will find it easier to bathe your newborn in the kitchen sink. (See Chapter 9 for tips on bathing a baby.)

That's really all you need to buy to care for a newborn. Once you've taken care of your infant's needs for food, clothing, cleanliness, sleep, and safety, you've provided every essential.

What Else Could You Possibly Want?

Of course, you'll want to offer your baby more than the mere essentials she needs to survive. You'll want something in which to carry the baby when you go outside, some things to entertain her, and some things to make baby care easier on you and your partner.

Here are some items you might want to consider buying:

➤ **Stroller.** Babies tend to like the outdoors, and it's healthy for them to get some fresh air. A stroller will take some of the tension off your back. Strollers now come in a wide variety, from lightweight "umbrella" strollers (not so sturdy, but the handiest for long-distance travel after your baby can sit up) to strollers that convert into carriages.

➤ **Baby carrier.** Baby carriers come in handy if you want to take a walk and don't want to push a stroller around. Some car seats have detachable basket-style carriers. If you want your hands totally free, try a cloth, front carrier with a harness that goes over the shoulders and around the waist, or a heavy-duty back-pack style carrier.

Daddy Dos and Don'ts

For tips on what to look for when buying everything from strollers and baby carriers to car seats and high chairs, consult a buyer's guide such as the *Consumer Reports Guide to Baby Products*. (*Consumer Reports* also has a web site (www.ConsumerReports.org) that might be helpful.)

➤ **Baby tub.** As mentioned earlier, the easiest way to bathe a baby is to take her into the tub with you or to wash her in the sink (after lining it with towels for a softer surface). When your baby gets a little bigger, however, you might want to try a padded baby tub—a small plastic tub with a detachable, sloped, and padded insert on which a newborn can lie without dunking her head. Then you can wash your baby almost anywhere and anytime.

➤ **Rocking chair.** Not for the baby, but for your partner and you. Gentle rocking can help soothe a nursing baby (or a baby with a bottle) and lull her into a drowsy state.

➤ **Pacifiers.** Babies like to suck on things, not just on breasts and on bottles, but on fingers, pacifiers, and anything that touches their lips. Your baby will use sucking not only as a way of eating, but also as a way of comforting herself. Although some hard-liners object to the use of pacifiers (and you should probably guard against over-using them), many parents find that babies really do enjoy them.

➤ **Toys.** Don't go overboard buying toys for an infant. Babies have little use for toys until they are three or four months old and can grasp objects in their hands. At that age, soft rattles make nice starter toys.

➤ **Mobiles and mirrors.** Though they cannot control the movements of their hands and feet, newborns can focus their eyes. A mobile that hangs over the crib or changing table will be appreciated very early in your baby's life. Rotating musical mobiles will usually hold a baby's attention long enough for you to change her diaper.

When choosing a mobile, hold it above your head to see how it will look from your baby's perspective. Babies respond best to bold colors and sharp contrasts such as black and white images and patterns. (Keep this in mind when you consider painting your child's room in pastel pinks or blues—colors that newborns find nearly invisible.) Then hang the mobile 7–12 inches above where your baby's head will lie on the crib or changing table.

Child-safe mirrors placed alongside the changing table or in your baby's crib will also entertain her. A changing-table mirror, for example, can often distract your baby from the messy task at hand.

Everything else—including staples of modern-day parenting such as baby swings, playpens, giant teddy bears, and even changing tables—might be nice to have but are far from essential, especially for a newborn. As your baby gets bigger, you will find that you want or need some of these or other items. For now, however, you really don't need to go wild in the baby mart.

Packed and Ready to Go

The final weeks before your baby arrives can seem endless. But if you keep yourself busy by taking care of last-minute details, the waiting should not drive you crazy. Of course, if you leave too many details to the last minute, the final weeks may seem way too short. Few new parents, however, end up thinking their baby arrived too soon.

You Can't Have a Baby without Paperwork

If you haven't already done so, you should take care of any required paperwork during the final few weeks before your due date. If you plan on having your baby in a hospital, for instance, you will need to fill out certain admission forms before your partner arrives in labor.

Most hospitals allow preadmission for childbirth or scheduled Cesarean sections. This means you and your partner can visit the hospital's admissions office in advance to take care of most of the required paperwork, including documentation of your insurance coverage, your partner's medical history, and the consent forms that allow the obstetrician to perform the delivery at that hospital and to administer anesthesia in case of an emergency.

To get an idea of how much all this will cost, check with your insurance carrier or HMO to find out how much of the labor, delivery, and post-partum care is covered under your health plan. Childbirth can be very costly, especially if a C-section becomes necessary, but most of it will probably be covered if you're insured. (A private room will, of course, cost more than a semiprivate room, and the difference will almost certainly come out of your pocket.)

As long as your partner has insurance or belongs to an HMO, don't worry about the cost of your baby's hospitalization. Upon birth, your baby is covered to the same extent as your partner (although you will probably have less than 48 hours to notify your insurance carrier of the arrival). Although all hospitalization costs will almost certainly be covered, the attending pediatrician's *post-partum* visits in the hospital may or may not be covered by your insurance.

Paterniterms

Post-partum simply means after separation—in the case of a mother and child, after childbirth.

What Did You Forget?

A couple of weeks before your due date, begin packing your bags (in case the baby arrives early). If you have taken a prenatal childbirth class, your teacher no doubt told your wife what to bring (pillows for wedging, tennis balls for pressing into the small of the back, and so forth). You might not have heard anything, however, about what you should bring to serve as her labor coach. For yourself, remember to bring

Daddy Dos and Don'ts

Remember to replace the fruit or sandwich you've packed every couple of days until the big day actually arrives. Nobody in the birthing room will welcome the sight and smell of a moldy sandwich or rotten piece of fruit.

➤ A stopwatch or a watch with a second hand to time your partner's contractions.

➤ Paper and a pen or pencil to note the timing of the contractions and to write down anything you might want to record for posterity.

➤ Relevant notes from your childbirth class.

➤ A portable CD player or tape deck and some of your partner's favorite relaxing tunes.

➤ Something to pass the time (magazines, newspapers, cards, or travel games), especially between the well-spaced contractions of early labor.

➤ Something for *you* to eat (fruit, cookies, a sandwich), since hospital cafeterias often close shortly after the dinner hour.

➤ Some loose change for the hospital's vending machines or to make phone calls after the delivery.

➤ The phone numbers of people you'd like to call with the news.

➤ Your insurance or HMO identification card and any phone numbers you'll need to call to notify your carrier of the newly insured.

➤ Some clean clothes to change into after the birth of your child.

➤ A bottle of Champagne or sparkling cider if you want that to be part of the post-partum celebration.

Daddy Dos and Don'ts

You also might want to bring a gift to present to your wife on your baby's birthday—a token of your gratitude, appreciation, and pride. You might want to choose something that has nothing to do with babies, something that shows her that you still see her as so much more than the mother of your child. When in doubt, pick something sexy—lingerie, silk or satin sheets, jewelry, or perfume. Though she probably won't use any of these for some time after the birth, they will remind her that you still adore her.

Lights, Camera, Action?

If you're a camera or camcorder buff, you'll want to have plenty of film or blank video cassettes to capture your baby's first moments in the world. Although I understand the desire to preserve this momentous occasion with photographs, I cannot comprehend (or support) husbands who choose to record the entire process of labor and delivery on videotape.

Look, I appreciate the desire to record such an important event for posterity. But the more attention you devote to the camera, the less you'll have to devote to your laboring partner. A few seconds away from your wife's side to snap some photos is one thing. But if you're playing Quentin Tarantino at your wife's feet throughout the final stage of labor and delivery, who's playing Phil Jackson at her head?

Father Knows Best

"It makes me feel a bit touristy and foolish to be taking pictures in such circumstances, but it helps to have something to concentrate upon besides the melodrama that is unfolding on all sides of me."

—Dan Greenburg

Before stepping into the birthing room, you need to decide whether you want to be coach or auteur. You cannot participate fully in the labor and delivery while directing a video. Chances are your wife needs your attention, your support, your encouragement, and your hand much more than she needs your skill at cinematography.

If you absolutely must capture your child's birth on video, you'll do better to ask someone else to take over one of the roles. If it won't make your partner uncomfortable, consider asking a friend (a very close friend) either to hold the camcorder or to serve as your partner's labor coach.

Whatever you decide will work best for you and your partner, figure it out now. If you're going to invite extra people into the birthing room, you'll probably have to clear it with your obstetrician or midwife in advance.

Daddy Dos and Don'ts

If the thought of a friend having such an intimate view of your wife when she's most vulnerable makes her uncomfortable but you both still want a video record of the event, it might make sense to hire a professional. After all, you'll be surrounded by other professionals—the obstetrician or midwife, nurses, and perhaps an anesthesiologist—who are relative strangers to you; will one more really matter?

Is There Gas in the Car?

Now that you're all packed and ready to go, don't forget that unless you're planning a home birth, you'll need some way to get to the hospital or birthing center. If you have a car, fill up the tank regularly. Like many expectant fathers, you may even want to practice the drive once or twice during the ninth month of pregnancy to see what you're likely to encounter on the way, to locate the emergency entrance, and to find out where to park.

Daddy Dos and Don'ts

Store a spare set of car keys in a magnetic box under your car's bumper in case you lock yours in the car in the excitement of the moment. (Hey, it happens!) Also consider loading the back seat of the car with pillows and blankets or towels on the off chance that your baby decides not to wait until you reach the hospital or birthing center.

Although you won't need to install an infant car seat just yet, you might want to put it in the trunk or back seat so that it's ready when you need it. You don't want to pick up your wife and newborn baby and then realize you don't have it.

If you've never owned a personal pager (and even if you hate the idea of having one), this might be the time for you to consider getting one. When labor begins, you'll want your wife to be able to reach you right away.

Finally, come up with one or two contingency plans in case your wife can't find you or you can't get to her right away when labor begins. Make arrangements with a friend to take her to the hospital or birthing center in a pinch, or put a list of the phone numbers of the nearest taxi companies next to the phone(s) and in your wife's purse. That way, you'll know she can get where she needs to be if you can't take her.

So Where's the Baby?

As your baby's due date approaches (and especially if it goes by without event), you may become increasingly anxious, concerned, and impatient. The car's gassed up, the bags are packed, and the nursery's ready. Your wife is as big as a Volkswagen, she complains of constant aches and pains, and she stopped working weeks ago. So what's taking that baby so long?

The Waiting Game

Maybe you've left yourself with too little to do. Try not to call a halt to all activities prematurely. Yes, the baby could come early and you want to be ready if he does, but just sitting around waiting through the last month of the pregnancy will drive you crazy. You could be sitting around twiddling your thumbs, becoming more and more anxious and irritable every day, for as long as eight weeks if you and your partner put your life on hiatus at the beginning of the ninth month.

The due date is just an estimate, a best guess about when your baby will arrive. It's not uncommon for a pregnancy to continue two or three weeks past the due date, so try to be patient.

Think of this waiting as practice for what you'll be in store for during the next 18 to 60 years. As you'll soon learn, almost nothing ever proceeds strictly according to plan with kids. You'll need to adapt yourself at least to some degree to your child's time-table: for feeding, sleeping, walking, talking, and learning. This adaptation often begins with the birth itself.

Father Knows Best

"Somewhere on this globe, every ten seconds, there is a woman giving birth to a child. She must be found and stopped."

—Sam Levenson

False labor also may add to your anxiety. It's not uncommon for women in their ninth month of pregnancy to experience a series of contractions that, though they help prepare the body for labor, do not indicate actual labor and delivery. Generally, these contractions subside after a while, but you can't just sit around assuming it's false labor. You'll spring into action, and then both you and your partner may feel let down when you discover that it was just a false alarm.

Unfortunately, even if you exhibit extraordinary patience and take the attitude that the baby will come when he's ready, the people closest to you may force their own anticipation of the happy event upon you. Friends and relatives may call daily; colleagues may ask about the baby every morning. If the anticipation is already making you tense, these well-meaning inquiries will only heighten your anxiety. And if you're laid back about the timing, you may start wishing your baby would arrive just so you'll have some news to share with all your well-wishers.

If your friends and relatives are unwittingly adding to your anxiety, let those with whom you feel most comfortable know it. They will no doubt understand and respect your wishes.

Cool Daddy Ohs

Births increase when the moon is full. The full moon's stronger gravitational pull, which influences the tides, also seems to affect the release of amniotic fluid.

Last Rest Stop for Miles and Miles

Instead of just sitting around waiting, spend some special time together, just the two of you. (And treat yourself to something special, too.) After all, it's probably the last chance you'll have for unfettered self-indulgence for quite some time.

So in these last few days (or weeks), relish both your solitude and your life as a couple. You know what you like to do, so go out and do it while you still have the chance. Here are a few suggestions:

Daddy Dos and Don'ts

Remember, sexual intercourse and orgasm have been known to induce labor at the end of pregnancy. So as long as your partner's water has not broken or her cervix has not begun to dilate, make love often.

➤ Go out on a date (with your wife, of course).

➤ Spend a quiet evening together at home.

➤ Spend an evening or two playing poker or going out with the boys.

➤ Go to the gym and get some exercise.

➤ Turn off the alarm clock and treat yourself to a good night's sleep.

➤ Make love; have wild, animal sex (again, with your wife).

Heck, any of these suggestions beats sitting around waiting, so go ahead. Indulge yourself one last time.

The Least You Need to Know

➤ If you can afford it, take at least some paternity leave soon after your baby is born.

➤ If you have only a limited time for paternity leave, consider when you will be most needed and useful at home.

➤ Line up as much help as you can for when your partner and child come home together.

➤ Here's all you really need to buy before the baby arrives: diapers, baby clothes, a baby bed, bedding, washcloths, a car seat, and a handful of medical supplies. Everything else you can buy at your leisure (if you ever have any) or do without completely.

➤ Don't just sit there waiting during the last weeks of pregnancy. Do something fun, something romantic, something entertaining, and definitely something time-consuming.

Chapter 6

Choose Your Own Adventure: What Kind of Father Do You Want to Be?

In This Chapter

➤ Some choices you need to make to define yourself as a father

➤ Fatherhood today: The more things change, the more they stay the same

➤ Figuring out how to split time between work and the other responsibilities of fatherhood

➤ Three kinds of dads: the breadwinner, the split personality and the full-time dad

➤ The dearth of role models for contemporary fathers

Few of us grew up wanting to be a father. Chances are, when you were a kid, you wanted to be an astronaut, the quarterback for the 49ers, or the center fielder for the Yankees. Perhaps you wanted to be a doctor, a scientist, a firefighter, a teacher, or even a writer.

Whatever you wanted to be when you were a boy, you probably thought little about becoming a father. Furthermore, you may seldom have even made believe you were a daddy. Indeed, perhaps the only time you pretended to be a father was when your sister or a female friend roped you into "playing house." Boys just weren't brought up to behave that way in those days (and, in most cases, still aren't today).

The models of fatherhood we observed growing up—our own fathers and those we saw on TV and in the movies—probably conformed to a very different notion of what it meant to be a father than the one most of us have today. Most of the fathers we grew up watching were distant, somewhat mysterious figures who were expected to

➤ Bring home the bacon (that is, earn money).

➤ Discipline the children (but only after finding out from their mothers what exactly they did that was so bad).

➤ See the children no more than 5–10 hours a week.

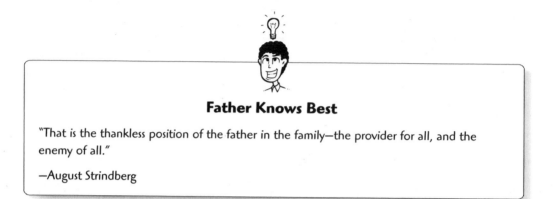

Father Knows Best

"That is the thankless position of the father in the family—the provider for all, and the enemy of all."

—August Strindberg

Given these cultural constraints, and the pressure to conform to them, most of our fathers did a pretty good job with us.

But now you're a dad—or you're soon going to become one—and you may (or may not) approach your role as a father very differently from the way your father approached it. With little play-acting experience and, in all likelihood, very distant role models, however, you may be unsure exactly how you would answer the following questions:

➤ How do you plan to approach fatherhood?

➤ How would you describe your new role as a father?

➤ What kind of father do you really want to be?

Typecasting: Filling the Role of Father

What does it mean to be a father today? It probably means something a little different to every man who becomes one. Fathers today have so many options that each is free to define, modify, and redefine the role in his own way. As a result of the choices they—and their partners—make, fathers may take very different approaches to issues such as

➤ How much time they devote to baby or child care.

➤ The expectations about the extent to which they must provide for their families financially.

➤ How to divide parenting responsibilities with their partners.

➤ How best to complement their partners' approach to parenting.

➤ How involved they become in their children's lives.

➤ What part they play in disciplining their children and molding their values and behavior.

➤ How they talk (and listen) to their children.

➤ What they do when with their children

No matter how hard you look, you will not find absolutely right or wrong solutions to these difficult parenting issues. The best you can do is to come up with solutions that are right or wrong for you and your partner.

Father Knows Best

"Before I got married I had six theories about bringing up children; now I have six children and no theories."

—John Wilmot, Earl of Rochester (1647–1680)

The choices you and your partner make in resolving these and many other open-ended parenting issues will depend upon a wide variety of factors, including the following

➤ Your personalities and temperaments.

➤ Your individual talents.

➤ Your upbringing.

➤ Your ethnic heritage.

➤ Your religious beliefs.

➤ Your values.

➤ Your education.

➤ Your financial circumstances.

➤ Other circumstances of your day-to-day lives.

With so many factors influencing you and your partner, the kind of father you decide to be is a highly personal decision.

Father Knows Best

"You know the only people who are always sure about the proper way to raise children? Those who've never had any."

—Bill Cosby

Rewriting the Roles

Changing social patterns have opened up new options for both men and women that permit new family arrangements. The women's movement, the subsequent increase of women in the workforce, and the need for many families to have two incomes just to survive or to maintain a comfortable lifestyle, have encouraged, allowed, or forced women to see themselves as more than just mommies and to move beyond the home as their sole sphere of influence. Among other things, these changes have heightened the demand for quality day care and caused many families to explore new ways of sharing parenting responsibilities.

Society as a whole changes very slowly, however. Despite all the changes wrought by the women's movement over the past 30 years, women are still the primary care-givers in most households. Although the advances of the women's movement may have fallen short of revolution, they have at least transformed the attitudes of most men and women and the household dynamics that grow out of them. As a result, many men are asking for—or being forced to accept—more child-rearing responsibilities.

Many men embrace these new challenges, though some still shy away from them. Today, the challenge for fathers is to balance the need or desire to devote time to parenting with the more traditional paternal responsibility of wage-earning. Although most men today still take on the primary responsibility of bringing home the bacon, some (in cooperation with their partners) have begun to break new ground. Today's fathers fall into one of the following categories:

➤ The full-time breadwinner

➤ The split personality

➤ The full-time dad

The Full-Time Breadwinner

The majority of families today still cling to the traditional idea of the father as the full-time breadwinner. Like many generations of fathers before you, you may embrace this model. After all, it does have certain advantages:

➤ It provides an efficient division of labor and a clear-cut understanding of each parent's responsibilities.

➤ The father's remoteness from his children's day-to-day lives provides little emotional entanglement, which some men regard as a blessing.

➤ The father's role in the home is relatively easy. Other than making money, he has very limited family responsibilities.

You may not see all of these as advantages, but some men are very comfortable playing such a limited role in their families. The traditional full-time breadwinner role also has its drawbacks, however:

➤ It allows the father little time to spend with his children.

➤ It significantly reduces the father's opportunities to get to know his kids—and for them to get to know him.

➤ The father misses out on most of the everyday joys and pleasures of family life.

Despite these drawbacks, you may find the breadwinner role best suited to your needs, desires, and abilities. Like many men, for example, you may find your work both more restful and more fulfilling than the demands of fatherhood. After all, you probably know how to do whatever you do in the workplace—and you've no doubt gotten good at it. You may not feel quite the same about baby care.

The traditional breadwinner and his family today are not quite the same as they were in previous generations. The primary difference is that today's father is often not the sole provider for his family. Very often, today's mother also works either part- or full-time, requiring someone else to care for the children.

Father Figures

Two-thirds of American women with dependent children hold a paying job.

The Children's Hour

Whether or not their partners also work full-time, the biggest domestic challenge faced by fathers who are full-time breadwinners is simply finding the time to play with, care for, and be with their children. Time constraints make it impossible for many fathers who work full-time to devote as much time to their children as they might like. (Mothers who work full-time, of course, face a similar dilemma.)

Do the math. Let's say you work 40–50 hours a week and it takes you 30 minutes to an hour to commute each way. That's already 45 to 60 hours a week devoted to the job (assuming you never work late or on weekends). Still, that leaves 108–123 hours a week at home—a pretty big chunk of time.

Unfortunately, if you're a nine-to-fiver, the kids—especially from infancy through the preschool years—are asleep most of the time that you're home. Depending on your child's age, he probably sleeps 9–14 hours a night. That's another 63–98 hours a week that you can't spend with your child. This means that even the most saintly (or masochistic) father who works full-time has only 10–60 hours a week to spend with his child. (Don't be deceived by that top figure of 60 hours a week, which seems like a lot of time. It's a rare full-time breadwinner who works just 40 hours a week, has almost no commute, and whose young children sleep just nine hours a night.)

But wait! This reckoning doesn't take into account time-consuming activities such as making home repairs, exercising or playing sports, participating in community service, or just plain spending time alone. Your child also will develop his own interests as he grows: friends, sports, clubs, scouting, TV, homework, and so on.

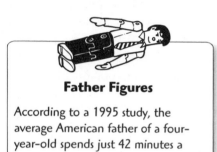

Father Figures

According to a 1995 study, the average American father of a four-year-old spends just 42 minutes a day alone with his child. That works out to less than five hours a week!

When you stop to think about it, you have relatively little time to devote to active parenting responsibilities if you work full-time—certainly far less time than you spend on the job or sleeping.

Sure you're tired when you get home from work. Of course, you just want to relax. But try to save a little energy for your kids. The hours you'll have to enjoy them, to play an active part in their development, and to drive them crazy and be driven crazy by them are relatively few, and they will become fewer and fewer every year.

Try not to turn parenting into something you do on automatic pilot. Watch, listen, and plan. Be spontaneous, creative, involved, and as invested in parenting as you are in your job. Although you won't get paid for this time, you will be rewarded—every time your child smiles spontaneously or shows affection for you, or every time you see him discover something new about the world or his own abilities.

The Split Personality

A handful of parents today are taking advantage of home workstations and flex-time scheduling to carve out a new type of parenting arrangement: split personalities.

In this setup, the father and mother share both bread-winning and child-rearing responsibilities. Although based on an ideal of equal partnership, this arrangement seldom achieves precise parity in practice. One partner usually spends a little more time making a living and less time caring for the child than the other. This kind of compromise does not mean you have to abandon the ideal of equal partnership, however.

Relatively few parents can manage this split-personality arrangement, although it has become somewhat easier in the past decade. It depends, in large part, on both partners' choice of careers as well as the concessions made to working parents by their employers.

To make the split-personality/split-parenting arrangement work, you and your partner must have very marketable skills, yet neither of you can work 40 hours or more a week on a regular basis. If either of you does work 40 hours, you may need to have somewhat flexible hours rather than a nine-to-five job. Many large employers now offer the option of "flex-time scheduling," which allows employees to choose hours such as 7 to 3 or 11 to 7 rather than 9 to 5. By taking advantage of flex-time scheduling, you can accommodate your partner's schedule and have more time to spend with your children when they're still awake.

The split-personality, equal-partnership arrangement works even better if one of you can work at home. Computers, fax machines, and the like have made it possible for more and more people to do some—or even all—of their work at home. If this idea appeals to you and the nature of your work makes it feasible, ask your employer. By doing some or all of your work at home, you can work whatever hours are most convenient for your family.

Although this kind of arrangement requires a certain juggling of responsibilities and a great deal of flexibility, my wife and I are living proof that it can work. I'm lucky enough to work for an employer who has been very understanding of my needs: me. (Running your own business makes this arrangement work better, of course.)

My wife Susie works 20–25 hours a week in a hospital on an 8 to 1 shift. While she's working, I take care of the kids, getting a little work in during their morning nap—when they consented to take naps. When she gets home, I go to my office to work. Because I work at home, I can start working within minutes of her arrival and get four to five hours in before dinner and, when necessary, more hours on weekends or weeknights after the kids go to bed.

Not Enough Hours in the Day

The biggest challenges faced by parents who try to work out this kind of equal (or nearly equal) parenting partnership involve making ends meet, maintaining productivity, and finding time for each other. Financially, two half-jobs rarely add up to one full job. Typically, a part-time job pays less than half of what a full-time job does. So two parents working part-time will probably earn less money than one of them would working full-time.

To drain your finances further, few employers provide health insurance and other benefit packages to part-time workers. In all likelihood, you'll have to pay for your own health insurance and set up your own retirement account.

In addition, if one of you works at home, you may find it difficult to keep up your productivity with all the distractions around you. Working at home requires a certain mind-set and a lot of self-discipline. To get your work done, you'll need to discipline yourself to get down to work at every opportunity. When your baby lies down for a nap, you have to get to work. When your partner gets home, you have work to do.

This kind of tag-team parenting, however, may leave you with little time for each other, especially if one or both of you work more than 25 hours a week. You and your partner will need to make a special effort to devote time to each other as well as to your kids and jobs. If you don't, your relationship will probably deteriorate—or at least stagnate.

The upside of working out this kind of split personality deal is that your kids get to spend sustained periods of time with each of you. (Of course, not every father sees this as a huge benefit, but many do.) This may not only be enormously fulfilling for you, but the models you provide of shared parenting responsibilities will prepare your children for when they become parents—a time when even more balanced parenting roles will almost certainly be the norm.

Mr. Mom

The most radical departure from traditional parenting roles, the full-time dad (also called the "house husband" or "Mr. Mom") is certainly not for every father. Some men (and some women, too) are extremely uncomfortable with an arrangement that stands traditional gender roles on their head. Nonetheless, it makes sense for some couples to explore this alternative.

Financial considerations motivate some couples to embrace these nontraditional roles. Though in general women are still not paid as much as men in the same field, many career women now earn more (or have the potential to earn more) than their husbands.

Again, do the math. If your wife makes $80,000 a year as a doctor or lawyer and you make $30,000 as a teacher or auto worker, it doesn't take a Forbes to figure out that the loss of her income will affect your lifestyle much more than the loss of your income. If you and your partner have decided that one of you will take care of your baby (rather than putting him into full-time day care), it makes good financial sense for the one who makes less money to stay at home.

Of course, financial considerations should not be the only criteria used in making this decision. You should also take into account your suitability as a full-time parent. Some men stay at home with the baby because they want to and know they'll be good at it. If you feel more "at home" with babies than your partner does, or if you're one of that rare breed of fathers who knows in his heart how nurturing he can be, then why should you conform to cultural stereotypes that paint you as less nurturing than your partner?

Father Knows Best

"He didn't come out of my belly, but my God, I've made his bones, because I've attended to every meal, and how he sleeps, and the fact that he swims like a fish because I took him to the ocean. I'm so proud of all those things. But he is my biggest pride."

—John Lennon

Is Anybody Out There?

The biggest challenge that full-time dads face is the same one faced by full-time moms: not going stir-crazy. Despite the fact that infants will go almost anywhere with relative ease, you will still probably find yourself spending the vast majority of your days at home.

As a result, full-time dads can feel very isolated—even more so than stay-at-home moms. Most full-time moms schedule classes or activities or arrange play dates for their children as much (or even more) for their own benefit as for their children's. (Play dates often begin in late infancy or early toddlerhood—long before children have the social skills to play with another child.) Play dates and classes allow stay-at-home moms to get together with other mothers, to see and talk to other adults who can share in the joys and hardships of their lives.

As a full-time dad, however, you will have few, if any, male peers who can identify with you. Oh, sure, you can go to "Mommy and Me" classes, too, but even the name may put you off a little and cause you to wonder whether you're really welcome there.

To avoid feeling totally alone as a full-time dad, you will need to reach across the gender gap. Though you will have difficulty finding other full-time dads who can commiserate or celebrate with you, you can find plenty of stay-at-home parents.

Some (and perhaps even many) of the moms you'll meet will look upon you with a degree of bewilderment, suspicion, or even hostility. Full-time dads are, after all, a rare breed. Yet simply by

Cool Daddy Ohs

If you're feeling isolated and unsupported, you may also find information and support on the World Wide Web, which has sites for all kinds of fathers, including stay-at-home dads. (See Appendix B for a listing of organizations and web sites for fathers.)

introducing yourself, sticking it out, and being friendly, you can often get past these initial doubts—or you can seek out those mothers who see you not as a freak, but as a marvelously uncommon type of man.

As a full-time dad, you need to make an effort not only to get out of the house with your child during the day, but also to get out of the house on your own or with your partner in the evenings. Go for a run, play poker with the boys, or hire a babysitter and go on a date with your wife. More than any other type of father, the full-time dad needs to make sure to carve out some personal time away from the kids.

Maintaining a Balanced Load

No matter which path of fatherhood you choose—full-time breadwinner, split personality, or full-time dad—much more balance in parenting roles is possible today. An increasing number of families, including those in which the father is the sole breadwinner, are seeing the emergence of a more involved, more nurturing father. Most fathers now share—at least in part, if not equally—in the child-rearing tasks once regarded purely as a woman's domain.

So you can—and many times will be expected to—share some of the tasks traditionally associated with "mothering," including the following:

➤ Changing diapers

➤ Feeding your baby

➤ Taking your child to the doctor

➤ Playing with your child

➤ Making lunches

➤ Driving your child to school

➤ Entertaining your child

➤ Taking your child on special outings

Who knows, you might even need to do your share of household chores, such as cooking, grocery shopping, cleaning, and doing the laundry.

Assuming a greater share of parenting responsibilities than your father and grandfathers did can bring a greater sense of fulfillment and give you a greater influence on your children's development and well-being.

Wanted: Role Models

Everybody needs role models, even new fathers. Yet models of modern fatherhood are not often easy to find. Your own father, in all likelihood, conformed to a view of fatherhood that has changed in many respects since his day.

If you look to the media for models of fatherhood, you may end up feeling even more clueless. The movies seldom dwell very long on father-child relationships, while network TV offers a spectrum of fathers ranging from saints to idiots with very few realistic portraits in between.

Memories of Childhood

If you and your partner decide that you best fit the traditional bread-winning model of fatherhood, you probably don't need to strain to find a role model. Your own father most likely conformed pretty closely to this definition. Whether you regard your father as a good father, a bad father, or somewhere in between, you saw how he fit the mold and formed ideas about how you would and would not like to be like him.

Even in adopting a traditional role, however, you will probably face many challenges that your father didn't. Your wife may expect you to take on at least some share of domestic duties, such as putting the kids to bed, giving them a bath, or doing the laundry. (Like my dad, your father was probably never expected to do any of these.)

If you decide you want to be a nontraditional father, you will probably have an even harder time coming up with an appropriate role model. Most of us rarely, if ever, had a chance to observe a role model of fatherhood that did not conform to the traditional pattern.

Most of us grew up with mothers who were omnipresent. Mom probably got your breakfast ready in the morning. She stayed at home with you until you went off to preschool or kindergarten. She packed your lunches or welcomed you home for lunch. And when you came home from school, mom was there waiting for you.

By contrast, most of our fathers were distant and mysterious figures. Dad worked hard, we knew, because he was gone 50–60 hours a week. If your dad commuted, he was probably gone by the time you came to the breakfast table and may not have come back until dinner or later. So you saw your dad for maybe an hour or two before you had to go to bed.

Father Figures

Today's dads want more role models. In 1999, *Sesame Street Parents* magazine surveyed its male readers and asked, "What would help you be the best dad?" The number one answer: more role models (chosen by 28 percent of readers). The other top answers were a more supportive work environment (23 percent), more dads to talk to (21 percent), and more encouragement from their wives or partners (20 percent).

Daddy Dos and Don'ts

In trying to figure out what kind of father you want to be, it might be helpful to evaluate your own father's fathering. What did your dad do with you that you liked? What did he do that you disliked? How would you like to be just like him? How would you like to be different? If you could have changed one thing about your relationship with your father, what would it have been? What's the best thing he ever did for you?

The answers to these questions can help steer you in the direction you'd like to go now that you're a father.

Your dad was probably home on weekends, but even then he may have had little time to devote to you and your siblings. He had many other things to do: mow the lawn, rake the leaves, paint the house, shovel the driveway, put up a fence, fix the drip in the bathroom sink, and put up the storm windows.

On holidays and family vacations, we may have had a better chance to observe, interact, and play with our fathers. (I don't know about your dad, but my dad even brought work with him on vacations.) But these special times always passed so quickly.

Father Knows Best

"[His children, now grown,] asked him how old they had been when they first crawled, walked, talked, and read, and he was embarrassed to say that he could not remember. 'Ask your mother,' he told them."

—John Updike

Sure, many of our dads took advantage of every opportunity they had to play, talk, or just share time with us. But our dads had so many other well-defined responsibilities that they simply didn't have much time for parenting.

In his role as the "head of the household," your father was probably the sole family provider and ultimate authority figure. His job description: to make sure his family had a roof over their heads, clothes on their backs, and food on the table, as well as to discipline the children. Though often feared and respected, even loved and honored, the fathers of previous generations were rarely well known by their children.

Father Knows Best

"... [M]y wife and I have tried not to make the mistakes that our parents made with us. For example, we have always been against calling the children idiots. This philosophy has been basic for my wife and me. And we proudly lived by it until the children came along."

—Bill Cosby

From the Ridiculous to the Sublime: TV Dads

Unfortunately, television, which has wielded a greater influence on our generation of parents than on any previous generations, provides few healthy role models for the modern father. Half-hour sitcoms and one-hour family dramas almost always paint their characters with very broad strokes, turning them into caricatures more than characters. Only rarely has network television offered fully drawn portraits of American fathers. Unfortunately, for every Jack Arnold on *The Wonder Years* (a detailed rendering of the bread-winning father as a good man who wants to play an important role in his children's lives), there are dozens of fathers portrayed as complete idiots or idealized beyond belief.

Tough Acts to Follow: Fathers on TV

Types of Dads	Actors	Shows
Well-meaning, but clueless	Fred Gwynne	*The Munsters* (1960s)
	Michael Gross	*Family Ties* (1980s)
	Tim Allen	*Home Improvement* (1990s)
Too good to be true	Robert Young	*Father Knows Best* (1950s)
	Andy Griffith	*The Andy Griffith Show* (1960s)
	Robert Reed	*The Brady Bunch* (1970s)
	Dick Van Patten	*Eight Is Enough* (1980s)
	Steven Collins	*Seventh Heaven* (1990s)
Not-so-lovable slobs	Carroll O'Connor	*All in the Family* (1970s)
	Ed O'Neill	*Married with Children* (1980s)
	Homer Simpson	*The Simpsons* (1990s)
Missing in action	None	*One Day at a Time* (1970s)
		Alice (1980s)
		Murphy Brown (1990s)
Relatively well-rounded	Dan Lauria	*The Wonder Years* (1980s)
	Bill Cosby	*The Cosby Show* (1980s)
	John Goodman	*Roseanne* (1990s)

On television, of course, fathers are almost always shielded from real-life conflicts and the issues that you and I will face regularly as fathers. When an episode does touch on "contemporary issues," by necessity they are almost always miraculously resolved in 24 or 48 minutes (or, in the case of a particularly thorny issue that requires special treatment, in a two-part episode).

Clearly, television—with its cartoonish depiction of fathers and its simplistic and tidy resolutions of conflicts—has little to offer in the way of usable role models of fatherhood.

Cine-Ma? What About Cine-Pa?

What about the movies? Can the contemporary father find any useful role models in the cinema? Perhaps surprisingly, the movies pay very little attention to the relationship between fathers and their children. The stuff of domestic drama has traditionally been thought of as a subject for "women's pictures." So Hollywood has offered female movie stars many good roles as mothers.

Male movie stars, however, have traditionally starred in action films, in which children have no part, or in romantic comedies, which focus on falling in love and marrying, not the aftermath (children). The tendency to ignore fatherhood is not a recent development or an outgrowth of the demand for spectacular special-effects blockbusters. It began with movie stars from the black-and-white era, Hollywood's Golden Age. How often did the stars from that era—or any since—portray fathers? And how often was fatherhood in any way central to these movies?

➤ Rudolf Valentino, Douglas Fairbanks, and Errol Flynn did not become stars playing fathers.

➤ Charlie Chaplin, Harold Lloyd, and other stars of silent movies almost always traveled solo.

➤ The only star from the era of black-and-white comedies who consistently portrayed a father was W.C. Fields, whose characters always hated children.

Father Knows Best

"Anyone who hates children and dogs can't be all bad."

—W.C. Fields

➤ Such legendary stars as Clark Gable, Humphrey Bogart, James Cagney, Gary Cooper, and Cary Grant never played a memorable father. (Rhett Butler adores his daughter, but their relationship gets very little attention until her death prompts his divorce from Scarlett.)

➤ Jimmy Stewart rarely played a father, and in his most notable portrayal of paternity (in *It's a Wonderful Life*), he tries to kill himself.

➤ John Wayne played no fathers of note.

➤ Spencer Tracy played a father in three memorable films (*Father of the Bride*, *Father's Little Dividend*, and *Guess Who's Coming to Dinner?*), but his children are already grown in all of them.

➤ Henry Fonda's best known portrayal of a father was the dying dad of a grown daughter in *On Golden Pond*.

➤ Marlon Brando's best known role as a father (in *The Godfather*) isn't exactly an ideal role model.

This cinematic neglect of fatherhood has only heightened in the age of the blockbuster. Consider the biggest box office stars of the past 25 years:

➤ Sean Connery's rare portraits of a father (in *Indiana Jones and the Last Crusade* and *Family Business*) came late in his career, when he had grown old enough to be a grandfather. In both films, Connery's grown sons rediscover their reprobate father.

➤ Clint Eastwood's best role as a father came in one of his least-watched films, *Bronco Billy*.

➤ Dustin Hoffman played a father in three notable films: *Kramer vs. Kramer*, *Death of a Salesman*, and *Hero*. In all three, however, he was a sorry schlepper (though redeemed to various degrees by his love for his sons).

➤ Warren Beatty has never played a father.

➤ Jack Nicholson and Harrison Ford have rarely played fathers in any meaningful way. When they did, however (in *The Shining* and *Mosquito Coast,* respectively), they went mad.

➤ Arnold Schwarzenegger's two turns as a father (in *Jingle All the Way* and *Junior*—the latter most noteworthy because Arnold gets pregnant) were performed tongue-in-cheek.

➤ In Tom Hanks' most notable role as a father (in *Sleepless in Seattle*), he can't even get a date without his son's help.

Among these movie stars—the biggest male box-office draws of the past century—only about two dozen of their films portrayed fatherhood in any significant way. (And that's out of more than a thousand movies that these stars have collectively made!)

Even these scarce portrayals of fathers often focused on aging, dying, or just plain bad dads. So the movies don't offer much in the way of role models for modern fathers either.

Daddy Dos and Don'ts

In addition to picking up pointers from books on fatherhood (like this one) or parenting magazines, you may also find help from local or national fatherhood groups. These self-help groups can help fathers cope with the ongoing demands of fatherhood. They also offer members the chance to hear the opinions of other fathers, share their own experiences, and benefit from different perspectives as they attempt to make difficult parenting decisions.

The development of self-help groups for fathers is a relatively recent phenomenon, so you may not find a group in your area. If you can't, contact a national fatherhood group for guidance in setting up your own local group. (See Appendix B for a list of national fatherhood groups.)

On Your Own

With few role models in real life, on television, or in the movies, fathers today find themselves pretty much on their own in defining their new roles. You may look to books such as this one for guidance or useful tips, but in the end you will need to trust your instincts.

With all the options open to today's fathers, you can pretty much write your own job description. What aspects of the job of fatherhood are most important? Personally, I would say the following:

➤ Sharing your time

➤ Showing your love

➤ Providing for your family

➤ Protecting your family

➤ Teaching your values

➤ Instilling self-discipline

➤ Serving as a role model

➤ Demonstrating respect—but not deference—to your child

In carving out your niche as a father, you might add other items to this list or disagree about the importance of one or more items that I've included. Even if you agree wholeheartedly with everything on the list, you and I might still disagree about how to prioritize them. When one paternal duty clashes with another, which takes precedence? Well, that's for you to decide.

The Least You Need to Know

➤ The choices you make—about what you do with your time, priorities, sharing and dividing of responsibilities, and so on—define the kind of father you'll be.

➤ There is no "best" kind of father. So just try to be the best father you can be.

➤ Fathers who work full-time should make the most of the little time they have with their children. Parents who split child-care responsibilities should take special care to devote time to each other. Fathers who stay at home with the kids should make sure to stake out some time just for themselves.

➤ You'll be hard-pressed to find a good role model of fatherhood on TV or in the movies. Your own dad probably provided your most useful role model, but he no doubt faced very different expectations.

➤ Trust your paternal instincts and make conscious decisions about the kind of father you want to be.

Part 2

Your Rookie Year: Fathering Infants

You made it through your partner's pregnancy, and now you have a beautiful baby. Congratulations! Now what?

No matter how much research on newborns you've done, you may feel unprepared and somewhat overburdened. Just the basics of baby care—feeding, changing, bathing, soothing, changing again—seem to eat up almost every hour of the day.

To complicate matters, your partner may not feel 100 percent for some time after delivery (especially if she had a C-section). Luckily (for both of you), newborns sleep even more than they eat, cry, and dirty diapers. Your baby's sleep needs will gradually decrease over the course of the year, however, so take advantage of your baby's down-time while it lasts. Before long, your baby will be sitting up, crawling, standing, and walking. Once your baby is on his feet, you'll constantly be on your toes. So get some rest while you still can.

Chapter 7

After Care: Post-Partum Recovery

In This Chapter

➤ Helping your partner recover from labor and delivery during her post-partum hospital stay

➤ Surviving on your own after bringing your baby home

➤ The causes of post-partum depression (yours as well as your partner's)

➤ Helping each other beat the baby blues

➤ Why traveling with a newborn is easier than traveling with a toddler

Congratulations! You made it through pregnancy, labor, and delivery, and now you have a beautiful baby to take home with you. (If you had a multiple birth, then multiple congratulations!)

Now that you have a newborn baby on your hands, you can expect your life to change dramatically. You will no doubt begin to wonder how someone so small can have such an enormous presence. For a while, at least, all your decisions—and even most of your thoughts—will center on what's best for the baby. Want some dinner? You'll have to squeeze it in between the baby's feedings. Will those Cajun spices affect your partner's breast milk and give your baby gas? Want to take a shower? Better take one as soon as the baby settles down for a nap. Want to go to a movie? Can you take the baby and hope she sleeps, or will you have to get a babysitter?

Because you have to consider—and, to a large degree, defer to—your child's needs, however, doesn't mean that you shouldn't consider your own needs, too. Your needs are by no means secondary to your baby's. *Gratification* of your needs, however, must be secondary. You can defer gratification; your baby cannot. Furthermore, your baby depends entirely on you and your partner to satisfy her needs, whereas you can satisfy many of yours—and have your partner and other resources to call upon to take care of the others.

Father Knows Best

"… [T]he children have to come first. It's no use putting off their evening meal for two months."

—Libby Houston

Although taking care of the baby may have to come first, taking care of yourselves and each other is an essential part of parenting. If you let yourself get run down, who will take care of the baby? If you don't eat well, sleep when you can, and stay in shape, how will you possibly keep up with your baby, whose energy and alertness will grow exponentially throughout the first year? And if you don't insist on some time to yourself, how will you avoid resenting all the time you devote to your baby?

I Want to Go Home!

In the days and weeks following labor and delivery, you will find yourself swamped with new responsibilities. Caring for a new baby—a tiny, lightweight, fragile, and delicate thing—is plenty of responsibility in itself. But in the immediate aftermath of childbirth, you will also need to take care of your partner—something you might never have had to do before. Your partner will need your strength, your help, and your love.

Under the weight of this overwhelming new load of responsibilities, you'll find yourself either drowning, merely treading water, or thriving. The way you handle the load depends in part on your personality and in part on your circumstances (your partner's delivery, your parental leave from work, and so on). But it also depends on how well you take care of *yourself*.

Leave It to the Professionals

If your partner is giving birth in a hospital (and most mothers in the United States still do), she will probably have just one day to recover from a vaginal delivery before she is sent home. If your baby was delivered by C-section, your partner will have just three to four days before being discharged. (If your baby is born in an alternative birthing center, you'll likely return home in less than a day. If your partner gives birth at home, you will have only a few hours of supervised recovery time.)

The time your partner has under supervised care is short, so take advantage of any assistance the nursing staff offers. Of course, the quality of nursing care in maternity wings varies, as it does in any hospital unit. You'll likely get at least one nurse who you like very much and, unfortunately, at least one nurse you don't. No matter how much the nurses bother you while you're in the hospital, however, you'll miss them when you're home.

No Sleep for the Weary

If you've decided to stay overnight at the hospital until your partner and baby are discharged, the hospital staff will likely leave your new family alone much of the time. This doesn't necessarily mean that you'll have a lot of privacy. The nursing staff will regularly stop in to:

➤ Monitor your partner's pulse, blood pressure, and other vital signs.

➤ Monitor your baby's vital signs.

➤ Offer lessons, suggestions, and encouragement to your partner in her first attempts at breast-feeding.

➤ Encourage and assist your partner in getting back on her feet, at least for short walks.

➤ Ask about how much your baby has eaten and about wet and soiled diapers.

➤ Whisk the baby off to the nursery for blood tests, a weight check, and a bath.

In addition, if your partner had a Cesarean section, the nursing staff will come in regularly to:

➤ Empty and remove the Foley catheter bag and record your partner's urinary output.

➤ Ask about your partner's bowel movements.

➤ Monitor your partner's *PCA (Patient-Controlled Anesthetic),* if one has been prescribed.

➤ Give your partner a sponge bath.

➤ Help your partner to her feet (after 24 hours).

Daddy Dos and Don'ts

When the nursing staff takes your baby to the nursery, feel free to join them (insist, if necessary). The hospital will probably require you to change into surgical scrubs or cover your street clothes with a hospital gown before you enter the nursery. Neo-natal nurses—especially if they're caring for a full house—often seem oblivious to the cries of babies because they need to test or bathe a baby quickly and then move on to the next. In such a case, you can offer your baby a *clean* finger to suck on or some other comfort during this time of distress.

Paterniterms

A **PCA,** or **Patient-Controlled Anesthetic,** administers a baseline dosage of a painkiller (typically morphine) through an intravenous line. When your partner feels pain, she can press a button that delivers more of the painkiller (as long as she has not yet reached the maximum allowable dosage, which is set by the anesthesiologist).

Getting Your Partner Back on Her Feet

To speed your partner's recovery from childbirth, encourage her to start walking as soon as she feels up to it. Walking will advance your partner's recovery in a number of ways. First, it will help stimulate the bladder and bowels, which need to resume normal functioning as soon as possible after delivery. (An undrained bladder can cause a urinary tract infection or prevent the uterus from descending into the pelvis, causing bleeding and even hemorrhaging.)

In addition, walking will help keep muscles from atrophying as a result of disuse. It also may help to relieve immediate post-partum depression. And it will hasten recovery in general. So help and encourage her to get back on her feet soon after delivery.

After a vaginal delivery, your partner should begin walking later the same day. A Cesarean section requires a longer recovery, but your partner should still be on her feet the next day after surgery.

You don't necessarily need to guide your partner on a hike through the Himalayas. She will no doubt be very sore and find walking difficult, especially if she had a surgical delivery. Just help her walk across the room, where she can sit upright in a chair for a while before returning to bed. Then later that day or the next, progress to a slow walk through the corridors, perhaps with her pushing the baby's bassinet ahead of her.

Where Are You Taking My Baby?

The nursing staff may become insistent—and sometimes even belligerent—about taking your baby away to the nursery for at least the first night. The nurses, concerned primarily with the safety of the baby and the recovery of your partner, have sound reasons for breaking apart your new family:

➤ Your partner's potentially poor judgment due to the painkillers.

➤ The inability of your partner to lift the baby out of the bassinet (due to incisional pain).

➤ The fear that your partner will drop the baby (again due to her discomfort or the affect of the drugs).

➤ Your partner's need for rest to speed recovery.

Nonetheless, if you and your partner decide you'd rather keep the baby in the room for the night, you have every right to do so. You may, for instance, find it unbearable to consign your child to the nursery for the night. No matter how many times the nurses ask if you'd like

Daddy Dos and Don'ts

The nurses will make less of a fuss about your decision to keep the baby overnight in the hospital room if you also stay in the room with your wife. (Many labor and delivery units now accommodate fathers who plan to sleep over with chairs that convert into extremely uncomfortable beds.)

them to take the baby, simply respond with a firm, "We're fine" or "We'll call you if we need your help." Don't let anyone bully you into making a decision you're not comfortable with.

While still at the hospital, you and your partner may decide to do most of the changing and *swaddling* yourselves, or you may choose to let the neonatal nurses do it for you. (For tips on changing diapers and clothes, see Chapter 9.) Either way, if you haven't got a clue about how to change a diaper or swaddle a baby, you may find it helpful to watch a nurse. Most nurses will be happy to show you how to do it.

The nurses also can help you bathe and feed the baby. Don't be so stubborn about doing everything yourselves that you refuse help. You and your partner will be on your own soon enough, so take advantage of help while you can.

Homeward Bound

Barring medical complications, your family should be home within a few days of your baby's birth. This is the period when your participation will be most needed and appreciated.

When your partner first arrives home, she will need to focus not just on the baby, but on her own physical recovery as well. To complicate things, her hormone levels will begin dropping to their pre-pregnancy levels. In addition, your partner may be hit with a cold blast of post-partum depression. Add a baby who wants to eat every two to three hours and you can see why your partner would welcome some help.

Where Does It Hurt?

If your partner delivered vaginally, she and the baby will probably be sent home after just a day of recovery in the hospital or birthing center. Your partner will not exactly be in peak physical condition, however. In addition to general exhaustion, your wife may feel sore from the strain of pushing out the baby. Specific areas, of course, will hurt more than others:

Paterniterms

Swaddling your baby means wrapping him tightly in a blanket. (Most babies don't like their arms and legs to move about uncontrollably.)

Paterniterms

An **epidural,** or epidural block, is a common means of delivering anesthetic during childbirth. The drug is delivered through a needle inserted into the back. An **episiotomy** is a controlled, surgical cut of the **perineum,** the area between the vagina and the anus. Obstetricians often perform episiotomies to prevent uncontrolled tearing of the perineum when the baby emerges from the vagina.

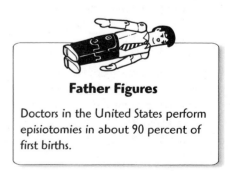

Father Figures

Doctors in the United States perform episiotomies in about 90 percent of first births.

➤ She may feel back pain or soreness around the site of the *epidural*, if she had one.

➤ She may feel uncomfortable, sore, or numb around the *perineum*—especially if she had an *episiotomy*, which usually takes 7–10 days to heal.

➤ She may find walking difficult for a few days, especially if she had an episiotomy.

➤ She may feel discomfort in her breasts as her body begins to produce milk.

Many of these symptoms may persist until (or even beyond) your partner's first post-partum visit to the obstetrician—five to six weeks after labor and delivery. She will need you to pick up as much of the slack as possible for several weeks (and, of course, to do your share of baby care after that, as well).

No Heavy Lifting

If your partner has a Cesarean section, she will need even more help and support from you during the first weeks (and even months) of your baby's life. A Cesarean section is major abdominal surgery and usually requires six to eight weeks of recovery.

After three or four days in the hospital, your partner will come home feeling sore and depleted. In addition to the post-partum complaints of vaginal deliveries described previously, your wife will likely feel the following in the wake of a Cesarean section:

➤ Pain not only at the site of the epidural, but around the incision as well

➤ Sharp and intense pain whenever *afterpains* tighten the skin around the incision

Pain around the incision should improve as time passes. Nonetheless, your partner may need prescription painkillers for another week or longer after the PCA (Patient Controlled Anesthetic) has been removed, and the area around the scar may remain sore and sensitive for many more weeks.

For a week or two, your partner won't feel up to much. Indeed, her obstetrician will probably advise her not to do any strenuous housework or lift anything more than

Cool Daddy Ohs

A new mother's body begins to produce milk even if she decides *not* to breast-feed her baby. Only when demand is absent (because the baby is being bottle-fed) will production of supply be discontinued.

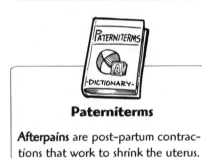

Paterniterms

Afterpains are post-partum contractions that work to shrink the uterus.

Daddy Dos and Don'ts

Letting the baby sleep in a bassinet or nap in a baby carriage will eliminate much of the strain in lifting and make it possible for your wife to get the baby on her own.

10 pounds. (The act of lifting could pop the stitches or staples used to repair the incision.) This means, among other things, that she should probably be discouraged from lifting your newborn out of a crib or placing the baby into it. She can hold the baby all she wants, of course, but should avoid lifting her from the crib.

The Baby Blues

In the wake of childbirth, with a new baby on your hands, you and your partner may feel either elated and exhilarated or depressed and disconsolate, or swing somewhat wildly between the extremes. To complicate matters, you may feel either increasingly confident in your ability to handle your new responsibilities or totally overwhelmed by them.

Oh, Mama!

Not all women suffer from post-partum blues. But it shouldn't be surprising that many new mothers do. After all, in the first weeks of your baby's life, your partner is being rocked by changing hormone levels, deprived of essential sleep, and forced to master on-the-job training. Even worse, unless you've taken an extended leave of absence from work, your partner has to deal with all these changes and hardships on her own.

Women who have gone through post-partum depression liken it to PMS with a vengeance. If your partner gets the post-partum blues, she will experience severe mood changes and profound depression. She may periodically suffer from unexplainable yet unstoppable crying jags. And she will feel buried under the weight of her new responsibilities as a mother.

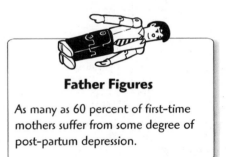

Father Figures

As many as 60 percent of first-time mothers suffer from some degree of post-partum depression.

Many factors contribute to a new mother's post-partum depression, including the following:

➤ **Hormones.** Much of the cause is, of course, hormonal. Now that she's no longer physically supporting two lives, your partner's body is changing once again. During the post-partum period, estrogen and progesterone levels drop dramatically. Hormones aren't the only explanation, however; they will stabilize within a week or two of childbirth, whereas her depression may last for several weeks (though it often passes within a few days).

➤ **Exhaustion.** Already sore and weak (especially if she had a Cesarean section), your partner may feel exhausted. Although yours may be the rare newborn who sleeps through the night, it's more likely that your baby will wake up every two to four hours for several weeks (or months). These regular interruptions of your partner's sleep cannot help but take their toll on her.

➤ **Anticlimax.** After the nine-month build-up of pregnancy and the excitement of childbirth, your partner may suffer from some emotional letdown. The return to a daily routine—albeit a new routine—may leave her feeling comparatively numb.

➤ **Isolation.** Despite the constant company of your baby, your partner's life may become increasingly solitary, especially if you can't afford to stay home with her. As the initial flurry of visits to see the newborn drops off, she may feel increasingly lonely.

➤ **Invisibility.** Your partner may feel pushed aside, invisible, and neglected as friends and relatives (and perhaps even you) turn their attention to the baby. (You may empathize with this feeling from your experience during the pregnancy.)

➤ **Ugliness.** She may feel unattractive or even unlovable when childbirth doesn't magically restore her figure to what it once was.

➤ **Helplessness.** Your partner may feel that she is losing control of her own life—first in the hospital, where she's at the mercy of the medical staff, and then at home, where your baby's schedule rules.

➤ **Lack of confidence.** Your partner may not feel up to the task of caring for the baby. She may feel tied down, overwhelmed, or unsure of herself in the face of her new responsibilities.

➤ **Disappointment.** Your partner may feel disappointed in your baby's appearance or behavior, which may not conform to the idealized stereotypes she may have imagined. And if everything didn't go as planned during labor and delivery, she may feel disappointed in her own performance in childbirth.

➤ **Nostalgia.** Your partner may miss her old life, with its comparative freedom and fewer (or at least different) responsibilities. She may also miss her old body and fear she'll never regain her shape.

➤ **Resentment.** Your partner may feel resentment or even anger toward the baby—and, by extension, toward you—for disrupting her life.

➤ **Guilt.** Above all, she may feel guilty about the negative emotions she's feeling. She may feel as though something is wrong with her because she can't accept the baby and her new role as mother wholeheartedly and without ambivalence.

Father Figures

Only about 1/10 of 1 percent of new mothers (that's 1 in 1,000) require professional counseling for severe post-partum depression.

Again, not all women experience severe post-partum blues. Some women embrace the new challenges of motherhood (though somewhat exhaustedly). But it should not be regarded—by you, by her, or by anyone else—as a personal failure if your partner cannot do so right away. After all, mother-hood takes a lot of getting used to.

Generally, post-partum depression strikes within the first week or two after childbirth. Fortunately, it seldom lasts for more than a few days or a week. So if your wife feels depressed shortly after childbirth, take comfort in the knowledge that it will probably soon pass, and reassure her of the same.

Mother's Little Helper

Helping your partner through post-partum depression requires understanding, compassion, and solidarity. If her new responsibilities are weighing her down, try to take as much responsibility for baby care as you possibly can.

To make sure she gets enough rest, encourage your partner to nap when the baby does, rather than immediately seizing the opportunity to clean the house or do the dishes or attend to other chores.

If the shape of your partner's body depresses her, encourage her to do some light exercise. Within a few months, she can get back her former figure (or something closely resembling it). Exercise, of course, has other benefits besides improving one's shape, including reducing stress, improving sleep, and providing a general sense of well-being.

You also should encourage your partner to stick to a sensible diet—but this does not mean going *on* a diet). Indeed, if she is breast-feeding, your partner should probably consume about 500 calories more per day than she did before the pregnancy. She should also drink plenty of fluids—eight to ten glasses a day. Although not going on a diet, however, your partner should watch what she eats. Too much junk food—especially fatty foods and sugars—will not only make it harder for her to return to her pre-pregnancy shape, but will likely leave her feeling rundown as well.

Whenever you can, encourage your partner to go for a walk—by herself, with you and the baby, or with a friend. Encourage her to take an hour or two between feedings to see a friend or just take some time for herself. Or, take the baby into another room while she visits with a friend. All of these breaks from baby care can help relieve your partner's isolation, depression, and the sheer weight of constantly caring for the baby.

Talking can also alleviate some of the isolation your partner may feel. Invite her to talk about her feelings with you and friends and relatives (especially those with young children), or, if necessary, with a therapist.

Daddy Dos and Don'ts

Once you return to work, get up early if you must, but take the baby for at least half an hour before you leave the house in the morning. Give your partner time to get ready to tackle the day ahead. Having the chance simply to take a shower and get dressed can make an enormous difference in how she feels about herself.

Finally, if your partner (or you) suffers from cabin fever, keep this in mind: Newborns are extremely portable! Although you don't necessarily want to expose your baby to crowds of people, you can take her almost anywhere. So get out, get out, get out of the house! Take long walks if weather permits. If you can afford it, take your family to dinner one or two nights a week. If you time it right, your baby might sleep through dinner—and maybe even a movie—allowing you a "care"-free evening together.

She's Not the Only One

It won't be easy to help your partner through her post-partum blues if you're suffering from your own case of depression. Many new fathers also suffer from post-partum blues, and for many of the same reasons that new mothers do (okay, maybe not the hormones). You, too, may experience the following:

➤ Exhaustion due to lack of sleep

➤ An emotional letdown after the immediate exhilaration of new fatherhood

➤ The burden of being tied down with new responsibilities

➤ A sense of isolation as the congratulations from friends and coworkers fade away and you realize you're pretty much on your own

➤ The difficulty of adjusting to your new life and a yearning for the more carefree life of the past

➤ Feelings of inadequacy as a father (which may be compounded by heightened financial concerns)

➤ A sense of being a fifth wheel, now overshadowed by both your wife and your baby

➤ Anger or resentment toward your baby

➤ Guilt about your ambivalent feelings regarding parenthood, your new baby, and your partner

Fortunately, some of the same suggestions that can relieve your partner's doldrums can work for you, too. Try some of the following:

➤ Get out of the house.

➤ Tell your partner you need a little time for yourself. (This one will go over much better if you return the favor, offering to give your partner some time to herself, too.)

➤ Go out to dinner.

➤ Drink heavily. (Just kidding.)

➤ Talk to your partner, to friends, and to relatives (especially new fathers), or, if necessary, to a therapist.

➤ Set your priorities. Figure out what you can let slide for a little while so that you and your partner can get the rest you desperately need.

Getting Away from It All

It's not running born, as previously mentioned, is extremely portable. Most infants tend to sleep through most car and plane trips, lulled to unconsciousness by all the "white noise."

In fact, traveling with your newborn, though it may seem unthinkable, is much easier now than it will be in about six or eight months. For one thing, as soon as he can walk, your baby will probably have little patience for the confinement of an airplane and will find it difficult to sit still for hours in a car seat. For another, once your baby starts eating solid foods, you'll need to carry more and more paraphernalia with you wherever you go: jars of baby food, baby spoons, bibs, and sipper cups. In addition, the older your baby gets, the more toys, books, and other entertainment you'll need to carry. Finally, in six months your baby will be wearing clothes and diapers that are twice as big as the ones he wears now. (He'll probably need his own suitcase.)

For now though, your newborn can go almost anywhere (as long as your pediatrician gives the okay). Besides a well-stocked diaper bag, all you'll need to pack are

Daddy Dos and Don'ts

No matter how fanatic you and your partner are about cloth diapers, when going on vacation, break down and buy some disposables. You don't need to pack enough for the entire vacation, since you can find them almost anywhere you go. Instead, just pack enough to get you where you're going (and then pack 10 more just in case).

➤ An armload of disposable diapers.

➤ Clothes. (Bring plenty of extra outfits in case of "accidents.")

➤ A first-aid kit. (See Chapter 10 for the first-aid items a baby needs.)

➤ A handful of your baby's favorite toys.

➤ Bottles and formula (if your wife doesn't breast-feed exclusively).

This may seem like a lot to pack, but believe me, when it comes to vacationing with kids, this is traveling light—and now may be your last chance to do so for years to come. Take advantage of it if you can. (See Chapter 21 for more information on traveling with your child.)

The Least You Need to Know

➤ Although all the decisions you make must take your baby's needs into consideration, this doesn't mean your needs don't matter. You may, however, need to delay gratification of your own needs (and those of your partner).

➤ While still in the hospital or birthing center, take advantage of the assistance and expertise of the nurses and midwives. You may learn a thing or two.

➤ Your partner needs you the most when she and the baby first come home. Consider taking a paternity leave from work, if possible, to help care for the baby.

➤ Many factors—including hormonal changes, exhaustion, and the strain of adjusting to your new lives as parents—can contribute to post-partum depression.

➤ Offering each other help and support—and giving each other a little time for yourselves—can help ease the post-partum blues.

Chapter 8

Crying Out for Contact: Soothing and Handling Your Baby

In This Chapter

➤ Learning to interpret your baby's cries

➤ Why you should respond quickly to your crying baby

➤ Attending to your crying baby's needs

➤ Recognizing—and coping with—a baby with colic

➤ Handling your baby with care

Parenting is equal parts intuition and trial and error. Your baby is crying, for example. What's wrong? What does she want to tell you? Is she hungry or tired? Does she need a diaper change? Did she bang her head or scratch her hand? Trust your instincts and go with what seems right to you. Don't worry, if you guess incorrectly, your baby will loudly continue to let you know.

For most questions that arise in parenting an infant, you will do well to trust your instincts first, and then learn through trial and error what works and what doesn't. Nonetheless, a few pointers on baby care certainly couldn't hurt.

The Crying Game

Nothing tears at the hearts of new parents more than the sound of their baby crying. Your baby's cry is a clarion call, summoning the troops to action. No doubt when you hear it you, your partner, or both of you at once will spring into action trying to soothe him. But what should you do? How can you interpret your baby's cries and know what he wants or needs?

Okay, So It Loses a Little in Translation

Let's start with the premise that your baby never cries without cause. Crying is not merely your baby's way of exercising her lungs or making noise; crying *means* something. Crying is, in fact, your baby's primary means of communicating needs and desires.

Your child, like every infant, is an individual, with her own particular needs and desires. Yet your baby has no verbal language and, therefore, no way of expressing her needs and desires except by crying.

What does your baby mean when she cries? Well, fortunately, a baby has very limited needs. So when your baby cries, she's trying to tell you that she needs your help because she feels one of the following (listed roughly according to frequency):

➤ Hunger

➤ Pain or discomfort (for instance, gas, a full diaper, diaper rash, feeling too hot or too cold, a bump, or a scrape)

➤ Tiredness

➤ Loneliness

➤ Boredom

➤ Frustration

➤ Fear

➤ Anger

When your baby cries, start with the assumption that she's reacting to one of these conditions. As soon as you figure out and take care of the cause, her crying should stop.

In dealing with a crying baby, keep this point in mind: Your baby cries in response to immediate and intense needs. She lives in the moment and does not yet have the ability to anticipate needs. In other words, your baby is saying, "I'm starving!" or "I'm totally exhausted!" rather than "I'm getting hungry," or "I think I'm getting a little sleepy."

Respond to your baby's crying—her desperate expression of need—as soon as you can. Don't be afraid that you'll spoil her by responding "too quickly." For crying out loud, you can't spoil a baby by giving her what she needs!

The way you respond to your baby's cries—which provides the foundation for your baby's trust in you—will have an enormous impact on her development. Studies have shown that when parents deal with the cause of their babies' crying quickly and effectively, the babies cry less frequently and for shorter times, as they grow older, than children whose parents ignore their babies' cries or delay the gratification of their needs. In addition, babies who receive immediate reassurance (through their parents' responsiveness) that their attempts to communicate work tend to develop good communication skills once they acquire a vocabulary.

So when your baby cries, don't just stand there; do something!

Stop Your Sobbing: Tricks of the Trade

Ah, but what to do? Well, no matter what your baby's complaint happens to be, soothing him almost always begins with picking him up and holding him. If you hold your baby close to your chest, your body will immediately begin to warm his and the steady sound of your heartbeat may have a calming influence.

In fact, if loneliness, boredom, fear, anger, or frustration brought on his cries in the first place, just picking him up may stop his crying altogether. Even if he's crying for another reason, holding your baby can magically transform his wails into sniffles and snuffles.

Father Knows Best

"Except that right side up is best, there is not much to learn about holding a baby. There are one hundred and fifty-two distinctly different ways—and all are right! At least all will do."

—Heywood Broun

If picking your baby up doesn't stop his sobbing, you'll need to try to figure out what's the matter and attend to it as best you can. You may find it helpful to try some of the following:

➤ **Feed your baby.** If your baby is hungry, don't hesitate to feed him. This seems like common sense, but some parents get the idea that they should feed a baby only according to a strict schedule. If you allow your baby to cry until it's "time" to eat, however, your baby will probably exhaust himself and have little energy left for eating well. And if he doesn't eat well, your baby will be crying for the breast or bottle again in half an hour or an hour.

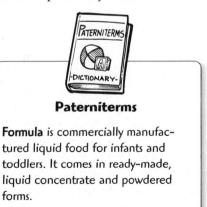

Paterniterms

Formula is commercially manufactured liquid food for infants and toddlers. It comes in ready-made, liquid concentrate and powdered forms.

Fathers of breast-fed babies like this suggestion because it lets them off the hook. After all, if your baby is hungry and doesn't drink *formula,* what can you do but pass him to your partner?

➤ **Change your baby's diaper.** It can't be pleasant to sit around in a wet or dirty diaper. A wet diaper can get cold pretty quickly if you don't attend to it. And a long time in a wet or soiled diaper can lead to an uncomfortable rash. If your baby isn't hungry but is still crying, check the diaper first. If it's wet or soiled, get him a clean, dry one.

While you're changing your baby, check for diaper rash. If you see redness that looks painful, smear on some medicated diaper cream before putting on the new diaper. Or, if it's warm enough and your baby doesn't object to being naked, try giving him some "naked butt" time, since airing out can also reduce diaper rash. Be forewarned: He could start spurting again at any moment and often without warning. So be sure to place a cloth diaper under his crotch before setting him down, and be ready to catch any eruptions with another one. (For more on changing your baby, see Chapter 9.)

➤ **Burp your baby.** Your baby's belly may ache either from eating too much or from taking in too much air while feeding. If your baby begins to cry within a few minutes of eating (or while eating), he may need to let out an enormous belch. To help your baby, hold him close to you so that his head rests on your shoulder. (You might want to drape a cloth diaper over your shoulder first in case he spits up.) Then, push up any air bubbles from his belly by firmly stroking upward on his back or gently patting his back with two or three fingers. (You can use your whole hand to pat his back, but using just two or three fingers will remind you to be gentle.)

If your baby has gas pains, he should burp within a few minutes (maybe just a few seconds). If your baby has overeaten, he will probably spit up, perhaps a surprisingly large amount. (Your baby won't mind the mess at all, no matter where it ends up.) If your baby neither burps nor spits up after several minutes, bellyache probably isn't the reason for his cries.

Daddy Dos and Don'ts

If you decide to use a pacifier, try to view it as the soother of last resort. Some parents fall into the trap of relying too heavily on the pacifier to stop any crying. But crying can indicate many needs besides the need for soothing, and an over reliance on pacifiers will make it impossible for you to find out what your baby *really* wants or needs.

If your baby uses a pacifier, try to break him of the habit by around six months. For one thing, it may be easier to break the habit while he's still young. For another, babies use their mouths a lot to explore and learn about the world. Every toy or spoon or book or washcloth you give your baby will go straight to his mouth. That's the first way he finds out about different objects and their textures—but your baby won't be able to do this if he always has a pacifier in his mouth.

➤ **Give your baby something to suck on.** If your baby cries even though he has already eaten and been burped, wash your pinkie finger, turn it upward so that the nail doesn't scratch the roof of his mouth, and let him suck on it. Even when not hungry, your baby will find the act of sucking in itself soothing. Sucking on something doesn't always work, but it may calm your baby when he's hurt, bored, angry, or tired—anything but hungry.

Once your baby has developed some hand-eye coordination (at around three or four months), you can guide his thumb to his mouth and teach him to become a self-soother. A pacifier can help, even at an earlier age, but until he can put it back in his mouth himself, you'll probably be doing a lot of "retrieving."

➤ **Rock your baby.** By holding your baby close and rocking him, you may be able to calm him down (whether he's tired, angry, bored, or scared). If you have a rocking chair, hold your baby so that his head is on your shoulder or against your chest and rock slowly, about one rock per second. (Holding your baby in a "nursing" position—cradled in your arms and looking up at you—will probably frustrate rather than calm him. Nonetheless, some babies like being held this way even when they're not eating.)

If you don't have a rocking chair, you can create a rocking motion by swaying from side to side, doing deep knee bends, or rocking back and forth on your heels. A ride in a stroller or car seat can also provide some soothing movement that may stop your baby from crying (and perhaps even lull him to sleep).

While rocking your baby, try singing a lullaby or a favorite song to him (no heavy metal, please). Or, talk to him in a soft voice or even a whisper. Your voice can often exercise a calming influence on your baby (and he doesn't care whether you can carry a tune).

➤ **Swaddle your baby.** Babies don't retain heat very well. If your baby gets cold at all, he'll cry (which not only lets you know that something's wrong, but actually generates some heat for him). If your baby's hands or feet feel cold to you, he needs more clothing or to be swaddled in a warm blanket. Wrapping your baby tightly in a blanket will not only make him warmer, but will also provide him with a snug, womb-like sensation. (Most babies don't like their arms and legs flailing

Daddy Dos and Don'ts

A quick lesson in swaddling: Lay a baby blanket on a flat surface. Now imagine it's a baseball diamond. Fold a corner of the blanket over by bringing second base to the pitcher's mound. Next, place your baby face up so that his shoulders lie on the fold you've made. Wrap third base around his torso and under his back. Next, bring home plate up to his chest. Lastly, take first base, wrap it around his torso, and tuck it in behind his back. Voilà, a bundled up baby!

about until they develop some idea of what to do with them—around three or four months.)

➤ **Put your baby down.** This doesn't mean you should start insulting your baby or calling him rude names. But if he's crying from being tired or as a reaction to over stimulation, the best thing you can do for your baby is to put him down and encourage him to go to sleep.

First, try swaddling, rocking, or giving your baby something to suck on until he calms down a bit. Then, as soon as his eyelids close or even start to droop a bit, set your baby down in his bassinet, crib, or carriage. If he immediately pops his eyes open, lifts his head, or starts to cry (loud cries, not mere snuffles or sighs), sleep may not be what your baby needs. But if he doesn't object, he'll soon drop off to sleep. (For more on getting your baby to sleep, see Chapter 16.)

➤ **Distract your baby.** If your baby is crying because he's upset, bored, or in pain, a little sleight of hand might do the trick. When he's very young (in the first few months), your baby won't exactly want to play, but he may enjoy looking at a black-and-white mobile or toy or a flash card with a bold design. Or you can try holding your fingers about a foot away from his face and slowly moving them back and forth so that he can track your hand with his eyes.

Of course, no visual distraction will work if your baby is crying so hard that his eyes are pressed shut. In this case, try getting his attention with something that makes an appealing sound. A toy that dings, squeaks, or makes music may induce your baby to open his eyes. Once you attract your baby's interest, you can use a visual stimulus to distract him from whatever happens to be distressing him.

➤ **Play with your baby.** At around two or three months of age, your baby will start to enjoy playing with you. If you suspect that loneliness or boredom has brought on his cries, try entertaining him.

Simple play and simple playthings will work best for the first year or so. You don't need to put on a clown suit or anything. Just try engaging your baby with a toy or two. Make some funny faces or play peek-a-boo. Gently bounce him on your knee while chanting a nursery rhyme. When he sits up, try rolling a ball to him or passing toys back and forth. When he starts to get mobile, you can play chasing games or even a primitive form of hide-and-seek. (For more on playing with your baby, see Chapter 11.)

➤ **Give your baby away.** No, you can't take the baby back to the hospital and get your money back, no matter how frustrated you've become trying to stop his wailing. But if you've tried everything you can imagine and nothing seems to stop your baby's crying for more than a minute or so, it's time to throw up your hands and surrender.

Pass your baby off to your partner and see what she can do. Don't become so obstinate in your determination to fix what's wrong that you refuse to take help from your partner. After all, you should be working together, not on opposing sides. (For more on the partnership of parenting, see Chapter 13.)

Even if your partner can't stop your baby's crying, let her give you a break from trying to calm him down. (Of course, it works both ways. If she's been trying without much success to calm the baby, you should offer to give her a break.) If your partner succeeds in calming him down, find out what she did. The next time your baby cries, try what worked for your partner (unless, of course, she offered the baby her breast).

Through trial and error, you'll find out which of these strategies work best to calm your baby. If none of these soothers work for your baby, try something new. Expand this repertoire with anything you discover that seems to work. Pretty soon, you may even be able to tell by the way your baby is crying exactly what he wants or needs.

It's Crying Time Again: Colic

Sadly, one type of crying will not respond to any attempts you make to calm your baby. This type of crying, which often begins around three or four weeks and can continue for up to three months, is called *colic*. Although babies who suffer from colic apparently emerge unscathed by the experience, parents of colicky babies go through hell for as long as it lasts. If your baby develops colic, you and your partner may feel increasingly frustrated, sad, angry, and, above all, desperate.

Generally, colic occurs only once a day, often in the late afternoon or early evening. But it happens *every* day and can last anywhere from one to four hours. If your baby has colic, no matter what you try, nothing will stop her from crying. (In fact, if anything succeeds in stopping your baby from crying for more than a minute or so, she doesn't really have colic.) Then, suddenly, the screaming will stop and your baby will once again seem perfectly normal.

Unfortunately, there's not much you can do but wait for it to pass. Oh, you can—and should—try the strategies suggested earlier in this chapter. But don't expect anything to work.

If your baby has colic, try to arrange it so that you or your partner—and ideally both of you—have nothing else to do during the time that it usually strikes. If you can help and support each other through your baby's colic, both of you will be less likely to harbor negative feelings toward your child.

Hang in there. Colic doesn't last forever. Indeed, it rarely lasts longer than 12 weeks (and often much less). So be patient. Together, you can get through this with most—okay, some—of your sanity intact.

Paterniterms

Colic refers to a pattern of inconsolable and intense crying or screaming. A baby who suffers from colic will often draw her legs up to her chest or belly, clench her fists, appear restless, and cry so hard that she turns red. Unfortunately, its cause is unknown and, therefore, untreatable.

Handle with Care

Your baby no doubt seems like a fragile, delicate creature to you. He's so small, so soft, so vulnerable, so helpless. In fact, your baby may seem so delicate that you fear hurting him in some way. Rest easy. Babies have survived fathers who were Neanderthals (literally, if you want to go back that far). They have survived fathers who didn't appreciate their fragility enough to even ask the questions you're asking. Your baby will survive your mistakes, too.

That said, you should observe certain ground rules when handling your baby. After all, your baby really is a fragile, delicate creature; you'll need to handle him with care.

Cool Daddy Ohs

Any sudden shift in position (or loud noise) will cause your baby instinctively to jettison her arms and legs, throwing them out spread eagle in anticipation of a fall. Then, just as quickly, she'll pull them back in to her body. It's almost as though your baby is trying to grab hold of the air to stop from falling. (This instinct is known as the **Moro reflex** or **startle reaction.**)

No Sudden Movements

Whether you're picking up your baby, carrying her around, moving her from your lap to your shoulder, or turning her from facing your body to facing outward, try to avoid any sudden movements. Move slowly, changing your baby's position gradually to avoid alarming her with the fear of falling.

For the first few months, your baby will prefer either remaining stationary or moving gradually and gently in the strong arms of one of her parents. Any other movement may seem somewhat dangerous to her. So, at least for a few months, hold off playing "whoops-a-baby"—throwing your baby up in the air and catching her on the way down.

Heads Up!

Playing "whoops-a-baby" with a young infant is also playing Russian roulette with the cardinal rule of baby handling: *Never drop your baby on his head!*

Your baby's head, though it may seem massive in comparison to the rest of his body, is actually very delicate. Indeed, your baby's skull won't be fully formed until he's about two years old.

Father Figures

At birth, your baby's head makes up an amazing 25 percent of his total body length. An average adult whose head took up that proportion of his height would have a head 15–18 inches long—about the size of a large watermelon!

When handling your baby, take special care to protect the two *fontanels* on his head. One fontanel, located on the back of your baby's head, should close within a few months of birth. The other fontanel, on top of your baby's head, will not disappear until the skull bones fully fuse—just before his second birthday.

The existence of the fontanels leaves a baby's brain somewhat unprotected. That's why it's so important to avoid dropping your baby on his head (or dropping anything heavy on his head). It's also important to avoid banging his head against anything.) Your baby's growing brain depends on it.

The Neck Bone's Connected to the Head Bone

Like the skull, many of the other bones in your baby's body are not fully set. Picking your baby up by her hands or arms—or worse, swinging her around by them—can easily result in a dislocated shoulder or collar bone. No matter how gently you lift her, the simple act of pulling can wrench an infant's bone out of place.

Instead of picking your baby up by the hands or arms, pick her up by her whole body. Slide your arms under her head and bottom and lift her all at once. This will not only avoid straining the muscles and bones in her arms, shoulders, and neck but will also provide much-needed support to her head and neck. Until your baby's neck muscles develop enough so that she can lift her own head and keep it up herself, you'll need to support and protect your baby's head and neck for her. (Your baby may lift her head within the first few weeks of her life. But until she can hold it up for more than a few seconds at a time, your baby's head and neck will still need your support.)

That's really all there is to handling your baby safely. All you need is a little gentleness, a little support, and a lot of love, and your baby will love being held in your arms. (And you won't think it's all that bad, either.)

Paterniterms

The **fontanels** are the two soft spots on your baby's skull where the bones have not yet fully joined. This lack of closure allows your baby's skull to change shape to pass through the birth canal. After birth, the fontanels allow for rapid growth in brain size.

The Least You Need to Know

➤ For practical parenting questions, trust your instincts first, but be prepared to learn through trial and error. (Your baby will teach you a lot about parenting if you pay attention.)

➤ Your baby cries for a reason. He's trying to tell you that he's hungry, hurt, uncomfortable, tired, lonely, bored, frustrated, afraid, or angry.

➤ Responding quickly to your baby's cries will not spoil her. It will help build your baby's feelings of security as well as a bond of trust between you.

➤ Soothing a crying baby *always* begins with picking him up. From there you can feed him, burp him, change him, rock him, sing to him, or whatever else takes care of his needs.

➤ Never drop your baby, especially not on her head.

Chapter 9

In One End and Out the Other: Feeding and Cleaning Your Baby

In This Chapter

➤ Supporting your partner's breast-feeding

➤ Feeding your baby from a bottle

➤ Introducing solid foods and spoon-feeding

➤ Dealing with dirty diapers and diaper rash

➤ Having a ball in the bathtub

During their first few months, babies spend most of their waking hours doing one of two things: eating and messing their diapers. If you and your partner have decided that breast-feeding is the only way to go for your baby, you won't have a whole lot to do on that score—though certainly you can offer help and support to her. If you've decided to feed your baby at least part of the time with a bottle, however, you should try to do your fair share of feedings.

In the interest of equal time, do you have to change all the diapers if your partner does all the feeding? Not on your life. After all, it wouldn't be fair if you monopolized all the fun jobs, would it? But again, you should take on your fair share of cleaning dirty diapers.

What's for Dinner?

The one area where you might legitimately feel left out of parenting is feeding your baby. If your partner has decided to breast-feed your baby—and especially if she plans to feed him exclusively from the breast—you may feel as if you're missing out on something. After all, nourishment serves as a metaphor for love, care giving, and providing what's needed for healthy development. As you watch your partner nursing your baby, his wide eyes staring up past the breast at her face, you can see a special bond between them. How can you possibly hope to compete with that?

The Wonder Dad: Offering Style, Support, and Comfort

Fortunately, parenting partners do not have to compete for their baby's affection (see Chapter 13). So try not to feel jealous of this one special thing that your partner can do for your baby, but that you can't. Instead, focus on all the special things that *you* can do for your baby. Keep in mind that breast-feeding is the *only* thing your partner can do for your baby that you can't. Everything else—from spoon-feeding to diapering, from bathing to soothing—you can do for your baby, too.

So don't just sit there sulking. Support your wife's breast-feeding efforts and help both her and your baby feel more comfortable.

Cool Daddy Ohs

Newborns see best about 12 inches in front of them—almost the exact distance between a mother's breast and her face. This makes nursing the ideal opportunity for bonding between mother and child.

Daddy Dos and Don'ts

While making sure that your partner drinks enough fluids, help her guard against drinking too much. More is not necessarily better. In fact, excess fluid can slow, rather than support, milk production.

Here are a few things you can do:

➤ **Make sure your partner gets enough fluids.** When your partner sits down to feed the baby, bring her a large glass of cold water. She needs plenty of fluids—eight to ten glasses a day—to stimulate milk production and to replenish the fluid she's losing.

➤ **Help her get comfortable.** If you don't have a chair that offers comfortable arm support for a mother holding a baby to her breast, get one. (A rocking chair will prove versatile, offering not only arm support for your nursing partner but a place where either of you can rock—and soothe—your baby.)

A foot stool may also come in handy, especially if your partner is petite (that's the word short women use instead of "short") and her feet don't reach the floor. A foot stool provides foot support and prevents leg and foot muscles from cramping or falling asleep. It can also make it easier for either of you to rock the rocking chair with your foot so that you don't repeatedly have to shift your upper body—and the baby.

Finally, offer your partner a pillow to support her elbow as she holds the baby to her breast. Even if her chair offers good arm support, a pillow will make it much more comfortable as the baby's weight presses her arm into the arm support.

A relatively recent addition to the baby-product market is a special horseshoe-shaped pillow for nursing mothers. It wraps around the mother's waist, providing both support and comfort as she nurses the baby.

➤ **Admire without envy.** Lactation is not a prerequisite for parent-child bonding. You can connect with and care for your baby in many different ways—just not this one.

So try not to feel jealous. Instead, just watch in wonder. That a mother's body can provide her baby with all the nourishment he needs is miraculous. Equally amazing is the love between them unfolding before your eyes.

It's 3 A.M. Do You Know Where Your Baby Is?

Another way to offer support if your partner breast-feeds exclusively is to help out with middle-of-the-night feedings. You can participate by getting your baby out of the crib and bringing her to your partner. You can change your baby's soggy diaper between breasts, after a feeding, or, if you're dexterous enough, during a feeding. (Trust me, the diaper *will* need changing in the middle of the night.)

Some new fathers view it as a point of honor to participate in mid-night feedings, and some new mothers view it as an important symbol that they and their partners are in this together. Other parents eschew this romanticism for a more practical approach.

The argument for practicality goes something like this: Your partner can—and really should—sleep while the baby is sleeping. (Of course, if you have other young children at home who don't allow your partner to sleep when the baby naps during the day, this argument goes out the window.) But if you've gone back to work full-time, you probably can't do the same. Since your partner, if she's breast-feeding, has to get up to feed the baby anyway, it might make more sense for you to miss out on the mid-night rituals.

Of course, logic cannot be the only consideration in making this decision. Some new parents find that shared sleep deprivation brings them closer together. It reaffirms their bond to each other and their commitment to the baby. Whether you and your partner ultimately decide to come down on the side of romanticism or practicality depends on your own personalities and your relationship. Talk it over with your partner and decide what's right for both of you.

Pass the Bottle This Way, Pal

Even if your partner has decided to nurse your baby, you might find it necessary to provide supplemental bottle-feedings of *expressed breast-milk*

Paterniterms

Expressed milk is milk that your partner has squeezed or pumped out of her breast between feedings and then stored in the refrigerator or freezer for later bottle-feedings. It is especially convenient for parents who want to maintain an exclusive diet of breast-milk for their babies while allowing the mother freedom to leave the baby for more than a few hours.

or formula. Unless required for medical reasons (low birth-weight is the main one), you should probably hold off on bottle-feeding, however, for at least several weeks after your baby's birth—to give her the chance to get the hang of feeding from your partner's breast. No matter how closely manufacturers design bottle nipples to re-semble maternal nipples, the sucking action required to draw formula (or expressed breast-milk) is not the same as that needed to draw milk directly from the breast. In fact, it's much easier for your baby to feed from a bottle. So trying to do both at first may confuse your baby or, worse, make her resist learning to drink from the breast.

If you and your partner decide to add supplemental bottle-feedings, you can handle most or all of them. And, of course, if your partner has decided not to nurse your baby at all, you can share equally in the bottle-feeding of formula.

A Formula for Success

You can buy (from most to least expensive) ready-to-use formula, liquid concentrate, or powder. Just follow the directions on the package. Be precise; adding too much water to a powder or concentrate can cause undernourishment, whereas too little water can lead to dehydration.

When the bottle is ready, cradle your baby in one arm and hold the bottle with the other. Make sure to tilt the bottle about 45 degrees at first (enough so that the inside of the nipple remains filled with formula). Then, as your baby drinks, gradually increase the angle to keep the nipple covered with liquid. If you don't, your baby will drink in a lot of air as well as formula, which can give him painful gas bubbles.

Avoid propping your baby up with pillows and shoving a bottle in his mouth. Not only will this probably cause your baby either to choke (from drinking too much too fast) or to develop gas pains (from sucking in too much air), it will also waste a valuable opportunity for you to bond with your baby. Remember, a baby sees best from about 12 inches away. This makes feeding time a terrific opportunity to interact with your baby. So if his eyes stay open, look into them. While he's drinking, coo, whisper, or sing softly to your baby (unless it distracts him from the bottle). Try to make the most of this special time to connect with your baby.

Daddy Dos and Don'ts

When using a mix, make enough bottles for the whole day. Formula will remain safe for up to 24 hours if refrigerated in a capped, sterile bottle. When your baby is screaming for something to eat, you'll be glad you did. It's much easier to grab a bottle, heat, and serve than to have to get out your chemistry kit and mix up a new one—especially if you try to do it while holding your baby.

Daddy Dos and Don'ts

If you use a microwave (and most parents do despite warnings to the contrary), be very careful. Microwaves heat unevenly, so you'll need to shake the bottle well after heating, let it set a minute, and then test the temperature by letting a few drops fall on your wrist. Make sure the formula is only warm, *not* hot (about room temperature).

Don't worry if your baby doesn't finish the entire bottle of formula. (You can't reuse it later, however, since the combination of formula and backwash provides a fertile breeding ground for bacteria.) By the same token, if your baby still seems hungry after finishing a bottle, make a couple more ounces of formula and see if you're right. Through trial and error, you'll soon get to know how much your baby tends to drink.

If your partner nurses your baby, your willingness to give the baby a bottle will become especially important when the time comes to wean your baby from the breast. While you are giving your baby a bottle, your partner can stay out of sight—and, hopefully, out of mind.

Spoon-Feeding

At around four to six months, your baby will start needing solid foods in addition to breast-milk or formula. (Solid foods, however, should be viewed solely as a supplement to breast-milk or formula for one or two more months.) So, even if you've never had a chance to give your baby a bottle, you can certainly get into the feeding frenzy now.

Spoon-feeding your baby will make a horrible mess. It will take some practice for you and your baby to get in sync, and for her to learn how to swallow more food than she spits out. But no matter how messy it gets, it can still be a lot of fun—for both of you.

Daddy Dos and Don'ts

If your baby starts to fuss or choke while drinking from a bottle—especially if you know he's hungry—the fault probably lies in the bottle's nipple. A blocked nipple, clogged with powder or formula, will prevent your baby from drinking. A nipple with too small an opening will make it difficult to drink so that your baby gives up after a short time (and then wants to eat again almost immediately). A nipple with too large an opening will release too much formula too fast, resulting in choking.

To fix a clogged nipple, gently squeeze the bottle or switch to a clean nipple. To widen a hole, use sterile scissors or a red-hot needle. If the hole is already too wide, replace it.

When introducing solids, start slow. Choose a time when your baby is alert and hungry, but not starving—perhaps after she's already finished drinking from one breast or had half a bottle of formula. Give your baby just a few spoonfuls to see how she likes it. At first, focus on getting a little food from the spoon into her mouth—one or two dozen spoonfuls at most—before finishing up with your partner's other breast or the rest of the bottle.

Introduce just one new food at a time, and then avoid introducing anything else new for a few days. That way, you'll be able to figure out the cause if she reacts to a particular food with indigestion or an allergy, which will manifest itself as diarrhea, a rash, or unusual crankiness. If this happens, hold off on that particular food for a couple of months, and then try again. Your baby may grow out of this allergic response.

Daddy Dos and Don'ts

For the first few weeks of introducing solid foods, just bring the spoonful of cereal or pureed fruit to your baby's lips. Don't try to shovel the food into her mouth. Let her suck it off the spoon. After all, that's the only way she knows how to eat.

You might have greater success if you give your baby her own spoon. Not that she'll suddenly dig into the bowl and start feeding herself, but the spoon will keep your baby's hands busy and allow you to get your spoon to and from her mouth without too much interference.

Start with baby cereal (rice, barley, or oats) mixed with water. Hey, it may not taste great to you, but your baby will probably love it. If she doesn't, try sweetening it a little by mixing it with formula, expressed breast-milk, or apple or pear juice. (Avoid adding processed sugar.)

After your baby has gotten used to cereal, you can begin opening up the menu little by little. Start by adding pureed vegetables (store-bought jars or homemade) and then pureed fruits. If you start with fruit, your baby is more likely to develop a sweet tooth and reject vegetables. Next, introduce a variety of breads and pastas, cut into small pieces so that your baby doesn't choke on them.

At around eight months, when your baby begins to rely more on solid meals and less on the breast or bottle for nutrition, you can begin introducing sources of protein: chicken, beef, tofu, brown rice, and beans of all kinds.

Even if she doesn't have any teeth yet, your eight-month-old probably can use her gums to chew food of increasingly complex texture than the pureed, soupy foods you've been feeding her. If you notice your baby has begun "chewing" her food (usually around seven or eight months), you can also start to introduce foods with more texture. The food should still be ground up, but not necessarily pureed.

Finger foods start to get fun at about the same time. Of course, what your baby considers finger foods may not match your definition. In fact, she probably considers *everything* a finger food. Good first finger foods for your baby include the following:

➤ Cooked vegetables, grated or sliced

➤ Small pieces of fruit (about half the size of a grape)—a sliced banana, for example

➤ Macaroni or spaghetti, cut into small pieces

➤ Rice

➤ Rice cakes

➤ Triangles of bread or toast

➤ Pretzels (preferably with little or no salt)

➤ Small chunks of chicken or meat

By the end of the first year, you can give your child almost anything to eat. The exceptions, which you should probably avoid until after your baby's first birthday, include the following:

➤ Foods high in acid content (citrus fruits, tomatoes).

➤ Common allergens (eggs, milk and dairy products, fish and shellfish, wheat, corn, and chocolate).

➤ Choking hazards (peanuts, popcorn, hot dogs, whole grapes, raw carrots, and the like), which you should probably avoid until your child is at least two years old—and then only with adult supervision.

➤ Foods high in salt or sugar.

➤ Honey, which should be avoided until age two because it can cause botulism.

Have fun introducing your baby to a varied diet and discovering the foods your baby likes and dislikes. Your baby's first reaction, however, can be misinterpreted, so don't give up on a particular food just because she spits it out the first time you offer it to her. Your baby may simply be full or distracted or be having difficulty getting used to this spoon-feeding business. You may have to offer a food three or four times before you can reach a solid conclusion about whether your baby likes it.

Father Knows Best

"There are times when parenthood seems nothing but feeding the mouth that bites you."

—Peter de Vries

If your baby doesn't like a particular food, don't force her to eat it. (Similarly, if she's full, don't force her to eat everything you've prepared.) Try to establish a relaxed, fun atmosphere, free of tension or pressure. If you can do that, your baby will enjoy eating.

Cleanliness Is Next to Impossible

The actual physical needs of an infant are very limited. Besides food and sleep and warmth and shelter, all your baby really needs from a physical standpoint is to be kept relatively clean. Of course, this sounds a lot easier than it turns out to be.

During your baby's first months, your life may sometimes seem like an endless stream of diaper changing. Later, when your baby begins eating solid foods, he'll feel sticky or gooey after every meal and can probably stand to have a bath five or six times a day. Then, when he begins to toddle, your baby will quickly discover the joys of dirt and mud. Given these obstacles, it may seem impossible to keep your baby clean for very long.

Father Knows Best

"A soiled baby, with a neglected nose, cannot be conscientiously regarded as a thing of beauty."

—Mark Twain

It's a Dirty Job, But Somebody's Got to Do It

Naturally, nearly everything that goes into your baby will come out sooner or later (more likely sooner). Since your baby still has an immature digestive system and her diet is all liquid, the food that her body doesn't absorb travels very quickly through her stomach and intestines—and into her diaper. As a result, you will need to change somewhere between eight and fourteen diapers every day.

Changing diapers isn't really so bad, however, especially if your baby stays exclusively on a diet of breast-milk for a few months. The excrement of breast-fed babies does not smell nearly as noxious as that of bottle-fed babies or those who've progressed to solids. In fact, it smells kind of sweet.

So don't sit back and let your partner have all the fun. Get in there and don't be afraid to, as they say, get your hands dirty.

Father Figures

It's not only amazing, it's downright frightening. Your baby will wet or soil more than 7,000 diapers in her first two and a half years. (And that's a conservative estimate!)

Father Knows Best

"The arrival of a baby coincides with the departure of our minds. My wife and I often summoned the grandparents of our first baby and proudly cried, 'Look! Poopoo!'"

—Bill Cosby

Get Ready, Get Set ...

Get everything you need ready first so that you can make the change as quick and painless for both of you as possible. You'll need

➤ A washcloth and a small bowl of warm water, or baby wipes.

➤ A clean diaper.

➤ Diaper cream, in case your baby has a rash.

➤ A change of clothes, in case your baby's diaper has overflowed.

... Go!

First, take off your baby's dirty diaper by unfastening the tape tabs of a disposable or separating the velcro of a diaper wrap. Be careful not to make any smearing worse than it already is. Before moving on to a washcloth or baby wipe, you can use any clean section of the diaper to wipe up some of the poop, making sure you always wipe from front to back.

If your baby wears disposable diapers, close up the dirty diaper and deposit it in a diaper pail. If he wears cloth diapers, separate the dirty diaper from the diaper wrap, drop the diaper in the diaper pail, and set aside the diaper wrap on the corner of the changing table.

Next, clean your baby's genitals and bottom with a baby wipe or wet, warm (not hot!) washcloth. You may also need to clean his belly, thighs, legs, and hands, as well as your own hands.

Whether your baby's diaper is wet or soiled, wipe the genitals first, front to back (especially if you have a baby girl, to avoid wiping poop into the vulva). Then, wipe off your baby's thighs and upper legs if they got wet or dirty. Last, but certainly not least, gently lift your baby by the ankles so that you can get at the bottom. You should always wipe the bottom thoroughly even if only the diaper is wet.

Unfortunately, the freedom of having his diaper off may occasionally prompt your baby to let out some more. To avoid getting sprayed (or worse) while changing, try one or more of the following:

➤ Have a cloth diaper available to catch and mop up any sudden sprays.

➤ Drape a cloth diaper over your baby's genitals (especially if you have a boy) from the second you remove the dirty diaper to the moment you're ready to put on the clean one.

Daddy Dos and Don'ts

Do *not* wipe inside the lips of the vulva or pull back the foreskin of an uncircumcised penis unless some of your baby's poop has managed to migrate there. You may cause, rather than prevent, an infection. If the inside of the vulva or foreskin is soiled, wipe it first with a totally clean wipe or washcloth.

109

➤ Pull your baby's shirt or one-piece outfit up to the chest and the pants down to the ankles (or even all the way off) to avoid getting his clothes wet.

➤ Move fast, try to hold on to your sense of humor, and if necessary, dive for cover!

All Red in the Cheeks

No matter how hard you try to prevent it, your baby will sometimes develop a red, often bumpy, diaper rash. If your baby has a rash, change his diaper more frequently, and treat the rash every time you change him. Try one or more of the following:

➤ Let your baby go naked for 15 minutes or so at a time, at least on his bottom. A good "airing out" can help eliminate the rash.

➤ Switch the type of diapers he wears (from disposable to cloth or vice versa). A change may help.

➤ Avoid using soap or diaper wipes that contain alcohol, both of which can cause dry skin and irritation. Water alone works just fine for cleaning your baby.

➤ Dry your baby's bottom completely after each washing. Trapped moisture can aggravate diaper rash.

➤ Try different diaper creams, especially those with zinc oxide, until you find one that works.

You don't need to use baby powder at all. In fact, some pediatricians warn that inhaling particles of talcum or corn starch can actually harm your baby.

Once you've cleaned his bottom and taken care of any diaper rash, you can put a clean diaper on your baby. Check his clothes to make sure they didn't get dirty or wet, and change them too, if necessary. That's all there is to it.

In five to ten minutes, check your baby's diaper again. Chances are he may need another change.

Call in the Toxic Waste Crew

After wrestling your baby into a clean diaper, lift her off the changing table, and put her in her crib or bassinet, or on the floor while you clean up. If she screams when you put her down, try cleaning up with one arm and holding her with the other.

Once your baby is in a safe place, throw away the used diaper wipes or dump the dirty washcloths in a pail of

Daddy Dos and Don'ts

Never leave your baby alone on the changing table, even for "just a second." If you've unwrapped her diaper and suddenly realize you need another washcloth or some diaper cream, don't leave her alone. Do your best to contain the mess and bring your baby along with you. Long before your baby can crawl or even roll over, she can move herself slightly with the kicking of her legs or the flailing of her arms. If you leave your baby on the changing table, even for a few seconds, she might suffer a nasty fall.

water and borax (which will cut down on offensive odors). If you use cloth diapers, what you do with the diaper wrap depends on how effusive your baby has been. If the diaper wrap isn't wet or soiled, you might want to save it for re-use. If it's wet or lightly soiled, place the diaper wrap in the laundry (or, better still, in a bucket of borax and water). If the diaper wrap is heavily soiled, you'll probably want to wash or at least rinse it off a little before dropping it in the bucket.

Now that you're officially done, wash your hands with an antibacterial soap. Believe me, you'll need it.

We're Having Some Fun Now, Aren't We?

Changing diapers doesn't have to be torture either for you or your baby. In fact, if you don't try to have some fun with it, you'll hate it—all 10,000 times—and so will your baby. So do whatever you can to make it more entertaining for both of you.

Need some ideas? Try these:

➤ Decorate a wall near the changing table, at first with black-and-white patterns (which your newborn sees best), and later with posters or fun, colored pictures from magazines.

➤ Hang a mobile—again black-and-white at first and later color—over the changing table to keep him occupied.

➤ Talk to your baby: about what you're doing, about your day, about the weather, about anything. If your baby seems to be listening, avert your eyes every few seconds from the nasty task at hand to make eye contact.

➤ Sing songs (lullabies, silly songs, rock, rap, whatever).

➤ Play "This Little Piggy" or other toe games. Your baby's on his back with his toes up—why not?

➤ Be silly and get your baby to laugh. Make goofy faces, put a diaper on your head, and talk in funny voices. Who's going to know?

Super Soakers: Bath Time

Your baby's bottom is not the only part of her that will get dirty. Although newborns tend to stay fairly clean, you still need to give yours a bath every now and then. Unfortunately, your baby probably won't like taking a bath, at least for the first few months. Most babies don't even like being naked, much less being plunged into water while they're naked.

Little by Little: Sponge Baths

Since your baby probably won't welcome the experience and really doesn't need everyday cleaning, limit the baths to one or two a week, until he develops a taste for them. Or, try giving him a sponge bath by carefully unwrapping one part of his body at a time, washing it, drying him off, and then wrapping him up again before moving on to another part.

You will need to stick to sponge baths at least for the first week or two, since the *umbilicus* should be kept dry until it falls off. You should clean the umbilicus two or three times a day by dabbing it with a sterile cotton ball dipped in alcohol (which helps to prevent infection).

Paterniterms

The **umbilicus** is what's left over after the umbilical cord has been severed and knotted after childbirth. When the umbilicus withers and falls off, what's left is the belly button.

Daddy Dos and Don'ts

Whether you bathe your baby in a sink or a tub, make sure she doesn't get burned by brushing against a hot water tap. If hot and cold water flow through the same faucet, *always* turn off the hot water first. This will allow the flow of cold water to cool down the spigot. If you live in an ancient home that has separate faucets for hot and cold water, make sure to wrap a washcloth or dishtowel around the hot water tap to prevent your child from touching it.

You should also stick to sponge baths for your baby until after his circumcised penis has healed. The penis should be covered with a small, sterile piece of gauze with a dab of petroleum jelly on it. You should change the gauze every time you change the baby until the penis heals.

The success of a sponge bath depends on how well you work with one hand. You'll need one hand to hold up your baby and support his head and neck. Choose any hold that feels secure and that you can maintain when (and I mean when, not if) he starts squirming. A good technique is to grip your baby under the underarm that's farthest from you and use your wrist and forearm to support the back of your baby's head and neck.

Once you have a grip on your baby, use your free hand to wash him, little by little, from top to bottom, with a warm, damp washcloth. If you must use soap, use very little, since soap can dry your baby's skin. Make sure to wash inside all the creases where the skin folds over itself; dirt and schmutz tend to accumulate in these places.

When you've finished sponging off your baby's front, it's time to clean his back. Flip him over so that your hand and forearm support the front of his head and neck. Wash your baby's genitals and bottom last, and then quickly wrap him up in a towel so that he stays as warm as possible. (Babies, you'll remember, do not retain heat well.)

You may want to slap on a diaper before your baby has a chance to take full advantage of his nakedness. (Whoops, too late!) Don't feel you have to rush your baby back into his clothes, though, especially if the bath has upset him. As long as you've got him bundled up in a dry towel, he'll stay warm enough. And being held in your arms may succeed in calming him down so that you can get him dressed with fewer tears.

Sink or Swim

Once the umbilicus has fallen off and the circumcision (if any) has healed, your baby can take the plunge and move on to real baths. To avoid straining your back—since you'll need to continue supporting your baby in the tub until long after she can sit up on her own—you may want to start out in the kitchen rather than the bathroom. Use either the kitchen sink or a portable "baby tub" that you place securely (no balancing or precarious perches) on a kitchen counter or other convenient large surface that's more than waist high.

If you decide to use the kitchen sink, line the bottom with a towel, rubber mat, or the foam-rubber insert from a portable tub before filling it with warm water. This will not only be more comfortable on your baby's bottom than stainless steel but will also keep her from slipping, sliding, and sinking. Also, after you've filled (or rather, half-filled) the sink with water (and before you've put the baby in), remember to swing the spigot away from the sink so that she doesn't bump her noggin on it.

When your baby gets too big for the sink or portable tub—or sooner if you don't mind kneeling on tile floors for long periods of time—you can move her into the bathtub. You can make this transition to the big tub at any age. After all, bathing your baby in a sink was for your sake—and the sake of your back—not your baby's. When you put your baby into the tub, she will be less likely to startle if you

Daddy Dos and Don'ts

No matter where you bathe your baby, always test the water temperature—using your elbow rather than your hands—to make sure it's not too hot or too cold.

Never leave your baby alone in the water—even for an instant. Believe it or not, an infant can drown in an inch or less of water. Even after your baby can sit up for extended periods of time by herself, you should never leave her alone in the tub. Let the answering machine pick up the phone, take her with you (wrapped up snug and warm in a towel, of course) if the doorbell rings, and avoid taking any foolish—and possibly tragic—risks.

➤ Hold her securely, with one hand supporting her bottom (and perhaps gripping a thigh) and the other supporting her neck and head (and perhaps gripping the far shoulder).

➤ Ease her into the tub rather than plunge her into it.

➤ Talk softly and calmly to her as you lower her into the water.

➤ Support her with your left hand or cradle her head and shoulders in the crook of your arm while you wash her gently with your right hand.

Pay attention to how your baby reacts. Remember, she doesn't absolutely have to take a bath yet. If your baby really fears the water, take her out and continue giving her sponge baths instead. Then, once a month or so, try to reintroduce her to the tub until she feels comfortable.

Even after your baby can sit up by herself—indeed, for many more months after that—you should make it a point never to let go of her while she's in the tub. Of course, the easiest way to maintain a secure hold of your baby is to climb in with her. But if you don't like baths—or don't like as many baths as your baby seems to enjoy—you'll need to kneel by the side of the tub and lean your arms over the edge to hold on to your child.

A bathtub safety seat, which sticks to the bottom of the tub with suction cups, can come in handy when your baby can sit up long enough to use one. But don't make the mistake of thinking that a safety seat means you can let down your guard. Babies can slump down and, by moving just one leg, even slide right out of a safety seat and under the water. You should support your baby with at least one hand until she can sit up for more than a minute or two—and even then, never leave her alone in the water.

Tubby Time Is Fun Time

Many fathers who work full-time outside of the home find that bath time is their time to shine with their babies. If you approach it with a playful attitude, bath time can be a lot of fun for both of you.

To make bath time a success, attitude and timing are everything. The attitude is easy: Have fun, play, enjoy. You should even encourage your baby to splash (which is a form of discovery), as long as he doesn't threaten to bury the house under water.

As for timing, choose an hour when your baby is not too hungry, not too full, and not too tired—and when you have enough time so that you don't have to hurry through the bath. An hour or two after the evening meal—his, not necessarily yours—is usually a great time for a baby's bath. Your baby won't be so full that he spits up all over the tub, but he won't be so hungry that he can't stand anything that delays his next feeding. Finally, the bath—and your good company—can help create a warm, relaxed feeling that can help make bedtime much smoother.

By the time your baby is three or four months old, he will probably love the water. He will enjoy running it through his fingers, trying in vain to catch it when you pour it from a cup, and feeling it buoy up parts of his body. Most of all, though, your baby will love splashing it with his arms and legs.

Now is the time to bring in a raft of bath toys. Your baby will probably have a lot of fun with

➤ Rubber duckies and other floating animals.

➤ Plastic cups or other unbreakable containers.

➤ Balls, boats, and bath books—anything that floats.

If you encourage your child to have fun in the tub, you will invariably rear a child who loves bathing. And since cleanliness is next to godliness, you may end up with a little saint on your hands. (Yeah, you wish.)

The Least You Need to Know

➤ You may not be able to breast-feed your baby, but that's the *only* thing you can't do for her. If your baby is on an exclusive diet of breast-milk, immerse yourself in all other aspects of baby care rather than focusing jealously on the one thing you can't do.

➤ If your baby drinks from a bottle, make sure to take your fair share of turns feeding him. If you make the most of it, feeding time can be a terrific opportunity to build your relationship with your baby.

➤ Introduce solid foods gradually, one new food every few days. This way, you can pinpoint foods that cause allergic reactions.

➤ Get used to changing diapers—and try to add some fun to it—because your baby will go through 7,000–10,000 in her first 30 months.

➤ Never leave your baby alone on the changing table or in the bathtub—even after she can sit up on her own.

Chapter 10

Daddy Doctor

In This Chapter

➤ How to tell if your baby's sick

➤ When illness calls for a doctor's attention

➤ Putting together a child-ready first-aid kit

➤ Treating minor accidents and illnesses yourself

➤ The basics of CPR for kids—and why you should take a course in it as soon as possible

---

Okay, so your kid is sick. He's puking rainbows of green and yellow gunk, so much that you have a hard time believing that his little body could have contained so much vomit. His fever is climbing faster than the thermometer on a hot summer's day—in Arizona. He seems to have lost interest in everything. When not throwing up, he just lies there like a beached whale (okay, a tiny beached whale): barely breathing, hardly moving, his eyes half-open in a blank stare.

So now what do you do?

Let's make the scenario even more interesting. Your wife has returned to work, perhaps just part-time, or she had to fly out of town because a relative was in a car accident. In any case, it's just you and your child, maybe for just three or four hours, maybe for a couple of days. What do you do if he gets sick?

Daddy, I Don't Feel So Good

If you take on any significant portion of baby or child-care (see Chapter 6), you will need to know how to care for a sick child. Yet as the scenario you just read illustrates, even if you have taken on a more traditional paternal role—working outside the home 40 or more hours a week and yielding almost all child-care responsibilities to your partner—a time will probably come during the first few years as a father when you alone have to take care of your sick child.

Caring for a sick child—especially a sick infant—can be scary. Illness hits small children hard. The same virus that has you dragging along all day, drinking tea and sipping soup and feeling generally miserable, can turn your child into a zombie. Nothing arouses her interest: not food, toys, or even TV.

It's easy to think a small child in this condition is in dire need of medical attention—that you can't handle it. But if you know what to do when your child gets sick, you'll prevent the scariness of her illness from building into a full-scale panic attack.

Is There a Doctor in the House?

To take care of a sick child, you don't need medical expertise—that's what pediatricians are for. But you do need common sense and a little bit of basic knowledge about sickness and health.

An infant, for instance, won't be able to tell you what's wrong—or even let you know that he doesn't feel well. So you'll need to know what to look for with a baby, not just to find out exactly what's wrong, but to know whether he's sick at all.

Naturally, you will recognize the most obvious signs of illness. If your child's skin scorches your hand when you touch it, you'll guess correctly that the fever probably indicates some illness. If he begins vomiting with the force of a tidal wave, you'll again have a pretty good clue that your baby is sick. (Of course, if your baby does both and his head begins to spin, it's a pretty good bet that he's been possessed by the devil.) But what should you look for in the absence of these obvious signs?

A good rule of thumb to apply is that any radical change in your baby's day-to-day behavioral patterns may (or may not) indicate illness. Most babies tend to develop general patterns of behavior: a feeding schedule, eating habits, how often they wet or soil their diapers, customary nap and bedtimes, the length of time they sleep, patterns of activity, even discernible patterns of crying depending on the cause, and so on. When these patterns change, it usually indicates some other major change.

Does a change in pattern always signal illness? Certainly not. A baby whose sleep needs suddenly increase may merely be going through a growth spurt or mastering a new skill, an effort that drains him of energy. An infant who wets fewer diapers may simply be drinking less (perhaps the weather got cooler).

Nonetheless, you should watch for radical changes in behavior or behavior patterns. Although they may not always indicate illness, such changes do demand your attention. If it's illness, you'll soon pick up other clues that will confirm your hunch. If it's not, you may have the joy of discovering—at the same time your child does—something new that he can do.

Patience! Patients!

While the challenge involved in caring for sick infants centers on figuring out what's the matter and then treating it appropriately, the challenge with older children who get sick is to remain patient, understanding, and loving. If you're like most people, the sight and sound of a sick infant will melt your heart. A sick baby is a sad, pathetic creature; you'll do anything to cheer her up or make her feel a little better.

Unfortunately, that's not always the case with older children. Once your child begins to speak, she will find it easier to describe how she's feeling. But she may whine or complain about it incessantly. That's where patience comes in.

With toddlers and older children, whining may in fact be one of the first signs of illness. When a viral or bacterial infection really takes hold of your child's body, it may knock her out just as illness did when she was a baby. But in the early stages of illness, a spreading infection may wear down your child just enough so that every minor setback or frustration makes her cry and moan.

So if your child—who is no whiner, of course—starts whining a lot more than usual, try to remain patient and understanding with her. Her complaints and short temper may indicate the onset of illness (or perhaps just over-tiredness). If you become impatient and snap at your child because of her whining tonight, you may feel guilty tomorrow morning when she wakes up with a temperature of 102.

A good bedside manner is essential for a father with a sick child. Yes, your child's whining might drive you crazy. Yes, she might throw up all over your best suit just hours before a critical business meeting. Yes, she might keep you up all night. But no matter how bad all this might make you feel, keep in mind one important fact: Your child feels worse than you do. So do your best to keep your composure, your compassion, and your love—or keep your distance.

Calling for Reinforcements

How sick does your child need to be before you call the doctor? Well, it all depends on you, your child, and his symptoms.

Different parents have different ways of dealing with illness. You or your partner might call the pediatrician at your child's first sniffle. Or you may be more of the wait-and-see types, handling the common colds yourself and only calling the doctor if your child's fever becomes alarmingly high or if it lasts more than a day or two. Either approach is fine if it works for you.

Of course, children also have different ways of coping with illness. Your child may be so cautious that he brings every little scratch in his throat or every minor ache or pain to your attention. On the other hand, your child may resist letting anything short of malaria slow him down. Or he may be somewhere in between. How your child responds to illness will depend on his personality. A little experience with him will allow you to gauge his responses to illness and act accordingly.

Finally, the symptoms themselves should of course have some bearing on your decision to call the doctor or not. Certain symptoms should not be minimized or ignored, no matter how they affect your child's immediate behavior or demeanor. The following symptoms almost always demand a pediatrician's attention:

➤ A fever greater than 102 degrees Fahrenheit in a child of any age—or any fever at all (that is, a rectal temperature greater than 100.4 degrees Fahrenheit) in infants under 2 or 3 months)

➤ Unusual and persistent crying

➤ Unusual listlessness or inactivity

➤ Noticeable changes in your child's color or behavior

➤ Sudden loss of appetite or other noticeable disruptions in his feeding patterns

➤ Inability to take in fluids or urinate

➤ Severe, persistent vomiting—that is, spitting up more than usual or throwing up with great force (often called projectile vomiting)

➤ Foul-smelling diarrhea, diarrhea in which you can see blood or mucus, or any diarrhea accompanied by a fever

➤ Constipation when coupled with vomiting

➤ Any show of blood in his vomit, urine, or bowel movements

➤ Convulsions, twitching fits, or other seizures

➤ Severe, persistent headache, especially if associated with fever and neck pain

➤ Any widespread or unfamiliar rash

➤ Wheezing, breathlessness, or any other difficulty in breathing

➤ A persistent cough

➤ Persistent redness of the eyes or any discharge of pus from the eyes

➤ Any discharge from the ears

➤ Ear pain, which a preverbal child may (or may not) signal by repeatedly turning his head or pulling at his ear

➤ Swelling or sinking of either *fontanel*

➤ Any burns that blister

Paterniterms

The **fontanels** are two soft spots in a baby's head, located where the bones of the skull have not yet joined. One fontanel, located at the back of the head, closes at about four months; the other, on the top of the head, disappears when the skull bones fuse—generally around a child's second birthday.

➤ Ingestion of any nonfood items or any suspected toxins

➤ Hives, swelling, flushing, or respiratory distress after eating a meal, receiving an injection, or being stung by an insect

➤ Any injury that causes him to cry for more than 15 minutes

➤ Vomiting or temporary loss of consciousness following a fall

➤ Extreme swelling, especially of an arm or leg, following a fall or other accident

➤ Severe pain to the right lower abdomen, sometimes accompanied by vomiting or appetite loss

If your child has any of these symptoms, consult your pediatrician. Of course, you can call your child's doctor about any other health or developmental concerns, too. If anything your child does worries you or your partner—or causes you to wonder whether it's normal—feel free to call the doctor. If something is really wrong, the earlier you call, the better. And if nothing's wrong, your pediatrician's reassurances will make you feel better.

Tell Me Where It Hurts

Whenever you call up your child's doctor or bring your sick child to the pediatrician, it will help if you have the following information on hand:

➤ **Current temperature.** Be sure to specify whether the temperature is rectal, *axillary* (obtained by placing a rectal thermometer under your child's armpit), oral, or *tympanic*.

➤ **Symptoms.** Provide information about when symptoms first appeared, in what order they appeared, and how severe they seem.

➤ **Medications.** Be sure to tell your doctor what medicines you have already given your child, and remind him or her of any medications your child takes regularly.

➤ **Vital statistics.** Your pediatrician no doubt has hundreds of patients. Remind him or her of your child's age, weight, and any allergies she has.

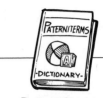

Paterniterms

Axillary temperature is obtained by placing a rectal thermometer under your child's armpit (which medical types call the "axilla").

Tympanic temperature is obtained by inserting a special thermometer inside your child's ear so that it presses against her eardrum (the "tympanum").

Daddy Dos and Don'ts

Rectal thermometers generally provide the most accurate temperature readings. Accurate oral readings depend on your child's ability to keep her mouth shut and the thermometer under her tongue for three minutes. Tympanic (eardrum) readings vary widely depending on the placement of the sensor in the ear. And axillary (armpit) temperatures are usually one to two degrees lower than rectal temperatures.

➤ **Pharmacy phone number.** If your pediatrician prescribes something over the phone, you'll want to have the phone number of your local pharmacy handy.

➤ **Questions.** Be ready with any specific questions you have regarding your child's symptoms, treatment, or medications. You may find it helpful to write them down before you call so that you won't forget.

When your child is sick and you visit the doctor, a nurse will collect much of this information: her age, weight, temperature, symptoms, and any medications she's taken. But while the nurse and doctor gather all the information they need, make sure you get all the information you need. Ask any questions you think will improve your ability to minister to your child, because once you leave the doctor's office, your child's health is once again in your hands alone.

Playing Doctor

You don't always need to call your child's doctor when your child is sick or injured. Certainly you should not hesitate to consult a doctor if your child's symptoms warrant it. But if you choose to handle a minor illness or emergency on your own, you'll need to have the proper supplies on hand at home. A well-stocked medicine cabinet, complete with an up-to-date first-aid kit, can mean the difference between quick relief and prolonged misery—or in a worst-case scenario, between life and death.

The Daddy-Doctor Motto: Be Prepared

Before your baby becomes mobile, he will probably need very little in the way of first aid. So you don't have to start filling your medicine cabinet with every type of gauze and antiseptic available to humankind until the second half of your baby's first year, when he starts pulling himself up to a standing position and then crawling. In all likelihood, that's when your child will begin injuring himself as he explores and expands his world. (To make your child's world as risk-free as possible and encourage him to explore in a safe environment, see the baby-proofing steps detailed in Chapter 15.)

For infants (those who cannot yet crawl or pull themselves up to a standing position), a rudimentary first-aid kit should contain

➤ A thermometer (for monitoring fevers)

➤ Acetaminophen drops (for treating high fever)

➤ A calibrated syringe or medicine dropper (to measure medicines accurately)

➤ Activated charcoal (to absorb and neutralize poison if your child swallows anything toxic)

Daddy Dos and Don'ts

Never, ever give your child aspirin or any medication containing aspirin unless your pediatrician specifically prescribes it. Aspirin has been associated with Reyes syndrome, a disease that can cause uncontrollable vomiting and permanent damage to the liver. So stick with acetaminophen (children's Tylenol or other brands) unless your doctor tells you otherwise.

or syrup of ipecac (to make your child vomit up poison)—but only after consulting your pediatrician or a poison control center first)

➤ Antiseptic liquid (for cleaning your hands both before and after administering medicines or first aid)

That's really all you'll need for the first few months. But by the time your baby has started moving around by himself, you should also add the following:

➤ Adhesive bandages of various sizes (for cuts and scrapes)

➤ Nonstick bandages (1"–2") (for larger cuts and scrapes)

➤ Sterile gauze pads and rolled gauze of various sizes (for large wounds)

➤ Adhesive tape (for holding gauze and non-stick bandages to the skin)

➤ Small scissors (for cutting gauze, bandages, and adhesive tape)

➤ Cotton balls or swabs (for applying topical medicines)

➤ Anesthetic and/or anti-itch spray, salve, gel, or stick (for relieving insect bites and bee stings)

➤ Calamine lotion or other soothing lotions (for cooling the skin and reducing the itch of sunburn, poison ivy, and other rashes)

➤ Hydrocortisone cream (for alleviating topical irritations)

➤ An antihistamine cream or oral antihistamine, such as Benadryl (for alleviating allergic reactions)

➤ Herbal or medicinal pain reliever (for teething)

➤ Acetaminophen in liquid, chewable, or suppository form (for toddlers and older children)

➤ Ice bag or cold pack (for reducing aches and swelling)

➤ Tweezers (for removing splinters)

➤ A complete family medical reference (for consulting before or after you call your pediatrician)

Daddy Dos and Don'ts

If your partner has filled and arranged the family medicine cabinet and normally takes care of your child when he's sick, it is especially important to take the time to familiarize yourself with all the contents of the first-aid kit. Be sure you know where everything is before you need to use it.

Daddy Dos and Don'ts

For safety's sake, all medicines, whether prescription or over-the-counter, should be kept either well out of reach of your child or in a locked cabinet—and preferably both.

Home Remedies

You don't need to rush to the doctor or emergency room for every cut or fever. In many cases, you can probably handle minor accidents and illnesses yourself—if you have the proper supplies on hand and know how to use them. (Of course, if you have any doubts at all about whether your child needs professional care during an illness or following an accident, even after you've given first aid, you should seek it immediately. Better to be safe than sorry, as they say.)

Treating cuts, scrapes, and even larger wounds is largely a matter of thorough cleaning—though not necessarily scrubbing, which might make your already nervous patient run screaming from the scene—and bandaging. (Don't worry, you'll recognize anything serious enough to require immediate medical attention: a deep wound that might require stitches, or a gash that doesn't stop bleeding, for example.)

Although they don't always demand removal, splinters can be taken out with tweezers if they bother your child. You might find it easier after a bath, when your child's skin becomes softer and more pliable. (Sometimes the mere act of soaking in the bath will cause the splinter to emerge.) Depending on your child's personality, you might need to distract her while you work the tweezers—but if she wants to watch, by all means let her.

Rashes can be treated initially with topical lotions or ointments. If they don't show improvement within a day or two, though, you might want to have your pediatrician take a look.

Daddy Dos and Don'ts

Whenever you (or your partner) call your child's doctor to ask about the dosage of a certain medication, write down the pediatrician's answer on a small piece of paper and tape it to the bottle. Include the name of the drug on this handmade label (in case it falls off the bottle), as well as the current recommended dosage, how often you can give it to your child, and at what age (or weight) your doctor recommends that you'll need to increase the dosage.

Perhaps the most commonly misused items in family medicine cabinets are over-the-counter pediatric medicines. With prescription medicines—vitamins, antibiotics, and so on—your pharmacist will write the correct dosage on the bottle: one pill three times a day, for instance, or half a teaspoonful before bedtime. Assuming you follow the instructions on the bottle, you probably won't run into any trouble.

With over-the-counter drugs, however, the correct dosage for your child might not always be so clear. To dispense medicines safely, you'll need to know exactly how much to give your child at her current age (or, more accurately, her current weight). Most over-the-counter pediatric medicines now include dosage charts based on weight and age on both the box and the bottle. (If, according to the chart, your child's weight doesn't fall in the range that corresponds with her age, use her weight as a guide to determine proper dosage.)

However, if your child is under age two—or, in many cases now, under age six—the instructions will advise you to consult your doctor to find out the proper dosage. So until your child is older, be sure to check with your pediatrician before giving her any medicine. Even with older children, call your doctor first if you have any doubt about how much medicine to give.

A Spoonful of Sugar

Once you've measured out the proper dosage of medicine for your child, getting him to take it can sometimes be a nightmare. Yes, it's hard to believe, but your angel may turn into a devil when it's time to take his medicine. If your child resists taking medicines, you may need to add a metaphorical spoonful of sugar to help the medicine go down.

First of all, try to avoid turning medicine-taking into a battleground. Don't start out with the assumption that your child will give you a hard time. Begin with a reasonable and straightforward approach, helping him to understand that he has to take the medicine—no matter how awful he thinks it tastes—in order to get better. If you simply tell your child it's time to take his medicine and act as if you have no doubts that he'll do so, the force of your own personality will probably carry him through it. If, on the other hand, you signal any doubts you have about his cooperation, your child may pick up on it and begin resisting.

If your child doesn't fight, giving liquid medicine is easy. With an infant or toddler, sit the child on your lap (not lying on his back, which can cause him to choke on the medicine). Tuck a cloth diaper under his chin and over his shoulders to catch any spills. Then simply place the end of the syringe or medicine dropper in a corner of your child's mouth and squirt the medicine inside the cheek—not too far back, where it might cause your baby to choke, nor too far forward, where it might dribble out (or be spat out).

With older children you can switch to chewable tablets—although some older kids enjoy squirting liquid medicine themselves, too. (Measuring spoons and cups aren't nearly as much fun.)

If you run into continued resistance, try any or all of the following:

➤ Mix liquid medicine—or a pill crushed into powder—into a tiny amount of applesauce (just about a spoonful, so that he doesn't have to eat an entire bowl to get the proper dosage). But let your child know that that's what you've done—to try to make the medicine taste better. If you try to trick him, your child will know after one taste, and will never again trust the applesauce you serve him.

➤ Try "serving" the medicine to a favorite stuffed animal first—and praise the animal for its cooperation.

➤ Pour a glass of water, juice, or your child's favorite drink before offering the medicine. That way it will be ready to wash away the taste of liquid medicine — or wash down a pill or capsule.

125

➤ Bribe him. Offer him a favorite story, game, or other activity as a reward for his cooperation.

➤ Stuff a pill inside a small slice of soft banana and ask your preschooler or elementary-school child to swallow it without chewing.

Daddy Dos and Don'ts

For safety's sake, never allow your child to get or measure medicine himself. All medicines should be given under adult supervision. Also, never compare medicine with candy in an attempt to win your child's cooperation. This strategy may backfire, leading your young child to search relentlessly for more "candy."

Daddy Dos and Don'ts

In addition to preparing yourself for any possible emergency, you may also want to prepare your child—especially an older child—for the possibility. Contact the hospital where you would go and see whether you can arrange an advance tour of the emergency department. In addition, check your local library for children's books on hospitals or medical emergencies. Your child will remain calmer in an emergency if he has already formed an idea of what to expect.

One of these strategies should work if your child doesn't like to take medicine. By convincing him to cooperate in this way, you'll avoid the need to force him to take his medicine—a strategy that can not only lead to choking, but will no doubt become self-perpetuating. No matter which strategy works for you, don't forget to praise your child afterward. Children generally want to please their parents, so the praise you offer now may lead to greater cooperation later.

In Case of Emergency

No father likes to think that his child might have a medical emergency. But accidents happen and illness sometimes strikes without warning. If something unthinkable happens to your child, will you know what to do? If he gets hit by a car or falls off a swing set and loses consciousness, if his temperature soars above 104 degrees or he suddenly stops breathing, are you ready to spring into action?

Ready for Anything?

With any luck, your child will never experience any kind of medical emergency. But if he does, you'll need to be prepared. If you don't know whom to call, where to go, and what to bring, take some time now—when you're not in a mad rush to get to the hospital—to plan ahead.

The first person you call in a medical emergency should, of course, be your child's pediatrician. He or she will tell you whether to come to the doctor's office or head straight for the hospital. At night or on weekends, however, your doctor may not immediately be available. The doctor's answering service will certainly contact your pediatrician as quickly as possible, but in an emergency, you may not want to wait for a return call.

If you need to get your child to a hospital immediately, how will you know which hospital you should go to? Your doctor may have no admitting privileges at the hospital nearest to you. So find out in advance at which hospital(s) your child's pediatrician admits patients. That way, you'll know exactly where to go even when your pediatrician cannot be reached right away.

Are Your Papers in Order?

What should you bring with you if you have to rush out to the nearest emergency room? First, you'll need your child's medical history and proof of medical insurance. This will not only speed admission into the hospital, but may remind your doctor (or inform a hospital's resident physician) of certain medical conditions or events that might have a bearing on your child's diagnosis and treatment. To avoid having to gather all your papers together in a frenzy, get in the habit of keeping all of your family's medical records in the same, easily accessible place. These should include

➤ Your child's (or your) insurance ID card

➤ Your child's medical history, including records of any ongoing medical problems, any previous hospitalizations, and her immunization schedule

➤ A list of your child's allergies—especially allergies to pencillin or other medications

➤ A list (or the bottles) of any medications your child is currently taking

The wait in an emergency room—even for a child—can be a long one. Depending on the extent of your child's injuries or the nature of his illness, she may get bored unless she has something to distract her, at least for a little while. So if you have time before you leave for the hospital, throw together a few toys, books, or games and bring them with you.

Finally, if you suspect your child has swallowed something poisonous, but don't know what specifically what she ingested, throw anything she might have taken—the entire contents of your medicine cabinet, for example, or the household cleaners from under the sink—into a bag and bring it all with you.

Daddy Dos and Don'ts

You might not be home with your child when he has a medical emergency. In such a case, you'll want your baby sitter to contact you as soon as possible. To make sure any sitter knows how to contact you immediately, prepare an emergency information card and place copies of it next to every phone in your home. (You will find a blank emergency information card at the beginning of this book. Fill it out, make copies, and post them throughout your home.)

In addition, to make sure you can be contacted in case of emergency, you may even want to get a cell phone or a personal pager, if you don't already own one.

The ABCs of CPR

The one medical emergency that makes every father's heart stop is the possibility that his child could stop breathing. A broken arm, a bloody wound, a raging fever—all of these can be treated medically and healed in the course of time. If your child stops breathing though, you have only minutes to get him breathing again.

You can—and definitely should—prepare for such a possibility, however. If you have not yet taken a course in cardiopulmonary resuscitation (CPR) for children, sign up to take one as soon as you read this. Check with your local chapter of the American Red Cross, the American Heart Association, or your local hospital. (See Appendix B for the addresses, phone numbers, and web sites of these organizations.) If they don't offer a course themselves, they can certainly direct you to a parenting organization or adult education program that will.

A CPR course will teach you everything you'll need to know if your child stops breathing. You'll learn to

➤ **Check your child's ABCs.** This means checking the Airway to make sure it's not blocked, determining whether your child is Breathing, and checking his Circulation (pulse).

➤ **Perform artificial respiration.** If your child has stopped breathing, you should lay him down, tilt his head back slightly to open the airway, and, placing your mouth over his mouth and nose, gently exhale five times into his mouth and nose. Your child's chest should rise with each breath.

➤ **Perform CPR.** If your child has no pulse, you should center your index finger between his nipples, and then place your middle and ring fingers next to it so they form a line down the center of his chest. When you lift your index finger, your two other fingers will remain on your child's breastbone. Then between each breath of artificial respiration, you should press down on the breastbone sharply about one inch deep, five times in three seconds. After every five breaths, you should recheck the pulse.

Daddy Dos and Don'ts

Do not make the mistake of considering the brief overview of CPR techniques offered in this book a detailed description of what you would need to do in a respiratory emergency. For details and hands-on experience, you *must* take an approved CPR course.

In a CPR course, instructors will not only show you exactly what to do if your child stops breathing, but they will also provide you with hands-on experience and the chance to practice on a child-size dummy. By the end of the course, you will be able to demonstrate CPR techniques yourself. In fact, that's the only way you'll pass the course and get your CPR certification.

If you never need to use it, count your blessings. But if you do need it, your knowledge of CPR could someday save your child's life.

The Least You Need to Know

➤ Any radical change in an infant's behavior may—or may not—indicate illness. Check with your pediatrician to make sure.

➤ Although certain symptoms always demand a pediatrician's intervention, you should feel free to call the doctor whenever you have concerns about your child's health or development.

➤ Until your child is six, always consult your pediatrician to find out the correct dosage of over-the-counter drugs.

➤ Keep all medicines in a locked cabinet, or out of your child's reach—or both.

➤ Sign up now for a course in CPR for infants and children—and hope you'll never have to use what you've learned.

Chapter 11

1:00 PLAY
1:30 LUNCH
2:00 NAP
4:00 PLAY

Making Time for Baby

In This Chapter

➤ The many ambivalent feelings you might have toward your newborn baby

➤ The importance of time well spent: building a bond with your baby

➤ Picking out appropriate toys for your baby's first year

➤ Playing with your baby according to his rules

➤ How to read to your baby

Love at first sight? Can such a thing possibly exist? Sure it can. When you first saw your baby emerge from the birth canal or the incision in your partner's belly, you might immediately have felt filled with love for this small, bawling creature, the offspring of your love for each other.

All of us would like to respond this way to the first glimpse of our children. Our initial reactions, however, may or may not match up to the idealized preconceptions we might have. Many new fathers react to their newborn babies with a tremendous amount of ambivalence, and a mixture of sometimes surprising feelings that may include:

➤ Wonder

➤ Bewilderment

➤ Pride

➤ Disillusionment

➤ Affection

➤ Detachment

➤ Numbness

➤ Alienation

➤ Protectiveness

➤ Warmth

➤ Discomfort

➤ Joy

➤ Distaste, or even disgust

➤ The weight of duty or responsibility

➤ Fear

Father Knows Best

"As for children, I keep as far from them as possible. I don't like the sight of them. The scale is all wrong. The heads tend to be too big for the bodies, and the hands and feet are a disaster."

—Gore Vidal

But don't worry if you felt (or still feel) any of the "negative" feelings, or a combination of "positive" and "negative" emotions, when you first saw or held your baby. All are common paternal reactions.

After all, your initial reactions to your baby reflect not only your own personality, but many other influences as well, including

➤ How you felt about having children in the first place.

➤ The intensity or duration of your partner's labor.

➤ How your relationship with your partner is going in general.

➤ Outside concerns (finances, job satisfaction, your relationship with your own parents, and many more) that may seem totally unrelated to your baby or family.

You have no control over most of these "outside" influences. So don't let your initial reactions to your baby spook you. You may or may not feel boundless love for your baby at first sight, but you aren't necessarily doomed as a father if you don't.

Take Your Time, 007

If you feel an instant bond (James Bond) to your child, an immediate understanding and rapport, congratulations! You're one of the lucky ones—or one of that rare breed with a boundlessly open heart and an infinite capacity for love. For the rest of us, however, establishing a secure bond with our children may take a little more time, and even a little effort.

The Stranger Among Us

When your child was first born, for instance, you might have looked upon her as a complete stranger—or even an alien. And why not? Your newborn *is* a complete stranger to you—one who depends totally on you and your partner to take care of her, but a stranger nonetheless. And as for being an alien, well, the evidence is clear:

➤ The blue-gray skin color at birth (Martian!)

➤ The unnaturally large and misshapen head (Conehead!)

➤ The white goo called *vernix* that may have covered her body (Body Snatcher!)

➤ The rashes of white or red bumps, or the red or bluish-gray birthmarks on her skin (Cardassian!)

➤ The shriveling, blackish-purple, knotted cord where the belly button should, and eventually will, be (Klingon!)

Paterniterms

Vernix is a white, waxy or greasy substance that protects the skin of a fetus inside the womb. The skin will absorb much of it in the first weeks after birth, but you may find accumulations of *vernix*—which eventually turns to a powder—in folds of the skin, around the genitals, and under the fingernails.

Father Knows Best

"To be a successful father ... there's one absolute rule: When you have a kid, don't look at it for the first two years."

—Ernest Hemingway

If you're wondering what planet your baby came from, relax. Most of these signs of "extraterrestrial" origins will fade or entirely disappear within a few months of birth. So give your baby some time. She'll look human before very long.

What's the Rush?

New fathers who don't feel an instant connection and affection for their babies often feel disappointed in themselves—judging themselves as somehow lacking in either the basic instincts of fatherhood or in their capacity to love. Don't be so hard on yourself.

Parent-child love, or what has come to be called parental *bonding*, usually takes time to build—just like any other kind of love or bond. A few comparisons may help you view your brand-new relationship with your baby a little more objectively. If you adopted a child, would you expect an instant bond to exist between you and your new child? If your partner already had a child by a previous relationship when you first met her, would you expect to love her child—and have the child love you—instantly? Of course not. You'd allow the relationship time to grow and deepen.

But because this child is your flesh and blood, the fruit of your loins, you might feel differently—or believe you should feel differently—about your newborn baby. Well, if you feel an immediate bond with your newborn, that's great. Build on that base and expand on those feelings. But if you don't feel that instant intimate connection, don't give up on the relationship. You can create bonds and nurture love through repeated contact, getting to know and feel comfortable with your baby, and many loving and caring interactions.

Bonding for Beginners

Bonding with your child can begin with the first time you hold him in your arms, soothe his tears, sing to him, change his diaper, and the first time he smiles at you. Every moment you spend doing something for your baby or interacting with him will help strengthen the bond between you.

The bond between father and child (like that between mother and child) develops in a circular way: At first, you hold, rock, change, comfort, and feed your baby because you love him and feel responsible for him; yet the more you hold, rock, change, comfort, and feed him—and later, read to and play with him—the more the love between you grows. In short, the more time you devote to caring for your baby, the more (and sooner) you will get to know and love each other.

Sharing time with your baby can begin as soon as he is born. In fact, in all likelihood, your caring will seldom be more needed or appreciated than in these first days and weeks. So during your partner's hospitalization and the first weeks of her at-home recovery, take advantage of all the opportunities available to hold and care for the baby. Until your partner feels better after the physically, not to mention emotionally, traumatic experience of childbirth, she'll probably welcome equal parenting. Indeed, she's probably depending upon you to assume an equal parenting role during this time. And although you might need to give up this kind of "co-parenting" when you return to work after your paternity leave (assuming you were able to take one), the time you've already devoted to your newborn will have established a solid foundation for many years to come.

Newborns use their sense of touch more than any other to awaken to the world, so creating and maintaining a loving relationship with your newborn depends on warm, gentle physical contact. That's why holding your baby—to feed him, rock him, bathe him, and so on—is so important (see Chapter 8). The more you hold your baby, the more solid and secure your relationship will become.

Father Knows Best

"What is there about babies which makes us hug and kiss and fondle them, so that even an enemy would give them help at that age?"

—Desiderius Erasmus

If your partner breast-feeds your baby, she will bond with the baby not just then, but also in the countless other times she picks up or holds him. And though you cannot breast-feed, you can begin forming a solid bond between yourself and your child in every other way: by holding him, rocking him before putting him in the crib, giving him a sponge bath, and yes, even changing his diaper.

So even after your partner has recovered from childbirth, continue to do as much baby care as you possibly can. Not only will your partner appreciate it, but your baby will (literally) love you for it, too.

That's Entertainment!

Another terrific way to further your loving relationship with your baby—especially after the first couple of months—is to play with her. Now, you may think you have no time for such stuff and nonsense. After all, a man of your position may gladly take on the responsibilities and duties of parenting, but really has no business engaging in child's play.

If you think this way, you need to rethink the way you see child's play. For an infant—and later a toddler, preschooler, and even an elementary-school child—play is not just fun and games. Young children *learn* through play:

➤ They discover new abilities they didn't even know they had.

➤ They practice and learn to master physical and mental skills.

➤ They explore the world.

➤ They discover new things about the world.

➤ They even learn basic academics: counting, color recognition, and the alphabet.

So child's play actually is one of your parental responsibilities, because through play your child will learn about herself and the world. Besides, it's a heck of a lot of fun!

A Feast for the Eyes (and Ears)

For the first few months, your baby won't need a whole lot of toys and games. In fact, until your baby discovers his own hands (at around two to three months), he won't have the slightest idea what to do with a toy. So entertaining your baby in these first few months consists primarily of providing visual and auditory stimulation.

Decorate the area around your baby's crib or bassinet and around his changing table with two or three bold, black-and-white patterns (checkerboards, bulls-eyes, and the like). Hang a mobile over the crib and/or changing table. Place a child-safe baby mirror inside his crib or on the wall next to his changing table. When he is about two months old, change the decorations or add to them with bold primary colors: reds, yellows, and blues. All of these will provide visual stimulation for your baby (and make diaper changing go easier).

Daddy Dos and Don'ts

When you talk to your baby, don't worry about making sure that what you say is "simple" or age-appropriate. Any speech is appropriate for an infant. After all, your baby doesn't yet understand any of the *words* you say. What your infant gains through listening to your speech is not vocabulary or comprehension, but simply learning the patterns and rhythms of human speech (in your own language, of course).

To stimulate your baby's ears, at about six to eight weeks you can begin shaking a rattle for him. In the third month, you can place a rattle in his hand. Grasping it and listening to the sound it makes may help him discover his hands—and find out that he controls them. By producing a sound when he shakes or moves it, a rattle can provide your baby's second instructive demonstration of cause-and-effect—and of his own power. (The first, of course, is that when he cries, someone comes to help him.)

An activity board in the crib also combines visual and auditory stimuli. At about three or four months, your baby will start swiping at the rollers and dials himself. But even before then, he will delight in the bells, rattles, and ratcheting noises made when you push the buttons and spin the dials.

In these first few months, however, you will be your baby's favorite toy. More than any store-bought gadget, what your baby wants and needs are your time, love, and attention.

You can provide visual stimulation by making funny faces at your baby, by bringing your face in toward his for a "close-up" and then pulling back, and repeating this zooming in and fading out. Your child will enjoy it even more if you make some silly sounds while you zoom in and fade out.

You can stimulate your baby's hearing though singing songs, reciting nursery rhymes, cooing and babbling to him, even just talking to him.

As soon as your baby gains sustained control of his neck muscles, you can start getting into the physical play that dads stereotypically enjoy. Don't get too rough until your baby gets a little older, but you can start bouncing him lightly up and down on your knee or pulling him gently up to a sitting position. Or you can start playing airplane—either by letting your baby rest on your bent knees while you're on your back or by holding him by the waist and "flying" him across the room.

Toy Story

In all likelihood, even before your baby was born—and almost certainly shortly afterward—you began receiving or buying toys for her. But how do you know how to choose the best toys from the thousands on the market?

If you're wondering whether to buy that cute teddy bear that squeaks when you squeeze its tummy, the see-through plastic rattle with the tiny balls inside, or the curious configuration of concentric rings with a ball in the center, evaluate toys for your baby according to the following criteria:

➤ **Age appropriateness.** Select toys that match the skills your baby is currently developing or mastering—or skills you know she will soon develop. Age-appropriate toys either stimulate further development of the senses or make use of developing abilities. With the right playmates (that's you and your partner), age-appropriate toys can enhance and even accelerate her learning and her newfound abilities. If you give your baby a toy that's beyond her abilities, it will probably frustrate or bore her. On the other hand, if you give her a toy too late, it will almost definitely bore her. So pay attention to what she's doing and choose a toy that will fit her skills.

➤ **Safety.** Any toy you buy for your infant must be extremely durable to stand up to a year or more of banging, dropping, throwing, biting, and sucking. Also, the easier it is to clean, the easier it will be for you to minimize the long-term build-up of germs. For safety's sake, avoid any toy during the first few years that has sharp edges, glass parts, or toxic paint. Also avoid any toy heavy enough to hurt your child when she drops it on her foot (because you know she will) or small enough to swallow. (A safe toy for infants and toddlers will have no parts smaller than 2" in diameter.) Finally, you should make sure that any strings or ribbons are less than 6" long, because a longer ribbon could strangle your baby if she accidentally wraps it around her neck.

➤ **Simplicity.** Infants and toddlers like simple toys best because they are the most versatile and durable. The fewer parts and pieces, the longer it will last—and the more uses to which it can be put. In addition, simple toys are easier to clean.

➤ **Diversity.** Try to avoid acquiring too many toys that are similar to one another. Instead, strive for diversity in color, texture, shape, sound, and function.

Using these criteria, you'll find a wide variety of toys that your child will love. During the third and fourth months, your baby will especially love any toys that she can hold, bang, mouth, and suck. This is the way she explores the objects in her world. So look for toys that will excite your baby's senses of sight, touch, sound, taste, and even smell. Texture books, like the classic *Pat the Bunny*, as well as items that offer different textures or make different noises, are terrific toys for this age. So are crib activity boards, beanbags (as long as you make sure they stay in good condition, because if the beans get out, your baby will surely swallow them), and a variety of rattles (soft plastic, hard plastic, cloth-covered, squeakers, shakers, and so on).

Another fun toy during the third and fourth months (and beyond) is a set of soft blocks. Your baby can grasp or squeeze them, and of course use them to build and knock down towers. (At first, you'll have to do all the construction and she'll take care of the demolition.)

What your infant enjoys playing with doesn't even have to be what you would think of as a toy. Your baby considers almost everything a toy: oranges, plastic spoons or spatulas, colanders, and many other household objects. You can even make your own rattles by filling—and securely sealing—kitchen containers like coffee cans and plastic food containers with rice, beads, marbles, or small bells.

A crib gym will also come in handy at around four months. While lying on her back, your baby will love kicking, batting at, and grasping the rings and bars that hang down from a bar stretched over the top of her crib. You should take care, however, to remove the crib gym after she learns to sit up on her own (because she could use it to boost herself up and out of the crib).

At this point, your baby will also begin really enjoying your local playground (or a swing set in your yard). Small slides may be fun (although some children don't begin enjoying them until late in the first year—or even later.) Even more of a sure thing: swings and sandboxes. So take your baby on frequent trips to the playground; it's the perfect father-child outing.

Daddy Dos and Don'ts

Baby bouncers and baby walkers should be used only under strict adult supervision. The hooks or clamps that support baby bouncers can pop loose, dropping your baby to the ground. Baby walkers—because they allow mobility—can be very dangerous, especially around stairs. (In fact, the American Academy of Pediatrics advises parents not to use walkers at all.) Don't rely solely on a safety gate, which can give way under the impact of a baby in a walker, to protect your child. Instead, block off all access to stairs behind locked doors, chairs, or tables.

Some infants also have a lot of fun bouncing up and down in baby bouncers—canvas seats suspended by elastic cords secured to a door frame. A baby walker—a canvas or plastic seat set inside a table-like frame with a wheel at the base of each leg—can also expand your infant's horizons. Both bouncers and walkers provide a new upright perspective on the world, while walkers also offer a certain degree of mobility.

If you do get a baby bouncer or a baby walker, use it sparingly. If your baby enjoys them, that's great. But neither exercises or develops the skills your baby will need to crawl or walk. She'll develop these skills—rolling over, getting up on her hands (or at first, elbows) and knees, sitting up and balancing on her own, and finally crawling, pulling herself up to standing, and toddling—by frequently being placed on the floor. A favorite toy placed just out of her reach can sometimes motivate your baby to attempt and master these new tricks—but only when she's ready to do them.

Finally, when your baby can sit up for longer than a minute, she will start to enjoy playing with a ball. (Even earlier, she'll like holding, squeezing, and "eating" balls of different textures and resiliency.) At first, try just rolling a ball to her so that her outstretched legs stop it. Before long, she'll start to anticipate and reach out to "catch" the ball. After that, you can encourage your baby to roll it back—and then let the games begin.

Father Figures

Incredibly, nearly 25,000 infants a year receive medical treatment for injuries sustained in walkers.

Power Trip

You won't have to throw away any of your child's "baby" toys during the second half of his first year. In fact, most of the games and toys you've introduced in the second three months will continue to entertain your baby for months—and even years—to come.

During the second six months, toys that reward your baby's efforts to play with them will have a special appeal for him. Rattles, squeak toys, and crib-side activity boards—all of which make noise in response to his actions—will lose none of their appeal as your baby masters the art of playing with them. In addition, you can now introduce jack-in-the-boxes (you'll have to turn the handle yourself for a while) and simpler pop-up toys like busy boxes, in which animals or cartoon characters reveal themselves in response to a pushed button, pulled lever, dialed telephone, and the like.

Any toys that illustrate cause and effect—where your baby's actions serve as the cause and the toy demonstrates some effect (often involving sound)—will give your baby a growing sense of his own power. Through playing with these toys, your baby will learn that by acting in a certain way, he can produce a result that he likes. He finds out that he has some control over the world around him.

Accidental discovery shows your baby that what he does produces an effect. If he flicks a switch, Big Bird pops out of the busy box. If he tips a cup of water (hopefully while in the tub), the liquid pours out. After the first few accidental discoveries, your baby will begin flicking and pouring with intent, as a purposeful demonstration of his own power.

Simple musical instruments—especially rhythm instruments such as drums, tambourines, or even a pot and a wooden spoon—also reinforce the concept of cause-and-effect and add to your baby's sense of power. As a bonus (for your baby, not for you), these toys make a hell of a lot of noise.

Anything that pours or allows filling and emptying (cups, plastic bottles, or other containers) will also delight your child during the second half of his first year. A set of seven or eight nesting cups (cups of varying size that fit inside one another) is particularly versatile. Right now, your baby can probably fill them and spill them. Later, he can try fitting the cups inside one another. Eventually, he'll even build—and of course knock down—a tower with them.

As he begins to crawl and later walk, your baby will also begin enjoying games and toys that challenge or encourage his developing mobility. A riding toy that moves when your baby coordinates the movement of his feet and legs will be fun. So will pull toys (especially those that make noise), which both crawlers and toddlers enjoy pulling along with them on their journeys. Your crawler or toddler will also love pushing or kicking a ball in front of her and then chasing it down.

Near the end of the first year, a small plastic slide on a carpeted floor offers a safe and fun way to master climbing a small flight of stairs. You can even use it—along with a play tunnel, chairs to crawl under, and pillows to climb over—to create a homemade obstacle course that your baby will love to master.

Finally, you can encourage and reward your crawler's—and later your toddler's—increasing mobility by playing a game of "Catch me if you can." As long as you're not too threatening as the chaser (after all, you don't want to scare him out of his wits), your baby will love this game. And he'll love it even more if you let him catch you or, on the other side, elude you—triumphs that will add to his growing sense of power and mastery.

Play Nice

If you've never played with a baby before the birth of your own, you might (understandably) not feel up to the task of entertaining, amusing, and thereby educating, your infant. You might not know exactly where to begin.

How can you play with your baby in a way that both of you enjoy? It's easy. Just observe the following guidelines, developed through long hours of painstaking research:

➤ **Don't overwhelm your baby with toys.** Your baby can focus on only one toy at a time, so don't bother spreading out a bunch of toys around her and expecting her to "choose" the one she wants to play with. Whichever one you hold up before your baby's eyes or place closest to her is probably the one she'll "decide" to explore.

Father Knows Best

"What a dreadful thing it must be to have a dull father."

—Mary Mapes Dodge

Again, with a young infant, you don't even need toys to entertain and educate her. You can give your baby a fun workout while she's lying or sitting in your lap. Try bouncing her on your knee, or pulling her up to a sitting or standing position. Or try holding her by the waist—*not* the hands or arms, which could result in a dislocated shoulder—and helping her do knee bends and "jumping."

➤ **Don't be afraid to repeat yourself.** Repetitive games that you play with your infant will help her learn to anticipate what will happen next. The more your baby anticipates, the more she will delight in the result. At around three or four months, once she recognizes her fingers and toes as her own, your baby will love finger and toe play ("This Little Piggy" and the like). Encore performances of short kids' songs and nursery rhymes also combine anticipation and reward, especially when complemented with activities that your baby—with a little help from you—can do: clapping songs or rhymes ("Pat-a-Cake"), counting songs ("This Old Man"), finger-manipulation songs ("Itsy Bitsy Spider"), and so on.

Beginning at around four to five months, your baby will delight in another repetitive activity: playing peekaboo. Like all other play with infants and toddlers, peekaboo is not just fun and games—although it certainly is that, too. When you hide your face or a toy and then quickly reveal it, your baby will begin to master the concept of *object constancy*. (If you hide the object for more than

Daddy Dos and Don'ts

The limited attention span of infants renders them easily distractible. Understanding, appreciating, and using this fact to your advantage will make your life as a parent much easier in the first year or two. When you need to change your baby's diaper, distracting her with a mobile or a song will make her fuss much less. When your baby gets hurt, if you can entice her to focus her attention on something else (a squeak toy or you making a funny face), she will calm down more quickly.

a couple seconds, however, your baby will probably forget all about it.) Your baby will no doubt love peekaboo so much that by six or seven months, she may be hiding her own face and encouraging you to find *her*.

➤ **Be patient and "helpfully unhelpful."** Toys and games allow your child to master new skills *if you let her do so*. For instance, if your baby is just learning how to reach out and grasp objects, don't become so impatient watching her that you grab the object and give it to her. This cuts short—and in fact bypasses—the complex process your baby needs and wants to master. Grasping requires a difficult combination of awareness of her hands, gauging and re-gauging of distance, and hand-eye coordination. All of this is new to her.

Paterniterms

Object constancy is the comprehension that just because something disappears from sight, it doesn't necessarily cease to exist. As a rule, babies cannot appreciate object constancy until at least their fourth or fifth month.

So restrain yourself from automatically "helping" your baby by doing for her what she's trying so hard to do for herself. Naturally, if she becomes fretful or frustrated, that's the time to intervene—but don't confuse your frustration with hers.

➤ **Be your baby's biggest fan and cheerleader.** When your baby demonstrates a new skill—and not just the first time, but whenever she repeats it, too (at least for the first 100 to 1,000 times or so)—lavish her with praise. Rah-rah sis-boom-bah, yeah, baby! Don't be shy or hold back. After all, as the description of the mechanics of grasping illustrates, what may seem easy to you is actually quite an accomplishment for your baby.

Father Knows Best

"Infancy conforms to nobody: all conform to it, so that one babe commonly makes four or five out of the adults who prattle and play to it."

—Ralph Waldo Emerson

➤ **Pay attention to your baby's mood and responses.** Looking intently at and/or reaching for a toy means that your baby likes it. Turning away, fussing, or crying means she doesn't—at least, not right now. Seems rather obvious, doesn't it? Yet parents eager to entertain and educate their children sometimes ignore these signals.

Also, just because your baby liked a certain game or toy yesterday doesn't mean she will today. If you watch your baby's responses, she'll let you know—long before she can talk—whether she wants to play with a particular toy right now. (Similarly, just because your baby didn't like something yesterday doesn't mean she won't today. So when your baby's first response to a particular toy or game is negative, you can always try again in a few days or weeks.)

➤ **Be flexible.** Adapt as much as you can to your baby's moods and desires of the moment. Babies live very much in the moment: They have no past, no future, only now. So to play successfully with a baby, you need to be in the moment, too.

Try to avoid rigidity in the way you play with certain toys. You might know the rules of a particular game or the "right" way to play with a particular toy. But that's only from an adult, rule-oriented perspective. Babies, however, are anarchists, and they have no understanding or respect for "the rules" (at least, as defined by you). Fortunately, your baby is probably ingenious enough to come up with many new ways to play with a toy or to play a game. So back off a little and let your baby play the way she likes.

➤ **Don't be relentless.** Your baby will most likely lose interest in even the most fascinating toys and games within a few minutes. She is a baby, after all—and therefore has a very short attention span. So when you see her interest flagging, don't start shaking the toy or waving it in her face to regain her attention. Move on to something else or—gasp!—give it a rest. Your baby doesn't need you or your partner to entertain her all day. She needs "down time" just as much as you do—unfortunately though, not always *when* you do.

By the Book

Most babies will have at least some interest in books by six months, if not sooner. Books, of course, are terrific learning tools. They can stimulate language development by establishing connections between words and objects. Books can also open a window on the entire world outside, introducing your baby to objects, creatures, and activities that he probably doesn't see every day.

When introducing books to your baby, start with sturdy picture books with simple illustrations in bold colors. Don't worry whether the book has a story yet, because your baby doesn't need a story—just a single object per page and its name. Favorite subjects for infants include babies, animals, vehicles, fruit, and toys.

Ideal early books have no more than a dozen pages, no more than eight or 10 words per page, and can be "read" (or flipped through) in two or three minutes. Your child will probably have little patience for anything longer than that during his first year.

Sturdiness is an important quality of books for infants and toddlers. If you want your baby to develop a love for reading that will last a lifetime, you need to own books that

143

he can handle by himself, books that will stand up to all the abuse he can dish out. Publishers know this, so you will find a large selection of plastic, bath, board, and even fabric books in your local bookstore.

When you and your baby "read" together, try to make it a quiet, special time for the two of you to share. Sit your baby on your lap, facing out so that he can see the pictures you're talking about. Repeating the words two or three times will reinforce the connection between objects and their names.

Don't feel you have to stick to the text as written, word-for-word. Books for infants and toddlers, no matter how simple, can open up a world of possibilities to those parents who take advantage of them. So no matter what the book tells you to say, talk about what you see. If your child reaches out and turns more than one page, don't feel you have to go back to "finish" the story. After all, most early books don't tell a story anyway, so why be a fanatic about reading every page?

Near the end of the first year, when you introduce books that tell a story and feature more complicated illustrations, make games out of reading. Ask your baby, for instance, to point to certain objects in the illustrations. (In the classic *Good Night Moon*, for example, every color spread has a small mouse somewhere in the picture. Can your baby find the mouse? Can you?)

In playing games with books, you may be surprised at how quickly your baby seems to comprehend new words. But if your baby can't yet point out specific objects, make sure that you do it before you turn the page. Saying something like, "There's the mouse!" will help build the association between words and the objects they signify. These associations are the building blocks of language.

The Least You Need to Know

➤ Just because you're not filled with boundless love for your baby at the first sight of her doesn't mean you're doomed as a father. Building a bond with your baby may take some time and effort.

➤ The more time you devote to holding your baby and other simple acts of baby care, the more (and sooner) you will get to know and love each other.

➤ For a young child, play is neither idle nor frivolous. Play is your child's first and best way to learn about himself and the world.

➤ Try to choose toys that are safe, simple, versatile, and age-appropriate. Then follow your child's lead in how to play with them. Just because you know what she's "supposed" to do with a particular toy doesn't mean that what she's actually doing is the "wrong" way to play with it.

➤ You can build your child's love for reading and expand his world simply by reading to him every day. But don't feel you have to read every word on every page. Your baby won't care in the slightest.

Chapter 12

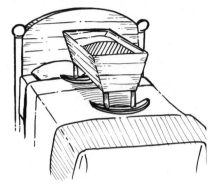

Baby in the Bedroom: Is There Sex After Childbirth?

In This Chapter

➤ Why you may not have had sex since your baby was born

➤ Why either or both of you may still need more time

➤ Fears, feelings, and circumstances that may inhibit your own or your partner's post-partum sexuality

➤ Getting in the mood for making love again

➤ Helping to get your partner in the mood, too

Now comes the big question—the one that invariably worms its way into the scant chapter usually set aside for fathers in most books on pregnancy and early parenthood. After all, everybody knows that we men have little or no interest in anything else. So here goes: Is there sex after childbirth?

The simple, reassuring answer is: Of course there is. But this simple answer gives rise to another, more pressing question: Who wants it?

In all likelihood, during the first few months of your baby's life, you or your partner will be feeling at least three of the following:

➤ Exhausted due to simple lack of sleep

➤ Wiped out by the intensity of childbirth, so that everything that follows (yes, even sex) feels somewhat anticlimactic

➤ Drained by the seemingly incessant demands of your newborn

➤ Preoccupied with your new responsibilities

➤ Never alone, especially if your baby sleeps in your bedroom

➤ Constantly tense or at least unable to relax fully, never knowing when your baby will next cry out

➤ Pressed for time, with too much to do and too few hours in the day

➤ Desperate to carve out just a little time and space for yourself alone, a time when you don't need to attend to anyone's needs but your own

➤ In the grip of post-partum depression (see Chapter 7)

➤ Critical or embarrassed of your own and/or each other's bodies, which may have lost some of their shape and tone during pregnancy

➤ Jealous of the time, love, and care the other devotes to the baby

Feeling turned on yet? Feeling sexy? Well, it shouldn't be surprising if you or your partner are not. All of these feelings and conditions diminish both sexual energy and sexual desire.

What's more, your partner has gender-specific conditions that may also have an impact on her libido. First of all, her body needs to heal from the trauma of childbirth (whether vaginal or surgical), recovery that usually precludes sexual intercourse, at least for a while. In addition, your partner's shifting hormone levels—which won't stabilize at "normal" (i.e., pre-pregnancy) levels until after she has her first post-partum menstrual period—may also diminish both her desire for and her comfort with sexual intercourse. Finally, if she nurses your baby, this too can have an impact on sexual energy, comfort, and desire.

Ready or Not, Here I Come?

So if either you or your partner or both of you aren't feeling up to making love again in the weeks—or even months—following childbirth, it's no wonder. Human sexuality needs time, energy, and attention in order to flourish. And with a new baby in the house, neither of you has much time, energy, or attention to spare.

Although you and your partner may have set a new personal record for abstinence during the end stages of pregnancy and these early stages of parenting, try not to worry too much about it. When both of you are ready for it, sex will still be there. It's like riding a bicycle: Just because you haven't done it for a while doesn't mean that you've forgotten how.

Cleared for Takeoff

Having sex after childbirth is like returning to the football field after tearing some ligaments: You'll need to get medical clearance first, and then you'll have to take it easy at first. (You may even need to work your way back into game condition.)

So before you and your partner have post-partum sexual intercourse, make sure you've consulted her doctor. The particulars of your partner's labor and delivery make a big difference in when you can resume having sex (that's why you need to ask her obstetrician/gynecologist). In general, however, the doctor will probably advise you to wait anywhere from four to six weeks (or more) before having intercourse again.

If your partner had a vaginal delivery, the period of abstinence depends entirely on the nature of her labor and delivery. An episiotomy (see Chapter 7) or tearing of the perineum requires weeks to heal. So if your partner had either, most obstetricians would advise a four- to six-week healing period. Even without surgery or injury to the perineum, however, your partner's perineal area is likely to be sore for several weeks after labor and delivery. In addition, the cervix needs to heal, and the flow of *lochia* should stop before you resume intercourse. So wait at least until your partner's first post-partum visit to the doctor—and ask for the go-ahead then.

If your partner had a C-section, you will definitely need to abstain from any sexual activities involving penetration for at least four to six weeks after surgery—and maybe longer. But take heart. You may have a slightly longer waiting period than you would if your baby had been delivered vaginally. But when you do start making love again, your partner will probably find intercourse much more comfortable than she would after a vaginal delivery.

Remember: Although you should ask your partner's obstetrician when you can resume sexual intercourse, sexual relations don't necessarily have to involve intercourse. So if you and your partner both have the urge before getting her doctor's okay, feel free to explore other avenues to sexual fulfillment.

Paterniterms

Lochia is the medical term for a post-partum discharge of excess blood, tissue, and mucus from the uterus. The flow of lochia, heaviest during the first few days post-partum, will gradually lighten in color, volume, and frequency—but may last for up to six weeks after childbirth.

Okay, Okay, Don't Rush Me!

Just because your doctor says it's okay doesn't mean that you two immediately have to jump back in the sack together. Take your time. Despite medical clearance, either or both of you may feel:

➤ You're not yet ready.

➤ Your partner is not fully healed (despite her doctor's reassurances).

➤ You don't have the energy.

➤ You're just not in the mood.

It may take six weeks (or less)—and it may take six months (or more)—before sexual desire returns for both of you. (If it takes six *years*, then you should worry.)

A problem may crop up if you and your partner find yourselves on dramatically different sexual wavelengths. One possibility: You may feel eager to test the waters of your sexual relationship again much sooner than your partner. If so, by all means, let your partner know you're interested. Make a pass, lay out your best seduction scenarios, and pull out your most effective pick-up lines.

At the same time, however, if your partner indicates she's clearly not yet ready, willing, or able to start having sex again, try to avoid putting a lot of pressure on her. (Even if she does want to make love, try to avoid putting a lot of pressure on her; after all, she's probably sore and tender all over.) Talk to her, find out what she's feeling—remember, it's a conversation, not an interrogation—and show as much patience and understanding as you can.

On the other hand, if you're the one with cold feet (okay, so maybe it's not exactly your feet that are cold), let your partner know if you feel she's putting too much pressure on you. At the same time, let her know what's behind your hesitation: whether fears, exhaustion, apprehension, simple lack of libido, or whatever. In making a pass at you, your partner has left herself vulnerable. Don't leave her wondering why you said no. Keep in mind that with all that pregnancy did to her body, she may not feel especially attractive or sexy even though she wants to make love to you. So unless you agree with her assessment, reassure her that you still think she looks terrific—but that you're not yet ready for this, that, and the other reason.

In trying to get your sex life going again, avoid the dangerous game of keeping score or keeping count. Try not to worry too much about how soon, how much, and how good. Time and sleep will allow you both to get back on your feet—or rather, off your feet—again.

Daddy Dos and Don'ts

If you and your partner can't get on the same sexual wavelength—or can't accept the fact that you're on different wavelengths—and it starts to become a source of significant tension in your relationship, don't be afraid to seek short-term marital counseling or sex therapy. A good therapist can quickly help bring you to a better understanding of each other, if not necessarily complete agreement, by helping you express whatever may be contributing to your disparate libido levels. A therapist can also offer suggestions on how to jump-start your stalled sex life.

So What Are You Afraid Of?

Childbirth—and the tiny yet immense presence that follows—can create a network of fears and concerns that orbit around the act of sexual intercourse like so many satellites. These fears and concerns almost always have a dampening effect on new parents' sexual passion—especially when added to the difficulties created by exhaustion, preoccupation with the baby, and the sheer logistics of arranging a time and place for making love.

Although the fears and concerns that may be keeping you and your partner from getting back into bed together may rise to irrational levels, none of them are irrational.

In fact, the most common concerns that new parents have about sexual intercourse—concern about the possibility of causing (or feeling) pain, worries about getting pregnant again, fears that somehow sex will be different now, and the ever-present prospect of coitus interruptus—do have a basis in reality.

But don't let your fears of post-partum sex slow you down too much. Fortunately, you can take steps to get around most of them.

You're Such a Pain

One of the reasons that you—like so many other new parents—may not rush into post-partum sexual intercourse is the fear that you will cause your partner pain or do some sort of internal damage. (Your partner may fear essentially the same thing: that post-partum sex will hurt or injure her.)

Unfortunately, your fears are not entirely groundless. If your doctor has not yet given you the thumbs up (again, the wrong part of the anatomy), intercourse could do some damage. Penetration could cause an internal infection, tear stitches, or even cause hemorrhaging. Time heals all wounds, however. And once your partner has healed and you've gotten a medical okay, you can make love without fear of creating this kind of damage.

Pain, however, presents more of a problem. Post-partum intercourse can be painful—although it isn't always and when it is, it doesn't last forever. Especially if your wife had an episiotomy or tore her perineum during childbirth, the perineal area may remain sore or uncomfortable for weeks (and occasionally months). Even if your partner had a Cesarean, she may still feel tender and painfully sensitive around the perineum.

To complicate matters further, your partner's vagina may also be very dry (and her sexual desire diminished) due to the post-partum decrease in her hormone levels. This dryness—which doesn't necessarily indicate a lack of sexual excitement—can leave your partner's vagina much more sensitive to friction, making intercourse somewhat painful. For some mothers, this dryness continues for as long as they nurse their babies.

You and your partner can take heart in the realization that this post-partum pain and dryness, if any, won't be a part of your sex life forever. And in the meantime, as long as you're aware of the potential for causing pain, you can take steps to relieve it.

Using K-Y Jelly or some other lubricating cream until your partner's vaginal secretions resume, for example, can alleviate much of the discomfort caused by dryness. To avoid hurting your partner's perineal area, you can be gentler and try different sexual positions that put less pressure on the perineum. For instance, your partner will have more control of the force and degree of penetration—and thus the pain it may cause—if you aren't on top of her. So keep trying new positions—and have fun doing it—until you find one or more that works for both of you.

Deja Vu?

Another concern that inhibits the sexuality of many new parents is the fear of getting pregnant again too soon. Anyone who finds the burdens of new parenting overwhelming, exhausting, or merely demanding would naturally think twice before doing anything that might risk doubling those burdens. In fact, even if you and your partner are flourishing in your new roles as daddy and mommy, the prospect of adding another child before the first one can walk and talk, much less go the bathroom by herself, may leave you both feeling less than aroused.

Father Knows Best

"The most effective form of birth control I know is spending the day with my kids."

—Jill Bensley

This fear, like the one of doing damage to your partner, does have some basis in reality. Unfortunately, there's no accurate way to predict when your partner will begin to ovulate again after childbirth—and therefore she might get pregnant again when and if you have sex.

We do know that mothers who nurse their babies tend to resume ovulation and menstruation much later than non-nursing mothers, so the longer your partner nurses, the longer menstruation might be suppressed. But if I were you, I wouldn't rely on breastfeeding as a contraceptive unless you're both prepared for the possibility of having another infant nine months from now. Too many parents who buy into the myth that a woman can't get pregnant as long as she's nursing find themselves juggling babies before a year is out.

You may feel safe as long as your partner hasn't yet had any post-partum menstruation. Big mistake. If you think back to those 10th-grade health classes, and if you and your buddies weren't snickering too hard to miss the information, you'll remember that menstruation occurs when a woman's body rids itself of an unfertilized egg. This means that ovulation will definitely—and fertilization and pregnancy could potentially—happen *before* your partner begins to menstruate again. In fact, it's possible for her to go from pregnancy to breastfeeding and back to pregnancy again without ever having menstruated at all.

So unless you and your partner want—or at least wouldn't mind—back-to-back pregnancies, you should avoid regarding breastfeeding as your sole contraceptive method.

As long as your religious beliefs allow the use of contraceptives, by all means use them if you want to avoid that second pregnancy, at least for a while.

What kind of contraceptive should you use? You should probably consult your partner's doctor. Many obstetricians advise nursing mothers to avoid birth-control pills, because the pill's hormones can interfere with milk production and may pass through the breast milk. (The effects of these hormones on a nursing infant are not yet known.) Barrier methods (condoms, a diaphragm, or a sponge) are generally effective and will do nothing to harm a nursing baby.

Three's a Crowd

A third fear that inhibits many post-partum couples from resuming their sex lives is the fear of interruption. Like the other fears that may get in the way of new parents' sexuality, this one doesn't exactly come out of left field. It's true: You seldom, if ever, have any time alone anymore. Your little baby has an immense presence; he is always there. If your baby sleeps in the same room with you and your partner, you may fear waking him with your sexual gymnastics and/or acutely feel the lack of privacy. But even if he sleeps in a room of his own, you probably keep a monitor on to keep track of him.

Daddy Dos and Don'ts

If you and your partner opt for a diaphragm, she will need to have her gynecologist refit her for a new one after pregnancy and childbirth. If you instead opt for condoms, your partner might find penetration more comfortable if you choose the lubricated type or use condoms in conjunction with a lubricating cream.

Because it's true that your baby might interrupt you at any moment, you might have to plan ahead when it comes to sex—or settle for a quickie whenever you can get it. The two most practical logistical strategies both require you and your partner to work around your baby's feeding and sleeping patterns:

➤ **Now's the time!** Spontaneously seize the moment. Your baby finally fell asleep, the two of you are home alone together, and no one's at the door or on the phone. Quick, let's get naked and do it right here and right now.

The drawback of this method is that by the time these rare and precious moments actually arrive, you or your partner (or both of you) might be too exhausted to take advantage of them. On the plus side, however, are the excitement of spontaneity and the illicit charge you get from stealing these moments.

➤ **Do you have an opening next Thursday at 9:30?** Plan ahead, making an appointment with your partner. Okay, as soon as the baby falls asleep tomorrow night, forget everything else, we're going to make love.

The down side of this strategy, for some, is that it lacks spontaneity and transforms the act of making love into an obligation, conditions that can strip sex of

151

its passion. Now that you have a baby, though, nearly everything else—from shopping to eating dinner to taking a shower—requires planning. So why shouldn't sex? The up side is that in explicitly making time for sex, you and your partner show each other that you feel your sexual relationship is important enough to schedule into your day.

Despite the best-laid plans or quickness in seizing the moment, you can expect interruptions at least some of the time. It may be hard, sometimes really hard, but try to see the humor of the situation. If your baby decides to pull himself up to a standing position in his crib for the first time while you and your wife are making love, try to recognize that this is pretty funny when you look over and see him staring at both of you. If interrupted in flagrante delicto, stop what you're doing and laugh it off. You can always try to pick up where you left off later.

Everything's Changed

If, like most fathers today, you have witnessed the birth of your child, your whole perspective of your partner may have changed. Whatever your new or renewed feelings may be, they will probably affect your sexual relationship with her. After seeing this miracle, the emergence of your baby from your wife's womb, sex with her—and for her, sex with you—may seem like something totally new, like exploring virgin territory.

Delving into anything that seems new or different often awakens some degree of fear of the unknown. Both you and your partner may wonder

➤ What will sex be like now?

➤ Will it feel different?

➤ Will I (or he) still fit inside her (or me)?

➤ Can this possibly still work?

The only way you'll find out the answers to these questions is to try it and see what happens. Then you'll find out for yourself that sex does indeed still work after childbirth. (If it didn't, everyone would be an only child.) True, sex will probably be somewhat different—in terms of lubrication, emotion, and energy level, if nothing else—but different doesn't have to mean worse.

The experience of witnessing childbirth occasionally gives birth to another obstacle that can get in the way of resuming sexual relations. Some new fathers, after having seen their baby emerge from their partner's vagina, find it unappealing or even disgusting to contemplate intercourse with their partner. A new sense of the functionality of the vagina—or the memory of the blood and baby flowing out of it—may trump sexuality, inhibiting any desire to have sexual intercourse.

If you (or possibly, your partner), feel this way, time and abstinence will probably bring you around to an acceptance of the multifunctional nature of the human genitalia. After all, the fact that you urinate with your penis probably never stopped you from using it sexually before. So why let the fact that the vagina has more than one use stop you now? (If time does not diminish your distaste for sexual intercourse, you should probably seek professional counseling.)

Similarly, some new fathers have a hard time seeing their partner's breasts as sexually pleasurable after seeing their baby feeding from them (although other fathers find it somewhat sexy). You may feel uncomfortable fondling or kissing your wife's breasts, perhaps because it seems to put you in a competition with your baby, who puts those same breasts to such good practical use. (Leaking milk, which sometimes occurs during sexual stimulation, and the tenderness of your partner's breasts to your touch can further complicate such feelings.)

Again, you will need to come to terms with the fact that female breasts have more than one function: as nutrition centers for your baby and as pleasure centers for you and your wife. In the meantime, if stimulating your partner's breasts makes you feel uncomfortable, leave them out of your foreplay. Your baby won't be feeding from your partner's breasts forever; maybe when she stops nursing, you'll feel differently.

In the Mood?

Given all the obstacles to resuming sexual relations with your partner—the exhaustion, the constant demands on both of your time, the new fears and feelings, and the lack of privacy—it may take a little effort for either or both of you to get into the mood. So what can you do to improve the mood for lovemaking? How can you prime yourself and your partner for an affair to remember?

To reestablish a healthy sex life after childbirth, you and your partner may need to smooth the way by trying any or all of the following:

➤ Treating each other with patience and understanding

➤ Rekindling romance

➤ Making use of relaxation techniques

➤ Warming up to intercourse

➤ Talking about sex, even if you're not doing it

➤ Employing ingenuity and creativity

➤ Availing yourself of technology (marital aids)

➤ Seeking out professional help

Of all these, the most important by far are patience and understanding. Neither of you has any need to rush into sex again. If you take your time and share your feelings with each other, the renewal of intimacy will soon bring you back into the bedroom together.

Take Your Time

Certain factors that may be inhibiting your post-partum sex life are, unfortunately, out of your control. You cannot do anything to change the instability of your partner's hormone levels, minimize the impact of nursing on desire (hers and yours), eliminate the need for your partner's body to heal from the trauma of labor and delivery, or relieve the sheer exhaustion that both of you feel. Fortunately, however, these influences—with the possible exception of fatigue—almost always improve with the simple passage of time.

In the meantime, because you have extremely limited control over these factors, all you can bring to the table (or bed) are patience and understanding.

It's a Date!

One way to start rekindling the fires of passion is to find or make some time to devote to each other. Paradoxically, though you may be spending more time together than ever before, you probably spend much less time alone together than ever before. Baby makes three—and three is very often a crowd.

Given your exhaustion and your new focus on the baby, it's far too easy to neglect your relationship with your partner. But to keep it strong and growing, you still need to pour energy—sexual and otherwise—into your relationship. So try to avoid taking your partner for granted. Make your relationship with her a priority, too.

Think of it this way: Nurturing a deep love for each other is a great gift to your baby. After all, what child wouldn't want two loving parents who care deeply for each other?

Father Knows Best

"The most important thing a father can do for his children is to love their mother."

—Theodore M. Hesburgh

Before you can start reviving the romance in your lives, you may have to wait until things settle down a bit—but just a bit, for things may never truly settle down until your kids grow up and (with any luck) move out of the house. After a month or two, start dating again—each other, of course. Get a sitter (or a relative) to take care of the baby at least once or twice a month so that you can have some fun together as a couple.

Exactly what you end up doing on these "dates" matters far less than the fact that you're doing it together—and demonstrating to each other that your relationship means enough to both of you to devote special attention to it.

Once you find yourself alone at last with your partner, try to avoid spending all your time talking about the baby. Certainly you can talk about the baby a little. After all, if one of you has returned to work full-time and the other stays at home with the baby all day, sharing what's going on in your lives apart will have to touch on life with baby. But other things are happening in your lives, too, right?

So talk about what you're doing when you're not together. Talk about what's going on in the world, about a book you're reading, or a TV show you saw. Talk about your feelings and your needs—and how they've changed since you became a father. (This is not talking about the baby; it's talking about *you*.) Heck, you can even talk about all the sex you're not having.

Don't forget to let your partner do some of the talking, too. And really listen to her. Show your partner understanding, compassion, and love. Hold hands. Compliment her on anything you admire about her, whether as a mother, as a woman, or as a lover. In short, remind her how important she is to you.

If you end your "date" by making love, that's great. But if you don't, that's okay, too. After all, you've spent the entire evening strengthening your relationship. And though making love is an important ingredient of this relationship, it's certainly not the only one. So don't think you've failed each other just because exhaustion, tension, preoccupation, or some other circumstance prevents the evening from building to a sustained and mutual orgasm. You can always go for that tomorrow night.

Relax, It's Only Sex

The tension and pressure of non-stop baby care—guessing what your baby wants when he cries, attending to all his needs, trying desperately to get him to sleep, and so on—or the pressure of working all day and coming home to find that now it's your turn with the baby, can leave you and your partner frazzled, frayed at the edges, and totally unable to relax. No matter who takes on the bulk of daytime childcare, neither of you ever seems to get a break.

Because unrelieved tension can diminish sexual desire, increase impatience, shorten tempers, and even contribute to (horrors!) impotence, you and your partner could probably both use an opportunity to relax. Because newborns sleep a lot, the opportunities for relaxation do exist—but they often go unrecognized, rendered invisible by the urge to get other things done when your baby nods off.

But relaxation is important—not just to your sex life, but to your physical and mental health. So instead of rushing to change the oil in your car or mow the lawn when your baby finally falls asleep, first take some time to break out your favorite relaxation techniques:

➤ **Get physical.** Go running or swimming; lift weights, ride a stationary bike, or do any other exercise that invigorates you and leaves you feeling relaxed at the end.

➤ **Get wrinkled.** Take a long, hot bath—and don't get out until your fingertips look like raisins.

➤ **Get entranced.** Meditate, contemplate your navel, repeat your mantra, whatever works for you.

➤ **Get nostalgic.** Think back to the childbirth classes you and your wife took during pregnancy. Did either of you learn any relaxation techniques that might come in handy now?

➤ **Get pampered.** Give each other a long full-body massage—an activity that is not only relaxing, it's sensual. Focus on areas that often become overworked in early parenthood or that tend to become repositories for tension: the lower back, the shoulders and neck, the feet, even the hands.

➤ **Get drunk.** Okay, maybe not drunk, but break open a beer or have a glass of wine or two with your partner. (Be careful not too drink too much, because alcohol can infiltrate her breast milk—and sabotage your erection.) In moderation, alcohol can relax your fears, loosen your inhibitions, and even numb or dull any pain that intercourse might cause your partner.

If your baby never seems to sleep, or sleeps at times when relaxation is inconvenient, it doesn't mean that you and your partner have to give up any hope of relaxation. You may not be able to take the time to give each other massages, but you can take turns giving each other breaks in which to relax using other methods. If your partner, for example, is having more trouble relaxing than you are, you might offer to take the baby for an hour so that she can take a warm bath, go running, or meditate—whatever leaves her feeling most relaxed and refreshed.

Daddy Dos and Don'ts

Once you do resume sexual relations with your partner, try not to become obsessed with bringing her to orgasm. Some women have difficulty achieving orgasm for several weeks or even months after childbirth. Many women maintain that orgasms aren't always necessary to their sexual pleasure, that the closeness and intimacy of sex is more important to them than the orgasm anyway.

Warm-Up Acts

If either or both of you doesn't feel like it yet or feels uncertain about it, don't rush into intercourse. Start slowly. Try some hugging, cuddling, holding, whispering sweet nothings, kissing, fondling, and more serious kinds of foreplay. One distinct advantage of foreplay: You can resume foreplay of most kinds—anything that doesn't involve vaginal penetration—much sooner than you can resume intercourse.

Penetration does not always have to be the be-all and end-all of sex. If you can avoid becoming fixated on intercourse, a wide range of possibilities will open themselves up to you: everything from holding hands and hugging to mutual masturbation and oral sex. All of these are good ways to start reclaiming your sexual relationship—and you can start them as soon as you both feel up to it, way before you get a doctor's go-ahead.

Talk Dirty to Me

No matter how reticent you may have been before now, start talking to each other about sex—even if neither of you is doing anything about it. If you or your partner (or both) have little or no interest in post-partum intercourse or in other sexual activities, you owe it to each other to talk about why. Your partner may feel just the same way you do—or she may have other fears or concerns that are inhibiting her post-partum sexuality.

Talking about sexual obstacles or problems may not necessarily solve them, but by not talking about them, you let each other's imagination run wild with speculation. If, for example, your partner's breasts had always been a focus of your sexual foreplay before pregnancy and childbirth but you feel uncomfortable stimulating them now, she might wonder why you suddenly adopted a hands-off approach. If you don't talk about it, she may blame herself. She may feel unattractive, unsexy, or unappealing.

Of course, you can't make your feelings, fears, or concerns go away just by talking about them, but letting your partner in on your feelings can get you to a common starting place where you can at least begin to explore solutions. Who knows? In the example above, maybe your wife's breasts are so sore and tender that she's perfectly content to leave them out of sexual foreplay. But you'll never find this out if you don't open the discussion.

Once you've begun to have sex again, continue to talk about it. Your partner needs to trust you and remain open to you—and vice versa. So find out if post-partum sex is painful for her, ask her what makes her feel good and what hurts her, and talk to each other about what each of you wants to do sexually.

Hey, I've Got an Idea!

Talking to each other about sex can lead to an exploration (both verbal and physical) of new ways of giving pleasure to each other. During her recovery from the trauma of childbirth, different sexual positions might be more comfortable for your partner than others. If she finds post-partum intercourse painful, experiment to find out what positions and techniques work best for both of you. Keep experimenting until you find one—or several—that causes her less pain or no pain at all.

We Have the Technology

Because both nursing and decreasing hormone levels tend to inhibit vaginal secretions, you may need to try using artificial lubricants, even if you've never used them before. You can apply lubricants directly on the vaginal walls or you can start using pre-lubricated condoms. Either will reduce friction and soreness.

If neither lubricants nor experimentation with different positions relieves the pain your partner feels during intercourse, consult her obstetrician/gynecologist. The doctor can prescribe a topical estrogen cream that may alleviate much or all of her pain.

Help!

If necessary—in other words, if you've tried everything else and nothing seems to work, or if you don't have the patience to try everything else—seek marital or sex counseling. Post-partum sexual difficulties seldom require long-term treatment. Very often, a professional sex therapist or marriage counselor can—in just a few extremely intense sessions—cut to the heart of post-partum sexual difficulties or correct the communication problems that sometimes underlie these difficulties.

After the problem is out in the open, a sex therapist or marriage counselor can then offer specific suggestions on what you can do about it. So you may learn a thing or two, pick up a few new tricks—and have fun doing it, too.

The Least You Need to Know

➤ Given your probable exhaustion; your new responsibilities and the tension they create; and the constant, inescapable presence of a third party, not to mention your partner's hormonal instability and need to recover from childbirth, it's amazing that you're even interested in *reading* about sex.

➤ Don't feel that you have to rush into post-partum sex to save your relationship. As long as you and your partner talk to each other about it, your relationship can survive.

➤ Common post-partum fears about sexual intercourse include the fear of causing (or feeling) pain, the fear of getting pregnant again, the fear that everything may have changed, and the fear that your baby will interrupt you. Unfortunately, none of these fears is entirely groundless.

➤ Relaxation, romance, extended foreplay, lubricants, new positions, and, if necessary, professional help can all help rekindle your sexual passion for each other.

➤ Though it may sound like a clichè, love, patience, and mutual understanding really are the keys to reviving your sex life after childbirth.

Part 3

Mapping Out Strategies for a Long-Term Parenting Partnership

You and your partner are in this for the long haul. Even if the unthinkable happens and you separate or divorce, the fact that you're reading this book shows your commitment to remaining involved and being the best father you can possibly be.

But long-term commitments require long-term strategies. You need to set goals together and figure out which take priority over the others. You need to come up with a common parenting philosophy, at least as far as the big things go. You also need to do some financial planning.

Finally, on those oh-so-rare occasions when you and your partner disagree about how best to fulfill your parenting obligations or achieve your common goals, you need to figure out a way to resolve your differences without bloodshed. When conflicts do erupt, keep one thing in mind: Both you and your partner want what's best for your child. Now all you need to do is figure out just what that is.

Chapter 13

Getting on the Same Page: Parents as Partners

In This Chapter

➤ Defining common parenting goals

➤ Coming up with priorities when goals conflict

➤ Resolving parenting conflicts without spilling blood

➤ Are mothers naturally more nurturing than fathers?

➤ How to offer—and receive—parenting suggestions without raising defenses

Unless you're a single dad, parenting is a partnership. It hardly matters whether you, your wife, or both of you work full- or part-time. The two of you need to work (and play) together, sharing the joys, responsibilities, and heartaches of parenting.

Though you and your partner share the common goal of rearing a healthy, happy, moral, and responsible child, you are not, of course, one person. Although you both want to do "what's best" for your child, you will not always agree on "what's best." Your partner will no doubt disapprove of some of your parenting choices, and some of the things she does as a parent will drive you crazy.

In such times of conflict, remind yourself that you do have common goals. To achieve them, you will need to talk to each other, develop a game plan for your family, and then cooperate with each other to bring that plan to life.

Goal Tending

If you have not yet taken the time to talk with your partner about the grand scheme of things (defining your goals as individuals, as a couple, and as parents; and developing a rough outline of plans to bring about those goals), now may be the perfect time for such long-range thinking. Early parenthood is a time of adjustment and reassessment. The dynamics of family life change dramatically with the birth of a baby. Before, you were a couple; now, you're parents. Before, you had only your own and your partner's happiness and well-being to worry about; now, you have the added concern of a child.

These transformations demand a shift of priorities for both of you. By discussing these new priorities with your partner, you will come to a better understanding of your common goals.

What Do You Want Anyway?

Not all parents, of course, have the same goals for themselves and their children. Your personality, the nature of your partnership, and other circumstances will make some of your goals unique to your family. Yet like most parents, you and your partner no doubt share most of the following goals:

➤ You want to do "what's best" for your child.

➤ You want to help your child to explore and learn, to grow and develop, to discover and hone her talents.

➤ You want your child to be as happy as she can possibly be.

➤ You want to nurture your child's physical development, intelligence, emotional well-being, and dedication to certain values.

➤ You want to help your child reach her full potential.

➤ You want to protect the health and well-being of every member of your family.

➤ You want to continue to grow as individuals, as a couple, and as parents.

➤ You want to build on the love that's already in your home and family.

➤ You want to thrive—or at least survive—financially.

You and your partner may have unique personal goals for yourselves as individuals, as a couple, and as parents that you would add to this list. You may have career goals (a job you care about, 100K a year, a key to the executive washroom). You may have lifestyle goals (a summer house in the country, a long-awaited vacation in Paris, or a huge power mower). You may have goals as a couple (maintaining both your passion for and friendship with each other, supporting each other as individuals, making love like bunnies). You may have goals as parents (instilling a love of music and art, getting your child into a good school, and training someone to fetch your slippers).

If you and your partner don't discuss them, however, your goals and hers might be somewhat different. Until you set all your cards on the table, you can't possibly begin to sort them out and decide what's most important to both of you.

When Worlds Collide: Conflicting Goals

If it were just a matter of setting one goal after another and then taking steps to achieve them, parenting (and working as partners) would be relatively simple. But goals don't arrive in neat succession; they come all at once and demand that you sort them out.

Unfortunately, not all your goals are likely to be compatible. When your baby starts to walk, for instance, your desire to protect him might conflict with your wish to nurture his development. You want him to learn to walk but hate to see him fall. Similarly, your commitment to spending time with your child may clash with your desire to provide a better standard of living. You may have to choose between overtime and baby time. Or, the time it takes to care for your child may take away from the time you have to devote to strengthening your relationship with your partner.

To further complicate setting goals for your family, you're not the only one with an agenda. Your partner will no doubt be setting her own goals, too, and they may not be exactly the same as yours. For example, you may butt heads trying to decide which matters more: your (or her) job or your (or her) baby-care responsibilities? Which takes precedence: your job or hers? Which should be treated as a priority: your mutual desire to stay at a party or your child's need to go to bed? Which is most important: cleaning the house or playing with your baby?

On an almost daily basis, your short-term goals will conflict with your long-term goals; your own goals will clash with those of your partner; and your personal goals as an individual, as a husband, and as a father will conflict with one another. As individuals, as a couple, and as parents, you and your partner will continually need to evaluate and re-evaluate your priorities.

What Do You Think?

When setting and prioritizing goals for your family, you really need to work together as a couple. First and foremost, this means talking to each other and making important decisions together.

It won't do for one of you to set goals and establish priorities unilaterally or to make important family decisions without consulting the other. Such unilateral decisions are arrogant and short-sighted, failing to take into account the other person's needs, desires, or opinions and failing to take advantage of the opportunity to benefit from the other's wisdom. What's worse, they also tend to raise hackles, creating anger and resentment that can eat away at the foundation of your relationship.

So talk—and listen—to each other before making any critical family decisions or mapping out plans for the future. In the course of these discussions, you may find out things you didn't know about your partner's—and possibly your own—thoughts, feelings, and priorities.

Doing the Right Thing

Of course, even after discussing major decisions or conflicting priorities, you and your partner may not agree on what to do. You know what she wants, she knows what you want, and yet you're still miles apart. In most cases, however, you cannot decide to take no action as parents just because you don't agree on what's best. You have to do something.

So what do you do?

Resolving conflicts that really matter is seldom easy, even when it's just one person wrestling with his or her own priorities. With two people, each with his or her own priorities and long-term agenda, decision making becomes even more difficult. Of course, you want to make family decisions that balance everyone's needs, desires, and interests. But when you and your partner disagree on how to accomplish this, how can you arrive at the "right" choice?

Whether arguing with your partner or simply plagued with self-doubt, you may find it easier to resolve many of your parenting conflicts if you recognize that you don't always have to make the right decision. In practical terms, parenting is often a matter of trial-and-error.

A few decisions, such as your choice to become parents in the first place, cannot be reversed. But many other decisions you'll make as parents—from disciplining your child to choosing a pediatrician, from picking a day-care provider to setting limits on television watching—can be fine-tuned, corrected, completely changed, or totally undone. So when you have to do something as parents, do something. If your decision doesn't work out, try something different the next time.

Father Knows Best

"If the new American father feels bewildered and even defeated, let him take comfort from the fact that whatever he does in any fathering situation has a fifty percent chance of being right."

—Bill Cosby

Crunch Time: Resolving Conflict

Okay, so you've decided that something must be done. How do you decide what to do, especially if you and your partner have dissenting opinions? Well, you could always sneak around behind each other's backs. You could pretend to cave in and reach a "mutual" decision, and then undermine it by discreetly doing what you wanted in the first place. But like unilateral decision making, this approach will quickly create anger and resentment and damage the relationship with your partner—not the healthiest or most honest approach.

Instead, try talking to your partner, not just about parenting conflicts in themselves but about how you will resolve such disagreements. Recognize when you can't come to an agreement and then decide—either as a general strategy or on a case-to-case basis—what you will do in such situations.

Most likely, you and your partner will rely on one of the following strategies to resolve apparently unresolvable conflicts:

➤ Persuasion

➤ Compromise

➤ Deferring to each other

➤ You always make the call

➤ Your partner always makes the call

➤ You split up authority according to the issue involved

➤ You try one of your solutions on a temporary basis

➤ You flip a coin

➤ You seek outside expertise

The Art of Persuasion

Whether you've decided that one of you will have the final word (or at least the final word on certain matters) or that you will make all major parenting decisions jointly, you and your partner should still discuss family matters thoroughly first. When you disagree about what's best for your child, the first and best solution is to talk about it, argue it out (civilly, of course), and try to convince each other that you are right. To make this work, both of you need to speak your mind and, even more importantly, to listen to each other with open minds.

The advantage: Parenting decisions reached through argument and persuasion are truly joint decisions, allowing both of you to present a unified front.

The catch: On some issues neither of you will be convinced by the other's arguments. You will reach a standstill, with each of you still insisting that you're right. What do you do then?

Mutual Compromise

If the art of persuasion doesn't work for either of you, some conflicts can be resolved through mutual compromise. Let's say you feel that daycare at a young age is not an option for your child, while your partner wants to go back to work. Perhaps you can iron out a compromise in which your partner works part-time and you (if you cut down on your own work hours) or a baby-sitter takes care of the baby during those hours. Neither of you may be completely satisfied, but both of you can arrive at a solution that works.

The advantage: Decisions reached through mutual compromise are made jointly and amicably, with each of you giving something up in order to get something else that you value.

The catch: Some issues do not allow for compromise. For instance, if you find spanking an acceptable disciplinary measure and your wife feels that under no circumstances should a parent ever strike a child, you will be hard pressed to find a middle ground. One of you will have to give way.

Deferential Treatment

If one of you feels particularly passionate about a particular parenting issue, the other—in the interest of family harmony—can simply agree to yield this time. You don't have to agree that your partner is right to see the value of parental unity on important issues.

Parental disunity almost always sets up one parent as "villain" and the other as "hero." If the two of you take different stands on issues as important as discipline or as trivial as snacking, your child will recognize it and use it to her advantage. This encourages the formation of secrets and alliances between one parent and the child against the other parent, who will naturally feel betrayed by and resentful of his or her partner and the child.

Far better to create an alliance with each other: not against your child, but for the good of your child (who may nonetheless feel betrayed and resentful toward both of you). To maintain this alliance, however, one of you will occasionally have to make a sacrifice and defer to your partner.

The advantage: Children benefit from consistency, from knowing what to expect from their parents, and from knowing they can't get away with performing an "end run" around one parent to get what they want from the other.

The catch: A strong-willed, extremely confident person will always feel passionately "right." This can mean that one parent always gets his or her way. The Lord of the Manor or the Domestic Goddess then consistently dominates the other parent and the family as a whole.

Lord of the Manor

Among many believers of orthodox and fundamentalist religions, the father acts as the ultimate authority in the family. This doesn't necessarily mean that the woman has no say in major decisions. In many such families, the husband explicitly seeks out his wife's advice, suggestions, and opinions before making a decision in certain areas. But when push comes to shove, mommy defers and daddy rules.

The advantage: With only one ultimate decision maker, there's less overt conflict.

The catch: It's not as popular as it once was, especially among women.

Domestic Goddess

Adhering to another popular tradition for deciding family issues, especially decisions centered around the home, some fathers cede virtually all authority in the home to their partners. Major child-rearing decisions are made, if only by default, by the mother, the queen of the castle.

The advantage: Again, a single authority—no matter how much inner conflict she may feel—makes decisions much more easily than two people with conflicting opinions.

The catch: Many fathers today want a greater hand in child-rearing than earlier generations of fathers had.

Father Knows Best

"Fathers should be neither seen nor heard. That is the only proper basis for family life."

—Oscar Wilde

Spheres of Influence

One way to combine the relative simplicity of the single authority figure and the desire of both partners for greater equality in deciding family matters is to define "spheres of influence" and recognize just one of you as the ultimate authority in each separate sphere. One of you, for instance, has the final word on discipline matters, whereas the other has the say-so on educational issues. One of you handles financial planning, whereas the other deals with vacation planning.

The advantage: By splitting up spheres of influence, you and your partner can take advantage of your unique talents and interests while maintaining an equal balance of power in your parenting partnership.

The catch: Life is messy. Areas of influence are not so discrete and frequently overlap. Financial planning, for example, affects vacation planning; questions of discipline spill over into issues about education.

Okay, Let's Try It Your Way

Again, in the interest of parental unity, one of you might agree to try it your partner's way—but only on a temporary basis. This solution works best when neither of you feels completely sure about your position.

Like "deferential treatment," this approach to conflict resolution involves one partner giving way to the other. But this approach requires both of you to agree that you're only "test driving" one partner's way for a limited period of time, trying it out to see how it works for everyone.

Let's say, for example, that you think your child should attend a private school but your partner considers it too expensive. You can see your partner's point. After all, you don't really have a lot of money to spare. She can see your point, too. Maybe the public schools in your area don't have the greatest reputation.

In a case like this, in which both of you are on the fence but leaning in opposite directions, one of you might agree to try it the other person's way and see how it goes. Your partner might agree to putting your child in private school for a semester to see how tight your financial situation gets. Or you might agree to enroll your child in a public school for a semester to see whether its reputation is well deserved. If you're unsatisfied with the results after a fair trial period (in this case, five or six months), you can try the other way.

The advantage: This type of resolution explicitly recognizes a point I made earlier in this chapter: Very few decisions that you make as a parent are completely irreversible. Though you can't take back the past, you can learn from it and use its lessons to change your approach to present and future parenting choices.

The catch: Both parents must be open-minded and flexible to make this type of conflict resolution work. Even if both of you initially agree to try something only on a temporary basis, once in place it can become entrenched and permanent.

Daddy Dos and Don'ts

Don't sweat the small stuff. If you and your partner can't come to an agreement on what you both recognize as a small issue, that's fine. No one in his right mind expects a mother and father to agree about everything. So don't use up all your time and energy arguing with your partner about the small stuff. Save it for the big issues—the ones where agreeing to disagree just won't cut it.

Calling It in the Air

Sometimes flipping a coin is the only way you'll be able to resolve a particular parenting conflict. When persuasion fails and compromise seems impossible, you and your partner will be stuck. In all likelihood, however, you will still have to make a choice. You can't just ignore an important parenting issue and hope it will go away. Going your own separate ways on important issues can be confusing and even damaging to your child.

When you and your partner are deadlocked in a parenting conflict, taking turns making decisions may be the only possible solution. Flipping a coin or cutting a deck of cards, for example, may truly be as good a method as any for deciding a hopelessly deadlocked issue. Or, you can establish a system not unlike college basketball's possession arrow: You get this one, I get the next.

The advantage: Except for the fact that it allows you and your partner to make a decision in a parenting situation that demands one, this method really has no advantages.

The catch: Keeping score of any kind is not generally good for a relationship. In addition, whether the "winner" is determined by a coin toss or by taking turns, the "loser" is unlikely to wholeheartedly support the decision. If you work together to come up with parenting solutions you can both live with, however, you probably won't reach this kind of impasse too often.

Asking an Expert

Another alternative if you arrive at an impossible impasse is to consult an expert. You can seek out more information on specific parenting problems or on ways to negotiate parenting decisions together by drawing on the expertise of others.

Do a little research on the issue. Look at books, magazine and newspaper articles, and the Internet. Talk to friends and relatives about what they would do in a similar situation. In certain cases, the advice of a pediatrician, a child psychologist, or a member of the clergy may be invaluable.

The advantage: Gathering more information can sometimes help one of you change your opinion about an issue or give you new ideas on how to resolve it. My wife and I, for example, initially disagreed about whether to circumcise our oldest son. Both of us felt strongly about it. After doing some research, however, she came around to my position. We later disagreed about the best way to get the kids to go to sleep by themselves. Extensive research gave us some ideas that might never have occurred to us, including some that we immediately put into practice. (See Chapter 16 for ideas on preventing bedtime from becoming a nightmare.)

The catch: Although an outside authority can provide information and concrete suggestions on how to resolve parenting conflicts in general, this method really involves little more than information gathering—a process that should play a part in any major parenting decisions. So even after drawing on the expertise of others, you and your partner will still need to decide for yourselves what is best for your child. Good luck!

Daddy Dos and Don'ts

If you and your partner frequently arrive at an impasse when trying to resolve parenting issues, you might find it beneficial to yourselves, your relationship, and your family as a whole to start seeing a family counselor. A good professional counselor can improve your general communication and conflict-resolution skills and offer you a safe place to practice them.

Breaking Up the Mommy Monopoly

Previous generations assumed that parenthood was a job suitable only for women. In establishing a parenting partnership for the new millennium, however, you can cast aside this outdated assumption. Parenthood knows no gender; fathers can perform the duties of parenthood just as well as mothers (with one obvious exception). You and your partner can write your own roles as parents, and then act out these roles as best you can. (See Chapter 6 for more on defining your role as a father.)

You can embrace the traditional models of parenting (Daddy works all day; Mommy stays home with the kids) if you like, but today you have a choice. You can share child-rearing responsibilities (and the far less pleasant duties of housekeeping) in any way that suits both of you best.

Cornering the Market

Even today, many men assume that mothers are just more naturally nurturing than fathers. They back away from active parenting because they believe their partners have an instinctive competence at mothering, while they have no corresponding instinct toward fathering.

Baloney!

Father Knows Best

"It's clear that most American children suffer too much mother and too little father."

—Gloria Steinem

Despite this common misconception, mothering is in fact no more innate to women than fathering is to men (except, of course, for the biological fact that women produce milk). In general, mothers are not "natural parents" any more than fathers are.

Of course, parenting does come more easily for some mothers than for their partners. Some parenting skills do begin with instinct. But this has little to do with gender. These mothers no doubt find parenting comes more easily for them than for most other mothers, too. And some fathers have the same kind of instinctive knack for parenting, too.

Few of the lucky minority of parents who do have an instinct for parenting, however, get by on instinct alone. Good mothers and fathers move well beyond whatever instinct for parenting they had to begin with. How? Simply by getting to know their children at an early age.

To develop your talents as a parent, all you need is a little practice. If you spend a good deal of time with your infant and engage and entertain him, you will get to know him and develop a close relationship with him. You'll know what he likes and dislikes. You'll learn what he wants when he cries in a particular way. The better you know your child, the better parent you'll be.

On-the-Job Training

Like any skill, parenting tends to become easier with practice. Not only that, but you get better at it, too. That's why mothers, who have traditionally taken on the bulk of child-rearing responsibilities, are regarded as naturals.

The late Joe Dimaggio put in a lot of hours on the ball field before he was regarded as a natural. But because he learned the game so well, Dimaggio made everything look easy. So it is with mothers. They don't assume the lion's share of parenting because they're naturals. In fact, it's just the reverse: They make parenting look easy because the time they've put in has improved their skills.

Although a nurturing instinct certainly helps, child-rearing is largely a trial-and-error process. Since they generally devote more time to their children than fathers do, mothers tend to learn more tricks and become more confident in their abilities. Through this kind of on-the-job training, women become more and more sensitive to the particular character traits, desires, and needs of each of their children.

If your partner assumes most of the child-rearing responsibilities, she will become increasingly proficient at them. But the same could easily be said of you. The more responsibility for child-rearing you take on, the more skills you will develop and the more confidence you will feel. However, if you shy away from feeding, diapering, bathing, playing with, and caring for your child, you will be less sensitive to your child's needs than your partner and, in all likelihood, increasingly less confident in your own parenting abilities.

So don't automatically defer to your wife's "expertise." After all, she doesn't have any more than you do, at least initially. In fact, unless she's baby-sat for a newborn before, she has exactly as much experience handling and caring for a baby as you do: zilch.

Remember: With the exceptions of pregnancy, labor and delivery, and breast-feeding, you can handle any aspects of parenting that your partner

Daddy Dos and Don'ts

If you're like most American couples, your partner will spend more time caring for your baby and getting to know her than you will. As a result, your partner will acquire a certain "expertise" in knowing what your baby wants and what works. So when you do your part in baby or child care, don't hesitate to ask for your partner's advice.

can. If you really want to do it, you can. Whether it's feeding your baby from a bottle, soothing her, putting her to bed, taking care of her during illness, singing to her, playing with her, changing her dirty diapers, bathing her, dressing her, or taking her to "Mommy and Me" classes, you can do it.

Learning to Share

As much as you possibly can, try to share child-rearing duties with your partner when you're not at work. Of course, you're tired when you get home from a long day on the job. Maybe all you really want is some peace and quiet.

Daddy Dos and Don'ts

Avoid being tag-team parents. Just because it's one of your turns to entertain and take care of your baby doesn't mean that the other should leave the ring and disappear. Sure, you want to take advantage of some time to be by yourself, but don't neglect to spend time together as a family, too. Play together, sing together, eat together, or just cuddle up together. When you're talking about daddy, mommy, and baby, three doesn't have to be a crowd.

But look at it this way: Why should you let your partner have all the fun? If you throw yourself into parenting when you get home, you may find that it can actually relax you and take your mind off work.

You and your partner can share the child-rearing responsibilities by taking turns or by specializing. If your partner gave the baby a bath and put him to bed last night, for example, perhaps tonight you can change him into his pajamas, rock him, and sing him some lullabies before putting him in his crib. Perhaps you love reading to your baby and your wife loves to sing. You don't have to take turns just for the sake of taking turns. You can establish specialized areas of expertise.

No matter how you and your partner split up the responsibilities (and the joys) of parenthood, make sure to ask for help whenever you need it and to do whatever you can when your partner asks for help. If your baby's poop leaks through his diaper and stains the crib sheets, who cares whether it's your turn to change the diaper or your partner's? If one of you takes care of the baby and one of you takes care of the crib, you'll both have more time to have fun playing with him.

Play Nice

You will work together best as a team if you both try to avoid carping and backbiting. Both of you want to devote time to your child. You truly want to share in the joys and challenges of parenthood. So begin with gratitude and appreciation for that simple fact.

Each of you, however, will have your own particular style, your own individual way of handling the responsibilities of parenthood. Because you change diapers, put your baby to bed, play with her, or stop her crying in a certain way doesn't mean your partner will do these things the same way. Your way is not the only "right" way.

By the same token, your partner's way isn't the only right way, either. Feel free to develop your own style of parenting. When your partner offers suggestions on how to do something, try them if you like—or try something else you come up with on your own.

If your partner sharply criticizes the way you change a diaper or bathe the baby, let her know—in the nicest way possible, of course—that though you may welcome suggestions, harsh words raise your defenses and make it harder for you to consider her advice. Of course, this goes both ways. You don't have to keep your mouth shut if you have a suggestion or some advice. You can point out, in a helpful way, that you feed the baby or entertain her somewhat differently and that it seems to work for you. But if you criticize or belittle your partner's parenting efforts, you can't really expect her to hear your suggestions.

To make the partnership work, avoid making each other feel defensive about parenting skills. If you can offer observations and suggestions and share experiences and expertise without questioning or attacking each other's parenting abilities, both of you will have the opportunity to learn from each other and become better parents. Instead of criticizing, offer each other thanks and appreciation. After all, neither of you will get a raise, a commendation, or a promotion for doing a good job.

Far too often parenting is a thankless job. The only people likely to recognize how well you are doing are your child, your partner, and, of course, you. If your child cannot yet speak—and, in all likelihood, even after she does—words of recognition or gratitude will not come from her. That leaves it up to you. Make a point of praising your partner when she does something especially loving or creative for your baby (or for you). You both deserve an occasional pat on the back for all your parenting efforts. If you don't commend each other, who will?

The Least You Need to Know

➤ Talk to your partner about long-term goals for you and your family. Only then can you sort out conflicting goals and decide what's most important to both of you.

➤ Many of the decisions you and your partner make as parents are at least somewhat reversible. Don't agonize too much over making the right choice all the time. If you make the wrong one, you can probably change it.

➤ You and your partner can resolve parenting conflicts in many different ways, but they all begin with talking to each other. Avoid making unilateral decisions.

➤ In general, mothers have no more innate parenting ability than fathers. What most mothers do have is more on-the-job experience.

➤ Offer observations and suggestions to each other, not complaints and criticism. You each deserve the other's appreciation and gratitude for your parenting efforts.

Chapter 14

How Much Is This Kid Gonna Cost, Anyway?

In This Chapter

➤ The bottom line: how much you can expect to spend on your kid(s)

➤ What you need to include in your will

➤ Life insurance: a necessary evil for most fathers

➤ What college will cost two decades from now

➤ Investing for a college education

Let's face it: You can't afford to have children. No one can.

With the cost of providing for a child rising every year, it's amazing that anyone chooses to have children anymore. In fact, many couples today have decided to delay having children until their 30s or even 40s, entertaining the optimistic delusion that they should wait to have children until they can afford them. If you know one of these couples, break the news to them slowly: You have no idea how expensive a child can be until you have one.

Just to provide the basics (shelter, clothing, food, medical care, and education) for your children, you and your partner may have to start scrambling for dough. Your wife may need to return to work sooner than she'd like. You may need to find a second job. You might even become desperate enough to start playing the lottery.

The *Real* Money Pit

No matter how hard you and your partner work, it can be difficult to make ends meet with a child or two thrown in the mix. Even the "start-up costs" can bring you to the brink of bankruptcy. Before your baby was born, you probably sank over $1,000 into necessary items like a bassinet, crib, changing table, stroller, car seat, and clothing—not to mention all those stuffed animals, rattles, and toys that you bought on impulse because they looked so cute. (See Chapter 5 on what to buy before your baby arrives.)

The spending spree doesn't stop there, however. The darned thing about kids is that no matter what you do to try to stop them, they just keep growing and growing. You'll keep buying more and more clothes, every month or two in the beginning, and then somewhat less frequently after the first couple of years. And you'll keep buying more and more toys, and then books, and later software, because you simply couldn't live with yourself if you didn't have age-appropriate materials to challenge and educate your child.

You'll be thrilled when your child first begins to speak—until you realize she's using her newfound ability to ask you for money. Trust me, I've been there. Not long after your child warms your heart by saying, "Mama" or "Dada," she'll start thinning your wallet by saying, "Mama, I want … " or "Daddy, can I buy …?"

Father Knows Best

" … [W]hen I … asked him [my father] for fifty cents, he would tell me the story of his life: how he got up at four o'clock in the morning when he was seven years old and walked twenty-three miles to milk ninety cows. And the farmer for whom he worked had no bucket, so my father had to squirt the milk into his little hand and then walk eight miles to the nearest can. For five cents a month.

"And I never got the fifty cents."

—Bill Cosby

You want to make your little one happy, of course, and if it costs a few bucks to make her beam with delight, you'll probably spend the money gladly. The trouble is, of course, that once it starts, it never ends. Your child, naturally enough, will always want you to spend more than you are willing—or more than you can afford.

Most children are not shy about making their wishes known. If your child wants something, you'll hear about it again and again and again. And chances are, what she wants will cost money.

Father Knows Best

"No matter how many Christmas presents you give your child, there's always that terrible moment when he's opened the very last one. That's when he expects you to say, 'Oh yes, I almost forgot,' and take him out and show him the pony."

—Mignon McLaughlin

Children: A Cost-Benefit Analysis

So what's the bottom line? In trying to provide for all your child needs and gratify at least some of his wants, how much can you reasonably expect to spend?

Estimates vary widely, but even the most conservative guesses place the cost of raising a child from birth to age 18 at $140,000–$280,000. Having two kids drops the cost per child to *just* $110,000–$225,000. And if you have three or more, the cost of each child becomes a relative bargain: $85,000–$175,000.

Though the total sum may seem like a lot, it can be manageable if you break it down into annual expenses of $5,000–$15,000. That's only $90–$300 a week! Now that doesn't sound so bad, does it?

But wait! If you plan to pay for your child's college education, you can add another $100,000–$400,000 to the total. We'll look at college expenses and how you can possibly afford them later. For now, let's look at some of the money you can expect to spend before your kid leaves the house.

Father Figures

The amount of money you spend on your child depends more on your income than on anything else. According to the U.S. Department of Agriculture, two-parent families who make less than $35,000 annually spend an average of $6,200 a year per child (if they have two children). Couples who make $35,000–$60,000 spend an average of $8,500 per child each year. Couples who make more than $60,000 spend about $12,400 per year on their children.

Where's All the Money Going?

Five to fifteen thousand dollars a year. At first, that sounds like a ton of money. But consider all of the essentials and incidentals involved in feeding, sheltering, clothing, and educating a child:

➤ **Housing.** Whether you're paying rent, paying off a mortgage, or just paying property taxes, you will pay more for the extra living space that becomes absolutely necessary with the birth of a child.

➤ **Furniture.** As long as you're already paying for the extra space, you might as well buy some things to fill it up. You will probably furnish your child's room with a crib, rocking chair, changing table, dresser, shelves, toy box, bed, desk, lamps, posters, and so on. Add a playroom and you'll need chairs, tables, and many of the same items needed for your child's room.

➤ **Food.** You think formula and jars of baby food cost a fortune? Just wait. Even before your child becomes a teenager, you'll spend more than $100 a month to feed her. That doesn't even count eating out—which can add up quickly once your child graduates beyond the children's menu.

➤ **Clothing.** For a while, at least, you can keep the cost of clothing down by buying second-hand clothes from consignment shops and by accepting hand-me-downs from friends and relatives. But once your child becomes fashion conscious, the amount you spend on clothes will double.

➤ **Diapers.** Unless you own and wash your own cloth diapers, you'll probably spend $2,000–$4,000 on diapers alone!

➤ **Household goods.** You'll need more of everything, from laundry and dishwashing detergents to soap, shampoo, and toothpaste. Your household consumption of paper products—napkins, paper towels, tissues, and toilet paper—will skyrocket. (Kids seem to think this stuff grows on trees. Okay, so what if it does?)

➤ **Medical and dental care.** You'll probably visit the doctor more times in the first year than any other time in your child's life. You'll schedule half a dozen well-baby visits in addition to all the times she gets sick. But this is offset by the fact that you won't need to take her to the dentist yet. And what if your child later needs orthodontia?

➤ **Day care.** Quality day care doesn't come cheap. In fact, if you have two or more young children, you may end up paying more for child care than the extra income earned with both of you working.

➤ **Education.** The bulk of your local public school's expenses are financed by your property taxes. If you—like many parents—choose to live in a

Daddy Dos and Don'ts

If both you and your partner work, the cost of child care that allows you both to work (or to look for work) is partially tax deductible. Before April 15th rolls around, get a copy of IRS Form 2441: Child and Dependent Care Expenses. *Note:* The form requires you to provide the Employer Identification Number of child-care facilities or the Social Security number of child-care providers. So if you pay a nanny or sitter "off the books," you won't be able to deduct the expense.

specific community based on the reputation of the local schools, you can expect to pay higher property taxes for the privilege. In addition, you will need to pay for any "extras" that you want your child to take: music or dance lessons, "Mommy and Me" classes, computer classes, swimming lessons, sports, scouting programs, and so on. Finally, if you want to send your child to a private school, add another $10,000 or so per year.

➤ **In-home entertainment.** Without something to keep her busy—and to stimulate learning and development, of course—your child will drive you and your partner up a wall. You will be her exclusive entertainment center. So to save your sanity, you'll invest thousands of dollars in toys, games, sports equipment, books, videos, software (all educational, of course), and art supplies.

➤ **Outside entertainment.** Even if you search out matinees, discounted prices for kids, and other specials, the high cost of entertainment—movies, bowling, miniature golf, swim clubs, zoos, museums, and the like—will probably astound you. Practically anywhere you go for entertainment—especially if you add the cost of snacks and other treats—will cost you a bundle.

➤ **Travel.** You can expect your travel and vacation costs to soar. By age two, and often before, your child will need her own seat on a plane or train; in most cases, that means another full-fare ticket. When you arrive at your vacation spot, you'll no doubt need more space there, too: a suite of hotel rooms, a bigger vacation house, and so on. This will cost more, too.

Father Knows Best

"I could now afford all the things I never had as a kid, if I didn't have kids."

—Robert Orben

What You Get for Your Money

Of course, you do receive some compensation for all the money you shell out. Okay, so maybe you can't count on your child taking care of you when you grow old. But in the meantime, your child can reduce your tax bill significantly—and that's got to be a plus.

For every child you have, you get to take an extra exemption from federal income tax (and almost always state income tax as well), which reduces your taxable income. You can also (since 1998) take a federal tax credit for each child (unless you exceed a maximum income level), which directly reduces the amount of tax you pay. In addition, some of the cost of daycare is tax deductible, as long as it allows both you and your partner to work (or look for work). Naturally, the exemption, child tax credit, and child-care credit won't even come close to covering the actual expenses incurred in taking care of a child, but hey, every little bit helps.

Down the road a little, if money gets tight, your child can always get a job of his own and contribute to the family income (or at least cover some of his own expenses).

Though having children provides you with some tax breaks, the true compensation you get for all the money you spend is, of course, your children themselves. For a mere one or two hundred grand, you get the privilege of raising a child: a priceless treasure.

Think of it this way: For somewhat less than a quarter of a million dollars per child, you get the following:

➤ Sleepless nights

➤ Countless worries

➤ A drastically curtailed social life

➤ Your child's resentment whenever you say "No"

➤ An inexhaustible supply of messiness

➤ Years of defiance

➤ An occasional smile, hug, or word that lets you know that your child loves you

I don't know about you, but it sounds like a bargain to me.

Daddy Dos and Don'ts

If you own your own business, put your child on the payroll. By paying your child, you increase your cost of doing business and therefore decrease your taxes. The salary you pay your child will no doubt be taxed at a much lower rate than the rate you pay in your income bracket. You'll pay less in taxes, and your child can start saving for college—all at the same time.

Father Figures

The number of deaths directly attributable to having drawn up a will? Zero!

If You Die, What Will You Do Then?

With all the expenses involved in rearing a child, you better get your financial house in order, if you haven't already. If you've never given a thought to long-term financial planning, you better start thinking about it now.

Though you may not be your family's sole provider, you probably include providing for your family as a major part of your role as father. So what would happen if you weren't around anymore? How will your wife and child survive financially if you die? What if you and your partner both die? Who will take care of your children? These are the kinds of questions that new parents must begin asking themselves.

Father Knows Best

"I'm not afraid to die. I just don't want to be there when it happens."

—Woody Allen

Where There's a Will, There's a Way

If you haven't written a will yet, you'd better write one now. Understandably, no one likes to think about their own mortality. You may fear that by planning for it, you will somehow bring about your own death. But writing a will won't kill you. And if the unthinkable happens—if you or your partner (or worse, both of you) should die in the near future— wouldn't you rather have a say in what happens to your child? Without a will, you won't.

You might say to yourself, "Why bother? My state has community property laws. When I die, my wife will inherit everything I own, and I trust her to take care of my child." Fair enough. But what if both of you die? Who will take care of your child then? And what will happen to your estate, no matter how little you think it amounts to?

Father Figures

Astonishingly, about two-thirds of the people who died over the past decade didn't have a will!

By writing a will, you can distribute your property the way you want, rather than rely on the rationality of your state's laws. In addition, you can spare your partner or relatives the burden of having to sort out your estate in the midst of their grief.

If you own a substantial amount of property, you would do well to consult a lawyer to draw up your will. If your estate is worth more than $600,000—the current amount exempt from federal estate taxes—or if you own property in more than one state or county, for example, you will probably need a lawyer's help with estate planning. A lawyer or financial planner can suggest ways in which you can reduce the amount of your estate to bring it closer to (or within) the tax limit.

You may need a lawyer's help in preparing your will even if your estate is less substantial. But if you have a relatively modest estate and intend to give it all to your wife and children, you may prefer to do it yourself and save the expense of a lawyer's fees (which vary greatly depending upon the size of the estate and the complexity of the will). You can simply pick up a last will and testament form for about a dollar. But if you want step-by-step instructions and perhaps some guidance as well, you can use any of the following:

➤ Last will and testament kit ($6–$8)

➤ Last will and testament book ($10–$15)

➤ Last will and testament software ($15–$50)

All of these items should be available at your local stationary, book, or office supply store.

Whether you prepare your own will or have a lawyer draw it up for you, make sure it includes the following:

➤ **Name of your executor.** Your executor has the responsibility to see that all the specifics laid out in your will are carried out. If you name your partner as executor, be sure to name an alternate who will take over if your partner dies before—or with—you.

Daddy Dos and Don'ts

When most people look for a place to store a will, they immediately think of a safe deposit box. Don't. Upon your death, many states require that any safe deposit boxes in your name—including boxes held jointly by you and your partner—be sealed until they can be opened in the presence of a representative of the state tax commission (just in case you're squirreling away hidden assets). If this happens, your will and testament will become totally inaccessible when it's most needed. So find a safe place in your home instead.

➤ **Distribution of assets.** If you want everything you own to go to your wife or partner, state this explicitly. If you want specific items to go to other relatives or friends, list these clearly and explicitly, and then go on to say that the rest of your property should go to your partner.

Again, take into account the possibility, however remote, that you and your partner might die at the same time. In such a case, you'll probably want the bulk of your estate to go to your child—perhaps set aside in a trust fund until she reaches adulthood.

➤ **Appointment of a guardian.** If you and your partner both die, who will take care of your child? Your will should name a legal guardian (or guardians) who will care for your child until she becomes an adult. (Of course, you'll want to ask your designated guardians about this first. No fair springing it on them when they can't say no because you're both dead.)

It's really not all that complicated. After making sure you included the preceding provisions, make at least two copies of your will. Sign and date each copy before two or three witnesses (depending on the state). (Choose adult witnesses who are not named in the will.) Give a copy of the will to your executor and one to your lawyer (if you used one), and keep the original for yourself. Store it in a safe place, such as a fireproof file cabinet or strongbox.

From time to time, you may need to consider revising your will. If you have more children, for instance, you'll want to split up your estate accordingly. Remember to make sure the legal guardian you appointed in your first will is still willing and able to assume custodial responsibility now that you have eight kids instead of just one.

When you update your will, be sure to retrieve and destroy all copies of the outdated will. Conflicting wills can result in the execution of the wrong will or in the need to settle your estate in court.

That's Life Insurance

Here's something else that almost no one ever likes to think about: life insurance. But if you want to help your survivors continue living in the style to which they're accustomed, a life insurance policy may be just what you need.

Father Knows Best

"There are worse things in life than death. Have you ever spent an evening with an insurance salesman?"

—Woody Allen

The amount of life insurance you need depends on two factors:

➤ The kinds of expenses you want covered when you die

➤ How much you can afford

An insurance specialist can help you determine how much coverage you need for the expenses you want to cover. For instance, do you want to replace your income—that is, the money lost because you're no longer around to earn it? If so, do you want to replace the lost income for your partner's lifetime or just until the kids are grown? Are there any other major expenses you want your insurance to cover—the mortgage on your house or your children's college education, for example?

A word of advice: Don't be awed by the numbers. The face value of your insurance policy may sound like much more money than your family needs. A death benefit of $200,000, for example, may sound like a heck of a lot of money. And it is. If your survivors, however, invest the entire sum and earn a 10 percent annual return, that's just $13,000–14,000 per year after taxes. If your survivors spend $25,000 a year, the death benefit (even if invested wisely) will be gone in less than twelve years. Keep this in mind if the insurance coverage your agent suggests seems way out of line.

Once you've settled on an ideal figure for your insurance policy, your agent will quote you a price. Seriously consider whether you can afford the monthly premium; if you can't, your policy will quickly be canceled.

Although you can get many types of life insurance, the two basic kinds are *term insurance* and *cash value insurance* (which includes whole life, variable life, and universal life).

Insurance agents compare the difference between term insurance and cash value insurance to the difference between renting and owning a home. With term insurance, you "rent" the policy for a term of one year (or five, 10, 20, or 30 years). As long as you continue to pay the "rent" (that is, your insurance premium), you can hold on to the policy. But when you stop paying, you will be "evicted" (your policy cancelled) and will own nothing.

Paterniterms

The basic difference between the two types of insurance? **Term insurance**, which costs less, provides nothing but insurance: a cash benefit paid upon your death. A **cash value policy**, which costs substantially more, not only provides insurance (a death benefit) but also builds up a cash value equity that you can draw upon later in life.

With cash value insurance, you "own" the policy. Premiums, though higher than those for term insurance, are more like mortgage payments than rent. As you pay mortgage payments on a home, you build up a cash equity in your home. As you pay premiums on cash value insurance, you build up a similar tax-deferred cash equity.

In general, a term policy perfectly fills the needs of young fathers with a limited income, whereas a cash value policy (which provides a kind of forced savings plan) may better suit your needs as you get older.

As the circumstances of your life change (your kids are grown up and through college, your mortgage is paid off, or you've won the lottery), you may no longer need the death benefit of your insurance policy. If you then cancel your term policy, you'll have nothing to show for all the money you've paid out in premiums. With a cash value policy, however, you can convert the money you've built up into an annuity, which will provide you with monthly income for the rest of your life. Or, you can borrow against the cash equity, using the accumulated cash value to help finance a major expense.

Choose life insurance wisely, being careful not to overextend yourself. The cash value of an insurance policy builds very slowly over the first few years. If you cannot keep up with the payments, you will have almost nothing to show for it—despite having paid premiums three to four times higher than you would for an equivalent term insurance policy.

College Bound

Naturally, you want the best for your child. Every year you read something new that emphasizes the importance of a college education. So you're determined that your child will go to college—perhaps even one of the nation's most prestigious universities.

But will you be able to afford it when the time comes? How much money should you be setting aside each month to build up a college fund? Will you be able to buy your child a diploma without having to sell your home?

The High Cost of Higher Learning

Four years of college entails an enormous expense today—and will be even more expensive 20 years from now. According to a survey by the College Board, the average private school charged $14,508 for undergraduate tuition and fees in the 1998–99 academic year. Add $5,765 for room and board and the cost of one year of higher learning was $20,273. And the cost has gone up since then!

Of course, you can save a bundle—more than 60 percent—by sending your child to a state school or other public college. The average undergraduate at a public school paid a total of $7,773 ($3,243 in tuition and fees and $4,530 for room and board) in the 1998–99 school year.

Father Knows Best

" ... [T]he bill for her first year [of college] had already reached thirteen thousand dollars. I looked hard at this bill and then said to her, 'Thirteen thousand dollars. Will you be the only student?'"

—Bill Cosby

As daunting as these figures are, they don't even take into account incidentals such as travel to and from school, phone calls home (and elsewhere), entertainment, spending money, and various discretionary expenses (like books).

Taken at face value, $7,773 (and especially $20,273) might seem high, but manageable. Unfortunately, if you plan on funding your child's college education, you won't be paying for just one year of school! If college costs were frozen at today's rates, four years of college would cost $31,092 for a public school and $81,092 for a private school. But if you think college costs are frozen, you're living in a dreamland.

A Diller, a Dollar, a Quarter-Million-Dollar Scholar

For decades, college costs have risen at a rate that outstrips inflation. For the last five years, for instance, the annual rise in college expenses has "slowed" to about a five percent hike every year.

What do rising college costs mean to you and your child? Well, for one thing, they mean that if your child is under six years old, you can safely anticipate paying double the current costs by the time your child receives his diploma (see the following table). If you have a newborn, the annual cost of his education will probably rise to nearly three times the current cost by his senior year of college.

Projected College Costs (Assuming a 5 % Annual Increase)

Academic Year	Private College Costs	Public College Costs
1998–99	$20,273	$7,773
1999–2000	$21,287	$8,162
2000–01	$22,351	$8,570
2001–02	$23,469	$8,998
2002–03	$24,642	$9,448
2003–04	$25,874	$9,921
2004–05	$27,168	$10,417
2005–06	$28,526	$10,937
2006–07	$29,952	$11,484
2007–08	$31,450	$12,058
2008–09	$33,023	$12,661
2009–10	$34,674	$13,294
2010–11	$36,407	$13,959
2011–12	$38,228	$14,657
2012–13	$40,139	$15,390
2013–14	$42,146	$16,160
2014–15	$44,253	$16,967
2015–16	$46,466	$17,816
2016–17	$48,789	$18,707
2017–18	$51,228	$19,642
2018–19	$53,790	$20,624

Academic Year	Private College Costs	Public College Costs
2019–20	$56,480	$21,655
2020–21	$59,303	$22,738
2021–22	$62,269	$23,875

Adding up the figures in the table, if your child of the new millennium enters college in the year 2018 and earns his undergraduate degree four years later, you will have shelled out nearly $90,000 if he attends a state school or a whopping $231,842—nearly a quarter of a million dollars—if he chooses a private college!

If inflation gets worse, you can expect to spend even more. At a six percent annual hike, college costs for the same four years (2018–2022) would be $109,055 at a public college and $284,429 at a private institution.

Where's All This Money Coming From?

In all likelihood, you will be expected (by your child and by her chosen college or university) to come up with most of the money to cover your child's tuition and room and board. (Of course, you could just tell your child it's up to her to finance her education. If you do, however, you can probably forget about your child taking care of you in your old age.)

Fortunately, you don't necessarily have to come up with all of the dough by your child's eighteenth birthday. If you can't cover all the exorbitant expenses through your own savings and investments, your child will have other funding options available to her:

➤ **Federal grants.** The federal government currently provides two different kinds of college grants to students in need of financial assistance: Pell Grants and Supplemental Educational Opportunity Grants. Both of these educational grants are based on financial need. If you've saved a significant amount toward your child's college education, however, you will probably not be eligible for federal grants.

➤ **Private grants.** Even if you don't qualify for federal grants, you can still apply for private grants, also called scholarships. Private grants are available from a variety of sources, which may include your high school Parent-Teacher Association, town council, employer, and local organizations such as the Elks, the Masons, or the Rotary Club. Many private scholarships are determined not by need but by some special ability or achievement. Your

Paterniterms

The difference between grants and loans? You do not have to repay the money you receive from a **grant**. You do, however, have to repay money received from a **loan** (though some students choose not to).

child may earn a scholarship based on her high school grade-point average, her college admission test scores, her athletic ability, her musical talents, and, of course, her beauty (think Miss America).

➤ **Federal loans.** The federal government offers loans both to students themselves (Guaranteed Student Loans) and to their parents (Parent Loans for Undergraduate Students, or PLUS loans). Guaranteed Student Loans have a low interest rate (three to five points lower than PLUS loans) and do not require any repayment until after your child leaves school. PLUS loans, in addition to having a higher interest rate, must begin to be repaid within 60 days of the loan. Unfortunately, limits on the amounts of these federal education loans mean that, even if you manage to secure both of them, they probably won't cover your child's expenses at a state college—and won't cover even half of the cost at a private college.

➤ **Personal loans.** If you don't qualify for a grant or scholarship and can't scrape up enough cash through government-backed loans, you may have to take out a personal loan. You can take out a second mortgage, set up a home equity credit line, or borrow against the cash value of your life insurance. As a last resort, you can even obtain a cash advance on your credit cards.

➤ **Work-study programs.** Your child can cover some of her educational expenses by entering a work-study program, sponsored either by the federal government or the college itself. Work-study jobs tend to pay little more than minimum wage, however, so it might make more sense for your child to look for a part-time or summer job that offers better pay.

➤ **Bank robbery.** If everything else fails, you can always hold up a bank. (For legal reasons, I have to point out that *this is just a joke*.)

Father Knows Best

"Because that's where the money is."

—Willie Sutton, when asked why he robbed banks

Investing Wisely in Education

The financing options discussed above are intended to supplement—not replace—the money you save and invest for your child's college education. You can't count on receiving grants; work-study programs and government-sponsored loans will cover only a fraction of the cost of a college education; and if you take out a personal loan, you will pay much more later than you would pay if you started saving and investing now.

So start setting aside as much money as you can, as soon as you can. Even if you can't save enough to cover all your child's college expenses, any money you can save now will be welcome down the road.

How much money will you need to invest? It's hard to say, because it depends on both the increase in college costs over the next decade or two and on the growth rate of the money you invest.

Suppose, for example, the increase in college costs holds steady at five percent until your newborn finishes college. You can probably finance tuition and room and board in full by investing $106 a month (per child) for a state college or $276 a month for a private college this year and increasing your contributions by five percent a year. These figures will be sufficient, however, only if your investments earn an average of at least seven percent a year. Given that the Standard & Poor's 500 Stock Index yielded an annual average return of more than a 17 percent over the last 15 years, a seven percent goal may seem modest. The standard disclaimer of reputable investment firms, however, certainly applies here: Past performance is no guarantee of future results.

The amount you need to invest also depends on the age of your child. If you begin investing as soon as your child is born (or even better, before), you will need to set aside much less per month than if you start when your child is five years old.

Where should you put this money? Well, that depends on how old your child is. The closer he gets to college age, the more conservative your investment strategy should be. If your child is not yet a teenager, the smart money would go into common stocks or stock mutual funds, which traditionally yield a higher return than bonds or money market accounts. Since the financial risk involved in stock investments is also higher than that associated with bonds, you probably shouldn't put all the college fund into stocks. If past performance holds, however, it wouldn't be unwise to put half or more of your money in the stock market.

You may wonder whether to put the assets of your child's college fund in her name or keep the assets in your name. The advantage of putting college funds in your child's name: The first $600 in income earned annually by these investments is tax-free; and the next $600 will be taxed at your child's rate rather than your own.

But the drawbacks of putting these funds in your child's name are significant. If your child applies for financial aid, he will be required to contribute nearly all of his own assets toward tuition and expenses. So substantial assets in his name will drastically reduce his chances of receiving financial aid. If the assets remain in your name, however, you will be required to contribute a much smaller percentage toward your child's educational expenses.

In addition, if you put your college-fund assets in your child's name, there's no guarantee he will use them for college tuition. When he turns 18, your child will have legal control over the account and can use his "college funds" for whatever he pleases: a fancy sports car, sex, drugs, and rock and roll, anything he likes. So think twice before making this transfer.

Bonds—U.S. Treasury bonds, municipal bonds, and corporate bonds—provide more safety than stocks and a steady rate of return. You can also invest in a bond mutual fund rather than purchase bonds (which are often sold in cost-prohibitive denominations of $5,000, $10,000, or $100,000) directly. When investing in bonds, be sure to time the maturity dates so that they correspond to the years when you'll need the money.

U.S. savings bonds don't provide as high a potential return as many other investments, but they are one of the safest investments you can make. An additional plus for savings bonds—at least for most American families—is that if you cash them in to cover college costs, the interest earned is either tax free or taxed at a reduced rate (depending on your income). Only the wealthiest families are fully taxed on savings bonds redeemed to finance higher education.

Unless you exceed certain income limits, you can also deposit up to $500 a year per child in an education I.R.A. Contributions are made from after-tax money, but later distributions—if used for qualified education expenses—will be tax-free.

Daddy Dos and Don'ts

If you have waited until your 40s to have children, you can build your child's college fund by putting as much money as the law allows into an Individual Retirement Account (IRA) or a Keogh plan. Once you have reached age 59^{1}/2—which you will by the time your child is in college—you can withdraw money from your IRA or Keogh to help fund your child's college education without having to pay any penalty.

A Roth I.R.A. can also serve as a college savings account. Contributions are not tax-deductible, but rather taken from after-tax money. After five years, you may withdraw contributions without penalty for any purpose. The key advantage of Roth I.R.A.s: Until you withdraw an amount that equals or exceeds your total contributions, the withdrawal is considered to come from the principal rather than the earnings (making the withdrawal tax-free).

No matter how well you've done in the stock market, by the time your child becomes a teenager you should probably begin shifting your college-fund holdings into more conservative investments. Sure, you might not make as much money, but when your child gets close to college age, it's important that your college fund remains intact. When your child enters her teens, reduce your risk by gradually moving investments into interest-earning securities, short-term bonds, certificates of deposit (CDs), and money market funds.

If you invest regularly, diligently, and wisely, you will go a long way toward paying your child's college bills. You may not be able to cover all the expenses, but if you invest what you can, you'll significantly reduce the damage.

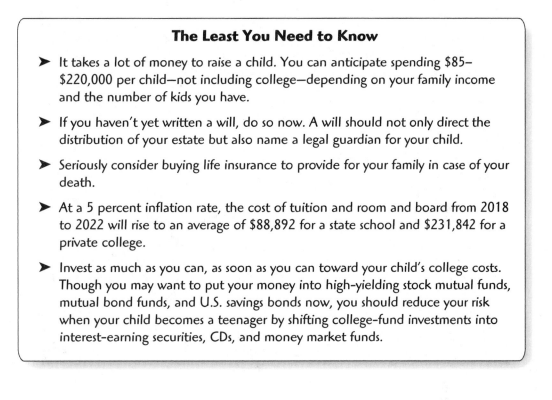

The Least You Need to Know

➤ It takes a lot of money to raise a child. You can anticipate spending $85–$220,000 per child—not including college—depending on your family income and the number of kids you have.

➤ If you haven't yet written a will, do so now. A will should not only direct the distribution of your estate but also name a legal guardian for your child.

➤ Seriously consider buying life insurance to provide for your family in case of your death.

➤ At a 5 percent inflation rate, the cost of tuition and room and board from 2018 to 2022 will rise to an average of $88,892 for a state school and $231,842 for a private college.

➤ Invest as much as you can, as soon as you can toward your child's college costs. Though you may want to put your money into high-yielding stock mutual funds, mutual bond funds, and U.S. savings bonds now, you should reduce your risk when your child becomes a teenager by shifting college-fund investments into interest-earning securities, CDs, and money market funds.

Part 4

Nuts and Bolts: Fathering Toddlers and Preschoolers

Congratulations! You've made it through the first year with your baby. Having fun yet? Good. You'll have even more fun with your baby's first steps (however tottery) and first words (however indecipherable).

Now the mischief-maker begins to emerge. Your toddler will get into everything in the house. Then, during the terrible twos (the only age that comes with a warning label), your child's language skills, physical strength, and coordination will expand dramatically. When she doesn't want to go to bed, she'll tell you in no uncertain terms—and maybe even put up some physical resistance.

But your child will also become increasingly social, great fun to play with, and independent (sometimes defiantly so). Hard to believe, but in just four more years she will be ready to go out into the great big world—or at least kindergarten.

Chapter 15

Helpful Handyman: Childproofing Your Home

In This Chapter

➤ Why childproofing? Why now?

➤ Keeping dangerous objects and substances out of your child's reach

➤ Preventing big falls and minimizing the risk of little ones

➤ Taking steps to avoid burns and electric shocks

➤ Teaching safe behavior

If you feel more comfortable holding a power drill than holding a baby, now is your time to shine. To make your home safe for your little one, you have a lot of home-improvement projects ahead of you.

So whip out those power tools and strap on that tool belt, there's work to be done—and you're just the man to do it.

Don't worry, though, if you're not the most handy handyman in the world. You don't really need to be Norm Abrams, Master Carpenter to childproof your home. In fact, you can probably do everything to make your home childproof with nothing more than a drill, a set of screwdrivers, and a hammer.

Is This Really Necessary?

Why do you even need to childproof your home? After all, you may never have had any accidents more serious than tripping over a throw rug or bumping your knee on the coffee table. How can the same home be so benign for you but a potential house of horrors for your child?

Mini-Magellans and Newtons in the Nursery

The basic reason to childproof your home is, of course, to keep your child safe. Childproofing fulfills an even deeper purpose, however. It encourages your child's growth and development by providing her with a safe learning environment.

Your child is an explorer, an adventurer. That's how she learns. Over the next few years, your child will thoroughly explore every inch of your home that she can reach. At first, she'll just want to put everything she "discovers" in her mouth. But soon she'll start examining everything with much more care. She'll experiment with objects, working to discover the unique properties of every thing in her world:

➤ Does this fit into that?

➤ What happens when I tip this container?

➤ What happens when I drop this object?

➤ What sort of noise can I make when I push this or pull that or throw something else?

Before long, she'll start sorting objects according to similarities and differences (though the categories she uses may be totally incomprehensible to adult eyes).

Your child is a scientist, too. Your home is her laboratory; the objects in it are the raw materials for her experiments. You want to encourage your child, of course, but before you can allow your child the freedom to explore and learn, you need to make sure that anything she can possibly get her hands, feet, or mouth on won't harm her.

Of course, you won't be able to prevent all accidents. Accidents do happen, especially when a child is around. But you can take steps to keep accidents to a minimum and to minimize the chances of serious injury from those that do. These steps are what childproofing is all about.

Once you've made your home as safe as possible, your child can explore to her heart's content, and you and your partner won't have to worry … much.

Right Here, Right Now

When is the best time to childproof? Some parents begin right when their child is born. If that suits your style, fine. But childproofing really isn't necessary as long as your baby remains essentially immobile. After all, how much trouble can he get into when he can't move from place to place? In fact, as long as you make sure to put him down in a safe place (and trim his fingernails regularly), your baby runs little risk of seriously injuring himself during the first few months.

Ideally, you should begin taking at least some child-proofing measures before your child began to crawl. If your child is already a crawler and you haven't yet childproofed your house, do so now. He'll only have more opportunities to get into trouble when he begins to walk.

Just because you've childproofed your house once, however, doesn't mean you're done for good. Each new physical ability your child masters—walking, running, climbing—requires a re-evaluation of your home's safety.

Staying Out of Touch

Your main focus in childproofing is to keep potentially hazardous items in places where your baby can't get to them. For young children, out of sight usually does mean out of mind. And out of touch means out of trouble.

You can use a number of strategies to keep potential dangers out of your child's reach. You can completely remove certain dangers from your home. Others you can move up high, well out of your child's reach. And still others you can store under lock and key. As long as your baby can't get her hands on anything that might harm her, she'll stay relatively safe.

Being a conscientious father, you would, of course, never think of giving your child anything to play with that is:

➤ Heavy enough to damage toes (if—rather, when—dropped)

➤ Made of glass (which becomes quite treacherous when broken)

➤ Sharp along the edges (or anyplace else)

➤ Poisonous or made of toxic materials. (If she can get her hands on it, you can bet she'll put it in her mouth.)

➤ Small enough to swallow (for the same reason)

➤ Made with a string longer than 6". (A young child can strangle herself with a long string.)

But since everything in your child's world is a plaything to her, you'll need to make sure that anything that she can get her hands on—anything kept in unlocked cabinets, drawers, or on open shelves low enough for her to get on her own—meets the same safety criteria.

Locked Up Tight

You cannot remove every possible hazard from your home. Houses need to be cleaned; things need to be repaired; hedges need to be trimmed; medicine has to be on hand. Although you can't rid your house of every potential danger, however, you should do as much as possible to keep them inaccessible to your child.

Paterniterms

Child-safety locks are devices, usually plastic, that make it very difficult for children—and some adults—to open drawers or cabinet doors. Locks for cabinets with double doors fit on the outside, joining the two door handles together. Locks for drawers and single cabinets are installed on the inside, preventing the drawer or door from being opened more than an inch or so. Both kinds of locks can be released fairly easily by adults who know the trick.

Start by installing *child-safety locks* on any low cabinets or drawers that contain anything even remotely dangerous to your child. And when your child becomes a climber, place the locks on high cabinets as well. The following household items should be kept in locked cabinets or behind locked doors:

Daddy Dos and Don'ts

You can leave some low drawers or cabinets unlocked, but only after making sure they don't contain anything potentially dangerous to your child. Your child will enjoy exploring these drawers and cabinets, which might contain child-friendly items, such as plastic cookie cutters and measuring cups, cookie sheets, pots, pans, and pot lids. Remember to check the contents regularly to make sure nothing dangerous has accidentally found its way inside.

➤ Household cleaning products (commonly kept under the kitchen or bathroom sink), such as furniture polish, shoe polish, mothballs, deodorizers, and air fresheners

➤ Plastic bags

➤ Sharp objects, such as knives, cleavers, and scissors

➤ Tools, such as screwdrivers, saws, and hammers

➤ Gardening equipment, such as rakes, hedge clippers, and lawn mowers

➤ Laundry supplies, such as detergent, bleach, and fabric softener

➤ Oil- and gas-based products, such as kerosene, lighter fluid, and charcoal starter

➤ Barbecue tools and supplies

➤ Cosmetics

➤ Pesticides, fertilizers, and plant food

➤ Foods that your baby can choke on, such as nuts, popcorn, and hard candy

➤ Alcohol, cigarettes, and other drugs, including all medications (even vitamins)

Father Figures

The most common cause of poisoning deaths among U.S. children under the age of six is not an obvious toxin such as household cleaners, bleach, or alcohol. According to the American Association of Poison Control Centers, *iron supplements* cause more fatal poisonings among young children than any other cause. So lock away those vitamins.

Better yet, move as many of these items as you can to higher cabinets (and still install child-safety locks). The trouble with using low cabinets is that you—or, more likely, house guests who have no children of their own—may forget to re-lock them. If, for example, you keep both liquid drain cleaner and extra rolls of toilet paper under your bathroom sink, anyone who kindly replaces the toilet paper may unthinkingly leave the drain cleaner accessible to your baby. So move the dangerous items to high cabinets whenever possible.

In addition to keeping them behind locked doors, always keep household cleaners, paints, medicines, and other toxic substances in their original containers. Most toxic substances now come in child-proof—or close to child-proof—containers. Take care never to leave bottles out and unopened just because you're "using" them. Instead, take what you need and immediately recap the bottle and lock it away.

Finally, use hanging planters or high shelves for potentially toxic plants, such as rhododendrons, daffodils, hyacinths, irises, buttercups, lilies of the valley, laurels, willows, and tomato leaves.

Do Not Enter

Contrary to what you may think, you don't necessarily have to childproof every room in your home. Childproofing a basement, garage, workshop, or tool shed would not only be a monumental task, but would most likely make those areas completely non-functional. The smartest and easiest child-proofing strategy for these areas is to make them completely inaccessible by putting locks on the doors.

Locked doors won't do any good, however, unless you and your partner get in the habit of locking them. You'll need to pull the door tight and lock it no matter which side of the door you're on.

In most of these areas, young children are not safe even when accompanied by an adult. A young child, for instance, does not belong in a workshop. If you're doing any kind of work there at all, you can't safely supervise your child at the same time. No child can safely play on the floor while you're running your band saw or drill press. Keep your child out of these areas altogether.

The locked-door policy, of course, applies to all doors that lead outside, too. Keeping a dead-bolt locked will prevent the frightening possibility that your little one might wander outside on her own. In a few years, when your child gets old enough to lock and unlock doors on her own, you may find it useful to attach bells to your door (like those in the shops of old black-and-white movies). That way, you'll hear it whenever your child opens the door. (This trick may also come in handy when your baby becomes a teenager.)

Daddy Dos and Don'ts

If your child eats something poisonous—or you suspect he might have—contact your pediatrician or a poison control center immediately. Until you have spoken to a doctor, however, do *not* give your child syrup of ipecac, which will cause him to vomit.

Daddy Dos and Don'ts

If you have reserved one or two rooms exclusively for you, your partner, and adult company, making them completely inaccessible to your child, to be fair you should make the other rooms entirely child-safe. Your child should be allowed to roam freely and safely through the rooms she spends the most time in: her bedroom and the family playroom, for example. Exercise special care to make sure these rooms are completely safe for your child.

Keep Away

In addition to keeping hazardous items behind locked doors, you might want to consider removing certain pieces of furniture and houseware and putting them in storage for a few years. These include delicate decorative objects, glass-topped tables, any furniture with very sharp corners, wobbly wall units (such as bookcases), table lamps, and anything else that might injure your child or break if he gets his hands on it.

Daddy Dos and Don'ts

With certain rooms, such as the bathroom or your child's bedroom, your main concern is not keeping the door locked so that your child can't get in, but making sure she doesn't accidentally lock—or just shut—herself in. With these rooms, try putting tape over the latch or lock to keep it flush with the door.

If you and your partner don't want to put some of these items in storage, at least move any decorative objects kept on coffee tables, end tables, and bedside tables to a high shelf or mantelpiece. Similarly, glass or china dishes and crystal glasses should be either moved to high cabinets or placed in storage until your child is older.

Tablecloths can pose a danger to your child, too, especially if you keep candlesticks, a centerpiece, or other decorative items on the table. By grabbing one corner of the tablecloth, your child could pull everything on the table down on top of him. To avoid this, you may want to forego using any for a couple of years.

To prevent a similar disaster in the kitchen, store small appliances (coffee makers, can openers, blenders, and food processors, for example) well away from the edge of the counter, and tuck or wrap up the electric cords behind them. If your toddler can reach the cord or the appliance, he can easily pull the whole thing down on top of himself. In addition, you should make it a habit to unplug appliances when you're not using them, making it impossible for your child to turn them on by accident.

Though it is sometimes difficult to enforce, pet food and pet bowls should also be kept out of your child's reach when your pets aren't using them. The combination of exposed food and dirty bowls provide an ideal breeding ground for bacteria.

Your baby's bedroom should be kept completely safe except for such diaper-changing supplies as diaper cream, diaper pins, and so on. Store these items out of your baby's reach (but well within your reach so that you'll never have any reason to leave your baby alone on the changing table). You can put one or two shelves on the wall behind the changing table, or you can install a wall hanging that has handy pockets designed specifically for changing supplies.

Your partner's purse probably contains many objects—cosmetics, coins, keys, and so on—that could be dangerous for your child to get his hands on. To keep her purse off limits to your child, make sure she hangs it on a high hook or the top "branch" of a coat tree whenever she comes inside.

Similarly, coins, jewelry, pins, buttons of all kinds, and office supplies (staples, paper clips, thumbtacks, and the like) should be kept not only out of reach, but out of sight as well. Store these items on top of your dresser, on high shelves, or in high cabinets.

Higher hooks may also be necessary for storing ties, belts, and scarves in your closets. Search your closets for any old dry-cleaning bags, which can suffocate a small child, and get rid of them at once. When you have clothes or blankets dry-cleaned, dispose of the bags as soon as you bring them home.

You can no longer safely keep shampoos, conditioners, soaps, and razors on the edge of the tub, where your child can get his hands on them. If you don't have a shower caddy (miniature shelf that hangs from the shower nozzle), get one now.

Finally, power tools, nails, screws, hammers, saws, screwdrivers, and other tools of the trade should be stored well out of your child's reach, ideally along a wall at the back of a tall workbench in that securely locked workshop. If you don't have a workshop or workbench, however, move your tools into high, closed drawers or cabinets that your child can't reach. Even ladders, when possible, should be hung on high hooks in the basement or garage, keeping them safely out of your child's reach.

Hazardous Waste

Though often overlooked during childproofing, wastebaskets and kitchen garbage pails are treasure-troves of objects hazardous to young children. If she can reach it, a young child will quickly dump any wastebasket or garbage pail. In addition to being messy and unsanitary, this "toxic waste dumping" can be very dangerous.

Anything that you've thrown away will immediately become accessible to your child: used razors, empty pens, toxic printer cartridges, spoiled food, expired medications, poisonous cosmetics, almost-empty bottles of household cleaners or laundry supplies, plastic bags, and things too tiny for you ever to have intentionally given your baby to play with. All the work you've done to keep these objects out of the hands of your child will be undone if she can get at them when they're "thrown away."

To prevent the dumping of hazardous waste

> ➤ Minimize the number of wastebaskets and garbage pails in your home. The more you have, the harder it is to monitor what goes in each of them.

> ➤ Think twice before you throw anything in an open wastebasket.

Father Figures

According to the Consumer Product Safety Commission, "desk supplies" account for five times as many children's visits to emergency rooms as fireworks do. So consider installing a child-safety lock on at least one desk drawer—and be careful what you put in your office wastebasket.

➤ Get garbage pails with secure lids (available in a variety of sizes) rather than open wastebaskets or garbage pails with lids that open easily.

➤ Empty your wastebaskets regularly.

Similarly, in your baby's bedroom, try to keep the diaper pail as inaccessible as possible. This is not always practical or even feasible. But if you put your baby's changing station next to a closet, you can keep the diaper pail behind a closed closet door. In any case, make sure it has a secure lid that will keep both diapers and their smell locked up tight.

Short Falls

Once you've made poisonous objects and choking hazards inaccessible to your child, you'll need to turn your attention toward trying to prevent the second most common cause of accidents among young children: nasty falls.

You can't escape the fact that your child will suffer some falls. He'll fall as he learns to pull himself into a standing position. He'll fall as he learns to walk. He'll fall as he learns to run. He'll even fall for no apparent reason whatsoever. Although you can't stop him from falling, you can make it safer for your child to fall.

A fall from a height that might give you a couple aches and bruises could prove much more serious for your young child. His bones are thinner and less set than yours. To avoid the possibility of traumatic injury, you need to do all you can to prevent serious falls.

What Goes Up Must Come Down

Stairs are particularly hazardous for crawlers and toddlers. To keep your crawler or toddler from trying to master the difficult art of going up and down stairs unsupervised, install safety gates at both the top and the bottom of every staircase in your house. Most parents readily concede the need for a safety gate at the top of a staircase, but some question the need for one at the bottom. After all, your baby isn't about to fall "up" stairs.

True, but if your baby steals away and climbs the staircase (and especially if she encounters a locked gate at the top), she could very easily fall back down the stairs. What goes up really does come down—and you don't want it to be your child.

What kind of safety gate should you choose? Basically, you have two options: those secured on one side with hinges and closed with a latch on the other side, and those held in place by the pressure of expandable rods against a wall on one side and a newel post on the other.

A pressure gate works just fine for the bottom of the stairs. If the gate pops loose because your baby bangs on it, uses it to pull herself up, or falls against it, she won't have far to fall. (In this case, she actually *will* fall upstairs.) You will no doubt hear the crash, come running, and find your baby lying on top of the gate. But if this happens at the top of the stairs, the gate may come crashing all the way down the staircase—with your baby right behind it (or on top of it). Don't take this chance. Instead, install a latched gate at the top of every staircase.

In addition to installing safety gates, you also need to install railings on any staircases that don't already have them. An open stairway is an invitation to disaster.

When installing a stair railing (or checking an existing one), make sure the bars are no more than four inches apart. Anything bigger and your baby might get her head wedged between them.

The same 4" rule applies to the spacing of bars and railings on outdoor porches, balconies, and decks. You should also avoid any crossbars (horizontal bars) that might allow your baby to climb up and over the top.

Of course, you can't keep your child away from stairs forever. Indeed, the sooner your child starts negotiating the stairs, the better. After all, it's a skill she will have to master some day. She should never practice, however, unless you, your partner, or someone else you trust is right there with her every step of the way. Until both you and your child become confident that she can handle climbing up and down stairs, your baby needs a "spotter."

Daddy Dos and Don'ts

Since a pressure gate is not permanently secured to a wall or newel post, you can move it into almost any standard doorway. This can keep your child safely inside a baby-safe room, temporarily turning the entire room into one of the world's biggest playpens.

So when your child seems ready to crawl up stairs, stay with her, ready to catch her if she falls. Once your child has mastered the somewhat easier task of climbing up stairs, you can teach her to come down them—at first by crawling backwards. Again, stay just one step below her, ready to avert disaster, until she reaches the bottom. Continue to spot your child even after you feel confident in her ability on the stairs. It's just too easy for a young toddler to become distracted, even while concentrating on the challenge of negotiating a staircase.

Avoiding Window Pains

Like doors, windows should be kept locked so that your child can't open them (on purpose or by accident) and fall out. Unfortunately, unless you have central air conditioning, you will need to open windows when it gets hot. When you have to open the windows, try one or more of the following:

➤ Install grates on the outside of windows—especially upper-story windows—to make falls virtually impossible. (Many U.S. cities require landlords to install such grates apartment windows above ground level.)

➤ Open only the top half of a window, not the bottom half.

➤ Install window guards that prevent windows from being opened more than four inches.

Unfortunately, windows carry additional risks besides falling. Large plate-glass windows and sliding doors are sometimes nearly invisible; a young child on the run might crash right through them. To make plate-glass windows and doors more visible, you might place stickers, reflective tape, toys with suction cups, or stick-on toys like Colorforms at your child's eye level.

The final hazard posed by windows is not the windows themselves, but the cords of blinds, shades, and drapes. Toddlers and young children can easily get tangled in cords that hang down too far—and even strangle themselves. To prevent this, get in the habit of tying up or shortening all cords so that your child can't reach them.

Refinishing the Furniture

Another way to minimize the injuries caused by nasty falls involves rearranging or removing certain pieces of furniture. Moving your child's crib—and all other furniture that might tempt him to climb—away from the windows, for instance, can eliminate one source of dangerous falls.

You might also consider removing any glass-topped tables (especially low ones) and tables with sharp corners. If you decide not to remove end or coffee tables with sharp corners, be sure to fit them with rubber or plastic bumpers to soften the blow if your baby's head crashes into one of them. Take the time to cushion the underside of table corners as well; your crawler is more likely to raise his head and hit the underside of a table than to fall down and hit the top.

You also might be wise to put folding chairs in storage for a few years. Folding chairs collapse far too easily, especially with a toddler or preschooler standing on them. Your child may crash to the floor, or his fingers or toes may get trapped and crushed by the collapsing joint.

Free-standing shelves, which to the child's eye look a lot like a ladder or a set of stairs, pose another risk. To minimize the risk posed by free-standing shelves, secure them to a wall with screws. Although this won't prevent your child from attempting to scale Mount Bookshelf, it will stop him from accidentally pulling the shelves down on top of him when he does.

Along similar lines, you may decide to furnish your child's bedroom with low, open shelves rather than tall

Daddy Dos and Don'ts

If you decide you need a toy chest to keep your child's room uncluttered, make sure it has a device to prevent the lid from slamming down and crushing tiny fingers. Most contemporary toy chests have protective devices already installed. If you buy or inherit an antique toy chest, however, you may need to build your own lid-slamming protection. You can easily do this by gluing small blocks of cork onto the front inside corners of the chest.

shelves, closed-door cabinets, or toy chests. Low, open shelves allow your toddler or preschooler to get the toys or books he wants all by himself. This not only increases your child's opportunities to exercise his independence, but makes it unnecessary for him to climb on the furniture to get something.

Rugs and carpeting can soften the impact of your toddler's repeated falls. But if you have rugs in a room your toddler spends a lot of time in, you'd do well to secure them to prevent them from slipping out from under his feet. Non-skid rug pads deepen the cushioning effect of rugs and keep them from sliding around on the floor. While your child is indoors, you'd also be wise to leave him in bare feet (or, if it's cold, in slipper socks with non-skid bottoms). Shoes actually make it more difficult for a young toddler to walk, and regular socks make slips and falls more likely.

In the bathroom, where a wet tiled floor and a running child can spell disaster, it's especially important to keep rugs and bath mats securely in place. Since the floor of a wet tub can also be treacherous, cover it with a rubber, non-skid bath mat. Cover the spigot in the tub with a foam "tub guard" or drape a washcloth over it to soften the impact of any bumps or scrapes. Finally, make it a firm rule never to stand or jump in the tub.

The Heat Is On

Heat, fire, and electricity are very dangerous for young children. Unfortunately, you can't really do without them. Houses get cold in the winter; gas stoves won't cook without fire; and electricity is indispensable in the modern home. So, rather than severing your ties with the local gas and electric companies, focus on keeping the gas and electricity you use safe for your child.

Don't Get Burned

Burns are a common source of injury to small children. Yet you can minimize the possibility of serious burns with a little attention to their most common causes: heat sources, cooking surfaces, ovens, fireplaces, and hot-water sources.

Exposed radiators, now found almost exclusively in older homes, can get so hot that a young child can burn herself by touching them. If you have an exposed radiator, enclose it in a wooden cabinet or cover.

Space heaters pose even more danger. Since they turn a lovely bright orange when they're on, they naturally attract a toddler's curiosity. So if she is already mobile, *never* use a space heater in the same room as your child. Better yet, avoid using one altogether.

In the kitchen, consider installing plastic covers on the controls of your stove, oven, or range, or remove the knobs when you're not cooking. These knobs will fascinate your young child, and you don't want her turning on the stove whenever she wants.

Oven doors can be dangerous, too, even when you're not baking or broiling. An oven door can crush little fingers that try to open it only to have it snap back shut. So if your oven door comes equipped with a lock, get in the habit of using it.

If you have a fireplace, make sure that the protective screen is the right size, in good condition, and fits securely. All matches, including fireplace matches, should, of course, be stowed out of your child's reach.

Hot water is another common source of burns. If you haven't done so recently, check the temperature of your hot-water heater. Make sure to set the temperature at a maximum of 130 degrees Fahrenheit, a temperature that will not cause any serious burns unless your child is exposed to it for more than 30 seconds. Even after resetting the hot-water heater, however, make sure to check the temperature of the bath water before putting your child in the tub. (Young kids, bizarre creatures that they are, actually prefer barely warm water to hot water anyway.)

Shock Treatments

You can reduce much of the risk of electric shocks and electric fires fairly easily. First, check to make sure that all electric outlets are grounded (that is, they have holes for three-pronged plugs rather than just two).

Second, make sure that you have made *every* electric outlet in your home inaccessible to your child. In the case of outlets used for relatively permanent objects (TVs, floor lamps, stereos, and computers, for example), use a child-safety outlet box that fits over both plug and outlet. A safety box makes it virtually impossible for your baby to pull the plug (unless he is unusually handy with a screwdriver, which he shouldn't be able to get his hands on anyway). With outlets that get a lot of play (frequent plugging and unplugging), use two-pronged plastic outlet shields that fit tightly into a socket. Once the safety devices are in place, all you need to do is make it a habit to put a shield or guard box over the outlet after using it.

Electric cords can be hazardous, too. Your toddler can trip over them, of course, but he also may find it comforting to chew on them, especially when teething. Hide as many electric cords as possible under rugs or behind furniture to keep them out of sight. You probably can't hide every cord, however. If you must leave a few exposed, secure them in place with electric cord staples or heavy-duty tape.

Finally, check all electric cords regularly for signs of wear and tear (or teeth marks). If you notice any frayed or cracked cords, replace them immediately.

Where There's Smoke ...

Despite all the precautions you may take to prevent a fire, you should still plan for that frightening possibility. If a fire does start in your home, you need to know exactly what to do.

First, you need some sort of warning that there's a fire. Make sure you have working smoke detectors in place on every floor—and ideally (and in some states by law) in every bedroom. Since they won't do any good if they're not working, replace the batteries in all of your home's smoke detectors every six months.

You may be able to put out a small fire on your own, but only if you have a working fire extinguisher. You should definitely keep one in your kitchen—and ideally at least one on every floor of your home. Like smoke detectors, fire extinguishers should be checked regularly to make sure they work.

Lastly, plan what to do in case of an emergency. You and your partner should come up with at least one fire-escape route from every room of your home. (This may require installing rope ladders in the windows of some upper-story bedrooms.) That way, even if the worst case scenario happens, you'll be able to make the best of it.

Something's Out There!

Before you start patting yourself on the back for a job well done, take a look outside. If you have a yard, you need to eliminate certain hazards before your child can safely play in it.

First, a little landscaping. Level the ground in your yard as much as possible to eliminate ditches and holes that might fill with water. A large puddle not only represents a drowning hazard for your young child, it can quickly become a breeding ground for all sorts of bugs.

Mow your lawn regularly to prevent grass from growing high enough to encourage ticks and other insects to make your yard their home. If your yard doesn't offer much shade, you might also want to consider adding a tree or two to help protect your baby's delicate skin from the sun.

If you put up a swing set (which will provide your child with a lot of fun for years to come), make sure to put a couple of inches of sand, wood chips, or other loose material underneath it to cushion any falls. Also, regularly check the swing set for rust and exposed bolts and screws. Any bolt that your child can reach should have a protective plastic cover.

If you have a swimming pool, put up a fence to keep your little one out. If you have a wading or kiddie pool, empty the water after every use and never let your child "swim" unsupervised.

Finally, good fences make good neighbors. You can keep your yard safe for your child by putting up a fence or growing thick hedges, which not only keep your child inside the yard, but keep unwelcome animals out.

Safety First

In addition to enhancing the safety of your home through various improvements, you may need to alter your behavior to keep it safe.

In the kitchen, for instance, make sure to use the back burners of your stove or range rather than the front burners whenever possible. When you're cooking, turn all pot handles toward the rear of the stove. And never hold your baby while using the stove or oven.

In the bedroom, avoid giving your baby an electric blanket; a wet diaper and an electric blanket can have shocking consequences. Also, get in the habit of pulling up the side rail of the crib to its locked position every time you put your baby in the crib (even if just for a minute). It might even prove worthwhile to develop the habit of double-checking, just to make sure.

Father Figures

One cup of boiling liquid can cover as much as 80 percent of your baby's body with third-degree burns. So exercise caution with your hot beverages. If you drink hot tea or coffee, never put your cup where your little one can reach it.

When your child gets old enough for a "big bed," try starting him off with a mattress placed directly on the floor. Or, move one side of the bed against a wall and use a temporary safety rail on the open side.

To keep dangerous drugs out of your child's hands, *never* leave a medicine bottle out as a reminder to take the medication. Instead, write a note or set an alarm if you or your partner have to take a particular medication daily.

Teach Your Children Well

Once you've reduced or eliminated as many dangers as possible from your home, you can start teaching your baby about the ones that remain. From about six months on, a sharp "No!" works as a deterrent to danger. Your baby will quickly grasp that "No!" means she's doing something she shouldn't be doing. So use this as your first tool in teaching your child the rules of safety.

Your baby will understand many words long before she speaks—and even then she will comprehend many more words than she can say herself. Around her first birthday, you can begin teaching her with words like, "Ow! That's sharp! Don't touch!" or "Blecch! Poison! Don't touch!" Be dramatic to drive the point home and repeat the lesson often; infants and toddlers almost always need more than one lesson in order to learn something.

With some safety rules, you can set up visual cues as signals to your child. For instance, you might decide to make it a practice to turn on the oven light whenever you or your partner is baking or broiling. A few words can then teach your child to keep a safe distance away whenever the light is on.

Before long, your child will begin understanding—and usually obeying—your safety rules. If you don't pile the rules on too thick, you'll soon see your child absorbing and adopting them as her own. She'll stop at a street corner and hold her hand up for you to take. She won't pretend that the bathtub is a trampoline. She'll buckle her own seatbelt whenever she gets in the car. Who knows, someday she might even stick to the speed limit when she's driving your car.

In Case of Emergency ...

Despite your best efforts, you will probably not escape parenthood without at least one or two accidents or illnesses that qualify as emergencies. What will you do? Well, it pays to be prepared. In addition to maintaining a well-stocked first-aid kit and taking a class in CPR (see Chapter 10), you should take the time to prepare an emergency information card and place a copy next to every phone in your home.

Your emergency information cards should include the following:

➤ Your name, your partner's name, and your child's name

➤ Your child's age, weight, blood type, and any allergies or special medical conditions

➤ Your address and phone number (in case a relative or baby-sitter has to make the call)

➤ Both of your work addresses and phone numbers

➤ Your pediatrician's name, address, and phone number

➤ The address and phone number of the nearest hospital

➤ The names, addresses, and phone numbers of nearby relatives or neighbors who might be helpful during an emergency

➤ The phone numbers of the police, fire department, and poison-control center

With any luck, you'll never need to use this card. But if you do, you'll be glad it's there.

Start All Over Again

Think you're done childproofing? Satisfied that you've made your entire house completely childproof (though really there's no such thing)? Good. Now put it to the test.

You could, of course, use your child as a guinea pig. (Over the next few years he will undoubtedly find things you missed.) But for the first test, it's much safer to use yourself or your partner as test subjects.

Start by getting down on your hands and knees and crawling through each room. Look around at about the same height as your baby (or maybe even a little taller since he's growing so fast). Using your "crawler's-eye" view, search every corner of every room.

What do you see? What catches your eye? What can you reach? Do you see that outlet behind the end table—the one you forgot about because you never use it? Do you see those paper clips on the floor under your desk? Can you reach that cord for the venetian blinds? Make sure you didn't miss any small objects that your baby could try to eat. You can bet he'll probably find them if you don't.

Keep in mind that if you're on your hands and knees and can reach something, your child can get his hands on it, too. Estimate your child's strength and tug a little harder than that (since we tend to underestimate a baby's strength) on anything that you can reach. Make sure that you have removed all obvious hazards or at least have placed physical impediments in the way to keep them off limits for your child.

Childproofing is not a one-time chore; it is an unending job that requires constant vigilance. Even after completely childproofing your home, however, you will need to keep an eye on your baby. Through his explorations, your child will discover dangers you never thought of. So remain close, alert, and aware of what your baby is doing. Nothing will keep your child as safe as your watchful eye.

The Least You Need to Know

➤ Your child will explore everything she can get her hands on. So make sure that anything she can get her hands on is safe.

➤ Lock away, move up high, or completely remove anything in your home that is poisonous, sharp, heavy, made of glass, small enough to fit in your child's mouth, or that comes with a long string.

➤ Any room that you can't make completely safe should be made completely inaccessible to your child.

➤ No matter how diligently you childproof, your child will find a way to have an accident. Prepare yourself for emergencies by posting emergency information cards, planning fire-escape routes, and learning CPR.

➤ The best way to evaluate—and fine-tune—your childproofing efforts is to get down on your hands and knees and do a test run. Anything you can reach, your child can reach.

Chapter 16

Beating the Bedtime Blues

In This Chapter

➤ Establishing relaxing bedtime routines

➤ Teaching your baby to fall asleep on his own

➤ Eliminating midnight snacks

➤ Dealing with sleep disturbances

➤ Coping with a bedwetting problem

Whether their children are four weeks old or four years old, one thing nearly all parents seem to want is a good night's sleep. Catching up on all the sleep you have missed since your child was born might be impossible, but is one good night's sleep too much to ask?

Fortunately, when your baby reaches about six months, you can take steps to help her become a sound sleeper. Although most babies can sleep through the night by this age, there's no guarantee that yours will.

Whether she's eight months old, eighteen months old, or three years old, your child needs to learn three skills before she will begin sleeping straight through for eight hours or more:

➤ Going to sleep by herself

➤ Eliminating midnight feedings

➤ Drifting back to sleep when something wakes her in the middle of the night

Your child will have to master all these skills eventually, so you might as well start teaching her now. After all, the sooner you and your partner can help her learn them, the sooner the three of you can settle down to a long winter's nap.

Sleeping Like a Baby

Newborns tend to sleep a lot. Unfortunately, because they have small stomachs and need frequent feedings, newborns seldom sleep for more than a few hours at a shot.

Father Figures

The average newborn sleeps about 16^1/$_2$ hours a day for the first month, and then about 15^1/$_2$ hours a day for the next few months. The number of hours your baby sleeps may be much more or much less. Some babies sleep as many as 20–22 hours a day, whereas others sleep for as few as 10 hours. Either extreme is considered "normal.

Daddy Dos and Don'ts

Try to take a nap or two during the day. Even if you don't fall asleep, 15–20 minutes of shuteye can reinvigorate you. In addition, alter your schedule so that you sleep more when the baby sleeps at night. Once your baby settles down for the night (or at least the first few hours of the night), don't stay up too much longer yourself. Get to bed so that you can get a reasonable amount of rest.

That's why most parents of newborns have such dark circles under their eyes. Adults often have difficulty adjusting to the sleep rhythms of a newborn baby. In all probability, you and your partner are not used to taking three-hour naps or splitting your nighttime sleep into three-hour segments. Like many new parents, you may persist in observing your usual bedtime, wake at the usual hour (or perhaps an hour or two earlier), and then wonder why you're so tired. (Could it have something to do with being awakened two or three times during the night and, unlike the baby, needing more than 30 seconds to drift back to sleep?)

Babies tend to sleep very soundly unless some sudden disturbance wakes them. Normal noise levels (even steady loud noises like the hum of a vacuum or the swish of a dishwasher) and even bright lights will probably not wake your child. Though you may want to avoid blowing a bugle, setting off an alarm, or dropping an encyclopedia next to his crib, you probably don't need to tiptoe around the house or whisper.

In fact, it's probably a good idea *not* to establish a cocoon of dark silence around your sleeping baby. If you do, he will soon start to react to normal noises as if they were sudden noises. The slightest disturbance may wake him. In short, you may very well train him to be a light sleeper.

Instead, go about your business as usual. With the exception of loud, sharp, sudden noises, little will wake your child other than the demands of his body:

➤ Hunger

➤ Gas

➤ A dirty diaper

➤ A stuffy nose

➤ Feeling too hot or too cold

➤ Some other cause of pain or distress

Rites of Passage

Infants sleep so much that you may not think you need to pay much attention to how your baby goes to sleep or how long she stays asleep during the first few months of her life. But establishing good sleep patterns begins with infancy—as does forming bad sleep habits. If, for instance, you or your partner habitually nurses (or bottle-feeds) your baby to sleep (so that she actually falls asleep while eating), she will come to depend on your comforting presence and attention to fall asleep.

Young children—whether infants, toddlers, or preschoolers—tend to like routines, which establish a sense of security in their day-to-day lives. And whether you realize it or not, you have probably already established a bedtime routine for your baby. Unfortunately, you may have unwittingly set in place a bedtime routine that depends on you or your partner as a constant presence. If so, you need to establish a new routine that encourages your baby to fall asleep on her own—or get used to playing an active role in getting your child to sleep for many years to come.

To change your child's bedtime routine, start by establishing a consistent bedtime and fairly regular naptimes. This doesn't mean that your child has to go to sleep at 7:30 on the dot every night. If she took a long nap late in the afternoon, your child might not be tired. If she took only a short nap, she may collapse a little earlier. Remember to take these kinds of circumstances into account.

If possible, however, avoid disrupting your baby's sleep schedule. An extra-long nap, for example, will probably push her bedtime back, which will influence when she next awakes. This, in turn, will carry into the next day, making it harder to re-establish routine naptimes and bedtimes. Similarly, if you keep your infant up late, her over-tiredness may cause her to sleep more fitfully in the night. She may then try to make up for the lack of rest with an extra-long nap or two the next day, which will make it hard for her to go to sleep at her usual bedtime that night, and so on, and so on.

Daddy Dos and Don'ts

When your infant wakes in the middle of the night, the longer you wait to attend to him, the more distressed he is likely to become, and the harder time he'll have getting back to sleep. On the other hand, if you respond immediately to every whimper, you'll train your baby to wake with every minor start and depend on you to fall back asleep. So try to take the middle ground. Don't jump up the instant your baby makes a noise in the night, but if the whimpers persist for a few minutes or escalate to cries, go to your child as soon as you can.

Daddy Dos and Don'ts

While trying to establish or stick to a fairly regular sleep schedule, remain flexible. Again, adhere to the middle ground. Automatically plopping your baby into the crib at "bedtime," even when you can tell she's not tired, may make it harder for her to go to sleep in the future. It's even worse to force your baby to stay up until bedtime if she seems ready to collapse an hour or two earlier. Studies have shown that over-tired babies actually sleep less restfully and wake up more often than babies who go to sleep when they're tired.

The Calm Before the Snore

When creating a bedtime routine for your child, make sure to choose quiet and relaxing activities that promote a warm, loving, happy, and calm atmosphere in your baby's bedroom (or your baby's corner of your bedroom). Rowdy play with your child is fun for both of you, but it makes no sense right before bed. Instead of crashing, your baby will become energized by the excitement, making it even harder for him to fall asleep.

Father Knows Best

"People who say they sleep like a baby usually don't have one."

—Leo Burke

Daddy Dos and Don'ts

If at all possible, you and your partner should avoid nursing or bottle-feeding your baby to sleep. A baby who regularly falls asleep while feeding will not only form the habit of needing a meal at bedtime, but whenever he wakes in the middle of the night as well. Some experts advise parents to feed their babies as soon as they wake up, rather than just before bed. By feeding your baby first, then allowing him to play or cuddle, you avoid training your baby to associate feeding with sleeping—and help teach him to fall asleep by himself.

The following bedtime activities have worked for generations of parents:

➤ An after-dinner stroller ride, which can soothe your baby with rhythmic motion while dusk brings the day to an end.

➤ A warm, relaxing bath an hour or so before bedtime. (See Chapter 9 for tips on bathing your little one.)

➤ Changing into pajamas or a nightgown, which can become a cue that bedtime is drawing near.

➤ Nursing, bottle-feeding, or, when he gets a little older, snacking a half hour or so before bedtime. A relatively full stomach can promote drowsiness and keep your baby sleeping longer before waking.

➤ Darkening the room, by drawing the shades or closing the blinds, can help induce the right atmosphere for sleep. If your baby (or later your toddler) doesn't like complete darkness, a small night light will usually do the trick.

➤ Singing songs or putting on a tape or CD of lullabies.

➤ Rhythmic motion—rocking in a rocking chair, slowly walking and swaying, or doing gentle knee bends while cradling your baby in your arms—can have a hypnotic effect on your baby.

➤ Comfort items like a baby blanket or a favorite teddy bear can help keep your baby calm.

➤ Gentle massage or soft caresses while your baby lies in the crib can help calm and relax him.

➤ Sucking, whether on a pacifier or his thumb may help your baby soothe himself enough to drop off to sleep.

➤ Saying "good night" or some other sweet parting words brings a close to your special, quiet time together.

When your infant becomes a toddler (and even when he becomes a preschooler), he might still enjoy many of these activities before bed. But your toddler or preschooler also might enjoy it if you add or substitute one of the following:

➤ Reading books or reciting nursery rhymes, which allows your soothing voice to lull your child into a drowsy state.

➤ Telling bedtime stories, especially ones that feature your child (or someone just like him) or you when you were a child as the hero.

➤ Looking around the room with him and saying good night to some of the animals, dolls, and other objects in his room—just like the bunny does in *Good Night, Moon.*

➤ Helping him put all his teddy bears and other stuffed animals "to bed." Your child, of course, gets to be tucked in last.

With a few of these suggestions—and perhaps a few of your own—you can create a bedtime routine that will help your baby fall asleep for months or even years to come.

Try to keep it relatively simple. Choose activities or strategies that you won't mind doing every night for the next few years—because you probably will be. Also, make sure that whatever you incorporate into your child's bedtime routine is something that either you or your partner—or on occasion, a friend, relative, or other sitter—can do.

No matter what you choose to include in your baby's bedtime routine, try to spend the last 15–30 minutes of his day near your baby's crib or toddler's bed. Ideally, you will end the bedtime routine and put your child to bed while he's drowsy—neither wide awake nor fast asleep. This will give your baby the valuable practice of falling asleep on his own.

Breaking Up Is Hard to Do

What if your baby has already grown accustomed to your presence when she falls asleep? What if your wife has always nursed her to sleep, or one of you has always given her a bottle? What if your child is already one year old (or two or even three), and every night either you or your partner still has to pull out your entire bag of tricks—nursing, feeding, reading, singing, holding, rocking, cuddling, massaging, taking her for a drive—just to get her to go to sleep? Can you break these bad habits without breaking your child's heart—or your own?

Does Your Child Need You to Stay—Or Merely Want You to Stay?

The skill of falling asleep on her own is something your child will have to learn sooner or later. The longer you wait, the harder it will be to break the habit of falling asleep in your arms or at your partner's breast. In fact, if you wait too long—for instance, until your child is a toddler or, worse, until after you've moved her out of the crib and into a big bed—you will find it much more difficult to get her to go to bed on her own. Your child will soon figure out that just because you put her to bed doesn't mean she has to stay there.

In the first few months, things were different. When your baby cried, she absolutely needed something: food, a diaper change, another blanket, and so on. But by the age of six months, your baby has learned to cry not only to signal that she *needs* something but also that she *wants* something. And though you have a parental duty to fulfill your baby's needs as best you can, you do not have an obligation to gratify all her desires.

Certainly, your baby *wants* you or your partner to stay with her or hold her or suckle her until she falls asleep. Wouldn't you? But even though it may have become a long-standing habit, your baby does not necessarily *need* you to do any of these things in order to fall asleep. Unless you plan on moving into her college dorm room with her in 17 or 18 years, your baby needs to learn how to get to sleep by herself.

The key, at first, lies in timing; put your baby down when she's very sleepy but not actually asleep. If you put your baby in her crib too soon, she'll pop up and start screaming her head off. If you put her down too late, then she's fallen asleep in your arms again. But if you time it just right, your baby won't have the energy to object for too long.

Oh, she'll object all right. This is not how it's supposed to be, she'll think. No fair, you're changing the rules. Everything's been fine up to now, but now you're ruining everything! Why have you abandoned me?

So, to let you know that she wants (but not necessarily needs) you to come back, your baby will cry out. Then what do you do?

Making Hard Choices: Which Is the Lesser Evil

Basically, you have three options, none of which your child will like a heck of a lot:

➤ **The crying game.** Let your baby cry himself to sleep. After saying good night, leave the room and don't return no matter how hard your baby cries. This may

216

go on, for anywhere from 20 minutes to more than an hour, at least for the first night or two. Although it may seem like a cruel shock to the child and a sign of heartlessness on the part of the parents, those who stick with this method generally report success, with the time spent crying quickly dropping to five or ten minutes within a few nights. Within a week, many babies subjected to this method go to sleep by themselves with little or no fuss.

For some children, however, this method is too traumatic. Sleep becomes terrifying and dangerous. From the moment you put him down in the crib, your baby may desperately pull himself up to his feet and start screaming and trying to cling to you. Bedtime becomes a torment for the baby—and for his parents.

➤ **I'll be back.** If the "crying game" seems unbearably cruel to you or your partner, you might have better success by moderating this strategy with periodic check-ins. After saying good night, leave the room, but then return every few minutes (unless your baby has already stopped crying and settled down). Or, if he's old enough to understand (and understanding comes much sooner than his ability to express it himself), let him know before you leave that you'll be back to check on him in five (or three or seven) minutes. Be sure to keep this promise; your child needs to trust you, to know that he can depend on you, and to learn that you can go away but that you'll always come back if he really needs you.

When you do return, try to calm your baby any way you can without picking him up. Offer a pat or stroke on the back or the head and soft words of comfort. Try to be reassuring but relatively boring. In other words, do not try to entertain him to get him to stop crying. Just make sure he's all right. Avoid picking up your baby unless: his hysteria has caused him to throw up; the intensity of his crying has made it hard for him to breathe; he's somehow managed to escape the crib; or his fury has caused his crib to spontaneously combust.

Keep the contact short and sweet. After just a minute or two, say good night and leave again. Continue checking on your baby at regular intervals until he falls asleep. Again, don't be afraid to be boring. Go through the same calm motions every time you come back. Let him know that you're there to reassure him, not to entertain him.

On each subsequent night, try to extend the interval that you stay away a little longer. Parents who stick with this method also report success in getting their children to sleep on their own. Some complain, however, that their babies cry even harder and seem even more upset when they return and then leave again than they would be if the parents just left and didn't come back.

➤ **Hanging out.** A more gradual approach involves sitting in the same room with your baby for a short time after putting him in his crib. Some parents prefer sitting across the room in a rocking chair where the baby can see them. Others pull a chair right up to the crib and rub the baby's back for a few minutes. After five or ten minutes, whisper good night and leave the room.

217

Daddy Dos and Don'ts

Even if you may not be home for most naptimes, the strategy for getting your child to go to sleep on his own should be basically the same. Consistency between naptime and bedtime routines will help your child adjust to falling asleep on his own. On the other hand, keep in mind that your child's need for naps will fluctuate with age and other circumstances. So if it doesn't seem likely he'll to go to sleep when you put him down for a nap, don't let him cry for long. You can always try again a little later.

Daddy Dos and Don'ts

Never use your child's bed, bedroom, or bedtime as a punishment. If you discipline your toddler or preschooler by sending her to bed, or even just to her room, she will soon dread going to bed. All your efforts to make bedtime enjoyable and relaxing will fall by the wayside.

Unfortunately, chances are your baby will start crying when you leave (or sometimes even before you leave). At that point, you'll need to fall back on either the "crying game" or "I'll be back" strategy.

If you and your partner don't have the resolve to stick with one of these three methods, you'll need to come up with a fourth option of your own or else surrender completely. If either of you is inconsistent—sometimes rushing in and "saving" your child, other times "toughing it out"—your mixed signals will confuse your child. Not knowing what to expect, your child may figure out that as long as he cries long enough or hard enough, you'll eventually give in to what he wants. And is that really a lesson you want to teach your child?

Independence Night

Once you have established a sleep routine that works, you can keep it essentially unchanged for years. Toddlers and preschoolers enjoy lullabies, baths, and stories even more than infants do. If you and your partner have made your child's bedroom fun, comfortable, and cozy, she probably won't put up any resistance when you suggest that you both go there. And if you have helped your child grow accustomed to falling asleep on her own, she will continue to do so—at least on most nights—throughout her childhood.

When your child becomes old enough to leave her bed, however, she may want to challenge you with her new freedom at bedtime. If you've already said good night and your child comes out later to find you, put her back to bed quickly and leave her there. No matter how many times she leaves her bed, simply scoop her up and put her back again.

To ease any separation anxiety, promise your child that you will check on her in 10 (or 15 or 20) minutes—just to make sure she doesn't need anything. Make sure to keep your promise. Otherwise, you can safely assume that unless she falls asleep by some fluke, your child will come looking for you again—defying your rule about staying in bed.

Father Knows Best

"To make sure that you don't get out of this crib, we've placed over a hundred black poisonous snakes around your crib. And if you so much as put a toe out there, they're gonna bite you, you're gonna swell up, and be dead until morning."

—Bill Cosby

Things That Go Bump in the Night

Think you're done with bedtime hassles now that you've trained your baby to go to sleep on his own? Think again. Your child (and you) may also suffer from one or more different kinds of common sleep disturbances. These include:

➤ Midnight feedings

➤ Other midnight wake-up calls

➤ Sleepwalking

➤ Nightmares

➤ Night terrors

So don't count on getting that good night's sleep quite yet. You and your partner probably have a few more nighttime challenges to tackle first.

Midnight Snackers

Most babies wake in the middle of the night—most often because they're hungry (at least during the first few months). Unless your baby was born prematurely, however, he should have the stomach to sleep through the night by the time he's six months old.

Unfortunately, by then, your baby may have gotten used to being held, nursed or bottle-fed, and put back to sleep whenever he wakes in the night. So if your baby still wakes in the middle of

Daddy Dos and Don'ts

You may have better success in getting your toddler or preschooler to stay in bed if you let her know that you have something important to do (wash the dishes, go to the bathroom, or take a shower, for example). Let her know where you'll be and promise that you'll return to check on her as soon as you're done. Again, though, you need to follow through on your vow. A broken promise will not only erode your child's trust in you but will give her an excuse to get up again.

the night after six months, it may be nothing more than a bad habit. Sure, he may *want* a feeding, and he may very well fall right back to sleep after eating, but he probably no longer *needs* a feeding.

To break the habit of midnight snacks, you may need to put more effort into filling your baby's stomach before he goes to bed. Try feeding your baby breast milk, formula, or a bedtime snack (when he's older) a little closer to bedtime. At the same time, however, avoid feeding him so close to bedtime that he's too tired to eat. You may also want to encourage your baby to eat more so-called "solid food" during his daytime meals.

More importantly—and here's where you definitely come in—use feeding as the "soother" of last resort when your baby wakes in the middle of the night. Instead of automatically handing your baby to your partner for nursing, sing him a soft lullaby, caress him gently on his back, or run your fingers through his hair. If your baby doesn't calm down, pick him up and try rocking or just holding him for a few minutes.

Indeed, if you really want to eliminate midnight feedings, try to leave your partner out of these midnight encounters entirely for the first few weeks. When your baby sees your partner in the middle of the night, he cannot help but think of feedings. After all, that's what your partner has always given him up to now.

On the other hand, if *you* go to your baby first, he won't automatically assume its time to chow down. Because you don't have breasts that may distract and excite your baby, you might have a more soothing effect in holding, rocking, or singing lullabies to your baby than your partner would. This gives you a much better chance of calming your baby and putting him back to sleep without feeding him—at least after the first couple of nights, when he will probably raise holy hell because he wants to be fed.

Even if you finally give up and your partner ends up nursing the baby, you will have lengthened the time before his midnight feeding by stalling—which just may encourage your baby to wait a little longer tomorrow night. Given time and patience (the greatest assets of fatherhood), you can eventually stretch that interval out until morning.

Hey! I'm Awake Here!

Even after you have helped your baby break the habit of midnight snacking, by filling her stomach before bed or exploring the rest of your calming repertoire, your infant or toddler may still wake up for good reason in the middle of the night. She may, for example, have a dirty diaper that's irritating her skin. Or she might have worked up a sweat because she's too hot, or is shivering because she's too cold.

In these cases, ignoring your child's midnight cries will not make the problem go away. Something is disturbing her sleep and your baby can't take care of the problem herself. Try not to get annoyed or angry that your baby is now disturbing your sleep, too. She can't help it. Go see what's wrong and see what you can do about it.

If she's too cold, give her a blanket. If she's too hot, loosen her clothes or take a blanket off. If her diaper is a mess, by all means change it. If she has a fever that's disturbing her sleep, give her some children's acetaminophen. (Remember to check the label and the dosage before you give any medicine to your baby, especially in the middle of the night when you're sleepy.)

Now if one of these problems wakes your child (and you) every once in a while, it probably won't bother you a whole lot. You'll take care of the problem, pat your baby on the back, and she'll probably drift back to sleep easily. (I wish I could say the same for you.) But if the same problem recurs night after night, you might want to try to forestall the problem with a preemptive strike. If your toddler or preschooler regularly wakes up because she is

➤ **Cold.** Put an extra blanket over her after she falls asleep. Before you go to bed, make sure she hasn't kicked off the blankets.

➤ **Poopy.** Change your baby's diaper after her bedtime bottle rather than before. If your toddler or preschooler no longer wears diapers, encourage her to go to the bathroom before she goes to bed.

➤ **Startled.** Cut down on outside noises by putting up heavy curtains, and use a rotating fan or other source of "white noise" to screen out other sounds.

➤ **Lonely.** Work on getting your child to go to sleep on her own at bedtime. Once she has mastered this skill, the fear of being alone, which might have awakened her in the past, may now not wake her at all.

➤ **Afraid of the dark.** Turn a light on! There's no rule that says a child has to fall asleep in complete darkness. Many kids fall asleep more easily with the lights blazing. Try a night light, a flashlight, or a lighted fish tank. If these don't work for your child, keep a bedside lamp on all night.

➤ **Unable to find a pacifier.** If your child finds it soothing to suck on a pacifier but keeps losing it in the middle of the night, strew a half dozen or more in her crib. Or, if she's old enough to remember where it is, rig up a small cup on the bars of her crib and fill it with pacifiers every night.

➤ **Thirsty.** Encourage your child to drink more before bed. (As long as she still wears a diaper, this won't create more problems than it solves.) Or attach a travel cup (one with a straw) to one of the vertical bars of her crib so that she can help herself to a sip in the middle of the night.

➤ **Hungry.** As suggested earlier, try to eliminate midnight snacks.

Exercise Some Restraint (You, Not Your Child)

Once you've broken your child's habit of midnight snacking (the most common cause of middle-of-the-night wake-up calls), you can gradually eliminate the other ways he depends on you to get him back to sleep at night: holding, rocking, rubbing, singing, and finding his pacifier for him. By no longer helping him to get back to sleep, you will train him to help himself.

All of us, adults and children alike, wake up during the night—if only slightly. But unlike your baby, who may not know how to do this yet, we have learned to fall back asleep again. By contrast, when your child wakes, even slightly, the disturbance of waking in itself may upset him and cause him to wake up fully.

You and your partner unintentionally may be adding to the problem by springing to the rescue every night. Here's what to do: Instead of running to your baby at the slightest whimper or sound (as no doubt he has trained you to do), you and your partner need to show a little more restraint. If you wait just a few minutes to see what happens, your baby may surprise you by calming himself down and falling back asleep.

If, however, your baby begins to make more noise, crying loudly and steadily, you will still have plenty of time to go to him. Try repeating the same techniques you used to encourage him to fall asleep on his own at bedtime. Try to calm him down quickly (but not hurriedly) and without picking him up, if possible. If you hold him, put him back in the crib as soon as he's calm again. Don't try to entertain or talk to your child except with brief, soothing whispers. Then leave, returning only if his crying persists for more than a few minutes. Before long, your child will be "sleeping like a baby." (Okay, you knew that line was coming sooner or later.)

Little Runaway

Not every child sleepwalks. But if your child does, try not to worry too much about it. As long as you secure a child-safety gate at the top of the stairs before going to bed and clear the floor of your child's room and the hallway of toys and other objects that she might stumble over, your child will probably not hurt herself while sleepwalking.

Far more dangerous is the child who runs while barely conscious—usually in the direction of her parents' bedroom in the middle of the night. A child who frantically runs to her parents in the middle of the night desperately wants something from them (although she may well forget what it is by the time she gets there). But because she is essentially running blind in this state, anything slightly out of the ordinary—a box in the hallway or a closed door, for example—becomes a hazard.

The best way to prevent midnight runs is to stop them before they start. If you go to your toddler relatively quickly when she cries out for you in the middle of the night, she'll have no reason to come running to you. (Of course, this means that you'll be the one stumbling over the box or crashing into the door.)

Don't take this to mean that you should rush to your child every time you hear her whimper or roll over in her bed. Neither you nor your child would ever get a good night's sleep that way. But if you hear your toddler or preschooler crying out, climbing out of bed, or racing down the hall, go to her immediately and find out what she wants. If you can, try to cut her off before she gets out of bed; if not, in the hallway.

When you intercept her, scoop your child up in your arms and take her right back to her own bed. If she wants something reasonable (a drink of water, a trip to the bathroom), you can accommodate her. Try to stay with your child only for a moment, until she calms down, however, before returning to your own bed. Don't entertain or overindulge her. If you reward your child in any significant way for these midnight runs, you can expect many more of them to follow.

Similarly, if you allow your child to snuggle in your cozy bed with you, this reward may soon motivate her to make nightly visits. So think twice before inviting your little one to share your bed with you. It could easily become a long-standing habit.

Is Three a Crowd in Bed?

What's so wrong with sharing your bed with your child? After all, it's the normal custom in many cultures.

What some people call "the family bed" does have certain advantages—especially when your baby still nurses in the middle of the night. Think about it. When your baby wakes in the middle of the night, you could wake up fully, stagger out of bed, grope your way to your baby's crib or bedroom, carry him to your bed, and then get up again 20 minutes later to take him back to his crib. Or you could reach over to the baby sleeping in the same bed, put him to your partner's breast, and then drift back to sleep (all three of you). Which sounds easier? When your baby is little, the family bed is by far the most convenient of these two options.

The family bed has drawbacks, too. If your baby (or older child) regularly sleeps in your bed, you and your partner will probably need to find another place to make love.

You will also need to decide how long to let this go on. The longer you let your baby sleep in bed with you, the harder you will find it to convince him to sleep anywhere else. The easiest time to move your baby out of your bed (or to change any element of his bedtime routine) is when he's still relatively young, before his rapidly improving memory helps him realize that he's missing out on something he used to enjoy.

So think about it, talk to your partner, and together make a decision whether to allow your baby in your bed, and, if so, for how long. You may decide it's right for you, but make a conscious choice. Don't just let your fatigue decide for you.

Daddy Dos and Don'ts

Do *not*, under any circumstances, take your baby to bed with you if you or your partner is drunk or if either of you sleeps extremely heavily. If you are unlikely to wake up in response to the sensation of rolling over on top of your baby or the loud objections he raises when you do, then it's just not safe for all of you to sleep in the same bed.

Nightmare on Your Street

Toddlers have a hard enough time figuring out what's real and what's imaginary without throwing nightmares into the mix. If your child has nightmares, she may scream out in terror or curl up and whimper. But no matter how she reacts, you can be sure she's frightened.

To help your child recover from nightmares, try to get to her as quickly as you can. Hold your child in your strong arms, stroke her back or hair, and offer calming words. Let your child know that it was just a nightmare. The quicker you get to your child, the quicker she is likely to calm down. She might have no memory of the nightmare or your comforting by the next morning. If you ignore your child's cries, however, her terror and her tears will likely worsen, and she will need to be comforted for much longer.

Since nightmares often express the dreamer's anxiety or stress (thank you, Dr. Freud), you should consider possible sources of your child's nightmares—especially if they recur over a period of several nights. A young child's anxiety most often springs from change. Perhaps your partner just returned to work or increased her hours. Or maybe you went away on a business trip. The start of a new daycare situation, a move to a new home, the birth of a baby brother or sister, the new freedom that comes with walking and running—all can make a young child anxious and sometimes lead to nightmares.

Certainly, you can't protect your child from every major change. You can't "take the new baby back," stay at home 24 hours a day, or stop your child from reaching new milestones, but you may be able to ease her through the transition simply by showing her that you love and understand her. Talk to your child about her dreams and about the source of her anxiety. What your child most wants and needs during such difficult transitions is your reassurance, your love, and your attention.

The All-Night Horror Show

During the preschool years (and sometimes into elementary school and beyond) your child may suffer from something called "night terrors." If he does, your child will awaken you with an ear-splitting scream in the middle of the night. When you rush to his room, you may find your child sitting up and staring vacantly in front of him, eyes wide with horror. Or he may continue screaming and flailing his arms and legs in terror. In either case, your child—though still asleep—will appear terrified, shaken, and perhaps furious.

Although he might appear fully alert at first, your child will ignore or even desperately resist your increasingly frustrating attempts to calm him down. Your child may cry hysterically or lash out at you, but he will remain asleep and unconscious of what he's doing. In all likelihood, he will wake in the morning with no memory of his terror.

Since your child will remain unconscious, you will probably find the experience even more unsettling than he does. Yet, no matter how disturbing you find night terrors, try to bear with your child for as long as they last. Don't bother trying to wake him or to talk him out of his terror. Your child cannot hear your appeals to reason.

Instead, just stay with your child and wait for him to calm down. If he lets you, hold your child in your arms, hug him close, caress him, and whisper soft words in gentle tones. But don't expect your attempts to soothe your child to have much impact. Your child may seem totally deaf to you, or worse, he may incorporate you into the terrifying scenario playing in his head. He may yell at you, shrieking that he hates you or that he wants to kill you, but try not to be put off by harsh words. He's shouting at someone in his head, not you. Stick it out no matter how unkind your child may seem to be. The terror will soon pass, and your child will sink back into a more restful slumber.

On rare occasions, children with night terrors will jump out of bed and race around in a desperate panic. If your child starts trying to escape his terrors in this way, you will need to run interference. Shut the door of his room and try to keep him from running into windows, dressers, or desks. You can try to pick him up, but this may only increase his terror.

If your child wakes up (or you gently wake him up), reassure him that he's safe, that the bad dream is gone now. Then, encourage him to go back to bed. Once your child falls back asleep and you see how calm and peaceful he looks, you can probably fall asleep again yourself.

Accidents Happen

Long after your child becomes toilet trained, she may still wake up in the middle of the night soaked in her own urine.

Understandably, you may get frustrated and exhausted by having to change your child's sheets for the fifth or sixth time in a week. But try not to get mad at your child. She has absolutely no control over bedwetting.

Almost all habitual bedwetting, or *enuresis*, results from some sort of developmental delay or slowness, not from laziness, apathy, defiance, or rebellion. Yelling at your child for wetting the bed will do nothing to solve the problem—and will almost definitely make your child feel guilty about not being able to "grow up," or to control something that's clearly out of her control.

Like the appearance of nightmares, a sudden increase in bedwetting may indicate stress and anxiety on your child's part. Again, talk to your child about what you suspect might be causing her stress and show her as much love and attention as you possibly can. Your love and understanding may help cut down on the frequency of bedwetting.

Paterniterms

If your pediatrician mentions the word **enuresis**, don't be alarmed. It simply means habitual bedwetting.

In most bedwetting cases, however, the best you can do is to remain patient. In all likelihood, your child will stop wetting the bed before her sixth birthday—and perhaps much earlier. In the meantime, you can try the following:

➤ Cut down slightly on your child's fluid intake before bed.

➤ Ask her to use the toilet right before turning the light out for the night.

➤ Cart her off to the bathroom just before *you* go to bed. (This actually encourages rather than discourages midnight urination, since your child probably won't wake up fully even when you prop her up on the toilet—but at least you won't need to change the sheets as often.)

Try not to think of bedwetting as a problem that you have to solve. That kind of thinking sets up both you and your child for failure. Instead, regard it as an accident (or maybe an extended series of accidents). If you don't make a big deal out of it, your child will eventually outgrow it. But if you berate your child for something that's out of her control, you may just make the problem worse.

Sleep Deprivation

As your child grows older, he will need less and less sleep. In response to his changing needs, you and your partner should gradually cut down on the number of naps your child takes. Unfortunately, the change in sleep needs occurs gradually. Your child won't wake up one day needing a full hour less sleep than the day before. So with each nap you cut out of your child's schedule, he will probably become over-tired for several weeks (or several months) as he adjusts to his new schedule.

Over-tiredness is an especially common problem in the months leading up to and following a child's second birthday, and then again around his fourth birthday. For many two-year olds, two naps are often too much and one is not enough. Similarly, many four-year olds could benefit from half a nap, but a full nap is out of the question.

Unfortunately, there's no way to take just half a nap, which puts your toddler or preschooler in an impossible situation. During the transition from two naps to one, and later from one nap to no naps, your child will become increasingly cranky as the day goes on and fatigue begins to take over.

Your child will probably become clumsier late in the day, having a harder time doing things (walking, putting objects inside one another, and so on) that he accomplishes with relative ease when not exhausted. To make matters worse, he will become frustrated much more quickly. When your child can't do or get something he wants, he may fall apart completely—screaming, having a tantrum, bawling, or breaking things. In all likelihood, he will become progressively more miserable, whiny, and totally unbearable.

All you can do during these transition periods is to remain flexible and patient. When phasing out a nap, for example, adjust your child's bedtime slightly to compensate for some of his lost sleep. Putting your child to bed a half hour earlier at night may make it easier for him to adjust to the sleep he's losing during the day. Also, be flexible enough to encourage your child to take an occasional "extra" nap even when you're phasing one out. Just because he's napping less doesn't mean that your child can't take one every other day or perhaps twice a week when he gets especially tired.

Be alert to the signs of over-tiredness. When you see your toddler (or later your preschooler) becoming increasingly frustrated, whiny, or tearful—the calling cards of over-tiredness—try to interest him in a quiet activity that doesn't demand much of him: listening to music or a story, drawing with crayons, and the like. Just sitting down quietly and calmly for a while can reinvigorate your child, renewing his energy, strength, and skills. Better still, your child might welcome the chance to sit and do something restful with you.

It won't be particularly easy for either you or your child to cut down on the naps he takes. But when he's ready, bear with it. Trust me, it won't last forever.

The Least You Need to Know

➤ Parents can train their babies to be bad sleepers who demand attention (holding or feeding) in order to fall asleep. They can also train their children to be good sleepers by undoing (or never establishing) these habits.

➤ Work on developing a simple routine that encourages your child to go to sleep by herself. Make sure it's a routine that you can live with for years to come.

➤ The longer you wait to teach your child to go to sleep on his own, the harder it will become.

➤ Your child does not necessarily *need* everything you provide her at bedtime or in the middle of the night (feeding, holding, special attention). She will *want* these things, however, as long as you seem willing to provide them.

➤ Bedwetting is a problem over which your child has absolutely no control. So don't get mad at your child if he regularly wets the bed.

Chapter 17

A Shift in the Balance of Power: The Arrival of Siblings

In This Chapter

➤ How having a second child will change all of your lives

➤ When and how to share the "good news" with your first child

➤ Getting everyone ready for the new arrival

➤ The first weeks at home with two kids

➤ Dealing with a lifetime of sibling rivalry

So you've decided to expand your family. Congratulations! What are you, insane? Did you learn nothing from having just one child? You thought having one creature in the house who thought she was the center of the universe wasn't enough? (I'm talking about your child, not your wife.)

Oh, well. There's no turning back now. You've made your decision and now you'll have to live with the consequences. You'll need to adjust a lot to cope with two children. Parenting two kids entails more than twice the responsibility of parenting one; not only do you have to feed and care for two kids, but you have to make sure they don't kill each other. But hey, you knew what you were getting yourself into, right?

The New Math: Two Times One Is Greater Than Two

If you felt overwhelmed—or even just strained—by the responsibilities of caring for one child, prepare for an even bigger shock if you're planning on having another. A second child will change the entire balance of power in your family.

Juggling and No-Look Passes

You may have thought you had your hands full with one child, but at least you could hand that child over to your partner. Now that you're having a second child, everything changes:

➤ Having two children means a lot of hand-offs: "Here, you take the baby; I need to spend time with the older child." "Whoops, baby needs to nurse; better switch back." You used to outnumber your children, so one of you could take a break now and then. Suddenly, you feel outnumbered—even if it's really only two on two.

➤ When one of you goes away—to work, a well-deserved night out, or a business trip, for example—the other must juggle two children, each of whom demands full attention.

➤ Your first child, who thought himself the center of the universe, will rudely awaken to the fact that someone else in the house feels the same way. (And seeing how much attention the new baby gets, he may suspect that his sibling is right.)

➤ You might have more health worries with your second child. Your oldest child will no doubt introduce the baby to every germ he meets in the park, on the playground, or at daycare—germs that you had taken great pains to keep away from your oldest child when he was a baby. (Despite appearances, the repeated exposure to germs and other disease-causing agents does not represent your oldest child's attempt to do away with your baby.)

➤ You can look forward to years of the following theme, played out in several variations: "Daa-ad, he bit me!" "Well, she touched my stuff first!" "Did not." "Did, too." "Did not." "Did, too." "Daa-ad, he bit me again!" "Hey, she hit me!"

➤ Your older child, whom you protected for several years from all sorts of nefarious influences (commercial TV, violence, curse words, soda, candy, fill in whatever you like) will see it as his responsibility to introduce these to his little brother or sister at as early an age as possible.

➤ Because they are at different developmental stages, even if only a year apart, your children may not find the same activities entertaining, making "fun for the whole family" an almost impossible goal. (See Chapter 21 for tips on reaching this almost impossible goal.) In addition, for the first few years, your older child will be playing with toys that are totally inappropriate for your baby (who will no doubt try to eat anything with small parts).

Knowing what you already know about small children, it's very brave of you to decide to have another. Having more than one child more than doubles the challenges of parenting. But most parents of more than one child would also agree that it more than doubles the joys, as well.

Age Differences

How will life change when your second child arrives? That depends on many factors, including the gender of both children, their personalities (especially that of your older child), your relationship with your partner, and your unique parenting styles. To a great degree, however, the way your lives as parents will change depends on how old your first child is when your second child is born.

If you have children two years apart or less, you will most likely have:

➤ Two kids in diapers at the same time.

➤ Two kids who for several years will depend on you for almost everything—not just changing diapers, but dressing, bathing, eating, and entertaining.

➤ Two kids who will probably play with each other (and fight with each other) a lot for the next sixteen years.

➤ An older child who will quickly forget what life was like when she was the only one.

On the other hand, if you have children more than two years apart, you will probably have:

➤ An older child who has at least some ability to entertain herself.

➤ Two kids who have very different skills, needs, and desires, making it difficult to satisfy both of them at the same time.

➤ Two kids who may occasionally play with one another, but who will probably travel in different circles throughout their childhood.

➤ An older child who will not only remember for a long time what life was like before the baby arrived, but who can—and frequently will—verbalize her wish that you would get rid of that thing.

In short, whether to have more than one child close together in age or spaced out by several years is entirely your own decision. Each choice has its advantages and disadvantages. Whatever you decide, good luck. You'll need it.

Is Everybody Ready?

Just as fatherhood began for you with your partner's first pregnancy, being a sibling should begin for your oldest child before the birth of your second child. It's only fair to give your child some warning about what to expect. Remember, when your partner had her first pregnancy, the nine months before birth gave you just enough time to get used to the idea of becoming a father and to prepare yourself for the changes to come. (See Chapter 1 if you need a reminder of what this adjustment was like.)

Well, the outcome of this pregnancy will change your child, transforming him into an older sibling. So it wouldn't really be fair to put off sharing the news with your child until you're on the way to the hospital or birthing center—or, worse, until you arrive home with a baby in your arms. No matter how old he is when you find out your partner is pregnant again, your child can use several months (or more) to get used to the idea of having a baby around the house.

When should you tell your child that you're expecting another baby? Whenever the time seems right to you. Certainly, if you're telling relatives, friends, and co-workers, there's no real reason not to tell your child. As long as she's at least about 16 months old, she will understand much of what you tell her. (If your child is under three, however, she will likely forget from time to time, so you'll probably need to remind her several times.)

Is Ignorance Really Bliss?

You may want to hold off on telling your child out of fear that if something goes wrong during the pregnancy—a miscarriage or some other complication—you will have introduced her to unnecessary grief. Understandably, no parent really wants his children to know death at an early age. But death is an inevitable part of life. If it does touch your lives, how much will your child benefit from your attempts to shield her from this kind of loss? (See Chapter 19 on how to talk to your child about death.)

Children pick up clues, signals, and emotional undertones much more readily than many parents give them credit for. If you and your partner are grieving over a miscarriage, your child will be confused and concerned if she doesn't know what's going on. "Why is mommy so sad? Why is daddy crying?" Even if your child doesn't yet have the words to ask these questions, she will clearly see your grief. Do you really want her to puzzle through the clues on her own, with no guidance or support from you?

Hearing about a miscarriage may indeed make your child feel sad, but seeing your unexplained grief will make her feel sad, too. Worse still, in searching for an explanation, your child may blame herself for your sadness. After all, it has to be something, and a young child tends to think everything in her world is somehow her own creation. The truth will at least help her understand what's really happening.

Nonetheless, some parents feel differently about this issue, and they are motivated only by good intentions. If you've decided to wait until well into the second trimester before sharing the news with your child, don't wait much longer than that. You should probably let your child know the news—and get used to the idea—before the third trimester begins. (If your child is more than three years old, she will probably notice your wife's belly expanding long before that. In this case, you should probably let your child know about the pregnancy as soon as your partner begins to "show"— which will probably be several weeks sooner than in the first pregnancy.)

Let's Talk Baby Talk

When you tell your child about the pregnancy, make sure to give him every chance to ask any questions about pregnancy, babies, and childbirth—and to tell you what he really thinks about it. You also might want to touch on what babies are like (you can start by letting him know what he was like as a baby), how a baby grows for nine months inside a mama's belly, and the answer to your child's big question: why you wanted to have another child in the first place.

When talking to your child about why you decided to have another baby, don't claim that you did it for your child or that you did it to give him someone to play with. Here's why you should avoid these arguments:

➤ Your child would probably rather pick his own playmates.

➤ Your baby won't really be able to play with her older sibling for months to come.

➤ Most importantly, it fudges the truth. Sure, you no doubt considered your first child in making your decision. You no doubt sincerely believe that growing up with a sibling *is* preferable to growing up as an only child. You may even have entertained some fantasies about the warm and loving relationship that will blossom between your children. But, bottom line, you're having another baby because you and your partner want one, not because you think your child wants one. (Chances are, at least if he's under age five, he doesn't.)

Give your child every opportunity to ask questions and share his feelings about the pregnancy and the baby to come. At the same time, however, try not to beat a dead horse. If your child shows no interest in the pregnancy or doesn't want to talk about the baby, don't force him to talk about it. (After all, he can't really see anything yet, so it may not yet be real for him.)

If your child's lack of interest disturbs you, mention it once or twice again, but don't be pushy about it. You cannot really force your child to talk about the pregnancy or the baby—or even to be interested in them.

When the subject finally does come up, you may want to take advantage of the opportunity to talk about how babies are made. Of course, with younger children, you don't need to go into a lot of detail. Try to simplify as much as possible. In general, you should probably avoid offering more information than your child has asked for. Listen carefully to his questions and then answer them in a way that will satisfy your child's curiosity without taxing his ability to understand.

For instance, your toddler or preschooler may ask questions like, "How did the baby get inside mama? Did she eat it?" Answer such questions as briefly, simply, and accurately as possible, perhaps something like, "No, mama didn't eat the baby. The baby grows inside mama." Often, the simplest explanation will suffice for young children. If your child wants more information, you can add something like, "When a seed from the daddy joins with an egg from the mommy, a baby starts to grow." Again, this explanation may very well satisfy your young child. But if he wants more details, try to explain as simply and directly as possible how the seed gets inside the mommy's body. (See Chapter 19 for more on how to talk to kids, both young and old, about thorny issues such as sex and death.)

In addition to answering any questions he may have, encourage your child to talk (as best he can, depending on his age) about how he feels about having a baby brother or sister. Of course, you can't stifle the feelings you don't like. Try not to be hurt or angry if your child calls the baby nasty names or expresses his anger or anxiety about the baby. By expressing unpleasant feelings, he might be able to make room for more pleasant ones.

Daddy Dos and Don'ts

You can prepare your child for the arrival of a sibling by telling her stories about when she was a little baby. If you have a photo album that includes her baby pictures, flip through them together. Or, if you have a camcorder, break out some of her baby videos and watch them together. While you're delving into these archives, talk to your child about what she was like and what she could do.

Accepting the Inevitable

Sometimes your child can accept the pregnancy (and sibling-to-be) more easily if you nurture a healthy sense of superiority in her. Let your child know well in advance that the baby won't be able to feed himself, wash himself, go to the bathroom by himself, walk by himself, speak by himself, or really do much of anything but sleep by himself. Finding out how helpless babies are might encourage your child to offer help (or at least tolerance) when the baby arrives.

You can also build a sense of acceptance by referring to the baby as "your baby sister" or "your baby brother" (or if you don't yet know the sex, "your baby brother or sister"). Repeatedly hearing these terms can instill a sense of "ownership" in your child—hopefully, pride of ownership.

You're Part of This, Too

You can help build your child's interest in and enthusiasm about your partner's pregnancy by including your child in the pregnancy. Take your child with you and your partner to the obstetrician once or twice—especially after the first trimester, when things start to get interesting.

When you're in the doctor's office, tell your child what's happening. Let him know that the odd sound he hears is the heartbeat of the baby growing inside his mama. If your partner has an ultrasound, bring your child along so that he can "see" the developing fetus, too. (Remember how real these made the first pregnancy for you?)

If you find out the sex of your baby in advance, let your child know, too. You may even want to ask your child's opinion on baby names (though don't give him the ultimate say-so unless you're prepared to name your baby Fluffy, Stupid, or Tinky Winky).

As the pregnancy progresses, encourage your partner to invite your child to feel the baby kicking. An older child will probably be more receptive to this suggestion than a younger child, who may have difficulty conceptualizing that the "kicks" he's feeling are from the baby inside his mommy's belly.

The more you encourage your child's involvement and keep him informed, the more he will feel a part of the pregnancy. And this may (or may not) make your child more receptive when your baby finally is born.

The Final Stretch

During the final two months of your partner's second pregnancy, you should start getting everything prepared for the new arrival, just as you did before the birth of your first child (see Chapter 5). This time, however, your preparation has to consider your first child and her needs. How can you best help your child make the smooth transition from only child to older sibling? Who will take care of her during labor and delivery? Should your child attend the birth of her sibling?

Having a Baby Doesn't Change Everything

Let's face it: Having a little brother or sister is going to be a big deal for your child. He will need to make some major adjustments in the way he views you and the world you represent. Things in your child's small world will change; you can't avoid that. But though you can't diminish the impact of having a new baby in the home, you can try to provide a comforting stability and order in the rest of your child's life.

Establishing an enjoyable routine well before the arrival of the new baby—and then maintaining it afterward—can keep your child feeling safe and secure. In the month or two leading up to the birth, stick as closely as possible to your child's normal routine. If your older child attends a

Daddy Dos and Don'ts

If you have not done so already, move your older child out of the crib and into a bed (or into a new bedroom) well before the birth of your new baby. (If your children are less than two or three years apart, of course, your older child may not yet be ready for a bed. If so, you'll need a second crib or bassinet for the new baby.) If you wait until the last minute (or even several weeks before the new arrival) your child will almost certainly feel resentful about being supplanted.

daycare center or preschool, for example, keep it up before, during, and after the birth of the new baby. Sticking to a routine will provide much-needed stability during this time of transition for your child.

Try not to introduce any major changes in your child's routine in the month or so before your partner's due date. The arrival of the baby will cause enough upheaval in your child's life without also having to cope with major changes such as

➤ Starting in a new daycare situation or enrolling in a new preschool.

➤ Getting used to a new baby-sitter.

➤ Establishing a new bedtime routine (see Chapter 16).

➤ Moving to a new house, especially one in a new neighborhood where he has no friends.

➤ Weaning from the breast. (If possible, this should be done no later than the second trimester of the pregnancy.)

By maintaining stability in other areas of your child's life, you can soften the blow of a new sibling's birth.

If you plan on taking paternity leave and handling most child-care responsibilities while your partner attends to the new baby, try to spend more time with your child in the final weeks of your partner's pregnancy. Even if you continue to work until your partner's due date, make a special effort to devote most evenings and weekends to your child.

Your child will benefit from consistency during his first few weeks as a sibling. If your partner has been doing most of the childcare, find out how she spends her days with him. Certainly, you don't have to do everything with your child the way your wife does, but little things—such as the way you cut sandwiches or set him up with watercolors and paper—may mean a lot to your child.

Daddy Dos and Don'ts

If you can afford to do so, start your paternity leave a week or two before your baby's anticipated arrival, and then take as much time off as you possibly can. The tricky part of starting a limited paternity leave early, of course, is that if your baby arrives a week or two late, you may have already used up most or all of your leave. You will be needed at home even more during the first few weeks of your new baby's life, when your older child needs attention and your partner needs rest and recovery time.

I Thought You Were Calling the Sitter

One detail you shouldn't leave until the last minute is lining up someone to care for your child during your partner's labor and delivery. The ideal arrangement for childcare during labor and delivery involves having someone (a friend, relative, or baby-sitter) stay in your home when you go to the hospital. If she stays at home, your child—who will probably miss both of you, even if you're gone only for the day—won't have the added burden of getting used to a strange place.

Once you have a sitter lined up, immediately arrange for a backup. If your first choice gets sick or fogged in at the airport or can't come through for you for some other reason, you'll need someone ready to fill in. You can't just leave your child home alone, and it might not be convenient to bring her along. So make sure you have a contingency plan ready, just in case.

Hey, Kid! Want to See Something Really Gross?

Although many hospitals don't allow children, especially young children, to attend the birth of their siblings, your child may be allowed to attend if your partner's labor and delivery takes place at a birthing center. If you plan on a home birth, your child can certainly remain with you. Now whether that's a good idea, only you and your partner can decide.

Daddy Dos and Don'ts

Ask your designated sitter to stay the night once or twice *before* your partner goes into labor. A "rehearsal" before the big event will give your child a chance to grow accustomed to the person who will be taking care of her. Having one or two "practice" nights is even more essential if your child will be staying at someone else's house during your partner's labor and delivery.

Of course, witnessing childbirth is not appropriate for every child. Many parents wouldn't even consider it, deeming it inappropriate, too distressing for their child, or too distracting for them. If you have no objections and your child expresses a desire to be there, however, why not at least think it over?

In deciding whether to include your first child in the birth of your second (or even to invite him to do so), you should consider carefully your child's age, temperament, and interest in the pregnancy and childbirth. Gauge your child's possible reactions by watching a video about childbirth with him. Keep in mind, however, that no matter how fascinated your child seems to be with the pregnancy or how much he anticipates having a baby brother or sister, the sight and sound of his mother's labor pains and the bloody delivery that follows may be disturbing.

Finally, if you decide that you want your new baby's older sibling present, make arrangements for another adult to be there to attend to your child's needs. After all, you cannot possibly satisfy the needs and demands of your children (who may get bored during a lengthy labor) *and* the needs of your laboring wife. No one needs this kind of juggling act during childbirth.

Take That Thing Back!

Despite all the preparations you've made, the arrival of a rival sibling will probably come as a shock and annoyance to your older child. She will no doubt need help making the adjustment from being an only child to being an older sibling—and that's where you come in.

Visiting Hours

After your baby is born, bring your older child to the hospital or birthing center as often as you can. Although children who are not related to the mother are not permitted in a hospital's obstetrical unit, almost all maternity wings now allow older siblings to visit their mother and the baby.

Don't worry if your child seems to pay almost no attention to his new sibling. Chances are the person he most wants and needs to see is mommy. Since hospitals are often foreign and forbidding places, your child may even need some reassurance that mommy is not dead or dying. So take the baby from her and let your partner give your older child a big hug.

No matter how much or how little your older child seems interested in the baby, avoid pushing the baby on him. Relationships take time to develop. Give your children a little space and time to develop their relationship.

Coming Home

Now comes the really hard part. Your child may have been excited about the prospect of having a baby brother or sister, but once you actually bring the baby home, the reality may be something of a shock for your older child. Despite wishes she may have to the contrary, your child will have to adjust to the idea that the baby is here to stay.

The first few weeks at home can set the tone for the relationship between your children. Your baby will, of course, command attention, but your older child, whether she demands it or not, needs attention, too. So put in an extra effort to make your older child feel special and loved.

Your child will not only welcome the special time she gets to spend with you, she will truly need you to be a stabilizing presence during this upheaval. She may never have spent so much time apart from her mother as she will during the first few weeks, when your partner will not only be consumed with baby care but will feel totally drained.

To ease your older child's anxiety, plan some special activities for your time alone with her. Take your child on a few special outings, or have some special playtime or reading time that just the two of you can share.

Just as important is giving your child the opportunity to have special times with her mother, too. When you can, take the baby so that your partner and older child can spend time alone together, just the two of them.

Will the Real Baby Please Stand Up?

Don't be surprised if your two- or three-year-old (or even your five- or thirteen-year-old) child begins acting more like a baby after the birth of a sibling. Your older child will no doubt want some extra attention now that he has a rival. Since the baby gets a lot of attention by crying, your older child may try to get attention that way, too.

Of course, it would be really helpful if your older child would dress or bathe or entertain himself for a little while when the baby needs a bottle or you're trying to get the little one to sleep. When he doesn't, you may feel particularly annoyed. Try not to be impatient with your child, however. Don't try to shame your child by exhorting him to "Act your age!" Instead, try humoring your child. Play along with the game of pretending he is a baby again. Hold him in your arms and rock him "to sleep" or let him drink from a bottle if that's what makes him happy. Now more than ever, he needs to know that you love and accept him even when he acts like a baby.

At the same time, however, let your child know that the reason you do all these things for the baby and not for him is not that you don't love him anymore, but that he no longer needs them, that he has outgrown them. If you give your child room to act like a baby, but also offer the choice to act like a big kid, he will probably play baby less and less as the weeks (or maybe months) go by.

Daddy Dos and Don'ts

Another way to encourage (though not pressure) your older child to give up regressive activities is to plan special days just for him. Take your child on a special outing: a trip to the movies or an afternoon at an indoor play space. Or make a spur-of-the-moment decision to go out for ice cream or some other special food. (After all, the baby can't eat anything but breast milk or formula, poor thing.) These kinds of treats can help your child appreciate the advantages of being "grown up."

Father Knows Best

"What strange creatures brothers are."

—Jane Austen

Continue to nurture a feeling of superiority and generosity in your older child. Encourage empathy for the poor baby, who cannot eat with a spoon or fork like your older child can, or walk or jump or do somersaults like he can. The baby cannot sing or even talk. The baby does not even know how to wait a few minutes like your older child can (if you remind him). You might even suggest that when the baby gets a little bit older, your older child can teach her a thing or two.

Father's Little Helper

One way to start building a good relationship between siblings is to ask your older child to do small things that might be helpful when you have your hands full with baby. Young children—especially from about $2^1/_2$ to 6 years old—love to please their parents. It will build your older child's confidence and help nurture empathy toward the baby if she can show herself (and you, of course) how helpful she can be.

Be careful not to overdo it, however. Watch your older child's reactions carefully. If she doesn't seem to want to get you a cloth diaper for the baby's spit up or pick out what the baby will wear, back off a little. You can always boost your child's confidence by asking her to help with something else, like painting a fence or washing the car.

Don't force your child to help—or really even expect her to help—with the baby. After all, this second baby business was your choice, not hers, and that makes taking care of the baby your responsibility, not hers. Certainly, you can ask your child to help, or even make suggestions about how she might help, but try to avoid putting any pressure on her.

Instead, try to understand why your child might not want to help. Remember, from your older child's perspective, the baby is probably a huge pain because

➤ He steals so much of your time and attention away from her.

➤ His crying bothers her.

➤ She has to be quiet when he's napping, which seems like all the time.

➤ His needs often mean that her needs have to wait.

So give your older child room to express her feelings instead of trying to force her to like the baby.

At around three months, your baby will start smiling, especially at familiar faces. Take advantage of this terrific opportunity to encourage your older child to develop warm feelings toward the baby. When the baby smiles at your older child, point it out and explain that it means he likes her. Your child will probably start to return the favor, finding it much easier to like the baby when she thinks the baby likes her.

Which One of Us Do You Love More?

There's really only one way to escape sibling rivalry: Never have a second, a third, or a fourth child.

But since you've got years of infighting to come, try to keep in mind (especially when their bickering threatens to drive you up a wall) that sibling rivalry is not necessarily a bad thing. Your family—and especially your children's relationships with one another—provides an experimental laboratory for social behavior. Just as your child first explored the world around him by treating the home as a laboratory, he will explore and test social relationships by practicing on his siblings. (And that's a good thing, right?)

The New Rival

During your partner's pregnancy, your child may have been eager for the baby to arrive. But once the baby actually comes home to stay, your older child cannot help feeling at least some jealousy toward the baby and anger and resentment toward you. No matter how much attention you lavish on her after the baby is born, your child will feel somewhat supplanted and replaced in your affections. Naturally, this will cause some friction between your children.

Both your children (or all your children) want—and truly need—your love and attention. And although you might have more than enough love to go around, you can't get around the fact that you have to divide your attention between your children.

Again, you can dampen some of the hostilities by making a point of spending special time every day with each child. Do something with your older child, especially when your partner is busy nursing or caring for the baby. And be sure to take the baby for at least a half hour a day to give your partner a chance to spend special time with your older child. If your partner handled the bulk of childcare before the baby was born, your older child will certainly miss her now that she's with the baby so much.

Daddy Dos and Don'ts

Avoid blaming the baby when you can't do something your older child wants to do with you. If you're constantly saying, "Can't you see the baby needs a diaper change?" or "Not right now, I have to put the baby down for a nap," you will rapidly set up an adversarial relationship between your two children.

No Fighting, No Biting

Although you should allow your child to express whatever he feels about the baby in words, make sure that you draw a clear line right from the start that forbids him from acting out hostile feelings. Your child can resent the baby, be bored with the baby, be annoyed with the baby, and even hate the baby. (Of course, he can also love the baby, feel proud of the baby, and be happy to see the baby.) But under no circumstances should your older child hit the baby, bite the baby, push the baby, or kick the baby.

Father Knows Best

"... [F]rom time to time children do like to share with siblings. For example, once in a while a brother will try to remove his sister's arm so he can play with it."

—Bill Cosby

With a child under four, appeals to morality will probably fail. In all likelihood, he just doesn't have a firm enough grip on the concept of right and wrong for this argument to work. You should certainly make the point that hitting, biting, and kicking are wrong and that these actions won't be tolerated. But instead of making an abstract moral argument, appeal to your child's self-interest instead. Point out that if he harms the baby:

➤ The baby will get upset, and her crying means that you have to pay even more attention to her.

➤ You will get upset and will have to punish your child for any deliberate attacks.

➤ He will feel guilty about hurting a defenseless baby—although it may take a few minutes (or days) for the guilt to sink in.

When both your children are still little, take an active role in trying to defuse situations that might turn violent. Although you may want them to learn how to work out conflicts on their own, most young children simply can't manage disagreements non-violently. So don't stay out of it on principle until someone gets hurt. Instead, step in and divert your baby or your older child's attention to some other activity. (Fortunately, young children are easily distracted.) Separate them, if necessary, but keep the peace any way you can. Rest assured, they'll have plenty of time to work out their differences on their own when they get older and are less physically mismatched.

Growing Up Together

You can't force your children to like each other or to enjoy each other's company (although given enough time, they probably will). You can encourage them to play together, but you'll need their cooperation. If they enjoy playing together (and they probably will if left to their own devices), great. But if they don't, that's fine, too.

Father Knows Best

"... [O]f course I wanted to share the doll's house with Bridget, because not only would that please Mother and demonstrate how generous and grown up I really was but because I knew that I loved Bridget very deeply and identified with her yearning as she tentatively touched the miniature grandfather's clock in the miniature hallway. ('Get your nasty little fingers out of there,' I wanted to scream, 'until I give you permission.')"

—Brooke Hayward

Keep thinking of your home as a social laboratory. As they grow up, your children won't necessarily like everyone they meet. So if your children don't like playing with each other, don't force them. As long as they can learn to get along with each other, they will have learned a valuable lesson. And as long as you can keep them from killing or maiming each other, you've done your job, too.

Unless arguments threaten to escalate to violence, I believe that older children should usually be left to settle their differences themselves. If your children come to you for help, you can offer suggestions on how they can resolve the conflict. But coming up with these kinds of ideas is a skill your children need to learn on their own, too.

One final word of advice about siblings as they grow older: If you want to maintain a reasonable semblance of family harmony, avoid making comparisons between your children. Nothing poisons a sibling relationship as quickly as listening to (or overhearing) parents who say things like

➤ Why can't you read yet? Jennifer was reading at your age.

➤ Her brother has a beautiful voice, but she can't carry a tune to save her life.

➤ You should see his sister: a born athlete. Matthew tries hard, but he's kind of clumsy.

➤ Why can't you be more like your brother?

➤ Why can't you be more like your sister?

Instead of drawing comparisons between siblings, recognize each of your children as an individual. They'll have certain talents, interests, and character traits in common (that's genetics), but each of your children will also have a unique personality, skills, and desires. Rather than holding up one child as a model for the other, try to appreciate their differences and encourage each of your children to improve his or her unique abilities.

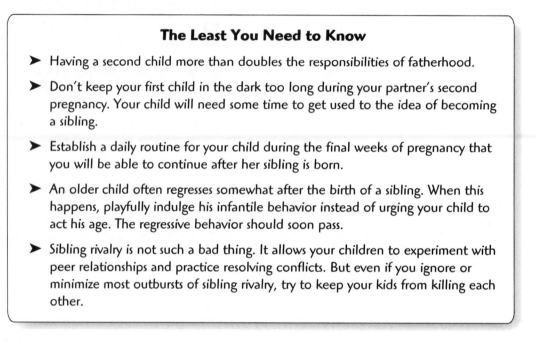

The Least You Need to Know

➤ Having a second child more than doubles the responsibilities of fatherhood.

➤ Don't keep your first child in the dark too long during your partner's second pregnancy. Your child will need some time to get used to the idea of becoming a sibling.

➤ Establish a daily routine for your child during the final weeks of pregnancy that you will be able to continue after her sibling is born.

➤ An older child often regresses somewhat after the birth of a sibling. When this happens, playfully indulge his infantile behavior instead of urging your child to act his age. The regressive behavior should soon pass.

➤ Sibling rivalry is not such a bad thing. It allows your children to experiment with peer relationships and practice resolving conflicts. But even if you ignore or minimize most outbursts of sibling rivalry, try to keep your kids from killing each other.

Chapter 18

The Serious Business of Child's Play

> ### In This Chapter
>
> ➤ The educational importance of toys and games
>
> ➤ How to play with your child
>
> ➤ Encouraging creativity and imagination through art and make-believe
>
> ➤ Helping your child get the most out of TV and computers
>
> ➤ Helping your child develop a love of reading

Fun and games, now that's serious. For your child, play is much more than just fun and games. Through play, your child will discover the world. She'll explore new objects, experiment with new textures, surprise herself with her own abilities, and rehearse new skills until she has achieved a certain mastery. So you can see this is serious business, this thing called child's play.

Toys and games serve as your child's best teaching tools. With your guidance and support, your child will develop physically, mentally, and socially. Best of all, it's fun. And if you can build a love for learning early, it may stay with your child throughout her life.

Class Is in Session

You and your partner are your child's first and best teachers; your home, his first classroom. Although it might seem like a huge responsibility when you recognize that your child will learn more from you than from anyone else, try not to feel as though you have a lot of pressure on you. If you relax and adopt a playful attitude, most of your "teaching" will be fun for both you and your child.

To teach your child and stimulate his development, you don't need to run out and buy a complete set of foreign-language tapes, flashcards, CDs, or Mozart. Everything that's already in your child's world will stimulate his senses. The sights, sounds, smells, textures, and tastes of your child's world will teach him a thing or two. So relax; all you need to do is open your child's eyes, mind, and heart by encouraging him to explore his world playfully.

You may not find this quite as easy as it sounds. Perhaps you're not a very playful person. But for the sake of your child, look at play from his point of view. Your child does not treat play as a time-filler or an exercise in self-indulgence. Play is the best way for your child to explore the world, discover its secrets, and grow. Through play, your child will not only learn about the world and practice new skills, he will enjoy what he learns. Who could reasonably object to that?

Father Knows Best

"For truly it is to be noted, that children's plays are not sports, and should be deemed as their most serious actions."

—Michel de Montaigne

Setting the Curriculum

You and your partner will serve as the primary filters for your child's experience during virtually all of her pre-kindergarten years. She can't play with a toy unless you buy it for her. (Indeed, until your child can crawl, she can't play with a toy unless you physically bring it to her.) Your child can't read books (or have them read to her) unless you buy them or get them from the library. She can't go anywhere unless you take her.

Through your choices of what to make accessible to your child, you and your partner set the curriculum for all of your child's pre-school learning. You alone get to decide what's appropriate for her to see, do, and learn.

Evaluating the Faculty

How good a teacher will you be for your child? What should you be teaching him to get him ready for school? How should you prepare your "lesson plan"?

Try not to worry too much about these questions. You don't have to fret about how much your child is learning through your play with him. Here's why: Whether or not you consciously set out to teach your child something when you play with him, he will learn something anyway.

Maybe your child will discover that wet sand holds its shape better than dry sand. Maybe he'll find out that balls can bounce and roll, but blocks can't. Maybe he'll master the manual dexterity needed to spin a game spinner or throw dice. Maybe he'll practice counting to six as he moves a game piece around a board. But count on it: Your child will learn something almost every time you play with him.

Since your child will learn something no matter what or how you choose to play, you don't need to worry about including an explicit element of teaching every time you play with him. On the other hand, if you really want to teach your toddler or preschooler a specific skill, make sure to include an element of play in the "lesson plan." After all, that's the way your child will learn best.

Your child will learn a lot through playful exploration of his immediate world. Yet you can enhance—and even accelerate—his learning by challenging him with age-appropriate toys and games. By devoting a little time, energy, and gentle guidance to your child (that is, simply by playing with him), you will help him learn.

Daddy Dos and Don'ts

You're an adult (or at least your driver's license says so), so you probably don't see all your parenting and household responsibilities as fun, but you should try to make household chores fun, especially those involving childcare. Splash around a little while giving your toddler a bath. Pretend the spoon is an airplane when feeding him. Sing a song or make funny faces while changing his diaper. The more playful an attitude you bring to baby care, the more fun both you and your child will have together.

Tips on Toys

From the time your child first discovers her hands, toys will be her most useful learning tools. Your child will use toys

➤ As a way of exploring and mastering new skills

➤ As materials for experiments that help her discover the properties of both the natural and the human worlds

➤ As puzzles that help her find out just how things work

Your choice of age-appropriate toys will help make learning fascinating and fun for both you and your child. The tips in Chapter 11 about purchasing toys for infants still apply throughout the toddler and preschool years. Buy toys for your child with an eye toward the following:

➤ Age-appropriateness

➤ Safety

➤ Simplicity

➤ Diversity

Using these criteria you can find dozens (or hundreds) of toys your child will love. You can get everything from balls, blocks, and stacking cups to ride-on toys, pushcarts, and pull toys; from bath toys and sandbox toys to shape boxes and jigsaw puzzles; and from LEGOs to Lincoln Logs. You will have fun choosing toys that allow your child to practice physical and mental skills such as stacking, pouring, riding, walking, sorting, matching, twisting, and building.

Although store-bought toys are often well made and versatile, you probably have plenty of safe household objects your child would love to play with, too. Remember the value of pots and wooden spoons and the appeal of plastic cookie cutters. Everything from paper-towel rolls to large cardboard boxes, from plastic rulers to colanders and funnels, can entertain your child for hours on end.

His and Her Toys?

When choosing toys for your child, especially during his early years, try to avoid automatic sexual stereotyping. Who knows, your son might like dolls or dressing up for make-believe play, or your daughter might like trucks and tossing around a football. But your child will never have the chance to find out if you limit yourself to buying toys that conform to stereotypes about your child's gender.

When you buy a push toy for your son, for example, why not get one that looks like a shopping cart? In all likelihood he goes to the grocery store with you or your partner, so it will seem familiar to him. Or when you buy a big kid's bed for your daughter, why not consider the one shaped like a racing car? After all, she probably spends a lot of time in a car and might enjoy the fantasy of driving off to dreamland.

If you encourage your child to explore all options for playthings, you will foster the development of a well-rounded child. As fitting in becomes increasingly important during the school years, your child will probably begin to conform to sexual stereotyping anyway (though a rare few rebel against it). But you certainly don't need to give sexual stereotyping a head start.

Everything Old Is New Again

Chances are, your child will accumulate more toys, games, and other playthings than she will know what to do with. Young children tend to play with no more than a handful of toys for weeks on end. It's almost as though they go on "binges"—playing Uncle Wiggly three or four times a day, for example, or playing with Barbies for hour after hour. And parents, eager to see their children find something that absorbs them, sometimes fall into a rut, too.

Young children enjoy repetition and draw comfort from routines in their lives. But if your child plays with the same toy (or handful of toys) over and over again, she will miss the opportunity to explore the world in greater diversity.

To encourage your child to play with a variety of toys, try rotating them every two weeks or so. Dig some of her forgotten toys from the bottom of the toy chest and put away some of the ones she has been playing with for a while. Your child can—and no doubt will—still go on toy binges, but if you increase her options, she periodically might transfer her obsession from one toy to another.

Game Hunting

At age three or four, your child can probably start to play simple board or card games with you. Like all child's play, games are not just fun—though they certainly should be that, too. Games enable your child to practice academic skills such as counting, matching colors, numbers, and shapes (the suits in a deck of cards, for example), and even comparing numbers. Because games usually last more than five or ten minutes, they can also give your child valuable practice in focusing his attention.

In addition, games encourage social interaction. While playing games with you (and later with other children), your child will get to practice social skills such as taking turns, waiting patiently, sharing, and being a good sport. You can reinforce the notion of being a good sport by emphasizing how fun the games are (even though your child may very well be obsessed with who's winning).

Games also provide a fun way to teach your child about following rules, honesty (no cheating!), and luck (both good and bad). Games can teach your child many valuable lessons about setting goals (playing to win), achieving them (winning), and handling the disappointment of not achieving them (losing). Best of all, your child will discover that even if he loses a game, he'll start out "even" with you the next time you play. For this reason, your child may want to play the same game over and over again.

Point-Shaving Scandals

The question of winning and losing brings up a thorny issue: Should you allow your child to beat you, at least occasionally? Certainly, if you're playing Concentration with a three-year-old, you could make almost all the matches yourself long before your child could. But should you rein yourself in to give your child a chance to make some matches, too?

Well, look at it this way: If you want your child to enjoy playing games and to learn the lessons that can by learned by playing games, she should win nearly half (if not more) of the games she plays. Though some children focus on the fun, adhering to the maxim "It's not whether you win or lose but how you play the game," no one likes to lose all the time. So your child will probably find it frustrating to play games with you if you win most of the time.

If you regard it as patronizing to let your child win half the time, or if you feel it would instill in her a false sense of confidence and competence, then fine, don't throw the games. But work at coming up with a way to even the odds.

One possible solution to this moral dilemma is to limit yourself to games governed entirely by chance and luck, at least until your child gets better at game strategy. Popular board games for preschoolers such as Chutes and Ladders, Candyland, and Hi-Ho Cherry-O, as well as card games such as War and Old Maid, depend almost entirely on chance.

Another solution, which may seem obvious if you're a golfer, is to handicap yourself in some way when playing games with your child that require more skill. When playing Go Fish or Concentration, for instance, you could start the game by giving your child five or six pairs of cards, and then play the game according to the rules. When playing checkers, you could remove two or four of your checkers at the beginning of the game. Or, when playing wiffle ball, your child could hit off a tee while you have to hit a pitched ball with the bat in just one hand (and not your dominant one). Through a little trial and error, you will soon arrive at an appropriate handicap—one that leaves the outcome of the game in suspense.

Winning will boost your child's confidence enormously, giving her a sense of joyful triumph—especially beating you, who are so big and clever in her eyes. At the same time, however, your child will master a valuable skill if she also learns to lose gracefully. After all, it won't be long before your child starts playing games with other children. And other kids are not likely to handicap themselves nor deliberately throw a game to let your child win.

Rules of Play

Even if you buy all the toys in the world for him, your child will still most often enjoy playing with you. As he gains greater and more graceful mobility, your child will enjoy playing tag, jumping on you, climbing all over you, wrestling with you, and chasing you around the house or yard. When you talk or sing or read aloud, your child will listen to you with great intensity. (Enjoy it while it lasts.) And if he can make you smile or laugh, your child will feel as though he just won a terrific game.

Since it will bring such joy to your child (and to you), make sure you give him a lot of playtime with you. But what's the best way to play with your child? What can you do to bring out the best in your child through play? How can you make sure your child learns something by playing with you? No problem. Let's start by going over the ground rules.

It's Only a Game

The first and most important rule to observe when playing with your child is that the way your child wants to play is just as valid, valuable, and important as the way you want her to play. Avoid ruling over your child's play with an iron fist. If your child indicates that she doesn't want to play with something at the moment, don't force the issue. Just because you want to build a block tower or play catch doesn't mean your child wants to. Pay attention to her moods and responses. If your child seems bored or frustrated with a particular activity, shift to something else. (You can always build that block tower after your child goes to bed.)

Similarly, if your child wants to play something the "wrong" way, let her. Don't expect your child to live by the maxim, "If you can't do something right, don't bother doing it at all." Your child has her own way of playing with things, which frequently involves experimentation and exploration. In fact, your child will often learn something valuable by playing with toys in her own particular way, even if it's the "wrong" way (at least in your eyes).

So if your child isn't playing a game according to the rules, or if she's playing with a toy the "wrong" way, regard it as an experiment rather than a failure. Who's to say your child's way of playing is any less valid than your way?

Father Knows Best

"There are few places outside his own play where a child can contribute to the world in which he finds himself. His world: dominated by adults who tell him what to do and when to do it—benevolent tyrants who dispense gifts to their "good" subjects and punishment to their "bad" ones, who are amused at the "cleverness" of children and annoyed by their "stupidities.""

—Viola Spolin

The second important rule when playing with your child is to have patience. You may want so much for your child to master a certain skill or activity (reaching out for a ball, for example, or counting the spaces on a game board) that you can't help reaching over and doing it for her. Try to restrain yourself from taking over when playing with your child, however. Have enough patience to give your child the time she needs to discover and practice how to play with a certain toy or plaything.

Of course, you can fit a shape into a shape box more easily than your child can. You can throw a pair of dice without throwing them off the table. You can count out play money faster. You're an adult; you're supposed to be able to do these things. Your child, on the other hand, needs to discover and master thousands of new skills like these in her first years. But she can't practice or master them if you do them for her.

So back off a little, big fella. Let the little one have a chance. In general, when playing with your child, help her only if she asks for your help—and even then, first encourage her to try again, unless she's already bordering on hysteria. When your child accepts the challenge and at last accomplishes what she wanted to do, she deserves congratulations. Don't forget to lavish her with hugs and praise.

Once you've mastered these two rules—flexibility and patience—you'll be well on your way to engaging your child in productive play. In fact, there's really only one other important rule: Have fun!

Playing the Part of Playmate

A father must assume many different roles when playing with his child. To help your child get the most out of play, you will need to shift fluidly among the following roles:

➤ **Playmate.** Your toddler or preschooler needs you to play with him. He can't play tag by himself. It's no fun throwing a ball if no one throws it back to him. Even make-believe is more fun when he doesn't have to pretend he's playing with someone, too.

➤ **Booster.** Your child takes great pride in mastering a new skill, but he feels even prouder when he can show it off to you. So applaud his efforts and cheer on his achievements.

Daddy Dos and Don'ts

Encourage your child, regardless of his age, to take a little downtime every day. Especially as he begins to cut down on the number of naps he takes—or, horrors, eliminates them entirely—your child will need you to provide at least an hour or two of quiet activities: reading, drawing or painting, listening to music, even watching television.

➤ **Know-it-all.** Your child will often need your guidance. He may want to know how something works. He may need suggestions on how to do something. He may have questions that he can't answer. When he asks for your help or advice, happily share it with him.

➤ **Lab assistant.** Your toddler or preschooler probably needs you to get the materials (books, art supplies, and so on) he needs to help him in his discoveries.

➤ **Crisis manager.** Learning is not always easy—even learning through play. In his rush to learn and develop, your child will no doubt want to do things he cannot yet manage physically or mentally. He will want to master new skills instantly. So when he reaches the breaking point, he will need your comfort, your encouragement, and, sometimes, your help.

Social Play

Social play—that is, playing *with* another child of the same age—will not really be an option until your child reaches age three or four. Oh, you can get a couple of one- or two-year-olds together and they might engage in some *parallel play* for a while, but actually playing and interacting with another child is not really possible for infants and toddlers.

By about age three, however, your child will start making friends. She will begin to have favorite playmates, and when one comes to play, your child may virtually forget that you exist. (Depending on your personality and attachment to your child, you may find this a relief or a blow to your ego; but, either way, it can't be helped.)

Because your child starts to play with others, however, doesn't mean that she no longer wants to play with you. Your child might ignore you when a friend comes over, but when the friend is gone she'll still want and need to play with you.

Paterniterms

Parallel play refers to the tendency of toddlers to play next to each other without actually playing with each other. A toddler engaged in parallel play may observe the other toddler out of the corner of her eye to see what the other is doing. She may even begin to imitate the other child. But toddlers rarely interact with one another in play.

Imagine That!

Most toddlers and preschoolers have a great deal of creativity and imagination. You can see it in the innovative ways they play with new toys and in the experiments they conduct with new objects to figure out how they work. You can hear it in the stories they tell and in the way they interpret misheard phrases. (A famous illustration is the child who loved the song about "Gladly, the cross-eyed bear," which turns out to be the hymn, *Gladly the Cross I'd Bear*.)

Although your toddler or preschooler will exercise his creativity and imagination no matter what, you can channel some of his ingenuity by providing outlets for his creativity and opportunities to explore his imagination. Two of the most enjoyable ways are through art and make-believe.

Art for Art's Sake

Toddlers and preschoolers love to create works of art. Art provides them with a wonderful opportunity to demonstrate their creative powers and to explore the notion of cause-and-effect that young children find so fascinating. They simply press a marker or crayon on a piece of paper and, voilà, a line appears. What a concept!

At one, two, and even three years of age, your child's artwork will be almost unrecognizable (if she intends it to represent anything at all). Toddlers are, by nature and ability, abstract expressionists. The process of creation matters far more to them than the final work of art. For your toddler, art is primarily a matter of manipulating and mastering various artistic media. So encourage your child to do fingerpaints and watercolors, scribble with crayons and markers, and sculpt objects with clay or dough.

The more practice your child gets with a particular medium, the more adept she will become at manipulating it. You will see her development increase in sophistication as the months and years go by. At age one or two, for example, your child will probably draw zigzag lines that run horizontally across the page. Before long, she'll draw vertical zigzags, and then spirals. By around three, your child may discover that she can make the ends of a line meet to form a circle or oval. (Okay, maybe not a perfect one.) She may also begin to notice that the lighter she presses down with a marker or crayon, the thinner the line will be.

Daddy Dos and Don'ts

If you don't immediately recognize what your child's artwork portrays, shy away from commenting on content unless your child asks you to guess what the painting represents. Even a question as innocent as "What is it?" may inhibit your child's creativity and exploration. Perhaps your child didn't intend it to represent anything. She was simply exploring the medium, trying out new brushstrokes, or experimenting with colors—in short, creating art for art's sake. If so, your question about content may inhibit her creativity by implying that all art should be representational.

As your child's hand-eye coordination and ability to manipulate different artistic media improve, her drawings and paintings will become increasingly recognizable. But you certainly won't recognize everything she creates.

You should not only exercise caution before asking about the content of your preschooler's artwork, you should avoid guessing it altogether. If you guess correctly, your child will beam and clap her hands as much for your cleverness in seeing it as for her own skill at creating it. But if you guess incorrectly, your child might feel discouraged about her artistic ability or think that you're a total idiot for failing to see the obvious. Either way, one of you loses. So, instead of guessing about content, simply admire the artistry—use of color, the brushstrokes, and the thoroughness with which she's covered the page with paint.

By age four or five, your child's artistic skill will really blossom, and, in all likelihood, she will seldom create art simply for art's sake anymore. She will no longer be content to put lines on paper and then see what she has created. She will become increasingly concerned with using art to represent something else. Moreover, your child will probably form a notion of what she wants to create before she even picks up a paintbrush, a crayon, or a wad of clay.

The Wonderful World of Make-Believe

From about age two, your child will enjoy playing make-believe, especially with your encouragement. So take the time to rummage through the attic or go to a few garage sales and pick up some dress-up clothes, hats, and props that will allow your child to pretend he's someone else. With just a few clothes and props, your child can instantly transform himself into a doctor, an engineer, a sports superstar, a cook, a firefighter, a police officer, a teacher, a construction worker, a truck driver, a nurse, a ballerina, a grocery store clerk, a librarian, a zookeeper, and of course, a mommy or a daddy.

Don't dismiss make-believe or pretend play as something done only by toddlers. Some parents of four-year-olds put so much emphasis on "school readiness" skills—the alphabet, numbers, shapes, and colors—that they discourage fantasy play, regarding it as idle entertainment, a waste of time. But the make-believe worlds your child creates actually promote intellectual, emotional, and social development.

Fantasy play offers a unique outlet for your child's imagination and creativity. In requiring your child to adopt a role (or many different roles), make-believe play fosters cognitive flexibility, the ability to shift ways of thinking from moment to moment.

Pretend play also allows your child to practice different ways of getting along with others, which will prove invaluable when he starts school. Playing house, for example, gives your child a chance to rehearse social interactions (most often based on observation and imitation of you and your partner) in a way that feels safe to him. Through this kind of practice, your child can build skills that will carry into his "real" friendships later in life.

Finally, by acting out grown-up roles in pretend play, your child can develop confidence and readiness for "real" excursions in the outside world (kindergarten, for example). The act of pretending can be very powerful for children (and adults, too). By playing a more mature and skilled role, your child will actually transform himself into a more mature and capable child.

Daddy Dos and Don'ts

Unless you are invited to take part, try to stay out of your child's make-believe games (though they can often be fun to listen in on). Your child will exercise his imagination much more if you keep your input out of it. Your child will create his own special worlds of make-believe—by himself or with a friend. If he asks you to play a particular role in his pretend play, however, don't hesitate to accept. But play the part strictly according to your child's script. Let your child weave his own scenarios rather than direct the plot yourself.

Why Do You Think They Call Them Monitors?

Television and computers, videos and the Internet: Aside from parents, these are the most pervasive influences on the majority of young children in America. (In some families, they probably have even greater influence than parents.) Is this cause for alarm or celebration?

Few parents see the pervasiveness of television and computers as something to celebrate. But parents who serve as their children's television and computer "monitors"—who place limits on the time spent at the television or computer and monitor what the kids watch or do—should not necessarily view this trend as particularly alarming.

As long as you know the content of the programs and videos she watches, the software she plays with, and the downloads she gets from the Internet, and offer her guidance in her choices, then these electronic boxes can often serve as valuable educational tools. And as long as you pay attention, you can keep the corrupting influence of these technologies at bay.

Welcome to TV Land

It's easy to point an accusing finger at TV. Yes, most of the stuff on the air—even the "educational" programs aimed at children—is crap. Yes, programs—even cartoons aimed at children—have far too much violence and sexual content. Yes, invasive commercials cast a seductive net, enticing children to pressure their parents to buy sugar-coated cereals, cookies, candy, and toys, toys, toys. Yes, television can even retard your child's creativity and imagination. And, of course, it consumes hours and hours on end—hours that your child might otherwise devote to reading, playing, exercising, or finding a cure for cancer.

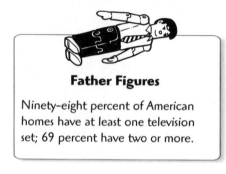

Father Figures

Ninety-eight percent of American homes have at least one television set; 69 percent have two or more.

But the answer to the often annoying and corrupt influence of television is not to throw the set out or turn it off forever. Even if this were the answer, most Americans would refuse the cure.

Monitored closely and viewed in moderate amounts, television can actually have a positive influence on your child. Television can help develop and advance reading, counting, and thinking skills and spur a young child on to further learning. Consider that TV can achieve the following:

➤ Take your child all over the world, introducing him to people, places, and experiences he might never otherwise encounter. (This, of course, is also one of the biggest complaints about TV.)

➤ Prompt your child to increase his vocabulary and language skills, learn to count, and recognize colors and shapes.

➤ Motivate your child to read more (or to want to learn how to read).

➤ Reinforce values such as respecting differences, being kind, and sharing.

Tossing out the good that television can bring just because it can also do harm is like (pardon the expression) throwing the baby out with the bath water.

Too Much TV ...

In all likelihood, television won't become too much of a problem during your baby's first year. To your infant, television offers nothing more than a blur of light and color. Televised images usually change so rapidly that they cannot sustain an infant's brief attention span.

All that can change in the second year, however, when many parents start to rely on the TV to keep their toddlers occupied for a "few minutes" while they take a shower, get dressed, make a phone call or two, or take care of a few household chores. From a practical standpoint, many parents wouldn't know what to do without the "electronic baby-sitter." But if those "few minutes" stretch into several hours, if you rely too heavily on TV to entertain your child or keep her quiet, you will dramatically shrink your child's opportunities to learn about the world in other ways.

Organizations interested in children's welfare—the National Education Association, the National Parent Teacher Association, and the American Academy of Pediatrics—recommend that parents limit the amount of time their children watch TV to 10–15 hours a week (in other words, an average of about two hours a day).

So, if you've decided to cut your child's TV time in half, what will you do with your child for those extra two or three hours a day? Well, let's face up to it: You or your partner will have to do a little more playing or entertaining. You can take out the crayons or paints and help her create something. You can read a good book or listen to some music. You can go to a park, a library, a museum, a carnival, or a local lake. If you have a preschooler, you can arrange for play dates with her friends.

It's up to you to keep your young child engaged when she's not watching TV, which probably is why so many parents encourage their children to watch it in the first place. Sure, keeping your child engaged and entertained may be harder work than sitting her in front of the boob tube, but often it's more fun, too.

Father Figures

The average American child sits in front of the tube 4 hours a day (28 hours a week). Sadly, children who watch 4 or more hours of TV a day tend to develop poorer reading skills, are less physically active, and get along less well with others than children who watch less than four hours a day. If you add it all up, the average child will spend nearly 25,000 hours watching TV by age 18. That's almost twice as much time as that same child will spend in school. Frightening, isn't it?

Father Knows Best

"One hour with a child is like a ten-mile run."

—Joan Benoit Samuelson

... Or Too Much Bad TV?

If you and your partner really want to avoid the corrupting influence of television, you'll need to pay attention not only to the amount of time your child spends watching it, but to the programming itself. Remember that you are the primary filters of your child's experience of the world during his first five years. You choose what he eats. You pick the books he reads. You decide which toys he plays with. You select the places to go on special outings.

How can you then turn on the TV and walk out of the room? In doing so, you turn over your role and responsibility as the filters of your child's experience to the commercial medium of the television. And do you really trust television programmers to make the same choices you would about what's appropriate for your child?

Father Knows Best

"If you came home and you found a strange man... teaching your kids to punch each other,... you'd kick him right out of the house. But... you come in and the TV is on and you don't think twice about it."

—Dr. Jerome Singer

If you don't do so already, you should carefully monitor what programs your child watches and guide his choices. If you're unfamiliar with a show that your child wants to watch, sit down and watch an episode (or at least part of an episode) with him. You can usually tell in just a few minutes (and often in just a few seconds) what's junk and what's not. Take a look at *Power Rangers,* and then check out *Reading Rainbow.* Which would you rather your preschooler watch: a show that features a dozen acts of violence in 30 minutes or a show that encourages your child to become a reader?

Believe it or not, you can find entertaining, intelligent, imaginative, and instructive TV shows for your children. If you want to avoid violence, hard-selling commercials designed specifically to appeal to young children, and programming that has little or no educational content, you'd do well to stick with the following:

➤ Shows on public television.
➤ Shows on The Learning Channel.

Father Figures

Astonishingly, nearly 85 percent of parents who have children age three to eight do not help their children pick out the TV shows they watch.

➤ Shows on Nickelodeon during the daytime, when all the commercials are sandwiched between shows (rather than interrupting shows in the middle).

➤ Certain shows on the Family Channel.

➤ Carefully selected children's videotapes.

If you have a VCR (and 78 percent of American homes do), your child need not ever watch commercial television at all. Forget the networks. You can be your child's television programmer. You can create your own video library by taping shows you like. You can even cut out the commercials, if any, while taping—or zip through them when your child watches the video.

In addition to taping shows directly from the TV, you can buy or rent thousands of different videos for your child. Most children's videos cost between $10 and $20, so if you find one your child loves (and you can tolerate), buying it will be cheaper than renting it a thousand times.

Daddy Dos and Don'ts

You should, of course, monitor the videos your child watches. Many of them offer the same violent, sexual, and questionable moral content that commercial TV shows offer. If possible, screen videos before buying them. If that's not possible, at least take a look at them before your child does.

Everybody's a Critic

Leaving aside that most TV programs stink and that commercials pitch junk food and junk toys to your kids, the main problem with television is the passivity of the medium. Most people who watch TV—adults as well as children—just sit back and absorb whatever is shown.

You can teach and encourage your child to view television more actively, to think critically about what she's seeing. While watching a program with your child, for example, you might consider the following:

➤ Comment occasionally on what you see.

➤ Ask questions to find out whether your child understands what's going on in the show.

➤ Play a game of guessing what might happen next.

➤ Play a game of guessing what a commercial is selling before the advertiser actually names the product.

➤ Help your child make connections between TV and real life by drawing associations between what you're seeing and your child's (or your own) experiences.

➤ Follow up on a subject or plot that your child found fascinating by doing further research. Go to a library or a museum to find out more about the subject. Or help your preschooler make clay models or paint pictures of what she sees on television.

Father Knows Best

"Television may be the only electrical appliance that's more useful after it's turned off."

—Mr. (Fred) Rogers

If you take a more active role in your child's television watching—limiting the hours she spends as a couch potato, monitoring and guiding her choices of programming, and training her to be a critical viewer—you can transform the television. In no time at all the idiot box will turn into an educational tool.

Welcome to the Computer Age

Like television, computers can bombard your child with junk. Yet, if you choose software carefully, computers can also promote and even accelerate learning in a wide variety of areas. The best software available for preschoolers (and kids in elementary school) can help your child practice and improve basic academic skills such as:

➤ Recognizing letters

➤ Associating sounds with letters

➤ Counting

➤ Telling time

➤ Adding and subtracting

➤ Sorting objects by color and shape

➤ Creating pictures by choosing colors and shapes

➤ Creating songs by choosing notes on a scale

Programs for slightly older children add to these skills by introducing:

➤ Computer-generated art

➤ Geographical adventures

➤ Synonyms, homophones, antonyms, and the like

➤ The concept of money

➤ Logic and problem-solving skills

Today, most elementary schools (and many preschools) have computers in the classroom. If you can at least familiarize your child with computers, he won't find them intimidating when he reaches school age. The best computer programs will not only delight and instruct your child, but will probably entertain him as well. So link up to the information superhighway before your child leaves you in the dust.

Helping your child get the most out of a computer requires even more of a commitment on your part than helping him get the most out of TV. The software might claim to be simple enough for a preschooler to operate on his own, but don't you believe it.

Chances are, your child won't be on the computer for more than a minute or two before he asks for your help. Until he gains some experience, for example, your child probably will need help manipulating the mouse and figuring out how its movement coordinates with the action of the arrow on the screen. In addition, although most programs for preschoolers emphasize graphics and the spoken, rather than the written, word, your child may need help with the small amount of reading they require.

Screening Software

Here's what to look for when buying software packages for your preschooler:

➤ Bright and entertaining graphics

➤ Clear sound quality

➤ Engaging sounds and graphics that are integrated with the essential activities of the program, not just incidental or unrelated to the primary activities

➤ Few written prompts or instructions, if any

➤ Easy-to-follow instructions presented graphically or through simple spoken words

➤ User-friendliness (keeping in mind that the user is a small child)—in other words, a program that requires only a mouse or one or two keyboard strokes to operate

➤ A graphical menu that allows your child to enter and exit the program easily

➤ Feedback that remains positive, encouraging, and upbeat even if your child makes a mistake—in other words, a program that encourages her to "Try again!" rather than one that displays sad faces or, worse, hurls "humorous" insults at her

➤ A limit on the number of wrong tries your child can make before the program supplies the right answer

➤ Educational value, yes, but also fun for your child (or what's the point?)

The computer software market changes rapidly. Although the best programs have some staying power, any list published here would neglect all the terrific programs developed since this writing. So ask for recommendations of age-appropriate software from friends, neighbors, and relatives who have small children. Ask your child's preschool teacher, the computer teacher at your local elementary school, and your software dealer.

Before buying a computer program for your preschooler, try browsing through it, if possible. Ask neighbors who have preschoolers what programs they have and see whether you can borrow them for a day or so. Check out your local library to see if it has children's programs that you can either borrow or use on a computer in the library. Or try some programs out on the computers in your local software store. However you do it, try to get some idea of what you're buying before you spend any money.

Although you will certainly find educational software programs that your child will love, keep in mind that the skills and concepts she hones on the computer can be taught in fun ways off-line, too. The computer should either complement and reinforce the concepts you introduce and practice in your everyday play with your child or introduce concepts that you then follow up on during your off-line play.

Daddy Dos and Don'ts

When testing out software in the computer store, bring your child with you. You may think a program is entertaining, cute, enlightening, and easy to use, but what appeals to you might not appeal to your child. If she finds a computer program boring or impossibly difficult to play, you will have wasted $20 or $30 if you don't find out until you get it home. (Because customers can sometimes download a program into their computer and thus get it for free, very few software dealers will accept returns with "no questions asked.")

Breeding Readers

Good children's books will not only introduce your child to a wide variety of silly characters, funny poems, and riveting stories, they will teach your child about colors and numbers, emotions and places. They will intrigue your child, increase his curiosity, and make him want to read more. In addition, the hours you devote to reading to your child may help improve his ability to express himself.

If you want your child to grow up to be a reader, start reading to him early and often. In fact, make a point of reading to your child every day. You can make reading part of your child's bedtime routine, for instance. (If you do, make sure to leave enough time to get through an entire book or two without rushing.) You can settle down to read a book whenever your child needs a break from being on the go or when over-tiredness has brought him to the brink of frustration. Or you can simply make reading one of the fun everyday things you and your child like to do together.

Learning How to Read to a Child

Reading will be a communal activity for years to come. In all likelihood, your child will not be able to read anything on her own until she is five or six years old. If you give your toddler or preschooler a book to "read" by herself, she'll quickly flip through the pages and be done in about a minute or two. But despite the tales about one- and two-year-olds never sitting still for more than a minute, most toddlers will sit for at least five or ten minutes if someone (like you) is reading a book to them. If you sit with your child, read her the story, examine the pictures with her, and piece together some of the words, she'll sit for much longer.

You can probably sustain your child's interest even longer if you try to make reading an interactive experience. Pause every couple of pages to ask what's happening (or what your child thinks will happen next). Examine and talk about the illustrations, and make sure your child knows what some of the more difficult words mean. Always let her know that it's all right to interrupt the reading to ask questions about anything in the story that's puzzling her.

Toddlers especially, but preschoolers, too, love repetition. Your child may ask you to reread the same book even before you've finished it the first time. Bear with the repetition and try to read with the same enthusiasm and energy the thirty-first time that you did the first.

Daddy Dos and Don'ts

When choosing books for your child, don't limit yourself only to the ones your child will understand every single word of. Your child's comprehension will surprise you. Even *if she* has to skip over some unfamiliar words, she can probably still follow the thread of the story. So you can read short stories to your child long before she can utter a complete sentence on her own.

In all likelihood, your child will get something new from each reading. She'll finally understand a word that she's glossed over during the first 80 readings. Or she'll notice a previously overlooked detail in one of the illustrations. Or she'll begin to memorize the book, which may help her recognize printed words before too long.

When reading to your toddler or preschooler, remember not to go overboard trying to remain faithful to the author's words. Your child may get bored with too many words on a page. (How much is too many? It depends on your child's age and interest in reading in general, as well as the particular book being read.) If so, feel free to skip to the next page. (You can always read the entire book on your own if the suspense is killing you).

Who Needs Pictures When You've Got a Thousand Words?

By age two or three, your child will probably begin to enjoy longer stories that use a combination of words and pictures to tell a story (although more basic picture books will not lose their appeal to him for quite some time). Stories that center on familiar places and situations (homes, nursery schools, friendship, and the like) will probably appeal to your child at this age.

As your child gets a little older, perhaps around age three or four, you can start him on the road to reading by occasionally pointing out certain words as you read to him. Choose simple words ("cat," "up," "tree") that you know will pop up throughout the book. When you pause to point out these words, tell your child the sound each of the letters makes. You may be surprised how quickly your child catches on. After just a few readings, your child may be able to figure out the word himself.

You can also pause to count particular objects in one of the book's illustrations. Counting books are designed explicitly for this purpose, but the illustrations in most children's books will allow you to do at least some counting with your child as well.

As your child gets older, begin choosing books for him that feature fewer pictures and more words. Although your child will probably need less of the story told through illustrations, he will still enjoy pictures—especially intricately complex illustrations that demand careful scrutiny.

By age four or five, your child's sophistication as a listener may have developed to such an extent that he can sustain interest in stories that can't be finished in one sitting. If he seems willing (and then maintains interest), try reading him a chapter or two from a good children's novel—one that features whimsical characters, funny situations, or children or animals as the central characters. (My children enjoyed *Pippi Longstocking, Charlotte's Web,* and *Stuart Little* at this age. Check with your local children's librarian for some other suggestions.)

Daddy Dos and Don'ts

As you tell your own tall tales, try to narrate the stories from a child's point of view. Imagine yourself as two or three feet shorter and tell the story from down there. This means that you will reach no higher than the bellies of adult characters in your story. As you stare up into their nostrils, you might see the ceiling or sky or birds behind these characters' heads. In addition, try to focus on exaggerated sensual details that will bring the story alive for your child: funny noises, vivid colors, and the taste of exotic foods.

Tale Spinning

Books aren't the only source of stories that your child will enjoy. In addition to reading to your child, you can weave stories of your own:

➤ True-life tales about your childhood or about your child when she was younger

➤ Made-up tales involving fantasy, adventure, and intrigue

➤ Stories that mingle true-to-life details with fantasy elements

➤ Stories featuring characters, actions, and settings suggested by your child

➤ Stories in which you and your child take turns saying what happens next

If you are well versed in creating stories for or with your child, take the time to tape them or write them down. (You and your child can even add illustrations to make a "real" book.) Before long, you will have a library of your child's favorite tales—stories she can listen to again and again.

The Least You Need to Know

➤ Play is not a waste of time for your child. It's the first, as well as the best, way for him to learn and grow. Best of all, your child will learn something through play regardless of whether you consciously set out to teach him anything.

➤ The way your child wants to play is as valid, valuable, and important as the way you want her to play.

➤ Monitor not just the amount of time your child spends watching TV, but the content of the programs he watches.

➤ Encourage active television viewing by following up TV shows with discussions or projects based on what you've seen. Complement computer learning, too, by practicing the same skills with off-line activities.

➤ Read to your toddler, preschooler, or elementary school child every day.

Part 5

The Wonder Years: Fathering Older Children

The kid's finally in school? Terrific, you did a great job parenting through preschool, and now you can go into retirement. After all, your child's teachers now have the responsibility for his education. And as your child moves from grade to grade, his friends will wield ever greater influence over his social behavior and opinions. (Yes, he has his own opinions now, and he won't be shy about sharing them with you.) So your job must be pretty much over.

Not so fast. Your child will still have questions—difficult ones about things like love and sex and death and right and wrong. Your child will need help developing a conscience—and encouragement to use it in guiding her actions. Your child will need help with school. Even as a teenager, though she would hate to admit it, your child will need your help and advice on those rare occasions when she allows herself to ask for them. So stick around. The best is yet to come.

Chapter 19

Love, Death, and Other Topics of Conversation

In This Chapter

➤ The importance of talking to your child about big issues

➤ What may happen if you try to repress your child's curiosity about sex and death

➤ How to talk to your child about sex

➤ Handling potentially embarrassing sexual situations

➤ How to talk to your child about death

Parenthood is a long conversation that begins when your child can't even understand a word you say and ends when she refuses to listen to every word you say. In the middle, however, your child will truly listen to you. She will want to know what you think and benefit from your wisdom. She will respect your knowledge, your experience, and your opinions.

This gives you a terrific opportunity from about age 18 months to age 16 (or if your child is precocious, 13 or 14) to help shape and mold the way your child thinks, but only if you take advantage of it. Open the conversation about big issues—about things like love, sex, death, religious beliefs, drugs, and morality—as soon as you feel your child can understand most of what you have to say. From time to time, whenever they come up (and if they don't come up, bring them up yourself), return to these issues, offering more detailed facts and opinions as your child's understanding becomes more sophisticated.

Your conversations with your child don't always have to be so weighty, of course. You should also talk to your child about your own interests—about sports or art or fishing or bird-watching or even politics—and about what interests her—school, friendships, TV, computers, and the like. The more you talk to your child about anything and everything, the easier your lifelong conversation will run and the easier it will be when you need to talk about the big issues.

Father Knows Best

"If men do not keep on speaking terms with children, they cease to be men and become merely machines for eating and for earning money."

—John Updike

Unspeakable Silence

From an early age, your child will demonstrate his curiosity, not just about the natural world, but about the human world as well. Your child will want to know more about sex and death as he becomes increasingly aware that they exist. Unfortunately, many parents never bring up the "difficult" topics of sex and death when talking to their children, perhaps because the subjects make them uncomfortable or because they want to shield their children from the distastefulness or the pain and sorrow that they associate with them. Sadder still, many parents change the subject or brush their children aside when the kids bring up these topics.

Father Knows Best

"I have answered three questions, and that is enough,"

Said his father. "Don't give yourself airs!

Do you think I can listen all day to such stuff?

Be off, or I'll kick you downstairs!"

—Lewis Carroll

Who Are You Really Protecting?

Most adults have a hard enough time talking about sex, death, and religion to other adults, much less explaining them to their kids. Sex—and to an even greater extent, death—make many of us so uncomfortable that we prefer not to talk about them (or in the case of death, even think about it) at all.

Yet you won't successfully shield your child from either the facts of life or the facts of death for long just because you refuse to talk about topics that make you feel uncomfortable. Your child will do what she needs to satisfy her curiosity. She will seek answers elsewhere. If you won't talk about sex and death, your child will most likely start asking her friends—children about the same age as she, with little or no more knowledge than she has.

Instead of forcing her to scrounge around for answers and in all likelihood receiving little more in return than distortions, myths, and fantasies, wouldn't you prefer to answer your child's questions yourself?

You may be afraid of "putting ideas" into your child's head, but your child is probably wondering about these things already. If you bring up these subjects, even while she's still a preschooler, you will probably find out she already has some shadowy knowledge about sex and that she thinks—or perhaps even worries—about death, most likely her own or yours.

No matter how young, your child already knows something about sex and death, but what she knows may not reflect either the facts or your opinions, beliefs, and values. So don't worry that your six-year-old will want to run out and try sex as soon as she finds out something about it. It won't happen. And don't shy away from talking about death because you want to protect your child from such sadness. She already knows something about it, and she probably needs your help to try to figure it all out.

Father Knows Best

"Two things are terrible in childhood: helplessness (being in other people's power) and apprehension—the apprehension that something is being concealed from us because it was too bad to be told."

—Elizabeth Bowen

Shhh! If We Don't Say Anything, Maybe It Will Go Away

Trying to repress or simply turn away your child's curiosity about things such as sexuality and death will not make it go away. But it may drive your child's interest underground.

If you refuse to talk about sex, for instance, your child will probably begin to see sex as something shameful or dirty. He may even begin to see his body, especially his genitals, as something dirty and shameful, too.

When your child has sexual thoughts, feelings, or urges (as you know he will), he will punish himself with feelings of guilt and shame. He may even start to see himself as a bad person. And when your child actually engages in sexual behavior—whether it's masturbation, a nocturnal emission, or even kissing (much less actual intercourse)— watch out. He may feel dirtier than ever, or he may completely reject the values that you failed to communicate and fling himself into sexually irresponsible behavior.

Similarly, if you shy away from talking to your child about death, he may begin to envision death as something dirty or awful, too. He will try to push any thoughts about death out of his mind. In doing so, he may become increasingly preoccupied with the subject. (For the next minute, try not to think about elephants. Aha! Caught you thinking about them already?)

What's worse, if someone close to your child dies, whether suddenly or after a long illness, your child will be ill-equipped to handle it if you've never before discussed the subject with him.

On the other hand, if you begin talking to your child about thorny topics such as sex and death early in his life, you may establish a pattern that will last throughout his childhood. If you take the time to talk about sex, you can help your child remain comfortable with his body and feel good about his sexuality, at least until adolescence, when most kids feel especially awkward about both their bodies and their sexuality. (See Chapter 23 for more on parenting teenagers.) If you take the time to talk about death before it's actually staring you all in the face, your child may feel a little less lost when he actually has to face it.

Everything You Know About Sex (But Were Afraid Your Child Would Ask)

From an early age, you can begin talking to your child about sex and satisfying her curiosity about the subject. By allowing and encouraging your preschooler (or even your toddler) to ask questions she has about sex and sexuality, you will open an on-and-off dialogue that may (or may not) continue throughout her adolescence.

The Body Shop

Your child's overt curiosity about sexuality will probably begin at around two or three, when he first begins noticing that the bodies of boys and girls—or the bodies of adults and children—are different. Your son, for instance, may begin to wonder why he has a penis but his sister doesn't. He may wonder why he doesn't have hair around his penis like you do. Your daughter may wonder why your partner has a pubic triangle while she doesn't. She may wonder why she doesn't have big breasts like mommy does or why daddy doesn't have big breasts, too.

When your child notices these physical differences and asks you about them, what will you say? Let's start with a basic premise: When he asks about sex, your preschooler doesn't want to know every last detail—not yet. So start with basic, simple answers. If this doesn't satisfy his curiosity, you can be sure he'll ask another question.

If your child asks about the physical differences between boys and girls, for instance, simply say that boys and girls have different bodies, that a boy has a penis and a girl has a vulva and vagina. (With a slap in the face to Sigmund Freud, you might want to point out that it's *not* that either boys or girls are missing anything. Each simply gets something unique and special of his or her very own.) If you want to relate it to something your child can easily appreciate, you can point out that this is why boys urinate while standing up and girls urinate while sitting down.

This may be all your child wants to know, so stop there. Resist the temptation to blurt out everything you know about sex now that he's brought the subject up. Listen to your child's questions, determine exactly what he wants to know, and offer only that information as simply and gracefully as you can.

That's all there is to it. If you offer your child simple and honest answers that satisfy his sexual curiosity, he will be more likely to turn to you for answers to other questions as they begin to develop in his mind.

Daddy Dos and Don'ts

Why do some parents refer to their child's penis as his "tinky winky," his "peepee," or some other cutesy name. What causes many parents to shy away from naming the vulva or vagina and instead resort to a nebulous phrase like "down there," which lends the female genitalia a dark, forbidden, and otherworldly air? Don't do it. When you talk to your child about the human body, use the real words for the genitals.

Hint: It Ain't the Stork!

Your toddler may also bring up the topic of sex if you and your wife are expecting a second baby. Whether your partner's second pregnancy begins when your child is a toddler, a preschooler, or in elementary school, the news that she can soon expect a new baby to join the family may prompt her to wonder where babies come from. When you tell her that the baby is growing inside her mommy's belly, your child may stare up at you in amazement.

If your child is three years old or older, finding out that the baby is inside her mama's belly will probably raise more questions than it answers. She may wonder how the baby will get out—or an even more difficult question: How did the baby get in there? Again, listen to your child's questions carefully and offer the simplest possible answer unless she asks for even more details.

Father Knows Best

"There's a time when you have to explain to your children why they're born, and it's a marvelous thing if you know the reason by then."

—Hazel Scott

If a child has the intellectual sophistication to ask a question, I believe she deserves a clear and honest answer. And by about four years old, your child can probably understand that when a father's sperm and a mother's egg join together, a baby starts to grow inside the mother.

If your child then wants to know how the sperm gets to the egg, why not tell her? What harm will it do a curious child to know the truth about how babies are created? It is, after all, a miraculous and beautiful process, not a dirty and shameful secret.

How your child responds to news about the miracle of creation will depend upon her age and her personality. When we told our six-year-old son how babies are conceived, he said, "Oh. Did you know I can bend my upper lip all the way up to my nose?" Our eight-year-old daughter had quite a different question: "Why would anyone want to do that? It sounds disgusting." (We're hoping she maintains this attitude for at least ten more years.)

If your child also wants to know when *she* can have a baby, you can color your presentation of the facts with a moral lesson. But don't gloss over the facts: Girls and boys can make babies when their bodies start changing, usually some time between age eleven and fourteen. But though children of this age have the physical ability to make babies—I hope you're listening, because here comes the whole point of this discussion—boys and girls

Daddy Dos and Don'ts

If you feel uncomfortable bringing up the subject of sexual intercourse (even in the context of conception) in a conversation with your child, you may benefit from an icebreaker. The children's department of your local library or bookstore probably has at least one or two age-appropriate books on sex, how babies are made, or both. By reading a book about sex to your child—or letting her read the book on her own—and then offering her the opportunity to discuss or ask questions about the book, you may find it easier to open this important conversation.

aren't grown up enough to take care of a baby properly. So you, my darling daughter (or son), should wait until you're an adult before you start having babies.

Just the Facts, Ma'am

Whatever your child wants to know about sex, try to provide simple and straightforward answers. Remember that all your child wants is information. Neither you nor your child should feel embarrassed that he wants to expand his knowledge.

After telling your child the facts of life, however, don't think to yourself, "Phew, I'm glad that's over with," for you will likely hear the exact same questions a month, a week, or a year later. When this happens, you may wonder whether you might have given him a lousy answer the first time. Don't worry: As long as you kept it simple, you probably did just fine.

Young children often don't absorb certain information unless they hear it more than once. (Just think how many times you've told your child to put his dirty clothes in the hamper or shut the door behind him.) So don't let the repetition of the same question faze you. Just tell him the same thing you told him the first time.

Caught in the Act: Handling Embarrassing Situations

Do you remember privacy? An outmoded concept, you probably gave it up as soon as your child began to walk. That's no doubt when she began to follow you into the bathroom or the shower or run into your bedroom in the middle of the night.

Lack of privacy can lead to some potentially embarrassing—and hilarious—situations. But if you handle them with grace, good humor, and frankness, both you and your child will suffer only minimal embarrassment. Don't just let these situations sit there like a dead weight though. Embarrassing situations almost always demand follow-up discussions, if not right when they happen, then at the earliest opportunity afterward.

Here's how to handle some of the most common sources of sexual embarrassment between parent and child:

➤ **Your child sees you completely or partially naked.** Your child won't be permanently damaged by the sight of your naked body. In fact, seeing you comfortably naked while getting dressed or stepping out of the shower may send your child the message that she, too, should feel comfortable and even proud of her body.

Nonetheless, some parents feel acutely uncomfortable, embarrassed, or ashamed when their children see them naked. If you feel this way, do whatever you can to prevent it from happening. Lock the bathroom or bedroom door behind you and keep yourself covered whenever you're anywhere else. If anyone in your home, you, your wife, or your child), feels uncomfortable with nudity, then it's only common courtesy to try to respect those wishes by keeping your nakedness to your self.

➤ **Your child bursts into your room while you and your wife are having sex.**
Whoops, there's that unlocked-door problem again. If you get caught in the act,
don't go into a panic. You haven't done any damage to your child that $80,000
of psychoanalysis can't cure. Seriously though, if you haven't yet talked to your
child about making love and sexual intimacy, now's the time.

Explain that you and your partner sometimes express your love for each other
sexually—that you touch each other in ways that make both of you feel good.
Make it clear that whoever was on top when she came into the room was not
hurting the other, a common misconception that children have when they
accidentally see a sex act. You might also add that by giving each other physical
pleasure, you feel very close and loving toward each other.

This situation also calls for a reaffirmation of the right to privacy in your home.
Especially if you don't want to lock your bedroom door, let your child know that
when the door to your bedroom is shut, she must knock and wait for an invitation before coming in. Make a promise to her that when she shuts her bedroom
door, you will respect her privacy in the same way.

➤ **You burst into your child's room while she is masturbating.** Hey, didn't you
just say that you would knock first? Well, too late now. You've caught your child
masturbating, and no matter how much you believe it's a perfectly natural means
of self-exploration and self-pleasuring, you probably found the sight at least
surprising, if not downright disturbing.

Try to take it in stride, though. Scolding your child or trying to forbid masturbation will send negative messages about your child's sexuality. So will ignoring it
since your child may begin to regard the subject as unspeakable. Talk about it,
though perhaps not at that particular moment.

Cool Daddy Ohs

Need any proof of the lingering
double standard? If you have both a
son and a daughter, pay attention to
your own reactions to your child's
masturbation. Chances are, you'll
probably find it much more disturbing to find out that your daughter
masturbates than that your son does.

Talk to your child about sexual excitement and
sexual pleasure. You might even want to explain
why the penis gets hard or why the vulva gets wet.
Finally, acknowledge the obvious fact that masturbation feels good and is perfectly natural—and
apologize for disturbing your child's privacy.

➤ **Your preschooler masturbates in public.** Masturbation is one thing; playing with oneself in public
is quite another. Many preschoolers have few
inhibitions about playing with their genitals while
sitting among a crowd of people. If your child
does this, let her know that it's perfectly all right
for her to masturbate, but that since it makes
some grown-ups feel embarrassed and uncomfortable, she should do it only in private. Drawing an

analogy between the private activity of masturbating and going to the bathroom, another natural bodily function best done behind closed doors, may make it easier for your child to understand.

➤ **You catch your child and another child "playing doctor."** Don't you *ever* knock? You may be disconcerted by the sight of your child and her friend carefully examining each other's naked bodies. But really, it's nothing more than another way for your child to explore the natural world, in this case, the physical differences between boys and girls. Instead of working yourself into a lather, look on the bright side. If your child is playing, "I'll show you mine if you show me yours," at least she has finally learned to take turns and share.

In all seriousness, try not to overreact to preschool sex play. Acknowledge your child's curiosity and let your child know that lots of preschoolers do this kind of thing. If you want your child to stop, let her know that you feel that certain parts of her body should be considered private. At the same time, however, offer her a book that explores the physical differences between girls and boys.

The Moral of the Story

As soon as you begin talking to your child about sexual intimacy, making love, or sexual pleasure, you can—and should—introduce the subject of sexual responsibility. At the same time that you're offering lessons about anatomy and talks about sexual intimacy, you can interweave some moral instruction regarding sexuality.

You and your partner probably have strong moral beliefs regarding sexual conduct, sexual responsibility, and sexual behavior (though your beliefs may differ from mine). If so, don't wait until your child is an adolescent (an age when he may not want to listen) before you start teaching these beliefs. When your child is still young and impressionable, use the opportunity of talking about sex and sexuality to relate your moral beliefs about sexuality, too.

For instance, when talking about making love, you might want to emphasize that:

➤ Making love, sharing sexual intimacy, is something very special.

➤ Ideally, making love is both loving and mutually satisfying.

➤ Only adults should share this kind of sexual intimacy (in other words, making love is not an appropriate activity for children, whether with other children or with adults).

In addition to these fairly universal beliefs, you probably have other opinions and beliefs about love-making that you may want to impart to your child. If so, seize the day. Take advantage of any opportunity that life presents you rather than waiting for a day in the not-too-distant future when your child's budding sexual feelings and behavior force you to have "The Talk."

The Talk

All of us have seen movies and TV shows in which a fumbling, nervous father sits his teenager down for "The Talk." The father, a model of incompetence, doesn't know quite what to say, but feels that he has a duty to provide some sort of sexual guidance to his child.

In my opinion, however, these exchanges represent far too little far too late. If you open a dialogue with your child from an early age—talking frankly, honestly, and regularly about sex in an age-appropriate way—you should never have to sit your teenager down for "The Talk." You won't need to instruct your child about "the birds and the bees" at the late age of 12 or 13 (or, whoops, really too late, 15 or 16). After all, if you've been talking about sexuality and providing moral instruction about sex since your child was a preschooler, what more do you have to tell her?

Father Knows Best

"A father... knows exactly what those boys at the mall have in their depraved little minds because he once owned such a depraved mind himself."

—Bill Cosby

As adolescence approaches, however, you may want to shift the emphasis of your talks to sexual responsibility. Sexual activity does have consequences: some are life-altering, others are life-threatening. Your child certainly needs to know this. Teenagers who have sex can get pregnant, they can contract sexually transmitted diseases, they can even become infected with the AIDS-causing virus. You owe it to your child to pass on these warnings (though hopefully in a way that doesn't whip up hysteria).

Father Knows Best

"I only have two rules for my newly born daughter: she will dress well and never have sex."

—John Malkovich

Even if you want your teenager to remain a virgin until the day she marries, your child may have some ideas of her own on the subject. You may urge abstinence on your child—even demand it—but if your child becomes sexually active despite your prohibitions, she will need to know about safe sex. Look at it this way: If, despite your wishes, your child becomes sexually active, wouldn't you prefer her to know how to have safe sex rather than throw herself into unprotected sex?

Stress abstinence all your want, but instruct your child in safe sex all the same. You may, for example, want to show your child (boy or girl) what a condom looks like, how it works, and how to put it on (use your finger, a cucumber, or a banana as a model). Maybe your child will never need this knowledge (yeah, in your dreams), but if she does, it may be a lifesaver.

The Mask of Death

Few children make it all the way through 18 years without having their lives touched in some way by death. Perhaps a beloved grandparent dies after years of illness. Maybe an aunt or uncle dies in a car crash. Maybe a high-school classmate commits suicide. One way or another, your child will probably need to cope with the loss of a loved one by the time he leaves home.

Unfortunately, many children are totally unprepared to deal with death. Our culture tends to conceal death under a shroud. Death remains a dark, mysterious, and terrifying force that no one likes to talk about. In fact, talking about death carries an even greater taboo than talking about sex.

But face up to it: All life ends in death—and death eventually touches everyone. If you refuse to talk to your child about death, you will leave him in the darkness. If someone close to him does die, he will feel totally lost and alone, without a clue about how to deal with his grief.

Death Is All Around Us

Too few parents take advantage of the opportunities that life presents them to talk to their children about death in a neutral way. Instead, most of us wait until we can no longer avoid the subject—when death claims someone we or our children love—and even then, we may try to brush aside discussion. Yet if you look for them, you can find dozens of situations that might prompt a discussion of death and its place in the life cycle:

➤ In autumn, leaves and plants wither and die.

➤ While you're driving, you may see a dead animal on the side of the road or, perhaps, one of your own pets dies.

➤ A character in one of your child's favorite videos may die (Simba's father in *The Lion King*, for example, or Bambi's mother in *Bambi*)

Don't let too many of these opportunities pass you by. If you use them to open a discussion, you and your child, no matter how old she is, can use these observations to share your thoughts and feelings about death. Instead of beginning the conversation with difficult questions such as, "Will you die?" and "Will I die," try to frame death within a larger, more neutral framework. You can introduce death in the context of the larger circle of endless change: the never-ending cycle of birth, death, and rebirth.

Within this discussion of death, you can bring in many other topics of discussion. For instance, your religious beliefs, including your faith (if any) in the afterlife, should play a part in any conversations you have with your child about death. You can also use these talks as an opportunity to reaffirm your reverence for life and/or your appreciation of the beauty of life.

Daddy Dos and Don'ts

As you did in talking to your child about sex, try to avoid using polite euphemisms when talking about death. Phrases like "passed away," "passed on," or "gone to a better place" may create misunderstandings and prevent your child from understanding the finality of death. Stick to the words "death" and "died" and describe it as the body no longer working. That will help eliminate confusion.

Bringing It Home

If you let your child know that you are willing to talk about death, in all likelihood, he will eventually ask you about your own (or his) death. When he does, try to answer his questions as straightforwardly as possible, but provide as much reassurance as you can, too. The notion of death—not in the abstract as before, but now on a personal level—can threaten your child's sense of safety and security.

Unless you, your partner, or your child has a fatal illness, provide your child with the reassurance that although everyone eventually dies, most parents stay alive until well after their children have grown up, moved out, and formed their own families. Let your child know that most people in the United States now live to be nearly 80 years old and that many people live many more years than that.

Point to the example of your own parents or grandparents (unless they died at a relatively young age, of course). Tell your child that you have every intention of becoming a grandparent yourself some day, so that you can have fun with his kids just like Grandma and Grandpa have fun with him.

As for his own death, your child may need a great deal of reassurance. Let your child know that the vast majority of children who survive their first six months go on to live well into adulthood. Tell him that you truly expect that he will live to be as old or older than his grandparents. (This will make a powerful impression on a young child, who probably sees his grandparents as more ancient than the pyramids.)

Good Grief

When someone your child loves dies, you should, of course, continue to talk about death. Chances are, if your child knew and loved the person who died, then you did, too. This means that both of you will be grieving at the same time, and you may not feel like talking about it. But by talking openly about your own feelings about the death and encouraging your child to do the same, you may be able to help each other through the grieving process.

The death of a loved one will reawaken any fears your child has had about her own death and yours. She will probably need a lot of love and reassurance at this time, hugs and soothing words that, despite your own grief, you alone can best provide.

Encourage your child to share her feelings and thoughts about death during this difficult time. Welcome any new questions she has about death or your beliefs about an afterlife and answer as honestly and reassuringly as you can. As your child tries to make sense of death, she will need you to provide her not only with guidance, but with a listening ear and an understanding heart.

Daddy Dos and Don'ts

Try not to cut short your child's expressions of grief. A child who is admonished to be brave or not to cry will actually find it harder, not easier, to mourn the loss of her loved one or get past this painful death. Remind your child that it's okay to cry, especially when mourning the death of someone she loves. (If your own grief has brought you to tears, let your child know it. She may feel more free to cry knowing that you have cried, too.)

The Least You Need to Know

➤ If you don't talk to your child about big issues such as sex and death, his knowledge about these subjects will never reflect your own understanding, beliefs, and opinions.

➤ Your child's curiosity about sex and death won't go away just because you refuse to talk about them. She may keep it a secret from you, but she won't lose interest.

➤ When your child asks about sex, offer simple, clear, and direct answers. Provide him with elaborate details only if he asks for them.

➤ If your child catches you in a potentially embarrassing sexual situation—or if you catch her in a similar situation—use it as a springboard for another talk about sex.

➤ When your child asks about death, provide straightforward answers, while at the same time offering reassurance to calm his fears.

Chapter 20

Just Wait 'Til Your Father Gets Home

In This Chapter

➤ Your role as an authority figure

➤ Setting limits and establishing rules: the cornerstones of discipline

➤ Appropriate punishment for young children

➤ Helping to create a conscience and foster self-discipline

➤ Older children and discipline

When I was growing up, the ultimate threat from mothers in my neighborhood was "Just wait 'til your father gets home." The father in question could have been the most benign and easy-going man in the world. But fathers in those days were automatically expected to take on the responsibility to come in and lay down the law.

Indeed, maintaining and enforcing discipline was one of the primary family responsibilities of fathers from the old school. A father could be absent from home for most of the day, earning money to "put food on the table," but when he returned, he was expected to listen to his wife's account of the day's infractions in order to determine and carry out appropriate punishments. Judge, jury, and executioner, the father was the ultimate authority in the home.

Times have changed. Yet even today, most fathers (though sometimes in tandem with their partners) still find that they are ultimately responsible for enforcing discipline in the family. Now it's *you* who is feared and respected. But how will you (and your partner) wield authority over your child? What should you do to discipline your child and help instill in him a strong sense of morality and responsibility?

Sizing Up Your Authority

Maintaining authority will play a big part in disciplining your child, yet you don't need to work very hard to establish your authority with her—at least initially. In fact, as soon as your child becomes conscious of your presence, she will regard you—and your partner, of course—as her ultimate authority figures.

Both of you have a natural authority, merely by virtue of your size. To your child, you are huge. Your sheer magnitude provides your child with a sense of security and protection (unless, of course, you use your size advantage to intimidate or abuse your child). From her earliest days, your child literally—and by automatic extension, figuratively—looks up to you. Your size affords you authority, your child's respect, and perhaps even her adoration.

Size Isn't Everything

In conveying your authority, your size isn't all that matters, of course.

You have also no doubt earned your child's respect by virtue of your competence. Nearly everything he *wants* to do, you *can* do—and almost always with relative ease. You can untangle what to him is a hopelessly gnarled yo-yo or necklace. You can prepare the foods he likes. You can drive a real car. You can build a tower of blocks long before he can even conceptualize such an idea.

Father Knows Best

"Don't demand respect as a parent. Demand civility and insist on honesty. But respect is something you must earn—with kids as well as with adults."

—William Attwood

As your child grows older and more capable, your ability to teach your child how to do many of these things will only increase your authority. Your child may now be able to do many of the same things himself, but it was you who taught him how.

The King Is Dead, Long Live the King

Time can only erode some of this natural authority and respect. As your child grows, she will see that you are not a giant as she once supposed. She will discover that you don't know everything and that you can't do everything. But that's okay. It's all part of growing up.

As she grows up, your child must acquire her own authority and mastery. Naturally, the more confidence your child develops in her own authority, the less authority you will have over her. But don't worry, this takes a lot of time to develop (18 years—or more).

The gradual relinquishing of some of your authority will not necessarily diminish your child's respect for you. Using strong-arm tactics in a vain attempt to hold on to absolute power, however, will almost invariably do so. So as your child becomes more mature and responsible, try to cede some of your authority as gracefully as you possibly can.

Setting Limits: Where It All Begins

From the onset of mobility until your child's second or even third birthday, your disciplinary efforts should focus on little more than setting limits on your toddler's behavior. Although you want to allow your child to explore his world freely, you still need to set limits that will:

> ➤ **Keep your child safe.** Examples: No sticking forks in electrical outlets, no jumping in the bathtub, no playing in the street.

> ➤ **Keep others safe from your child.** Examples: No hitting, no kicking, no biting, no eye poking, no hair pulling.

> ➤ **Keep your property safe from your child.** Examples: No drawing on the walls, no pancakes in the CD player, no throwing hard objects in the house.

In a perfect world, all you'd have to do is let your child know some of the ground rules, like the ones suggested above, to ensure his safety and protect others from him, and he'd salute and say, "Yes, sir," and that would be that. Unfortunately, your child does not yet have the understanding needed to make any sense of your rules—especially if they mean he can't go where he wants to go or do what he wants to do.

Ain't Misbehavin'

Toddlers are amoral creatures. They cannot grasp the distinction between "good" and "bad" behavior. If she can pour water in the bathtub, why can't she pour it into the VCR? If she can kick a ball, why can't she kick the cat? To a toddler, your rules seem arbitrary and nonsensical.

Your toddler understands very little about the world—and, therefore, should be forgiven for infractions that might merit punishment in an older child. Your child does not yet know that poking you in the eye or pulling your hair hurts. That's one of the things she will discover by exploring you in these ways. She cannot comprehend that climbing to the fourth shelf of the bookcase is dangerous. It's just another physical challenge that she has taken on for herself.

Father Knows Best

"Until a child is one year old, it is incapable of sin."

—*The Talmud*

When your toddler does these things, she's not misbehaving because she has no idea what it means to "behave." In your toddler's case, ignorance of the law *is* a valid excuse. What's more, her limited memory capacity makes it nearly impossible for her to learn from experience yet. If you say, "No!"—a word your child began to understand even before she could walk—it might stop your toddler from throwing her bowl of oatmeal this time. But the next time she gets a bowl of oatmeal, she will have forgotten all about your prohibition.

Father Knows Best

"[What is a baby?] A loud noise at one end and no sense of responsibility at the other."

—*Ronald Knox*

Spare the Rod

Given his limited memory, knowledge, and understanding of cause and effect, discipline during your child's early years should never involve punishment. To your toddler, who is just beginning to discover that causes have effects, that actions have consequences, punishment makes no sense. He cannot link your punitive behavior with his own bad behavior. Because the two behaviors seem totally unrelated to him, your toddler will see your punishments as arbitrary, unfair, and just plain mean.

What's more, punishment is not a deterrent at this age. Your toddler won't remember that the last time he did something, he got punished for it. So what's the point of punishing him?

Not only does punishment have no immediate or long-term impact on your toddler's behavior, it may backfire on you. If your toddler sees you (and your punishments) as cruel and arbitrary from the beginning—if he feels that you constantly disapprove of his behavior—he may, in time, give up his natural tendency to try to please you.

Tricks of the Trade

If punishment doesn't work, then how can you get your toddler to behave herself? Only by getting her to want to "behave." Your toddler will "behave" only if what she wants to do conforms to your definition of good behavior.

You do, however, have power and influence over how your toddler behaves. All you have to do is outsmart her. With a little ingenuity and trickery, you can steer your child away from bad behaviors and toward good ones. All you need to do is make good behavior something she wants to do. You can accomplish this in one of three ways:

➤ **Out-and-out trickery.** Make good behavior fun. Get your child to clean her room, for instance, by turning it into a game.

➤ **Redirection.** If it's not the activity in itself, but the object of her activity that's a problem, try giving your child something more appropriate. If, for instance, you put a ball in your child's hands, she'll probably put down the fragile object she was about to throw. If you give her a plastic slide to climb on, she'll most likely come down from the bookshelves.

➤ **Misdirection.** You can distract your one- or two-year-old very easily. By getting your child involved in some other activity or interested in some other toy, you can draw her away from activities or playthings that you find unacceptable.

Daddy Dos and Don'ts

Don't bother trying to get your toddler to behave by bribing or coercing her into making promises. Your toddler has no ability to remember, much less keep, a promise. To a small child, a promise is just a means to an end. Either she truly wants to please you by agreeing to do what you want, or she wants whatever you're offering in exchange for her promise and sees her assent as the quickest and surest way to get it.

The Nays Have It

Most parents get toddlers and preschoolers to behave almost exclusively by using the word "no." This word becomes a constant refrain in houses that contain toddlers.

In some cases, a sharp "No!" will indeed stop your toddler dead in his tracks, but sometimes, the appeal of whatever he's doing or trying to reach will be too strong for your toddler to stop. In such cases, you will need to take swift and immediate action. You'll need to take away the dangerous object or remove your child from any situation

Daddy Dos and Don'ts

Accentuate the positive. Don't guide your child's behavior solely through negative words and negative measures. Make a real effort to reinforce behavior that you approve of by showering your child with praise. Take note of the times when your child demonstrates kindness, generosity, or consideration or the rare occasions when he resolves a conflict peacefully. The more you praise your child's good behavior, the more you will see your child trying to repeat it.

that's dangerous (either to him or to someone else)—not in an angry or punitive way, but in a simple, matter-of-fact way.

Once you've eliminated the danger, briefly explain to your toddler why you've intervened. It doesn't matter if your child doesn't understand all (or any) of what you say right now. By explaining yourself, you will get into the habit of regularly reinforcing your disciplinary actions with words. Once they begin to sink in, these words to the unwise will help teach your child the difference between what's safe and what's unsafe—and between right and wrong. And that's the whole point of discipline, isn't it?

Hearing "no" all the time can be scary for a toddler. It feels dangerous to him to do anything that displeases you. Like all toddlers, your child truly wants to please you. When he doesn't, he fears you may not love him anymore. So try to limit the times you say "no" (more thorough childproofing—see Chapter 15—may help reduce the frequency with which you must say it). When you do say "no," make sure to follow it up with an explanation of why your child can't do whatever it is that he was doing—and reassurance that you still love him.

Setting the Ground Rules

Some time after your child's second birthday, she will become more able to understand and obey rules of behavior. Her increasing memory capacity now allows your child to learn from experience—though she may need several "lessons" before she truly appreciates a particular instance of cause-and-effect or actions and consequences. At this age, your child can begin to appreciate the difference between good and bad behavior. She just won't always know which is which.

Father Knows Best

"Let the child's first lesson be obedience, and the second will be what thou wilt."

—Benjamin Franklin

So at two (and three and four and five …), you should start teaching your child generalized rules of behavior (rather than just arresting particular actions). Your two-year-old needs you to begin helping her to distinguish the difference between right and wrong.

As already mentioned, it will probably take repeated lessons before your child begins to absorb your general rules of acceptable behavior. First offenses, though you shouldn't ignore them, should be treated somewhat lightly. Even a three-strikes-you're-out rule might be a little harsh for a two-year-old. If your child becomes a habitual or repeat offender, however, you will need to begin punishing her for breaking the rules. (See ideas and suggestions on punishment later in this chapter.)

I Can't Control Myself, So There: Why Your Toddler Misbehaves

Just as he did at one, your child at two will misbehave because he's exploring his world and his own abilities and still doesn't have an inkling of the difference between right and wrong. But through trial and error, your child this year will begin understanding which actions meet with your approval and which do not—in other words, he'll start knowing the rules.

Cool Daddy Ohs

Derived from the same root as the word "disciples" (students), the verb "discipline" originally meant to teach, not to punish. Try to keep this in mind as you discipline your children. Your ultimate objective should be to teach your child the difference between right and wrong, to instill moral behavior, and to encourage her to adopt most of your rules of acceptable behavior as her own.

Just because your toddler knows your rules doesn't mean he'll suddenly begin to obey them without fail. Why does he continue to break the rules even after he knows what they are? In general, toddlers disobey their parents for one of two reasons:

➤ Poor control of their own emotions and impulses

➤ The assertion of independence

Your child's control over his emotions—the ability to express anger and frustration without resorting to violence or destruction, for example—will come gradually with greater maturity, as well as your guidance and discipline. In the meantime, you can't do a whole lot to help your child gain control over his emotions. You can correct misbehavior repeatedly, and you can help your child find other ways to express anger (such as punching a pillow, banging a drum, running around outside, doing something loud, slapping clay around, or using words). But mostly, you'll just need to be patient.

Your child's inability to handle overwhelmingly powerful emotions will invariably give rise to temper tantrums. Fatigue and frustration also contribute to tantrums, so try to head these off through rest times or the use of creative distraction. When your child does have a tantrum, here's how to handle it:

➤ Ignore it unless you think he'll do damage. Show your child you're untouched by his tantrum.

➤ Don't yell. Someone has to stay in control.

➤ Don't appeal to reason. He won't hear it.

➤ Don't reward or punish a tantrum. Your child needs to know that a tantrum won't have any effect on you, positive or negative.

➤ Don't try to beg, bribe, or threaten your child out of a tantrum. It won't work, and it rewards your child with extra attention.

➤ Leave the room if your own anger threatens to get the better of you, but don't lock your child in a room. This may lead to hysterical separation anxiety and precludes the possibility of his apologizing.

➤ Finally (and this is the hardest one), don't treat tantrums any differently just because they occur in a public place. Sure, it's embarrassing, but hey, every child does it.

Most parents find the other cause of their toddler's misbehavior much more galling. In the first steps of a 16-year campaign to separate himself from you, to prove that you no longer completely control him, and to test your limits, your child will smilingly defy you and deliberately break your rules. You can see it in his face, for instance, as your child inches toward the TV that you've just turned off, all the time refusing to take his eyes off you and perhaps flashing a nervous smile. If he could put it into words, he'd say, "You can't make me!" By turning the TV back on after you've told him to stop watching TV, your child proves to himself that he doesn't have to do everything you tell him to do, that he is his own person.

Neither of these reasons for misbehavior—poor impulse control and a push for independence—warrant harsh punishment. Your child truly needs to demonstrate independence. And he truly has no control yet over the expression of his emotions.

Of course, just because you understand why your child is doing it doesn't mean you should allow misbehavior to continue. You need to start drawing a line for your child, setting clear limits on acceptable behavior. You can't allow your child to hit someone, for example, just because he can't stop himself. You can stop him—and you should. Similarly, you can't allow him to defy your rules just because he looks so cute when he does it. Consider leniency when imposing a punishment—but at the same time, do what you must to stop the behavior.

Daddy Dos and Don'ts

Try to avoid using candy or other sweets to bribe or reward your child for good behavior—or withholding them to threaten or punish your child for bad behavior. If you do this, candy and sweets will soon become symbolic of your love and approval. As your child begins to make this connection, he will repeatedly beg you for candy as a demonstration of your love. If you refuse him, your child may then feel unloved or under-appreciated.

You Are the Rules

At age two, your child will not be sophisticated enough to understand moral shades of gray. (In fact, she won't appreciate gray areas of morality until she is at least seven or eight.) So the rules you establish must be simple, clear, and consistent. To a toddler, "No!" has to mean "Never!" When you tell her, "No hitting," that's an absolute rule. It means she cannot hit another person under any conditions. If you start adding conditions—for example, "No hitting unless someone is hitting you and won't let you get away!—then the rule will become fuzzy in your toddler's already fuzzy mind.

Once you've established a "No!" rule, you must follow through with enforcement at all times. Failing to discipline your child, for whatever reasons, when she breaks one of these "No!" rules will only confuse your child. It will send an indirect message that your child may be allowed to bend the rules when it suits her.

The rules you set at age two, like the limits you set at age one, should continue to address issues of safety. Now's the time to develop the limits you imposed earlier—protecting your own child's safety, protecting the safety of others, and protecting your property—into rules designed to enforce these limits. But at two, rules should also begin promoting social behavior, encouraging courtesy and good manners. So in addition, try to develop rules that will encourage your child to

➤ Respect the feelings, thoughts, and rights of others.

➤ Be honest with you and other authority figures.

Polite Society

If you can instill in your toddler the habits of common courtesy and good manners, he will probably remain relatively polite and well-behaved as he grows older. At first, you can encourage politeness through an appeal to your child's self-interest. Let your toddler know that his politeness will often persuade adults to give him what he wants—or at least give his request more serious consideration.

Teach your child that certain words really do have a magical power, even over adults. Using these "magic words" may not always get your child what he wants, but they can make adults much more willing to consider giving your child what he wants or the help he needs. These magic words include:

➤ *Please,* which can make an adult more willing to help your child or give him something he wants.

➤ *Thank you,* which makes a grown-up even more willing to do the same in the future.

➤ *Excuse me,* which can make grown-ups stop a conversation or activity and pay attention to your child—or get a grown-up to move out of his way.

➤ *I'm sorry,* which can win the forgiveness of either an adult or child that your toddler has hurt or offended (even if only by accident).

When your child tries these magic words on you or on someone else, congratulate and praise him for speaking so politely. If he does want something, seriously consider giving it to him—and if you must refuse him, do so politely.

Daddy Dos and Don'ts

In trying to teach your child good behavior of any kind—whether manners, safe conduct, honesty, nonviolence, or kindness and consideration—keep in mind that even more influential than what you say is what you do. Your child will watch you carefully to make sure that your actions match your words—and will quickly catch you in any hypocrisy. If you're going to talk the talk, then make sure to walk the walk.

At first, you may need to remind your child many times to use these words. (He will also need to see you using them yourself—especially when you ask him to do something for you. After all, you can't expect your toddler to start saying "Please" and "Thank you" if you don't do the same yourself.) You may need to take a hard line, refusing to honor your child's demands unless he rephrases them as a polite question. But once your child sees how well these magic words work, he may start using them often enough to make them habitual.

How Would You Feel If ...?

Ultimately, the key to good manners and courtesy is the development of empathy, a fellow feeling for others, and consideration, thinking about what others might want or how they might feel before acting in a way that will affect them. When your child begins playing with other children—not just engaging in parallel play, but actually interacting with others—she will begin to develop the ability to empathize with others.

Of course, when push comes to shove, when consideration of others clashes with her own desires, your child will probably still choose self-interest over empathy throughout her preschool years. But when it doesn't cost her anything, your child will probably demonstrate increasing consideration and helpfulness toward others throughout her preschool years.

Over the next few years, you can encourage your child to recognize and respect the feelings of others and to consider how her behavior might affect other people's feelings in many ways:

➤ You can model empathy and helpfulness yourself. If your child witnesses you tuning in to the feelings of others (including her, of course) or offering help to someone—your child, your partner, a friend, or a stranger—she will probably begin to adopt a similar attitude. You can also model empathy when your child is upset simply by telling her, "I know how you feel," and trying to comfort her.

➤ Since self-awareness often precedes awareness of others, you can encourage your child to talk about her own feelings. Whenever possible, encourage your child to delve a little deeper, to try to figure out why she feels a certain way. She might also benefit from hearing you talk about some of your own feelings and what lies behind them.

➤ Voice concern about the feelings of others. Show your child that you care about how other people feel. By expressing your own concern for others, you may help nurture similar concerns in your child.

➤ Help your child to see connections between her own behavior and the feelings of others, connections that are far from obvious to a preschooler. Point out how she affects others in her world with comments like, "Look how happy you made him feel!" or "You poked her in the eye. That's why she's crying."

➤ Explain the reasoning behind certain moral choices that you make (especially those you make on your child's behalf). If consideration of others figured in your decision, emphasize it in your explanation. For example: "I know you still want to play with that toy, but it's Molly's turn now. If you take it back, she'll be very sad."

➤ Teach your child the Golden Rule: Treat other people the way you would want to be treated.

➤ Encourage your child to imagine herself in another person's shoes. For example, "How do you think you would feel if …?" Then make the connection explicit: "Well, Mikey probably feels just the same way you would."

Share and Share Alike

One prosocial behavior that might take years for your child to appreciate is sharing. Toddlers are by nature selfish and self-centered. For this reason, sharing is a completely unnatural behavior for a toddler. Your child won't give up something he wants just because another child wants it. Indeed, the fact that another child wants it might be the very reason your child suddenly wants it, too. To learn how to share, your child will need your help and encouragement. You will need to teach him how to share—and praise him whenever he does.

During play dates at your home, your child will necessarily have to share some of his things. Yet your child may go nuts when he sees his guest playing with one of his toys. He may even run up and snatch the toy out of his friend's hands.

When this happens, you will need to step in quickly. Take the toy from your child and return it to his guest. After admonishing your child with "No grabbing," suggest alternative ways that he might get a toy that someone else is playing with. For instance, your child might do one of the following:

➤ Wait until the other child is done playing with the toy.

➤ Ask the other child nicely whether he can play with the toy now.

➤ Ask for your help in setting up a system of taking turns.

➤ Offer the other child a trade so that both children end up playing with something they want.

Make it clear that even if none of these suggestions work, your child still doesn't have the right to grab the toy. To prevent your child from trying to grab it again, try to distract your child by engaging him in play with another toy or game.

If all else fails, take the toy away from both children and put it away rather than risk full-scale warfare. You might have better success at distracting both children if the object of their dispute has disappeared.

Preschoolers and elementary school children have a powerful sense of fairness. When your child gets a little older, you may have more success in encouraging sharing (and other prosocial behaviors) by putting it in terms of fairness. For instance, taking turns—one form of sharing—seems like a fair system to most four- and five-year-olds (as long as the length of the turns is roughly equal). At this age, your child will begin to comprehend—though not always welcome—the need to balance his rights and the rights of others.

Finding Punishments That Fit the Crimes

Coming up with punishments appropriate for young children is not easy. Certainly, you need to enforce discipline consistently. Your child needs to know that when she misbehaves in a particular way, predictable consequences will follow. Though punishment might not immediately serve as a deterrent to similar bad behavior in the near future, in the long run, your child will probably stop herself from misbehaving, at least occasionally, merely to avoid the punishment she knows will follow.

Certainly, not every "crime" deserves the same punishment. Where no violence or destructiveness is involved, for example, you might want to begin simply by issuing a warning and letting your child know exactly what you will do if she doesn't stop. If she obeys you, congratulate your child for her good sense and her self-control and help her find something less objectionable to do. If she ignores you, step in and immediately do what you said you would do. Threats that prove empty will only cause your child to become bolder in her misbehavior in the future.

Father Knows Best

"Children today are tyrants. They contradict their parents, gobble their food, and tyrannize their teachers."

—Socrates

Any "violent crime," of course, requires your immediate intervention. You need to stop your child from continuing her violence immediately. Comfort her victim if necessary, then remove your child from the situation forcibly and impose an appropriate punishment.

The Hot Seat: Time Out

For children from about two until age six, seven, or beyond, the punishment of choice these days seems to be the "time out."

Time outs usually work pretty well for two reasons. First of all, they forcibly remove your child from whatever caused or prompted the misbehavior. Secondly, they give your child time to regain some degree of control over his emotions and his behavior.

To impose a time out, start by picking a chair—one your child rarely chooses to sit in—and designating it the time-out chair. When your toddler commits a serious offense, pick him up immediately, tell him "No biting" or "No scratching" or whatever, and place him in the time-out chair. Make your child remain in the time-out chair for about one minute for every year of his age.

If your child gets out of the time-out chair before his "sentence" is up, simply put him right back. (With two- and three-year-olds, about two or three minutes of this back-and-forth business will probably be enough for both of you. At four years old or older, however, you may want to let your child know that if he gets out of the time-out chair, you will put him back in the chair and start timing all over again.)

When putting your two- or three-year-old into time out, you would probably do well to remain in the same room with him (he will probably try to get out of the chair as soon as you leave). Your child may already fear that you hate him because you are angry or are punishing him. If you then abandon him to his punishment, his separation anxiety will probably throw him into a hysterical panic. So put your toddler in the time-out chair, sit in the same room, but try not to interact with him, except to remind him why he's in time out, and urge him to calm down.

Daddy Dos and Don'ts

Any fear your child may have that you hate him will become aggravated if you call him a "bad boy." He will internalize this name-calling and begin to think of himself as a bad boy, unworthy of your love. When talking to your child about behavior, especially misbehavior, make it clear to him that you don't think he *is* bad. Instead, point to the specific offense and refer to that behavior as bad.

Daddy Dos and Don'ts

After any punishment—whether a time out, a loss of privileges, a grounding, or impounding the car—don't forget to remind your child that even when you're angry at him and disapprove of what he's done, you still love him. Especially when still young, your child almost definitely fears that he has lost your love or that he doesn't deserve it anymore. Let him know that he will always have it.

Keep in mind that to be effective, disciplinary measures should not merely be punitive, but rehabilitative. So when his time out is up, ask your child if he knows why you put him in time out. If he doesn't remember—and chances are he probably won't for the first few (or few dozen) times—remind him gently but firmly. It won't be long before your child knows the answer to this question: He'll know what he did wrong, and that's the first sign that your child has begun to understand your rules of conduct.

After he has served his time, try to get your toddler or preschooler involved in an entirely different activity. If you put him back in the exact same situation that caused his misbehavior in the first place, you will probably see a repeat performance.

Might Makes Right?

Let's not mince words. I don't believe parents should ever spank or strike their children. Now you may belong to the "Spare the rod, spoil the child" school of thought, but if you really believe this, I think you're wrong.

Spanking, often administered in the anger of the moment, can too easily slip over the line into punitive physical abuse. But just as bad is the spanking delivered coldly, without any overt emotion, well after the fact. A beating of this kind strikes the child—and me, too—as mean and vindictive.

Father Knows Best

"'I brought you into this world,' my father would say, 'and I can take you out. It don't make no difference to me. I'll just make another one like you.'"

—Bill Cosby

Besides, spanking does not teach a child anything. If you spank your child for hitting someone else, for example, you do not send her the message that hitting is wrong, but rather that hitting is allowed if you're bigger than the person you are hitting.

Remember that your child will behave not only according to what you say, but even more so according to what you do. If you spank or hit your child, she will probably demonstrate more aggressive behavior, not less.

Making Up Is Hard To Do

If your child actually hurts another person, especially another child, he needs to make it up to that person somehow. When your child is very young, you can begin teaching him how to make amends. At first, the best you can hope for is to get your child to say he's sorry to the person he's hurt.

At the same time, however, you can begin modeling caring, compassionate behavior toward your child's victim. Offer comfort to the other child even before putting your own in time out. Point out the injury and the victim's tears so that your toddler begins to understand that physical violence hurts people. In time, this approach will help build your child's empathy and a productive sense of guilt (the kind that motivates correction). Before long, your child may even run to get his victim a bandage or try to kiss the wound and make it better.

Profound Losses

With older kids, time outs may lose some of their effectiveness as both a punishment and a deterrent. You may need to devise a new strategy for keeping your preteen's or teenager's behavior in line. You'll need to come up with a new punishment.

Daddy Dos and Don'ts

Most toddlers and preschoolers tend to assume too much guilt rather than too little when they know they have done something wrong. Some children even abuse themselves physically, pinching or biting themselves. If you think your child is overdoing a guilt trip, help him overcome it by suggesting ways he can set things right. Although getting your child to apologize can help, it's sometimes not enough to say, "I'm sorry." You may need to help your child come up with appropriate ways to *show* he's sorry.

One punishment that often works well with preteens is the loss of certain privileges. Ideally, when stripping your child of particular privileges, you should choose ones that are related to the specific infraction your child committed. For instance, you might tell your child that she no longer has the privilege to have any friends over to the house since she refuses to clean her room. If she exhibits antisocial behavior—hitting or other violence or loud and insulting arguments with a friend—she'll have to sit out the next social occasion. If she throws food at the dinner table, she loses the privilege to eat with you for a week. If she drives after drinking, she loses the privilege to drive the car for a month or more.

"Grounding" is a special case of lost privileges. If you ground your child, it essentially means putting her under house arrest. With the exception of going to school (and perhaps meeting one or two other unbreakable obligations), your child may not leave the house unless it's on fire. Your increasingly social teenager may find grounding an intolerable punishment.

The Not-So-Stern Disciplinarian

As the house disciplinarian—even if you share the job equally with your partner—you will need to maintain a relatively even keel. Household rules should be fair, reasonable, and consistent if you want your child to understand and honor them. Similarly, punishments for breaking those rules should also be fair, reasonable, and consistent. Yet if you let your own emotions carry you away, you will have a hard time keeping a balanced perspective and meting out both justice and moral lessons fairly and consistently.

Whoa, Boy! Controlling Your Own Anger

Understandably, you will be furious when your child does something that warrants punishment. Whether your child hit, bit, or kicked someone, stole a bicycle for a joyride, or took your car without permission, you will be seething. But before you take any steps to punish your child, try to get some control over your own anger.

Calming down before handing down punishment has two benefits:

➤ Your punishment is less likely to be vindictive or overly harsh. Justice should be meted out dispassionately.

➤ You will provide your child with a good model. Anger management is difficult for children, especially young children. If you let your child know that you were angry, but waited to act until you regained some calm and composure, she may try to emulate this behavior.

My Mistake

Another way to maintain an atmosphere conducive to the teaching of moral behavior is to confess your own occasional guilt (rare though it may be). When you have done something wrong—whether you knew it at the time or only realized it later—promptly admit it, apologize, and try to make things right.

Admitting mistakes and asking for forgiveness will not automatically diminish your authority or eat away at your child's respect for you (though it depends, of course, on the nature of the offense), at least no more than the passage of time itself will. In fact, your child may respect you more for having the courage to admit mistakes and the moral strength to set things right again.

Letting your child see you admit a wrong and try to make amends will accomplish two valuable ends. First of all, your child will learn the valuable lesson that even parents aren't perfect. Secondly, you will serve as an instructive model for your child, showing him how he should behave when he does something wrong.

Listen to Reason

By around four or five, if not earlier, your child will no longer be inclined to blind obedience. Even if she abides by most of your house rules, your child will probably want and need some explanation of the thinking behind your rules. She will want to know exactly why she can't do something you've prohibited—or why she should do something you insist upon.

Instead of looking upon this as a direct challenge to your authority—which, of course, it is—try to see it as an essential building block in the formation of your child's conscience. By explaining what makes one action right and another wrong, you are teaching your child about moral principles and the consideration of others in an explicit way. You will be providing your child with the foundation of a conscience based upon reason and morality rather than fear of punishment or other reprisals.

Instead of waiting for your child to yell, "Why should I," start offering reasons for the specific behaviors you're trying to encourage. For example, "Would you please put your bicycle in the garage? If you leave it out in the yard, the rain will ruin it or someone might steal it." Or "Would you please stop banging on that wall? The baby needs to take a nap and that pounding is giving me a headache." This will let your child know that your rules are neither mean nor arbitrary, but based in reason, morality, and consideration of others.

What It's All About: Doing the Right Thing

For the first four to six years of your life, you will serve as your child's conscience. You will play Jiminy Cricket to your child's Pinocchio, setting the limits, establishing and enforcing the rules of safe conduct, and fostering ideas of fairness and consideration of others. In short, you will tell him how to behave.

But from about four years old on, you will need to start gradually phasing yourself into obsolescence. (Don't worry, it's a slow process that should take another 13 or 14 years.) Oh, you will still need to set limits, enforce rules, punish bad behavior, and encourage (and hopefully praise) good behavior for many years to come, but the ultimate goal of parental discipline should be to foster self-discipline. And as long as you're making all of the moral decisions for your child, he will never begin to move toward self-discipline.

Father Knows Best

"In the final analysis, it is not what you do for your children but what you have taught them to do for themselves that will make them successful human beings."

—Ann Landers

Soaking It All Up

By elementary school, your child should have absorbed and adopted many of your rules as her own. Your child by now knows many rules you've taught her in order to keep herself safe, to avoid hurting others, and to get along well with others. By identifying with your values, rules, and standards of conduct and claiming them as her own, your child will have begun developing a conscience all her own. (Identification is actually a form of empathy, so see what a huge impact you've already had on your child!)

In addition to internalizing your rules, your child will have started to internalize some of the productive guilt that makes her feel sorry when she has done something she knows is wrong. Generally, these guilt feelings will still come only after the fact, as remorse. But occasionally, throughout the elementary school years and even more so later, your child may feel "anticipatory" guilt feelings. When your child feels guilty before she has done anything wrong, these feelings may stop her in her tracks, actually preventing her from doing something simply *because it would be wrong*. What a big step: Your child will be exercising self-control, resisting her immediate urges, simply because to act on them would be wrong.

Though still developing, your elementary school child understands the basic concept of right and wrong (although only in absolute terms). She may not always know what's right and what's wrong in a particular situation, but you will have helped her develop a general moral code. More importantly, she can now choose to do the right thing not merely to escape punishment, but simply because she knows it is the right thing to do.

This is a huge step in your child's moral development. It means that your child has begun to take responsibility for her behavior. In all but the most extreme emotional states, she can control her behavior and make moral choices. (Unfortunately, elementary school children still fall into an extreme emotional state more often than they eat a meal.) In short, your child has begun to become self-disciplined.

Father Knows Best

"Selective ignorance, a cornerstone of child rearing. You don't put kids under surveillance: it might frighten you. Parents should sit tall in the saddle and look upon their troops with a noble and benevolent and extremely nearsighted gaze."

—Garrison Keillor

Back-Up Systems in Place

Okay, so where do you fit in now that your child is becoming self-disciplined? Well, think of yourself as having a dual role: as the supervisor, monitoring your child's moral progress, and as the primary back-up system, stepping in and taking over whenever the main system (your child's moral code and self-discipline) breaks down.

Just because your child now has a rudimentary conscience does not mean that he'll always behave well (as you would define it). Just because he now has the ability to choose to do the right thing does not mean that he won't—at least occasionally—choose to do the wrong thing. Just because he has developed some self-control does not mean he won't sometimes lose control (though hopefully this will happen less and less often as he grows older). Just because he has a moral code doesn't mean that he won't succumb to sudden urges or temptations to break that code. In other words, he's probably just like you.

Unlike yourself, however, your child has you and your partner to correct these lapses, to continue setting limits, to teach and re-teach your rules of conduct, to emphasize principles of moral behavior, and to reinforce them in a consistent and even-handed way.

Whether introducing a new rule or limit or reminding your child of an old one, you should certainly provide the rationale behind it by the time your child attends elementary school. Once your child sees how well-reasoned and fair your rules are, he's much more likely to adhere to them.

Daddy Dos and Don'ts

Whenever you foresee a situation or enticement that might tempt your child to stray from the straight and narrow, intervene in an attempt to head it off. Prepare your child to face the situation by asking him to repeat the rule you suspect he might be tempted to break. Putting your rule in his own words will accomplish two worthy goals: Not only will it remind your child of the rule, but it will also transform it into "his" rule, encouraging self-discipline by adding another building block to his growing conscience.

Father Knows Best

"Permissiveness is the principle of treating children as if they were adults; and the tactic of making sure they never reach that stage."

—Thomas Szasz

Educational Values

Your influence as the arbiter of values, rules, standards of conduct, and prohibitions will diminish somewhat as your child enters school and attempts to fit in with her peers. As unthinkable as it may seem, your child may turn away from or wholly reject some of the values you have instilled in her. By this point, however, you will already have provided at least a core set of moral values, which will remain relatively constant despite a little fine-tuning here and there.

Liar, Liar, Pants on Fire

When he was just a toddler, your child could not tell a lie. Of course, he could not really tell the truth either because he didn't know the difference. Until three or four, any untruths that escaped from your child's mouth probably resulted from either forgetfulness or from a belief in the magic of wish fulfillment—the same belief that convinced him that a dragon had once visited him in his room or that his invisible friend Binker lived under the bed.

When you asked your toddler, for example, whether he had broken your favorite coffee mug or had drawn on the wall with his new crayons—and you knew he had—he may very well have answered no. Why? Not because he wanted to deceive you or even to escape punishment. Your toddler may very well have forgotten having committed the offense—or because he knew that he shouldn't have done it, he convinced himself that he couldn't have done it.

Hopefully, you did not overreact to "lies" at this early age. After all, if your toddler didn't know it was a lie, how much of a lie was it?

Beginning around preschool or kindergarten, however, your child may begin to lie for a different reason: to cover up other misbehavior, avoid personal responsibility, and/or escape punishment. Though you may find them somewhat cute or funny, come down hard and fast on such lies, perhaps doubling the normal punishment (twice the time out, for example) and explaining to your child why you have done so.

Catching and punishing "cover-up" lies will accomplish two ends. First, it will discourage your child from lying to cover up misdeeds. Secondly, it may help break this habit when it's easiest for you to detect. At four or five, your child will probably tell whoppers, and you'll know immediately that he's lying. But if you brush it off and he sees that he can get away with lying, he will do it more and more—and what's worse, more and more skillfully as he gets more practice. Before long, your child will be telling lies that become harder to recognize as lies.

Don't let your child lie with impunity. Make it clear how seriously you regard lying and how much you value his telling the truth. This is an important lesson in your child's ongoing moral instruction. (Of course, you will probably need to repeat this one, like the others, more than once.)

While discouraging and even punishing lies, remember to reward your child for owning up to something, for taking responsibility for misbehavior. Don't fly off the handle if your child confesses to having done something wrong. (If you do, why would he ever want to own up to a misdeed again?) Though you should still probably punish the misbehavior, show a little leniency at the same time and definitely let your child know how proud you are of his honesty and acceptance of responsibility.

Upping the Ante: Encouraging Responsibility

You no doubt have a good kid. So as she gets older, trust her good intentions. Give her more and more responsibility to exercise self-discipline and regulate her own behavior. Most of the time, your child will probably try to do the right thing, but she might appreciate knowing that you are confident that she will, that you trust her good sense and her moral compass.

You can take a number of steps to help your child begin to accept personal responsibility for her own actions. Start by giving your child more responsibility to take care of everyday hygiene, grooming, and picking up. By five (or even earlier), your child should be able to pick out her own clothes and dress herself, brush her own teeth (with regular checks by you or your partner), bathe herself, wipe her own bottom, and wash her hands after going to the toilet. Also, she should be able to keep her room relatively neat—perhaps not as tidy as you or your partner would like, but tidy enough.

Doing chores that help family functioning (okay, they may not help much at first, but eventually they will) can also reinforce personal responsibility. Having a chore may introduce your child to the notion of working together toward a common good. It will help your child move beyond self-centeredness and begin to recognize the value of cooperation. Best of all, successfully completing a chore will increase your child's self-confidence and sense of her own competence.

By kindergarten, your child should be capable of helping out around the house in some way. Give your child a choice from among three or four chores, jobs that you know she can handle. (If you have more than one child, or even if you have just one, you might want to set up a "job wheel," rotating jobs weekly so that no one gets too bored doing the same thing week after week.)

Stressing that your child's actions have consequences will also reinforce personal responsibility. This means more than punishing her for misbehavior; it means helping her to see that what she does affects not only herself, but others. If your child gets caught in a lie, it makes it harder for you and others to believe her even when she tells the truth. If she steals something from a store, the store owner loses money, and all the customers will have to pay higher prices to cover shoplifting losses. If she hits someone or calls the person a nasty name, it hurts.

Try not to "rescue" your child from the consequences of her actions too often. If she forgets to put one of her school books in her book bag or knapsack, for instance, she will be less likely to repeat this forgetfulness if you don't automatically rush down to the principal's office with it. If you decide to show leniency the first couple of times something like this happens, talk to your child after school about her responsibilities and make it clear that three strikes, you're out. Any more than two "saves" on your part will remove any motivation your child has to accept personal responsibility.

Father Knows Best

"I learned what many young men have learned: If you leave your clothes on the floor of your room long enough, you can wait your mother out. Sooner or later, she will pick them up and wash them for you ...

"Fathers, however, are a little tougher about such earthy living. My father set my clothes on fire."

—Bill Cosby

The Least You Need to Know

➤ While still a toddler (or even a young preschooler), your child has no moral compass, no sense of right and wrong. You cannot reasonably expect your child to "behave" because he has no appreciation of rules. In such a context, punishing misbehavior makes no sense.

➤ Try to model good behavior. Your child will behave in ways that conform not only to what you say, but even more so, to what she observes you doing.

➤ In disciplining your child—that is, teaching him rules of moral behavior—try to balance all the "don'ts" with "dos." Don't just discourage and punish bad behavior, encourage and reward good behavior.

➤ The ultimate goal of disciplining your child should be to instill self-discipline and provide a moral foundation for her developing conscience. Your child's conscience should reflect the moral values she has absorbed from your teaching, but will probably also draw on the influence of her peers as she grows older.

➤ Trusting your child with more and more responsibility as he gets older will prompt him to exercise his own conscience and develop more self-discipline.

Chapter 21

Fun for the Whole Family?

In This Chapter

➤ Making the most of your weekends and other family time

➤ Family outings that everyone will enjoy

➤ Planning a family vacation

➤ How to fly with your child without flying off the handle

➤ How to drive long distances with your child without being driven crazy

Since most dads today still work full-time out of the home, the time they get to spend with their kids is usually in the evenings, on weekends, and on vacations or holidays. With so few hours to spend as a whole family, you will no doubt want to make the most of this precious family time.

Of course, you don't have to devote every hour that you're not working to family activities. For one thing, your partner will probably want at least a little time away from all of you once in a while. For another, you will probably need a little down time yourself every now and then. For a third, as your child gets older, he will have scheduled activities of his own—parties, play dates, athletic practices, and other after-school and weekend activities—that take him away from the family.

These limitations make the time you have together as a family even more precious. So whether you, your partner, and your child are spending the whole weekend or just the evening together, whether you have a day off for a national holiday or a one- or two-week vacation, try to make the most of your family time. If you waste it, you will never be able to recapture it.

Staying Close to Home

Much of the time you spend together as a family will probably be spent at home, but you may need to make a special effort to make sure that you share time with each other every day. On weekdays, for instance, try to arrange to eat dinner (and, whenever possible, breakfast) together. In their daily struggle to juggle work schedules, sleep schedules, and other activities, many families find that family meals are almost the only time they get to spend together.

No matter how much your child's table manners turn your stomach, make a commitment to eat most meals at the same table. Try your best to avoid turning the dinner table into a battleground. If you and your child fight over issues such as table manners and finishing all the food on her plate, you will miss the opportunity to turn dinner into a pleasant social occasion. (If you model good table manners and occasionally point out how your child's behavior could improve, she will, in time, emulate you.)

Instead of focusing on your child's table manners, focus on her day. Take advantage of the opportunity to talk to your child at dinnertime, and catch up on what she has been doing all day. You might want to share some interesting or funny details of your own day, too. (This will keep you from becoming a stranger to your child who, no doubt, wonders what you do all day.)

After dinner, a young child probably needs to begin getting ready for bed while an older child often has homework. This means everyone probably needs to split up in order to get all the essentials done before bedtime. If you work full-time, this means that you probably won't have any family time that's not a meal time until the weekend rolls around.

Avoiding Lost Weekends

Yes, I know you have chores to do around the house, things that you have to get done or nobody will do them. When you've finished these, you certainly deserve to settle down and watch a game (or two or three) on TV. Keep in mind, however, that the weekends also provide you with your best opportunity for family fun. If you consistently use up all your weekend time on chores, home-improvement projects, and vegging out, your child will grow up before you know it, and you will have missed out on your chance to share in family activities.

Make spending time as a family a priority on your weekends. If you need to pencil in family time on your schedule in order to make it happen, do it.

You don't always have to do something special to make the weekend worthwhile. You can have plenty of fun around the house:

➤ Play in the sprinkler when it's warm enough.

➤ Go sledding if it's snowy enough.

➤ Play freeze tag, catch, or Frisbee.

➤ Name your game: board games, card games, computer or video games.

➤ Have a family sing-along.

➤ Read aloud to your child.

➤ Watch TV together and talk about whatever you're watching.

➤ Get your child involved in fun chores with you, like painting a fence (shades of Tom Sawyer). Your child will probably enjoy helping you wash the car, water the lawn, or plant seeds in the garden. (Just add water to any chore, and you can almost always turn it into something fun for everyone.)

➤ Just goof around with one another.

Outing the Entire Family

In addition to exploring ways to spend time around the house as a family, try to plan special family outings. You don't necessarily need to do something special every weekend, but on the other hand, don't let too many weekends pass without going somewhere and doing something as a family.

Father Knows Best

"There is no such thing as fun for the whole family."

—Jerry Seinfeld

Planning family outings can be a tricky business. It's not always easy coming up with an activity that will keep everybody in the family happy, but if you think about what you and your partner like to do and ask your child what he enjoys doing, you will probably come up with a number of possible activities.

In selecting a family activity, feel free to share your interests. If you love fresh-water fishing, take your child to the lake or stream with you. (You might not catch as many fish, but you can still have a lot of fun together.) If you love modern or classical art, take your child to a museum once in a while. Go as a family to a sporting event, an auto show, or an outdoor rock concert. Planning activities around your own interests in this way will give your child a chance to develop his own passion for the things you love to do—and if this happens, it makes it easier to plan family outings for years to come.

At the same time, try to balance these kinds of "adult-oriented" outings with ones aimed primarily at exploring your child's interests. You might, for instance, want to look into whether your community (or one of the neighboring communities) has a children's museum, where your young child can engage in various role-playing activities, science experiments, and other educational play. Check out the closest natural history museum, where your kids can find out all about dinosaurs and other animals. Visit the nearest hands-on science center, where your child (and you) can explore the properties of the natural world through a variety of engaging activities. Now these kinds of places may or may not be up your alley, but to be fair, you should let your child drag you to a place he'd like to go if you're going to be dragging him somewhere you'd like to go.

Even harder than balancing the interests of parents and children is the challenge of balancing the interests of children of different ages. If you have children whose ages are more than a few years apart, you will have a tough time finding activities or outings that the whole family will enjoy. A trip to a park, especially one with a playground, for instance, will almost always delight a small child but may be a snooze for a teenager or even a precocious preteen. A family outing to the latest hit movie would probably thrill any child over age eight but may not be appropriate for your preschooler or toddler. (Attending the few movies that are suitable for this age will, of course, bore or even embarrass your older child.) Nonetheless, if you work at it, you can and will find activities that are fun for the whole family.

Ladies and Gentlemen, and Children of All Ages

Believe it or not, certain places do exist that can be entertaining for all children—from infants and toddlers to preteens and teenagers—and often adults, too. Some suggestions:

➤ **Visit your local library.** You should be able to find books that suit every reader (and prereader) in your family at your local library. Many libraries also sponsor activities (reading groups for young children, theatrical or magic shows, and the like) that your whole family may enjoy.

Father Knows Best

"I take my children everywhere, but they always find their way back home."

—Robert Orben

➤ **Take a hike.** If you live near a wooded area, take a family hike in the woods. Visit a local nature center and take advantage of the great outdoors. Family hiking not only gives all of you the opportunity to exercise and explore nature, but to talk in a leisurely way about both large issues and small.

➤ **Go jump in a lake.** Or a swimming pool or local swimming hole. Kids of all ages—and most parents, too—enjoy swimming and water play. Even before your child knows how to swim, she will probably enjoy having you bounce around the water with her in your arms or use "water wings" to keep herself afloat.

➤ **Play a game.** The haunts once known as bowling alleys, miniature golf courses, and arcades have now been rechristened as "family fun centers." But the new name fits. You, your partner, and your child—no matter how old she is—will probably have a great time bowling, putting, or playing arcade games. (You can even ask the manager of your local bowling alley to eliminate the gutters so that your small child can bowl more than a 3.)

➤ **Check out the local multiplex.** Having trouble finding a movie suitable for both your 4-year-old and your 11-year-old? If you and your partner take your kids to a multiplex theater and then split up once you're inside, one of you can take your younger child to a G or PG movie while the other takes your older child to a PG-13 or, if you think it appropriate, even an R-rated movie. That way, everybody is happy.

➤ **Hang around the mall.** Now personally, I would rather have every hair on my body pulled out than to spend a Saturday afternoon at the mall, even (or especially) in the company of my family, but some people seem to like this sort of thing—the shopping, the food, the rides, even the crowds. If you're one of them, then, by all means, consider a trip to the mall as a family outing.

➤ **You belong in a zoo.** Animals retain their fascination for most children well into their teens. So make visits to your nearest zoo (or "wildlife conservation center") a regular event on your family calendar.

➤ **Head for an amusement park.** Amusement parks, water parks, and other theme parks nearly always offer "something for everyone." (Also keep a lookout for billboards announcing the arrival of local carnivals, which offer many of the same rides on a much smaller scale.)

Daddy Dos and Don'ts

If you have more than one child who's still less than four feet tall, make sure the adults outnumber the children on a trip to a carnival or amusement park. Many carnival and amusement-park rides—including, of course, the most popular ones—require an adult to ride with any child under 48 inches tall (one adult for each child).

You can probably come up with dozens of other ideas for family outings if you put your mind to it. Take the time to sit down with your partner—and your child, who will no doubt have ideas of her own—and come up with an even bigger list of special things you'd like to do as a family. Your family will be closer because of it.

Vacation, Everybody Wants One

Ah, summer vacations. The sun, the beaches, the warmth, the sand in the sandwiches. You probably have warm memories of vacations you took with your parents when you were a boy. Now you have the chance to return the favor to your own kid.

Father Knows Best

"A perpetual holiday [vacation] is a good working definition of hell."

—George Bernard Shaw

Until you've actually traveled anywhere with a child, you have no idea how difficult it can be. Oh, you can make it easier on yourself by planning ahead. (In fact, those spontaneous trips to the mountains or the shore—much less Aruba or Aspen—for the weekend are almost definitely a thing of the past. After all, you probably can't even take your kid to the park without first spending at least 20 minutes of packing and planning.) No matter how much planning you do, however, you can never anticipate everything that might turn your dream vacation into a nightmare.

No matter how many hassles go into planning your family vacation, traveling wherever you're going, and getting used to living temporarily somewhere other than home, you will probably find it well worth the effort. Whenever you doubt it, remind yourself that your child—especially if he is four years old or older—will probably remember this trip for the rest of his life.

Ah, That's the Spot

The place you choose to go on your vacation depends on your own interests, as well as the age of your child

Daddy Dos and Don'ts

If you have close friends or relatives who have children around the same age as your child, consider planning a vacation with them. Whether your child is an infant, a preschooler, or a toddler, he'll have an easily accessible playmate for the whole vacation. (Of course, to make this work, not only the children, but the adults should like each other and get along together.)

and the amount of money you're prepared to spend. Especially if you have more than one child, you will need to try to balance the different developmental needs, interests, and abilities of all your children as best you can as you settle on a vacation spot. Certainly you can't please all of the children all of the time, but you can at least try to take their ages, skills, and interests into account as you make vacation plans.

If you have a baby or toddler, for instance, you might want to put off that skiing vacation for at least a couple of years. (You can't expect your child to ski if she can hardly walk.) On the other hand, a beach vacation may be very possible for your family this year. (Even if the waves sometimes scare your toddler, she will probably love playing in the wet sand.)

If you can't come up with any vacation ideas that would suit everyone in the family, you might find it helpful to consult your local travel agent. He or she can probably make many more suggestions than you could come up with on your own. In addition, your travel agent may know of economical package deals for families or clue you in to family resorts (Club Med for Kids and the like). Although family resorts seldom come cheap, you and your partner might find it worth the expense, since the many activities scheduled for kids may actually give you two some time to be alone together.

Daddy Dos and Don'ts

If you go on a beach vacation, be sure to bring one or more beach umbrellas and gallons of sunscreen. Since most children have had limited exposure to the sun, they tend to burn more easily than adults. Don't fool yourself into thinking that a beach umbrella will protect your child from sunburn. The intense reflection of the sun's light on the water and sand can burn your child even if she stays out of the direct sun. So at the beginning of the summer, buy plenty of sun block with an SPF of 15. Then use it whenever your child will spend more than a few minutes in the sun.

Reservations About Lodgings

Wherever you decide to go, you'll need a place to stay. Naturally, you'll want to stay somewhere that seems inviting and comfortable for the whole family.

Unless you've stayed in the same place before, try to find out how accommodating your vacation lodging, whether in a hotel, vacation home, or campground, will be toward your child. When making reservations, for example, be sure to ask what facilities are available where you and your child can have fun. Do they have an indoor or an outdoor pool? Do they have a game room or tennis courts? Is there a miniature golf course, if not on the property, at least within a mile or two of the spot?

In addition, a good test question, if you have a baby, is whether the hotel you're considering provides cribs—even if you don't need one because you're planning on bringing your own portable crib. A hotel that does not provide cribs will probably not welcome children or accommodate the needs of most families very well.

Adventures Abroad

If you, adventurous soul that you are, decide to take the whole family abroad, you will need to plan your vacation well in advance of your departure. For one thing, your baby will need to have a passport—you have yours already, right?—in order to travel to a foreign country.

In addition, you will probably need to take your child to the pediatrician—especially if he's still under six—a month or so before you plan to leave. Don't wait until the last minute, because if your child needs any additional immunizations—which some countries absolutely require—he may need a week or so to get over any adverse reactions to the shots.

In-Flight Turbulence

If you're taking a vacation far from home or visiting relatives across the country, there's no way around it: You're going to have to travel by plane. Oh, in the old days, you might have packed everything up in the car and put in at least 500 miles a day and driven across country in a week, but don't plan on any long road trips now that you have kids. With an infant, toddler, or preschooler, you'll be lucky to get in 300 miles in a single day, between feedings, bathroom stops, diaper changes, and ants-in-the-pants stops. And don't even think of doing the same thing two days in a row.

Get ready for an adventure: flying with your child. If she is older than about 18 or 20 months, your child may be very excited about getting to fly in an airplane. But that excitement may fade quickly once your child realizes that there's nowhere to go and little to do for the eternity of the flight. With a little advance planning, however, you can ensure a fairly smooth flight.

Having Reservations Already?

Whenever your whole family is traveling by plane, book your seats well in advance. If your child has already had her second birthday, you will need to purchase a ticket for her, too. Ask the ticket agent if any of the flights to your destination offer discounts for children traveling with adults. (Such discounts have become rarer and rarer, but it never hurts to ask.)

Father Knows Best

"In America there are two classes of travel—first class and with children."

—Robert Benchley

As for seat location, you will make the flight much more pleasant for yourselves, your child, and your fellow passengers if you ask your ticket agent for the following:

➤ **Aisle seats.** If you find yourself stuck in the middle of a seven- or eight-seat center row on a jumbo jet, you will probably have a very unpleasant flight and so will all the people sitting in your row. Children often have a very hard time remaining seated on a long flight. If your child needs to get up often—to go to the bathroom, to talk to the flight attendants, to get a drink, to walk up and down the aisles—you will quickly tire of asking the people in the aisle seats to excuse you. Even an infant in flight may need you to take her for frequent walks—though she's just as likely to sleep through the entire flight.

➤ **Nonemergency seats.** Your reservation clerk needs to know that you will be traveling with a child. Young children—including infants seated in their parents' laps—are forbidden from sitting in the same row as a plane's emergency exits. Those who sit next to the emergency exits are expected to help other passengers if needed in an emergency. Clearly, neither your child nor you (if you have a baby in your arms) could perform this service if it became necessary. Make sure to get seats in a different row.

➤ **Seats next to empty seats.** Ask your ticket agent how full the flight is and whether any other flights leaving that day are less crowded. If you can find a plane that's not fully booked (or nearly so), ask your ticket agent if you can reserve seats next to a currently unoccupied seat. If it remains unsold, you will have a free seat where you and your child can spread out a little. If you have a baby or toddler and have not bought her a ticket of her own, an empty adjacent seat can be a godsend, allowing her to sit in the empty seat for free. In addition, an older child who gets bored with a lengthy flight might appreciate the chance to lie down and take a nap or to use the empty seat as a playing surface for cards or a travel game.

➤ **Seats that surround an empty seat.** You might even consider buying a block of seats on either side of an empty one. Chances are, that empty seat—which will be neither an aisle nor a window seat, the most popular seats on any plane—will be one of the last ones sold.

➤ **Bulkhead seats or front-row seats.** If you have an infant, you will especially love having bulkhead seats, which have enough extra room in front of the seat to accommodate a baby carrier or even a bassinet. In addition, some bulkhead seats even come equipped with built-in, fold-away bassinets. This means you and your partner won't need to take turns holding the baby for the duration of a six-hour flight (though federal law requires one of you to hold your baby during take-offs and landings).

The Terror of Flight 606

Before you had a child of your own, you no doubt spent at least one airplane flight in the company of a child who didn't want to be there. Guess what? That may be your kid now.

Not all children are terrors in flight. So who knows? Your child may take the whole thing in stride. But just in case he doesn't, you may want to have an escape plan in place. (Don't count on the pilot to pull over and let you out—or even to lend you a couple of parachutes.)

You'll need an escape plan not to get off the plane, but to make the flight more tolerable for your child, for you and your partner, and for the 200 to 300 people packed in around you.

Curiously enough, although most fathers worry more about flying with an infant than with a toddler, preschooler, or older child, your infant will probably give you the least amount of trouble.

If you schedule your departure time to coincide with your baby's customary naptime or bedtime, your infant may sleep through most or perhaps all of the flight. Even if he seems wide awake when you board the plane, the "white noise" of a plane's engines will probably be too much stimulation for your baby, causing him to shut down and go to sleep. (This is normal and not a cause for concern.)

Daddy Dos and Don'ts

If your child is still in diapers, try to change him right before boarding the plane. Airplane bathrooms, built for function rather than comfort, do not often accommodate the changing of diapers (though some bathrooms now have fold-out shelves for this purpose). In any case, you probably won't be able to change your baby for another hour or more (the time it often takes to complete boarding, get on the runway, take off, and reach flight altitude).

With an infant, the only likely trouble spots involve taking off and landing, when the change in air pressure that causes ears to "pop" will often send a baby into a fit of crying. You can moderate this if you time your baby's feeding to coincide with takeoff and landing. Just as chewing gum, swallowing, or yawning can help equalize the pressure for you (and your older child), sucking on a breast or bottle and swallowing milk or formula can help clear your baby's ears even before they become painful. (Sucking on a pacifier will *not* prevent changes in air pressure from affecting your baby's ears, because both sucking and swallowing are needed to equalize pressure in the ears.) You can make a warm bottle of formula on a plane by mixing about an ounce of the boiling water used by tea-drinking passengers, a couple of ounces of cold bottled water, and an appropriate amount of powdered formula mix, then testing the temperature before feeding your baby. If your baby won't eat, crying, though it may disturb you and your fellow passengers, will also help clear his ears.

For a toddler or preschooler especially, but sometimes for an older child as well, flying can lose its thrill pretty quickly. Your toddler probably finds it difficult to sit in a high chair or a car seat for more than about 15 or 20 minutes. Now that he can walk, your child wants to be on the go constantly. If you don't figure out a way to offer your toddler, preschooler, or older child some relief, the cramped quarters of the cabin will seem like torture to him. After all, there are only so many times you can walk up and down the aisle between the seats.

Mapping Out a Flight Plan

What can you do to make a flight with your child more bearable for everyone involved? Provide plenty of entertainment that you and your child can do together without having to leave your seats:

➤ If you have an infant, bring along a handful of her favorite baby toys just in case she doesn't sleep through the whole flight.

➤ If you have a toddler or preschooler, bring along small toys she can play with on her tray, some favorite picture books, and coloring books or other portable art projects.

➤ If you have a child in elementary school, bring a few toys, some books that you can read together, art supplies, a deck of cards, and simple travel games.

➤ If you have a child in high school, have her bring a long novel or a new magazine, a portable CD or cassette player with headphones, and perhaps some cards or travel games.

Daddy Dos and Don'ts

You can make these diversions even more fun in flight if you buy a few new toys, games, coloring books, and special snacks (to supplement the airline food). Before you leave home, wrap them up as presents. As soon as you get on the plane, let your child choose a present to unwrap. Space out the presents, approximately one an hour, throughout the flight. In this way, your child will have something brand new—and special—to occupy her during every hour of the flight. (This strategy works well on long car trips as well.)

When the flight finally ends (congratulations, you made it), all of you will no doubt be anxious to get off the plane. Take your time, especially if you have an infant or toddler. Although an older child can—and should—be expected to lug her own carry-ons, your little one cannot. In fact, you or your partner may have to carry your child in addition to the diaper bag and other carry-ons. Sit back and relax for a few minutes. You will have a much easier time getting up the aisles with all this stuff after most of the other passengers have already gone.

On the Road Again

Traveling long distances with your child by car is only marginally easier than traveling by plane. But a five-hour car trip has one advantage that a five-hour plane trip doesn't: In a plane, you're stuck, while in a car, you can stop and get out whenever your sanity is threatened.

Take advantage of this ability to stop by leaving yourself extra time to arrive at your vacation paradise. You might even want to plan ahead, picking out one or two spots where you might stop and have a picnic, play some catch or Frisbee, and stretch your legs. (If you have an infant, make sure to take him out of his car seat at all pit stops, too.)

Pick places for pit stops that are about 100 to 150 miles apart, about the limit of a young child's endurance. Even if you've made plans, try to remain flexible. If you have to take a break before you arrive at one of your designated pit stops, you can always skip the next one. Or if everyone falls asleep (with the exception of the driver, of course), you might decide to skip a pit stop and see how far you can go before everyone wakes up and starts complaining.

In any case, don't count on going more than 300 miles a day if you're driving with your child. (Even the most patient of children would find it difficult to remain strapped in a car seat for more than about six hours in a day.) If your vacation spot is farther than 300 miles from your home, pick a place about halfway there and make reservations for an overnight stay. (If you're planning on driving more than 600 miles with one or more small children, you're nuts.)

Bon voyage!

The Least You Need to Know

➤ The time you have to share together is limited. So make the most of the time you've got.

➤ In selecting family outings, try to balance the needs of everyone in the family, adults and children alike. Share some of your own interests on certain outings, but make sure to focus on your child's interests on others.

➤ As long as you all get along well, sharing a vacation with another family can allow you and your partner to take turns at childcare with the other parents. This means that you and your partner may actually get to enjoy a vacation of your own.

➤ No matter how old your child is, bring along plenty of diversions and entertainment when you're flying together in an airplane. Your child—and your fellow passengers—will be grateful.

➤ If you're driving more than an hour's distance with your child, allow extra time to get there. You may be making frequent pit stops.

Chapter 22

School Days

In This Chapter

➤ Preparing your child for his first days—and years—in school

➤ Learning to work with your child's teachers and school administrators

➤ Developing and encouraging good homework habits

➤ Rules to keep your kids safe

➤ Introducing your child to organized sports

To judge by the literature available to parents on the subject, you'd have to call the time your child spends in elementary school the lost years. It's as if your job were over as soon as your child enters kindergarten. You've played with and educated your child, nurtured a love of learning, encouraged independence, curiosity, and responsibility, and instilled limits on her personal and social behavior. In fact, you've done such a good job at parenting during the first five years that you deserve a break: How does six or seven years off sound to you?

Experts and amateurs, researchers and soothsayers, psychologists and parents have written thousands of books, many of them still in print, on parenting infants, toddlers, and preschoolers. You can find hundreds of other books on handling the challenges of parenting during a child's adolescence, those "difficult teenage years."

But just try to find a good guide to parenting that focuses on the years from age 5 to 11. You'll find ten times as much literature on fetal development—when a child isn't even born yet—as you'll find on child development during the elementary school years!

But the early school years are *not* lost years. These years mark the time when your child will truly begin to exhibit her independence. Shoved (often literally) into a classroom with two dozen other children, your child may flourish and come into her own, blossoming into an eager and able student, a happy and helpful playmate, a kid that everyone likes. But your child may also flounder, struggling with her academics, not playing very nicely with other students, and dreading every single day that she has to go to school.

The parenting challenges you'll face during these years won't exactly be a piece of cake, either. You will need to teach yourself how to deal with school teachers and administrators to help your child get the most out of her schooling. You will need to help your child learn how to handle the responsibility of getting homework done—on time. You will continue to serve as your child's teacher, but now you'll have to share the job with her school teacher, and he or she (not you) will get to set the curriculum.

Socially, your child will use you as a sounding board, perhaps needing your help to sort out the various difficulties involved in making lifelong friends (and then sometimes "breaking up" with them). She may seek your advice on how to handle thorny social situations—like trying to juggle conflicting promises made to different friends. (It's hard to be so popular.) You may need to comfort your child's hurt feelings when, for perhaps the first time in her life, somebody says something deliberately mean about her. (Kids of this age can be brutally cruel.) In short, she will need you and your partner to listen to her day-by-day life story.

Father Knows Best

"...[G]ood gracious, you've got to educate him first. You can't expect a boy to be vicious till he's been to a good school."

—Saki (Hector Hugh Munro)

In addition, you will need to instill your child with street smarts. Now that she's going out into the world on a regular basis, you'll have to teach your child how to deal with strangers and how to keep herself safe when she's not with you. Don't fool yourself into thinking that just because nobody ever writes about it, parenting a child through elementary school (or being a child in elementary school) is easy. It's not.

Off to School

Going to school changes everything. If your child never attended nursery school or had only limited exposure to daycare, kindergarten will provide his first opportunity to develop social skills in a group situation, his first chance to pick out one or two kids from a crowd and try to make friends. No matter how well you've taught him the names of shapes and colors and numbers and the letters of the alphabet, kindergarten will also mark your child's first experience with formalized teaching.

Even if your child has already spent a year or more in a full-day or half-day preschool or daycare situation, kindergarten will look, feel, and be totally different to him. After being one of the oldest kids in daycare, he will suddenly be one of the youngest kids in the elementary school. After perhaps a six- or eight-to-one ratio of kids to adults in preschool, he will be thrust into a classroom with 20 to 25 kids (or more) and just one teacher (and perhaps an aide). Everything may seem or actually be bigger than the world he's used to—and your child may feel very small. Depending upon your child's personality, he may feel very excited, totally terrified, or a combination of the two.

You Have Nothing to Fear but Fear Itself

In the months leading up to her enrollment in kindergarten, you can help build your child's confidence and prepare her for her first days of school by doing the following:

➤ Talking to her about school and answering as many of her questions as you can (or finding out the answers from the school principal, the kindergarten teacher, or a member of the local parent-teacher organization).

➤ Not building up the start of school so much that you increase her skittishness.

➤ Encouraging her to practice talking to adults other than you and your partner: grocery store clerks, postal workers, bank tellers, the pediatrician, the children's librarian. By talking to these people while you remain safely at her side, she will gain confidence in her ability both to understand adults and to make herself understood.

➤ Taking your child to a reading group at the library, the beach on a hot day (remember her sunscreen), a play or concert for children, or the zoo—anywhere you can find lots of kids her age. This will help prevent her from feeling intimidated by the crowds of children in her kindergarten.

Daddy Dos and Don'ts

It will help allay some of your child's nervousness about going to school if she becomes more familiar with the kindergarten classroom, her teacher, and the school principal. Find out whether your local school has an open house, visiting day, or orientation day for new students. (Most schools host these either in May or August.) Or arrange with the principal to visit the kindergarten classroom with your child.

➤ Making sure she can take care of her own personal needs: dressing herself (including zipping or snapping her coat shut), going to the bathroom, washing her hands, blowing her nose, feeding herself, and the like.

➤ Familiarizing her with some of the material that she will be learning or practicing in kindergarten: the alphabet, colors, shapes, counting to 10, opposites. Your child doesn't need to master these before kindergarten (otherwise, what's kindergarten for?), but she will feel more comfortable and confident in school if she at least recognizes some of the subjects that will come up.

Rallying the Team

Just because your child now attends elementary school does not mean that you and your partner have given up your jobs as his first and best teachers. You still have a lot to teach your child. But you will now share the responsibility with a succession of elementary school teachers, who will in large part determine the direction of your child's learning. Throughout his elementary school years, you will need to work hand-in-hand with these teachers and the school's administrators to help your child get the most out of his formal education. You will need to work together as a team.

What can you do to help? First of all, stay involved. Don't brush your hands off thinking your child is now in the hands of the pros. No matter how sensitive, skillful, and creative your child's teachers are—some will be extraordinary, some ordinary, and some just plain awful—they don't know your child. In fact, even after a year in their classrooms, your teachers won't know your child nearly as well as you do.

You can help both your teacher and your child get to know each other. Start by attending school functions like Back to School Night or an open house for parents. Most schools host a Back to School Night in September, after the first two or three weeks of school. Teachers usually make a formal presentation designed to acquaint you with their general curriculum, their daily schedule, and their teaching methods. They will then hold a more informal question-and-answer period and finish by allowing you to look around the classroom and approach them individually.

Father Knows Best

"One of the disadvantages of having children is that they eventually get old enough to give you presents they make at school."

—Robert Byrne

Take advantage of this opportunity to introduce yourself to your child's teachers and to become informed of what they have in store for your child in the coming year.

Next, arrange for regular conferences with your child's primary teachers. Many teachers will have a sign-up sheet for parent conferences on their desks at Back to School Night. If so, make sure to arrange for a time when both you and your partner can attend. (Some teachers schedule early morning conferences so that working parents don't have to take time off from their jobs to meet with them.)

If you have a special concern about your child, no matter how old he is, you can schedule a conference as soon as school starts. (Or if your child is entering kindergarten, bring up your concerns during the orientation day or visiting day that precedes the first day of school.) Most teachers, however, prefer to wait until after Back to School Night to arrange parent conferences. This gives them three weeks or so to start to get to know your child and to have something to contribute to the discussion of his educational needs.

Daddy Dos and Don'ts

Another way to stay involved in your child's education is to participate in the parent–teacher organization (PTO) or association (PTA), or attend district-wide school board meetings. Perhaps because the school day coincides so closely with work, many fathers cede all authority on educational matters to their partners. In fact, you may be the only father to attend a meeting in your community (trust me, I've been there). Since most meetings are held in the evening, however, there's no reason for fathers not to join the PTO or PTA.

Father Knows Best

"In the first place, God made idiots. That was for practice. Then he made school boards."

—Mark Twain

In general, the closer you stay in touch with your child's teachers and school administrators as well as the parents of other kids in his class, the more you'll know about

➤ What's going on in the classroom.

➤ What's going on in the school as a whole.

➤ The educational progress your child is making.

➤ The difficulties your child may be having.

➤ The ways you can complement at home what your child is learning at school.

➤ The interests and abilities of other children in his class.

Stay involved in your child's education. Don't leave it all in your partner's lap, even if she is more available during the day. After all, we're talking about your child's education here. What could be more important—or more deserving of a father's time and attention?

Crisis Management

Do you see a problem? Is your child having difficulty mastering the lessons taught in the classroom? Or does it all come too easily for your child, so that you feel that she is not at all intellectually challenged in the classroom?

If you feel frustrated by the course of your child's academics—either because what she's learning seems way too easy or way too hard—you owe it to your child, her teacher, and the school as a whole to voice your concerns. Your child deserves the best education she can possibly get from your school system. Your child's teachers want the chance to address your concerns, but they can't do it unless you share these concerns with them. Your school can only get better overall if you and other parents air problems you have with certain aspects of the curriculum—or even with certain teachers.

Don't minimize your concerns by thinking it's "only" elementary school. Even though the elementary school years may seem easier (compared to either infancy or adolescence) for both your child and for you as a parent, they are not at all unimportant years. Keep in mind that your child's experience in elementary school can set the tone for all of her future years of schooling.

Father Knows Best

"Our children are not treated with sufficient respect as human beings, and yet from the moment they are born, they have this right to respect. We keep them children for too long, their world separate from the real world of life."

—Pearl Buck

So here's what to do if you have a problem with what your child's teacher is teaching or how he or she is teaching it:

➤ Go to the teacher first. Sometimes, children behave differently in school from the way they do at home (shocking, isn't it?). You may have an extraordinarily brilliant child (of course you do) who never stops talking when she's at home, but perhaps in a classroom full of children and in the presence of a more distant authority figure, she becomes shy and quiet. If so, your teacher may not yet have noticed your child's brilliance.

No matter what you see as the academic problem (a curriculum that's too slow, too fast, too unfocused, or too rigid), compare notes with your child's teacher as a first step. The teacher's observations and opinions of your child may surprise or even enlighten you. But since you know your child best, your observations and opinions will almost definitely enlighten her teacher. For this reason, your child's teacher will welcome any information you can provide about your child and her special talents or particular difficulties, especially at the beginning of the school year when he or she is trying to get to know two dozen children.

➤ Go to the teacher second. Once you have shared what you know about your child with her teacher, see if anything changes. If, after a month or so, your conference seems to have had no impact, little impact, or a negative impact on what you saw as the problem (or potential problem), schedule another conference. If you have specific ideas about how you'd like your child's classroom experience to change, suggest them to her teacher and see how he or she responds. If you only recognize the continuing problem but cannot come up with any possible solutions, state the problem as clearly as you can and ask for the teacher's help and specific suggestions. Perhaps together you can come up with a plan to improve the situation.

➤ Go to the principal third. If you still aren't satisfied after another month, contact the school's principal. After all, if the problem you have with the academics taught in your child's classroom hasn't gotten any better by Thanksgiving, it may never improve if you don't get some more heads thinking about it.

Don't feel you're ratting out your child's teacher by going over his or her head. Keep in mind that teachers have to deal with dozens of kids, all of whom have different abilities and temperaments. Your child's teacher may do a terrific job teaching the majority of students in that classroom, and the overall curriculum may be appropriate for most of the kids. Your child, however, is unique—and if you think your child is falling through the cracks, whether it's the teacher or the curriculum, you need to go to a higher authority.

When you approach the principal, be tactful (mindful of the truly difficult job teachers have). Instead of attacking either an individual teacher or the material that's being taught, tell the principal about your concerns for your child, framing the specific "problem" as an issue that will undoubtedly come up again and again throughout her elementary school years. As such, the problem demands a long-term solution, one that will require coordination among different teachers as your child advances from grade to grade.

This strategy may yield immediate results—as the principal, your child's teacher, and you work together to address your child's academic needs. But more importantly, it may yield long-term results. For now that you've made the principal aware of the problem and your concerns, he or she may help steer your child in future years toward teachers who can better address her unique academic needs.

Have You Done Your Homework?

Beginning in first, second, or third grade, your child will start bringing schoolwork home with him. Filled with the joy of learning, your child may rush home, head straight for his desk, and polish off that homework. On the other hand, he may not mention it or think of it at all—until you've told him (for the third time) to brush his teeth and head for bed. He may remember that he has homework but can't quite remember exactly what it is or where it is. Or he may know what he's supposed to do for homework but have left the book he needs at school.

In all likelihood, you will encounter each of these scenarios—even the one where your child rushes home to do his homework—at least half a dozen times in the first year or two that your child has homework. In a vain attempt to avoid the unavoidable, you may even get into the habit of asking your child every day, "Have you done your homework, yet?" But no amount of nagging will prevent your child from occasionally dropping the ball.

Establishing good homework habits in the elementary school years is important for several reasons. For one, your child will have homework to do for at least twelve more years. If he doesn't develop good work and study habits now, your child will probably need to face an academic crisis before he becomes motivated enough to change. For another, the skills of time management, creation of a good work environment, acceptance of responsibility, and organization that your child develops through doing his homework will prove useful throughout his adult life, too.

Most school districts encourage teachers to gradually assign more homework with each passing year. In first or second grade, homework is not a big deal. Your child may come home with 15 or 20 minutes of work once or twice a week as his teachers prepare him for the deluge to follow. By third grade, your child will probably have about 30–40 minutes of homework almost every night. By fifth or sixth grade, however, you can expect your child to spend an hour or more on homework every night.

Don't waste all your time, breath, or energy trying to get your child to do his homework. Your child's homework—and good teachers will back me up on this—is *your child's responsibility*, not yours. But you can help your child develop good work habits and set up a customary time and a place for doing homework.

Father Knows Best

"...[M]ethod acting has been brought to American schools. Before a child can play the part of a student, he has to say: 'Well, what is my motivation here? Why am I doing this homework instead of hanging out at the mall?'"

—Bill Cosby

Start by encouraging your child to get organized. He can't get his homework done if he doesn't know the assignment—what to do and when to turn it in. If the first or second grade teacher warns you (probably at Back to School Night) that your child will have homework assigned this year, shell out a buck or two for an assignment pad or school planner. Make this the one essential item that your child always keeps in his backpack, bringing it to school and then back home every day. (Hopefully, your child will also get into the habit of using it to write down any assignments the teacher gives him.)

Once your child begins receiving homework assignments, you can help him choose the best time to get it done. It will help your child develop self-discipline (and cut down on the times you or your partner have to nag him to do his homework) if he starts to do his homework at the same time every day. The options are fairly limited: after school (or after snack); the half-hour before dinner; or right after dinner. Talk it over with your child and let him choose the time (remember, it's his responsibility).

Next, you'll need to choose a regular place where your child can do his homework. Of course, you've probably bought him a desk for his room, and you think this would be the perfect place for doing homework. Silly grown-up. Some children work just fine at desks, but a child often views a desk as such a serious, austere place that it may actually inhibit him from doing his homework. (Don't worry, the desk will still get plenty of use, but mostly as a storage facility.)

Besides, homework in the elementary school years is still viewed as a social activity. Your child may

Cool Daddy Ohs

Go for Baroque (as background music, that is)! Studies have shown that Baroque music (think Bach) can stimulate nerve synapses and improve clarity of thought, perhaps because its strict tempo (60 beats per minute) matches that of the human heartbeat at rest. So break out the Bach and play it at low volume while your child does his homework.

want to bounce some ideas off you or his sibling(s) that occur to him as he does his homework. He may want to fool around a little in between assignments (or even in the middle of an assignment). As long as your child actually gets the work done and can concentrate enough to do it well (when he finally gets down to work), try not to see this as a problem. After all, unless you work alone, you probably have pretty much the same work habits.

If your child doesn't buckle down to working at a desk, choose instead a quiet, but not necessarily silent, place. A kitchen counter, the dining room table, a kid-sized table in a playroom or your child's bedroom, a coffee table in the living room—anywhere your child can get the work done is the best place for him to do it.

Smart Kids, Safe Kids

When your child begins elementary school, it will probably mark the first time that she has had some degree of responsibility for her own safety. Oh, she may have gone to preschool or daycare, but preschool teachers and daycare employees have to supervise children much more closely than elementary school teachers do.

In preschool, the playground was probably a small, fenced-in area where two or three grown-ups could constantly keep an eye on all of the children in their care. In elementary school, the playground is often set in an open field. When the preschool day was done, your child's teacher would stay with your child until you—or someone whom you had specifically introduced to the teacher and who was authorized to pick up your child—arrived to take her home.

Daddy Dos and Don'ts

By the time your child enters kindergarten, she should know both her address and her telephone number for safety's sake. If your child doesn't yet know these, teach her. In the meantime, however, until she can recite both her address and her telephone number (and recite them consistently), write down her name, address, and phone number on a piece of paper and put it in her pocket or book bag every day.

Now, kindergarten and elementary school teachers aren't dumb. They won't release your child into the hands of a stranger, either. But few elementary school teachers actually deliver their students to *anyone*, with the exception of kindergarten teachers, many of whom use an entrance and exit separate from the rest of the student body and actually do hold on to the kids until their caretakers arrive. After kindergarten, teachers may lead their students to the door, but cannot possibly make sure that all of their students end up with their parents or caretakers. (The logistics of 200 to 300 students, all getting out of school at the same time, make this impossible.)

This new independence from strict supervision can, of course, lead to new troubles. To avoid having the unthinkable happen, you will need to help your child become street savvy and responsible.

You don't need to make your child paranoid to keep her safe. Of course, you want to protect her against the sick people in this world who prey on children. Of course, the thought of her disappearance or abuse at the hands of a stranger is your worst nightmare, but you need not—and should not—make your nightmares your child's as well. What good will it do your child to know the graphic and horrifying details that keep you up at night worrying?

Father Knows Best

"When you are eight years old, nothing is any of your business."

—Lenny Bruce

Knowing that some adults try to steal children away from their parents will probably give your child horrible nightmares and paranoid daydreams. Knowing that some adults get their kicks by hurting children may be even worse. You do, however, need to teach your child certain unbreakable rules designed to keep her safe. What are these rules?

A Stupid Rule

"Never talk to strangers" is a stupid rule. Your child may be innately shy or outgoing, but if he is outgoing, do you really want to curb his natural friendliness? Perhaps you do, but only to the extent that it might put him in danger.

Besides, your child constantly needs to talk to strangers. When he first goes to school, your child's teacher will be a stranger. When you and your partner go out together, a new babysitter will be a stranger. When he goes with you on errands, the bank teller, the grocery store clerk, and the salesperson at the shoe store are all strangers to him.

Even scarier for a child drilled with the rule "Never talk to strangers" is the question of what to do if he ever gets lost or somehow separated from you or his caregiver. In this case, everyone—including police officers and others who might help him—will be a stranger. If your child can't talk to any

Paterniterms

A safe definition of **stranger** for your child should emphasize a lack of introductions by you, your partner, your child's caregiver, or his teacher. Until one of these trusted adults has introduced someone, your child should consider that person a stranger. Stress that a person may still be a stranger even if he or she knows your child's name (since the stranger may have overheard it). A person may also look nice and normal and still be a stranger (because not all strangers look strange and mean, like ogres).

strangers, how will he ever find his way back to you? (A better rule to teach your child is that if he ever does get separated from you, he should seek out the help of a police officer or someone else in uniform: a store employee, a fire fighter, a nurse.)

Even the word *stranger* may seem vague to your child. Though it seems self-explanatory to a grown-up, the word may require a clear and concise definition for a child.

Finally, the rule that forbids talking to strangers will not keep your child safe from those who, statistically, are much more likely to do him harm: people whom he actually knows.

Two Smart Rules

Your child will remain safe from anyone, whether she knows the person well or not, who might want to harm her if you repeatedly insist that she follow, strictly and without exception, two closely related rules:

➤ **Your child must tell you**—or whomever you've entrusted with her care (a relative, a sitter, or her school teacher)—**at all times exactly where she is.** This rule will make sense to your child (though she may sometimes forget it). Since she almost always wants to know where you are, she will appreciate the fact that you want the same thing. (This is the explanation to offer first if she asks why you want her to obey this rule.)

➤ **Never go anywhere with anyone, whether you know the person or not, unless you or your child's caregiver says it's okay.** Teach your child that if someone tries to deceive her, persuade her to break this rule, or to take her by force, she should scream bloody murder and run to the nearest trusted adult.

When you teach these safety rules, make sure you make it clear (and then make it clear again) that they are absolute and unbreakable. Your child must let you know even if she's "just" going to the next-door neighbor's house, the playground down the street, the toy section of the department store. You need to know wherever she's planning to go.

If your child never, ever breaks these two rules, she will remain safe. No one, with the sobering exception of you, your partner, and any designated caregivers, will be able to take your child anywhere without getting your permission first. No one will be able to entice her with promises of ice cream, candy, or a puppy. No one will be able to trick her with tales that you are sick or hurt. For your child will know that even if these temptations or horrifying stories are real, she will still need to ask you or her caregiver what you think first.

No Means No!

To keep your child safe from those closer to him who might physically or sexually abuse him, you will need to empower your child—to give him the right to say no. (Yes, it may make your job as family disciplinarian harder once your child recognizes this right.)

Empowering your child means allowing him to claim what is rightfully his: ownership over his own body. Teach your child that no one has the right to touch his body in any way that feels uncomfortable to him or hurts him. He has the right to keep his own body private and to refuse to let anyone touch him. If you want to get explicit, there's no reason not to let your child know about his "private parts."

Reinforce these teachings with your own behavior. If your child, perhaps out of embarrassment, begins to refuse or shy away from your public kisses or hugs, as some elementary school kids do, you need to respect that and back off.

In addition, you and your partner should avoid insisting that your child kiss or hug a relative or dear friend who has come to visit. You can ask, of course, but if your child doesn't want to give Grandma a kiss and a hug, he has every right to refuse. (And you need not apologize or make excuses for him when he exercises this right.)

Finally, teach your child that no one has the right to demand that he keep something "secret," especially something that makes him feel bad or uncomfortable or something that the person who made the demand insists should never be told to anybody. (Child abusers almost always warn their victims to keep quiet—or entreat them to keep the abuse "our little secret.") Teach your child the difference between "good secrets" (which are exciting, fun, and almost always temporary—a surprise for mama's birthday, for instance) and "bad secrets" (which feel terrible and are intended to remain secret forever). Let your child know that he should not hesitate to reveal these "bad secrets" to you, your partner, or another responsible adult.

Soccer Dads

When the school day ends, mom usually takes over, at least until dinner time, but when the week ends, dad often takes over, at least on the athletic fields and on the courts. Beginning as early as kindergarten, kids in elementary school are taking up sports as never before. Despite all the talk about soccer moms during presidential elections, soccer dads—at least in my neck of the woods—attend most of the games and do almost all of the coaching.

Father Knows Best

"Girls scream, boys shout;

Dogs bark, school's out."

—W.H. Davies

The Only Game in Town

Little League and Peewee Football, both played almost exclusively by boys, used to be the only games in town. But nowadays, both boys and girls in elementary schools all over the country have access to town or city leagues sponsoring such sports as:

➤ Soccer

➤ Football

➤ Basketball

➤ Indoor soccer

➤ Baseball

➤ Softball

➤ Hockey

➤ Tennis

Especially during the first few years of elementary school (before the games and practices start to get too serious for some children), your child may very well want to join one, two, or even three of these leagues (fall, winter, and spring). Of course, it does mean sacrificing weekends and sometimes one or two evenings a week to practices and games, but you should do everything you can to support your child in her athletic endeavors.

Father Knows Best

"I hate all sports as rabidly as a person who likes sports hates common sense."

—H.L. Mencken

Sports provide a healthy recreation for children. By their nature, they involve a great deal of physical activity, which will not only keep your child fit, but will also give her a healthy outlet for venting the normal frustrations and emotions of childhood. League sports also emphasize the value of teamwork, the notion of working together and depending upon one another to achieve or try to achieve a common goal. But most of all—and keep this in mind, all of you overzealous, win-at-all cost, failed or aging jocks who are trying to recapture the often-fantasized triumphs of youth through your own small children—sports at this age (if not at every age) are supposed to be fun.

Of course, sports can also expose young children to some not-so-healthy influences. Most of these come from parents and coaches, but also from other children, who take these games too seriously. (How some parents can take a game so seriously after watching 18 six-year-olds crowd around a soccer ball and repeatedly kick each other in the ankles or a five-year-old hit a baseball off a tee and then run in a daze toward third base is beyond me.)

Some fathers (and mothers) put too much pressure on their children to do well on the fields or courts. If you're standing on the sidelines, by all means encourage your child to do her best and help her improve her play by inviting her to practice (without insisting that she do so) on a weekday evening or a weekend afternoon. During the games, cheer her and her team on and perhaps even occasionally alert your child to concentrate and keep her head in the game instead of looking for four-leaf clovers in the outfield grass or talking with her friends on the other team.

Father Knows Best

"It matters not whether you win or lose; what matters is whether *I* win or lose."

—Darin Weinberg

After you've offered this support, back off a little. Don't berate your child or one of her teammates for making a mistake in a game. Don't get into arguments or hurl insults at referees, umpires, or opposing coaches. Don't get mad at your child's coach for trying to give everyone a chance to play every position. That's what these leagues are supposed to be all about: learning the games, getting some exercise, and having fun—not winning. So *siddown* and *shaddup* already!

Those Who Can't Play, Coach

Most town athletic leagues depend upon parents, often but not always fathers, to volunteer as their children's coaches or assistant coaches. Do you have the stuff to coach your child's athletic team? Well, if you're a good dad, you'll probably make a good coach for young children.

You don't need to have been an all-state selection on your high school team to coach young children well. You don't even need to have played the game yourself, at least if you're coaching five-, six-, and seven-year-olds. All you need is patience and a rudimentary knowledge of the game.

Daddy Dos and Don'ts

For insurance reasons, most town leagues require that all of their volunteers, both coaches and assistant coaches, gain state certification as athletic coaches. When you sign up your child for the program, the organizers of your local league can tell you how to get certified if you want to serve as a coach. It will probably require no more than one two- or three-hour evening class in which you will learn basic rules of safety, some tips on successful coaching, and hopefully some basic first aid.

Many town sports leagues do not even begin keeping an official score until the children playing are at least seven or eight years old (though you can be sure that many of the kids will keep an unofficial tally in their heads). So when coaching five- and six-year-olds, you should have no more lofty objectives than

➤ Teaching the kids the basic rules of the game.

➤ Practicing a few skills that they can use in games.

➤ Getting all of your kids some time at all of the positions they want to play.

➤ Just having fun and making sure the kids have fun, too.

If you can get the kids on your team running the right way around the bases, if you can get one or two kids to make a pass in the course of a soccer season, you should consider yourself a successful coach.

Sports get more serious the older the kids get. By third grade or so, your child's league will begin keeping score of games. The number of kids who stick with a sport past second grade will usually shrink as those who find it too boring, too hard, or too frustrating will start dropping out.

As the children become more and more skilled, your knowledge of the sport you're coaching will become increasingly important. If you remain (or become) a coach after your child gets to third grade you should start moving beyond the basics of the game in your teaching. While still stressing fundamentals, you will also need to begin to address more subtle aspects, like positioning and game strategy.

Father Knows Best

"A team should be an extension of the coach's personality. My teams were arrogant and obnoxious."

—Al McGuire

Now's when your character as a coach really comes into play. Sure, everybody wants to win; that's a given. But there are worse things in life than losing a soccer or basketball game when you're 9 or 10 years old. Remember that you're coaching not only in a competitive league, but also an instructional league. You will need to balance the desire to win (the overall team goal) with the need to provide your players with valuable experience, to build their competence and confidence (individual goals).

If your team has a six-run lead when you bring a new pitcher in for the final inning of a softball game, for example, give her a chance to show what she can do. If she can't seem to find the plate and walks the first two batters, don't immediately pull her out in favor of your team's ace pitcher. Maybe with a few more batters, she'll get better. But you'll never find out—and you'll destroy your player's confidence—if you give up on her so fast. Of course, you don't want the game to get out of hand, but you've got four more batters before the tying run even comes to the plate. Give your kids a shot. Maybe they'll come through for you. And finding out what they can do is what the elementary school years are all about.

The Least You Need to Know

➤ Parenting may become a little easier during the elementary school years, but these are important years for your child, and he will still need you.

➤ Your child's education is too important for just one parent to handle. Get involved and stay involved. Attend teacher conferences and find out what your child is doing in class.

➤ Help your child find a good work space, set a convenient time, and develop good study habits. Perhaps even ask your child if she has any homework, but stop short of nagging her. Your child's homework is her responsibility, not yours.

➤ Teach your child two important rules in dealing with other adults: He should always let you know where he is or where he's going and should never go anywhere with anyone without your permission.

➤ If your child plays an organized sport, try not to become obsessed with winning. The elementary school years are all about learning and developing confidence. Wins and losses will fade in time, but skills, knowledge, and confidence will stay with her forever.

Chapter 23

Teenage Wasteland

In This Chapter

➤ Trying to communicate with your teenager

➤ How to prevent your teenage driver from driving you crazy

➤ Talking to your teenager about alcohol, tobacco, and other drugs

➤ What to do if you find out your child smokes, drinks, or does drugs

➤ The long goodbye: researching and applying to colleges

Remember your own glorious teenage years? Those days when you felt capable of handling anything that came your way? Those thrilling days when your body started changing, your voice started changing, and life seemed full of possibility? Those unselfconscious days when neither you nor anybody else cared how you looked or how you dressed? Those days of universal brotherhood, when all teenagers came together and no one ever felt left out? Those wonderful times when you could talk to your own father about the issues that were really on your mind: sex and drugs and rock and roll?

What's that you say? That's not how you remember it at all? Well, that's okay. I don't remember it that way either. Few people do.

Adolescence is a terribly difficult time, probably the hardest time in all of childhood (if not in all of life). Everything changes so rapidly in adolescence that no teenager ever has time to adjust.

Let's start with your child's body, which will change overnight from a small, graceful package into an awkward collection of gangly arms and legs. Your daughter will suddenly sprout breasts and not know exactly what to do with them. Your son will start to shave and his face will break out with pimples. Your daughter will quite reasonably begin complaining about her menstrual period. Your son's voice will rise so high he could be a castrato, which he may wish he were because his hormones are flying out of control. All he can think about is girls, girls, girls. And all your daughter can think about is boys, boys, boys.

Then let's take a visit to the high school. Your child wants nothing more than to feel like she belongs, but all too often, she'll feel just the opposite. She'll feel like she doesn't fit into the right clique. Painfully self-conscious, she'll know—she'll just know—she doesn't dress right or look right.

Your child doesn't even feel she fits into a single age group. Your child is certainly not an adult, but she no doubt feels she has moved way beyond childhood.

Your teenager wants desperately to stake out her independence, to claim some ground as her own, but she still has to come home to you every night. It shouldn't surprise you if your teenager starts treating you with disdain and defiance. After all, you and your partner are the ones who are holding her back from her independence.

Father Knows Best

"Children begin by loving their parents. After a time they judge them. Rarely, if ever, do they forgive them."

—Oscar Wilde

Despite her attitude and her behavior though, your teenager still needs you and wants your love and support. For though she's definitely moving toward adulthood, she's not there yet.

How to Talk to a Teenager

The single most important thing you can to do to help your child through adolescence is to remain connected to him, to continue to show interest in what's going on in his life, and to keep the lines of communication open—even if he doesn't choose to take advantage of them.

Sounds simple? Well, try it with a teenager who answers all your questions with monosyllables. Try it with a teenager who doesn't seem to want to have anything to do with you. Try it with a teenager who treats every word you say as an invitation to argue with you. It's not easy at all.

Turning Down the Heat

Especially during her early teens, your child is likely to become increasingly defiant and rebellious. When you exasperatedly ask your teenager for the third time to do something, she may look at you defiantly and claim, "I didn't hear you." (Don't believe her for a minute.) When you offer an opinion, she will as likely as not dismiss it, sometimes with incredible disdain. To judge by your teenager's reactions, you'd think you had nothing left to offer her, that your usefulness to her had long since past.

Father Knows Best

"The four stages of man are infancy, childhood, adolescence, and obsolescence."

—Art Linkletter

Alternatively, your teenager may sullenly give you the silent treatment. During particularly moody periods, your child may choose to ignore you completely, but don't fool yourself into thinking she's not listening to you. She may not be reacting outwardly, but she's definitely watching for your reaction. Whether she chooses to respond negatively or not at all, you can bet that your teenager hears what you have to say.

You can probably brush aside an occasional bad mood from your teenager, but if all of your conversations seem to end in bickering or nastiness, you need to figure out a way to turn down the heat.

Try backing off a little. Without even knowing it, you have probably begun fueling the fire. So for a time, try to limit your conversation to absolute necessities. Speak to your teenager in as civil a tone as you can manage.

After a time, when you feel you can do it, begin trying to thaw your relationship by offering your teenager a compliment or two. By opening a conversation on more friendly terms, you have a better chance of keeping it going.

Mastering the Approach Shot

Your teenager probably won't make it easy for you to continue communicating, but that's all the more reason for you to put in an effort to do so. Don't give up on him.

The best way to maintain at least a semblance of communication with a teenager is to open a conversation when you're already doing something that both of you enjoy. Perhaps you have a barbecue every weekend that seems to put everyone in the family in a good mood. Maybe you still manage to schedule regular meals together. (With more and more time commitments, dinner may not always work out as a family meal, but maybe you could all get together at breakfast.)

If you and your partner both start talking to your teenager about the same issue, however, he may feel ambushed. Especially if you want to talk about something big, try to bring it up on a one-to-one basis so he doesn't feel outnumbered.

Daddy Dos and Don'ts

As a father, you may need to make a special effort to keep the lines of communication open with your child. Your partner probably sees more of your child than you do. But as a father—especially as a father who works outside the home for most of the week—you will probably have to try harder. So whenever possible, set aside some special time alone with each of your children (no matter how old they are).

Again, your teenager might be more receptive to something you have to say, especially something important, if you bring it up in the midst of a fun activity. So arrange to do something that he enjoys doing. (Ideally, you'll enjoy the activity, too, but it's much more important that your child enjoy it.)

You might want to get tickets to a sporting event or a rock concert and talk to your teenager either on the way there or the way back. (Unless you live next to an arena, you'll probably have plenty of time, you'll have a captive audience, your teenager will be excited but relaxed, and you won't need to make too much eye contact, which can often bring antagonisms to the surface.)

Even if you don't have anything special to talk about with your teenager, try to arrange it so that you and he do something special together at least once a month. (You should make it easy for your partner to do the same, too.) That way, you can talk about anything and everything in an even more relaxed way.

Keeping It Going

Once you've opened a conversation, you will stop it dead in its tracks if you begin

➤ **Lecturing.** Give your child a chance to respond.

➤ **Refusing to see it her way.** Your teenager has her side of the story. Let her tell it.

➤ **Criticizing.** The very fact that you don't like something your teenager is doing might steel her resolve to continue doing it. So just ignore it, especially if it's something little, and hope it goes away.

➤ **Nitpicking.** Choose your fights wisely. If you constantly battle over the little issues, you may never even get to the big issues, much less argue about them.

➤ **Nagging.** You won't get your child to change or to do something you want her to do simply by repeating yourself over and over again. So why bother? Find another approach.

➤ **Accusing.** Begin nonconfrontationally, perhaps with a question, and see what your child has to say.

➤ **Yelling.** Your tone will drown out your words, and your child really won't hear anything.

➤ **Laying down the law arbitrarily.** Your teenager is no longer likely to accept "Because I said so" as a valid reason for doing something.

Instead of trying to keep a conversation going with these negative approaches, here are some more positive guidelines that might keep your teenager talking (and listening):

➤ When your teenager talks about her feelings, validate them with comments like, "That must have been hard," or "I understand how you feel."

➤ Listen to what your child has to say, whether she's talking about something trivial or something earth shattering. If possible, give your child your undivided attention, especially if she wants to talk about something important (and nearly everything is important to a teenager). If you can't, reassure her that you want to hear what she has to say, and figure out the soonest time when you can give her all your attention.

➤ If you're confused, ask questions. But try to avoid sounding critical.

➤ Relate to what your teenager says. If she's talking about a fight with a friend or breaking up with her boyfriend, recall fights you had or break-ups you survived. Then, without getting too preachy, tell your child a story that conveys something you learned through your experience. Your teenager will appreciate your advice more if she knows you've been there before.

➤ Let your teenager know what's going on in your life. If you work outside the home all day (and you probably do), your child—even at this age—may have little or no idea what you do all day. If you open up a conversation by talking about your day-to-day trials and triumphs, your teenager may feel free to model her own style of conversation after yours: freely volunteering information instead of forcing you to pull it out of her with dental tools.

➤ Use "I" statements ("I think..." or "I feel...," for example) instead of "you" statements. When you begin a sentence with "you," it may sound to your teenager like an accusation—and put her on the defensive right from the start. She may think or even say, "You don't know anything about me!" On the other hand, "I" statements let her know how her behavior affects you or lets her know that you're simply offering your perspective or opinion.

➤ Be clear and concise. If you're stating a rule that's nonnegotiable, for example, clearly say so.

➤ Don't make every conversation with your teenager a "serious talk." Talk about sports, talk about movies, talk about TV. Goof around with her, share jokes, and make each other laugh. If your teenager has fun talking to you (at least most of the time), she may be more receptive when you need to talk about the big stuff.

➤ When you do have big stuff to talk about, map it out in your head first so that you can make sure to cover all the bases. As little as your teenager may want to discuss a particular issue with you, she'll like it even less if you need to bring it up again because you forgot something the first time.

➤ Accept whatever your teenager offers. You can't force her to talk about something if she doesn't feel like it. Let the bad moods slide and pray for a good one to show up soon.

➤ Let your teenager know that you love her no matter what.

➤ Show your teenager that you appreciate the opportunity to talk with her. You don't necessarily have to thank her for talking to you, but you might close your time together with a comment like, "I'm glad we had the chance to talk" or "I had fun talking with you."

Father Knows Best

"Parents are the bones on which children sharpen their teeth."

—Peter Ustinov

If you can move past both the argumentative reactions and the nonresponsiveness of your teenager, the days of rebellion will eventually pass. You may be pleasantly surprised one day when your child actually stops for a minute and talks to you. Whether it's about something trivial or something important won't matter. What will matter is that you will have succeeded in keeping the lines of communication open.

Driver's Education

Yes, the time you've dreaded has finally arrived. Your child has a driver's license—or at least a driver's permit—and he wants to drive your precious car. What can you do about it? Well, you could refuse to lend your teenager the car, but that won't exactly foster responsibility or improve his driving skills, will it?

If you decide to break down and let your child drive your car, you will, of course, want to know that he will drive safely and responsibly. Fortunately, you can take steps to make your teenager a better driver, one worthy of getting behind the wheel of your baby.

Easing into the Fast Lane

First of all, do what you can to make sure the car you lend your child is appropriate and safe for her to drive. This means not only having your car regularly inspected and tuned, but also choosing an appropriate car for her early driving experiences. A station wagon or midsize family car in good condition is the best first car for a teenager to drive (although it probably wouldn't be her first choice). A sporty convertible, a souped-up hot rod, or a Jeep with a roll bar (*these* would be your teenager's choices) may tempt a new driver to speed or drive unsafely.

Secondly, once your teenager gets a learner's permit, give her plenty of experience driving with you in the passenger seat. (Try to forget that this seat is sometimes called the "suicide seat" or the "death seat.") Take your child somewhere that gives her room to make mistakes without doing any serious damage to herself, you, or the car. (A swimming pool parking lot in the spring, fall, or winter can provide you with a great open space to practice, and so can the parking lot of a sports arena when no events are scheduled.) Then give her a chance to practice such fine points as parallel parking without causing dents (use traffic cones or garbage cans to mark off a space), backing up while looking backward, and of course, using the brakes without throwing you through the windshield.

Thirdly, ease your child into more difficult driving conditions. No rookie driver should have to deal with highways, darkness, or a driving rainstorm. Instead, your teenager's first on-the-road experience should be with you (or a trained instructor) sitting next to her on a daytime drive during good weather conditions on local roads.

Let your child show you how good a driver she can be under ideal conditions before you gradually allow her to drive in less-than-ideal circumstances. Then, as a reward for her responsibility, safety, and improved alertness and skill, you can lift your restrictions one at a time.

For instance, you might let your new driver try a solo flight under ideal conditions first, then perhaps a nighttime drive (with you back in the passenger seat), then a nighttime solo. Make it a point to be in the car with your teenager the first time she drives in poor weather and the first time she drives on a highway. Only when you are satisfied that your child can handle the new conditions should you allow her to do so on her own.

Daddy Dos and Don'ts

If your school district doesn't offer a driver's education course to high school students, sign your child up for a course at a driving school. Even if you feel you can teach your teenager how to drive just as well as any trained instructor, it is still well worth your while to insist that she take a driver's education course. The main reason: Many auto insurance companies will discount your premiums if you can show that your teenager has passed this course.

Father Knows Best

"Never lend your car to anyone to whom you have given birth."

—Erma Bombeck

Your Car, Your Rules

Unless your teenager runs out and buys himself a new car—and where's he going to get that kind of money without your help?—he will have to borrow your car in order to drive anywhere. Guess what? This means you get to set the rules. Make it clear before you let your teenager borrow your car that he cannot drive it unless he agrees to honor these rules:

Daddy Dos and Don'ts

Consider buying a cellular phone now that your teenager drives. If your child is 30 minutes late getting home with your car, you and your partner will naturally worry about where he is. A cell phone will allow him to call and let you know that the car broke down, he ran out of gas, or he's stuck in traffic. Make it clear that the car's cell phone is for emergencies and for calling home only. For safety reasons, insist that your teenager pull over to the side of the road before making any cell phone call.

➤ Everybody in the car must wear a seat belt.

➤ No one can drive the car but your child.

➤ No side trips without first asking your permission. You must know where he has taken the car at all times.

➤ No drinking in the car—by the driver or passengers.

➤ No drinking and driving ever.

➤ No smoking in the car. (Of course, your own perfect child would never think of smoking at all, but he shouldn't let any of his friends smoke in your car either.)

➤ No speeding.

➤ No driving through intersections when the light is yellow. (I know yellow means "exercise caution," but your teenager does not yet have enough driving experience to have good judgment and exercise caution in this situation. Until he does, your child should treat a yellow light just like a red light and STOP!)

If you catch your child breaking any of these rules, make sure you enforce them with a suspension of driving privileges. (How long the suspension lasts depends upon the seriousness of the violation.) Driving, as my father used to tell me, is not a right, but a privilege. If your teenager can't handle the responsibility, he should not have the privilege.

A Model Driver

No matter what rules you come up with for use of the family car, chances are that your child will drive in a way that more closely mimics the way you drive rather than the way you tell her to drive. Remember to model good driving habits. You can bet that your teenager will be watching you, ready to catch you in any hypocrisy. If you don't buckle your seat belt, obey traffic laws (including those suggested guidelines known as "speed limits"), and drive safely and defensively, how can you expect your child to do so?

Of course, when your child is driving alone or with friends, she may drive very differently from the way she drives when you're in the car with her. And you probably won't know about it unless she gets a traffic ticket for speeding or some other moving violation, she gets into an accident and you find out the details, or you see your car cruising down the main street of your town at 45 miles per hour with teenagers hanging out of every window. (These infractions, of course, must have consequences.) If you don't catch her in the act though, all you can do is tell your teenager the rules of the road—the guidelines aimed at making her a safe and responsible driver—and trust that she will observe them at least most of the time.

Daddy Dos and Don'ts

If your teenager begins using the car a lot, you may want to consider having him chip in to cover the cost of gas and maintenance for the car. At the very least, make it known that your teenager should never bring the car home with an empty gas tank. Whether your child contributes to gas and maintenance, make it understood that any tickets he gets for moving violations or illegal parking are entirely his responsibility.

Volunteering to Be the Designated Driver

Make it absolutely clear that your child should never drink and drive. Of course, you probably also insist that he never drink, so in adding this second rule about driving, you may fear you're undercutting the first.

But get your priorities straight. Urging sobriety while also forbidding drunk driving is a lot like advocating sexual abstinence but teaching safe sex (see Chapter 19). If your teenager breaks the first rule, do you really want him to be ignorant of the second? Of course not. You want him to get home safely.

Let your child know that if he has been drinking, he should call you—anywhere, anytime—and you'll come and pick him up. (He should also call if the driver of the car he's depending on to get him home has been drinking.) This will send important messages, in addition to the obvious one about drinking and driving. It will let your child know that his safety is of paramount importance to you. It will let him know that you can forgive certain transgressions. And it will let him know that he can do something wrong and still come to you for help.

Of course, if your teenager makes this call, you need to keep up your end of the bargain. Punish your child appropriately for his drinking, of course, but don't punish him further for owning up to his misbehavior. (Of course, if your child lies in an attempt to cover up his drinking, the lie should lead to additional punishment.) Certainly you'll be angry. But your teenager will never again confess to bad behavior if you fly off the handle when he does. (For more on dealing with cover-up lies and confessions, and on controlling your anger when disciplining your child, see Chapter 20.)

Father Figures

A sobering statistic: Every year, 5,000 teenagers die in traffic accidents, making it the number one cause of death among teenagers. Teenagers account for just 1 of 20 licensed drivers, but are responsible for more than 1 of 9 fatal auto accidents and 2 of 15 accidents overall.

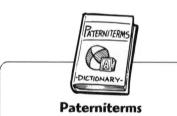

Paterniterms

Inhalants are common household products (paint thinners or airplane glue, for example) that kids inhale to get high because they're easily accessible. Any household product marked "Do not inhale" can be used to produce a high (dizziness, sleepiness), but the chemicals can also cause brain damage, kidney failure, loss of consciousness, and even death.

Accidents Happen

Does your teenager know what to do if she gets into a car accident? If she's going to drive the family car, she should.

Let your child know that if she gets into an accident while driving, she should immediately do the following:

➤ Call for an ambulance if anyone has gotten hurt, then call the police and call you.

➤ Remain at the scene of the accident until the police arrive.

➤ Exchange names, addresses, phone numbers, insurance companies, and driver's license numbers with the driver(s) of any other car(s) involved in the accident.

➤ Ask any witnesses to provide their names and phone numbers.

➤ Write down what happened, and later get a copy of the police report on the accident.

➤ Notify your auto insurance company as soon as she can.

Hopefully, your child will never have to go through all these steps. But if she ever has an accident, it may help calm her down if she knows exactly what to do.

Dangerous Habits

Teenagers, like toddlers, preschoolers, and elementary school kids, consistently test limits. That's part of growing up. But as a parent, you are no doubt concerned that part of your own teenager's testing may involve drugs: alcohol, tobacco, marijuana, cocaine, LSD, PCP, and even household chemicals used as *inhalants*.

An Ounce (or a Gram) of Prevention

What can you do to prevent, or at least discourage, your child from dangerous experimentation with tobacco, alcohol, and other drugs? Short of locking your child up in his room for four years, the best approach combines continued communication with your teenager and education about the dangers of drug use.

Here are some steps that might help:

1. Try to maintain a good rapport with your teenager. This can be difficult, but not impossible, during these years of hostility and rebellion, but don't give up trying. (Use some of the ideas suggested earlier in this chapter.)

2. Set clear limits prohibiting drug use (including alcohol and tobacco) and enforce any violations with a loss of privileges.

3. Keep tabs on your teenager. This doesn't mean spying on your child or rummaging through his room in search of evidence. But don't give up on the long-standing rule that you (or at least your answering machine) need to know where your child is at all times (see Chapter 22).

   If, for instance, your teenager goes to a friend's house, but then they leave to go to another friend's house, he should call you first, just to let you know. (You can help your teenager feel more grown up if you tell him that you need to be able to contact him immediately just in case there's an emergency.)

4. Since your child may have a perfectly innocent explanation for doing something that at first glance appears suspicious, regard him as innocent until proven guilty. Just because he went to a party where you heard that drinking was going on, for instance, doesn't necessarily mean your child was drinking, too.

Father Figures

Twenty percent of the nation's eighth graders have used inhalants at least once in their short lives.

Daddy Dos and Don'ts

Since many teenagers take up smoking or drinking because it makes them feel grown up, you may be able to head off this behavior by providing your child with other avenues to feel grown up. One way is to give your child more and more "adult" responsibility. You can also try giving him more "adult" control over certain family decisions.

The Rap on Drugs

If you have long talked to your child about serious subjects (see Chapter 19), your conversations about drugs should not be so different. Indeed, like your talks about sex and death, your conversations about drugs should begin long before your child becomes a teenager (especially since many children begin experimenting with drugs at age 12 or 13 or even younger).

Father Knows Best

"...[I]f you really pay attention to them from the very beginning, then you'll know the moment they start to swallow or sniff things that rearrange their brain cells."

—Bill Cosby

To get the conversation going, look for an opening (perhaps something you saw on TV, heard on the radio, or read in a newspaper or magazine) that will allow you to bring up the subject somewhat subtly. Try to avoid lecturing, which will turn your teenager off. Stay away from scare tactics, too, which your child will find meaningless. (Most teenagers have little or no appreciation of their own mortality.) Just talk and listen—and if your child has any questions about alcohol, tobacco, and other drugs, try to answer them as directly and straightforwardly as you can.

Of course, if you used drugs in your own youth, you may feel somewhat ambivalent or hypocritical preaching about the dangers of drugs to your child. If you tried drugs just once or twice, you shouldn't have any problem talking to your child about them. Level with your child about your limited drug use, but don't forget to let her know why you didn't want to try them again.

If you used drugs a lot when you were younger, you may have more trouble with this conversation. If you decide to tell all to your teenager, try not to glamorize your youthful drug use, no matter how fondly you remember those days. Unless you still take drugs, you stopped for a reason. So in talking to your child, focus

Daddy Dos and Don'ts

When you talk to your child about tobacco, alcohol, and other drugs, help her to come up with some responses that will allow her to resist peer pressure gracefully. Come up with some scenarios that allow your child to practice passive resistance. Saying, "I don't like the taste," will work for almost any drug, including alcohol and tobacco. Alternatively, she can honestly blame you by saying, "My parents will (*fill in appropriate punishment here*) if they find out."

on why you stopped rather than reminiscing about the concerts, the parties, and the colors you saw.

Even more problematic to preach against is alcohol because you might still drink alcohol—and drink it in front of the kids. Smoking has gradually become taboo in much of society, and illegal drugs have always been impermissible in most circles, but society as a whole (and perhaps your family as a small part of that society) accepts a certain level of drinking. This means that in discussing alcohol, you should probably emphasize moderation in adult drinking and prohibition of teenage drinking.

But Dad, You Drink and Smoke

No matter how antagonistic your teenager may seem toward you, he still sees you as a role model. If you smoke, drink alcohol (especially to excess), or use illegal drugs, your child may think it's all right—no matter what you say about it—to take up cigarettes, alcohol, and/or drugs, too.

Consider how your own behavior affects your child. If you smoke, try to quit long before your child reaches the teen years. If you use illegal drugs, cut it out. If you drink to excess, quit entirely. If you don't want to give up your occasional beer or glass of wine (or Scotch or gin and tonic), continue to drink in moderation. Let your child know that you think moderate alcohol consumption is okay for adults (though never for children)—as long as they don't drive afterward.

Of course, if your child asks *why* moderate drinking is okay, you probably have some soul-searching to do. You could talk about the possible health benefits of moderate drinking—though evidence of these benefits is thin and few people can honestly say they drink alcohol for their health. You could also talk about savoring (in moderation, of course) the pleasures the world has to offer. In the end, however, you may need to ask yourself why exactly you drink—and why you think it's okay.

You're Drunk!

Despite your prohibitions, your child may nonetheless experiment with alcohol, tobacco, or illegal drugs. What should you do then?

If you catch your child coming home obviously drunk, you need to sit her down for a talk, and it's okay for this one to sound like a lecture. But don't bother trying that same night. Instead, wait until morning when she has sobered up. Start the conversation over the breakfast table by asking your child to tell you what happened the night before. Give her a chance to give you the lowdown before you confront her with your own observations from the night before.

Father Figures

According to the U.S. Surgeon General, 50 percent of the nation's junior and senior high school students drink at least once a month. Another study found that by eighth grade—these are 13- and 14-year-olds!—55 percent of American children have tried alcohol.

After you establish that she was drinking, let your teenager know how disappointed you are, reminding her that you disapprove of teenage drinking or drug use. If it's a first offense, you might want to let your child off with a warning. (Her hangover may be punishment enough, and you should feel free to point this out.) Before ending the discussion, however, come up with an appropriate punishment that you will impose without fail if it happens again while she's under your roof. You might even ask your teenager what she thinks would be an appropriate consequence. (You may be surprised at the severity of the punishment your child comes up with.)

If it's a second offense, you have no choice but to impose the agreed-upon punishment—often some sort of restriction of liberty. If it happens again and again, however, you'll probably need help. Get in touch with a substance abuse counselor (whom you can find by asking your child's guidance counselor or a local community services agency for a referral).

You're Smoking!

Children take up smoking for a number of reasons only to find that once they've started, they can't quit a drug with addictive powers that a former Surgeon General has compared to heroin. Teenagers start smoking due to:

➤ Peer pressure (all their friends do it)

➤ Image (smokers are grown up)

➤ Perceived "benefits" (relaxation, relief of stress, weight control)

If you catch your teenager smoking, he may already have formed an addiction to nicotine. Punishment may not be the best way to accomplish your main objective: helping your child to quit smoking now. Again, the mortality argument doesn't work with teenagers, who cannot conceive of their own death and therefore cannot be motivated by it. If you want to encourage your teenager to quit smoking, focus instead on his current concerns:

Father Figures

More than one-third of American teenagers smoke cigarettes—and 3,000 more take up smoking every day. More than two-thirds of teen smokers wish they had never started and nearly half have tried and failed to quit.

➤ **Looks.** Smoking will age his face, giving him premature wrinkles. It also turns his teeth and fingers yellow.

➤ **Fitness.** Because smoking—as your child by now has found out—leaves him short of breath, it will impair his athletic skills and performance.

➤ **Romance.** Smoking stinks, gives you bad breath, and makes your mouth taste bad when you're kissing someone.

If any or all of these arguments motivate your child to want to quit, do what you can to help him out. Ask your pediatrician about the use of nicotine patches, nicotine gum, or drugs that suppress nicotine cravings. Suggest that your child spend more time in movie theaters, museums, stores, malls, and other indoor spaces where smoking is prohibited. Offer him an incentive, a reward you will give him if he quits smoking for six months. Best of all encourage him to tell a friend—one who doesn't smoke—that he's quitting. This approach will enlist the powerful agency of peer pressure, but this time to get your child to quit smoking.

You're Stoned!

In arguing against smoking pot in the first place or urging your teenager to quit if she has already tried it, appeal to your child's own self-interest just as you did in your discussions of smoking tobacco. (Long-term arguments still won't carry much weight). First, make the point that since possession of marijuana is illegal, your teenager might end up in jail if caught with it. (This argument, though true, may make little sense to your child, who may insist that she'll never get caught.)

So in addition, point out that smoking pot will disrupt:

➤ **Athletic performance.** In addition to leaving her short of breath, pot smoking slows reflexes and disrupts coordination, which will detract from her athletic skills.

➤ **Academic performance.** Since smoking pot tends to reduce the ability to concentrate and focus the mind and dramatically reduces short-term memory, it…uh…I forgot what I was going to say.

Father Figures

One out of every eight eighth graders has smoked pot. That number doubles to one of four among tenth graders. By senior year, one out of every three students has smoked pot.

Give It That Old College Try

Looking ahead to college can be an exciting—and nerve-wracking—experience for both teenagers and their parents. As you ruffle through various books and pamphlets that describe colleges your child is considering, as you shuffle through the endless sea of papers—college applications, financial aid applications, loan applications, test scores, and the like—you may become so bogged down in details that you lose sight of how much emotional investment your child is putting into this process.

Preparing for and applying to colleges marks the beginning of the end of your teenager's childhood. Unless he attends a local college, your child will be striking out on his own, not only leaving home, but also leaving behind almost everything he has ever known and loved. Even though he may not show it, your teenager will most likely feel excited, anxious, apprehensive, scared, ill-prepared, inadequate, and perhaps even incompetent.

Show your child a lot of understanding, love, and support during this time. He needs to know that even though he will soon leave home, he will always be able to come back. He needs your guidance, while at the same time having the freedom to make his own decisions regarding college. He needs to know that you have confidence in his abilities and his judgment (even if you're a little nervous, too). But most of all, your teenager needs to know that as he prepares to go out on his own, he will never be truly alone because you will always be there for him.

Father Knows Best

"This is the hardest truth for a father to learn: that his children are continuously growing up and moving away from him (until, of course, they move back in)."

—Bill Cosby

On the Record

Your teenager's academic record in high school will be an important asset (or liability) in her quest for college acceptance. Since college admissions officers look at the entirety of an applicant's transcript—not just the grades, but the courses taken—your child may need to begin looking toward the future as early as her freshman year in high school.

Daddy Dos and Don'ts

Keep in mind that not every child needs to go to college. If your child has never been a scholar and shows little or no interest in or inclination toward academics, forcing her to go to college may be a crushing experience. Besides, your child may have other talents—skills, crafts, artistic talent, people skills—that attending college will do little or nothing to enhance.

If your child plans to go to college, set up a meeting with her guidance counselor during her first year of high school. Begin by asking the counselor for recommendations about what courses she should take over the next four years. Your child's high school may offer a variety of courses to satisfy state requirements regarding English, history, math, science, and foreign languages. Every child who graduates in your teenager's class will have taken four years of English, two or three years of history, and so on. But in all likelihood, not all course offerings that satisfy state requirements will help prepare your child for college. (In addition, college admissions officers can usually tell whether an applicant has aced all easy courses and will prefer applicants who did well—even if not spectacularly so—in harder courses.)

Subsequently, you might want to meet with the guidance counselor once or twice a year just to talk about your teenager's progress in preparing for college applications. The guidance counselor might, for example, be able to suggest extracurricular activities that both suit your child's interests and abilities and will enhance the impression she will make on college admissions boards. The counselor can also keep you up-to-date on the standardized tests your child will need to take and when they will be offered.

Off the Record

What your teenager does when he's not in class or studying will also matter to most college admissions officers. Although colleges certainly want to admit students who demonstrate academic excellence, most colleges also look for well-roundedness in their applicants. So encourage your child to explore and expand his nonacademic interests, as long as they don't eat away at his academic performance. In evaluating students, college admissions officers will probably award "bonus points" for:

Daddy Dos and Don'ts

If your child will be taking certain achievement tests, which measure the amount she has learned about a specific subject, you might want to encourage her not to wait until her junior year to take all the tests. If, for instance, your teenager takes biology as a freshman or sophomore in high school, then the best time to take that achievement test would be in June of that year, when the material remains fresh in her mind. This will eliminate the need for your teenager, in the already busy junior year, to bone up on a subject she took a year or more earlier.

➤ **Leadership.** Does your child want to participate in his high school student government? Or would he want to run for election as one of his class officers?

➤ **Volunteer work.** Does your child have a special concern for the environment? Does he want to do something to help the homeless? Would he like to help or cheer up the sick or the aged? Civic mindedness—whether demonstrated by volunteer work in a homeless shelter, an environmental group, a hospital or nursing home, or any other organization that contributes to your community— counts for a lot in the eyes of college admissions officers.

➤ **Club memberships.** Does your child's school sponsor clubs that match your teenager's interests, academic or nonacademic? Many schools sponsor after-school clubs in areas as diverse as science, chess, photography, foreign languages, cooking, and public service, to name a few.

➤ **Participation in the media or arts.** Would your child enjoy working on the high school newspaper or helping to organize the class yearbook? Does your high school have a radio station (even just an in-house station piped into the cafeteria during lunch)? Would your child like to try out for the high school band or orchestra or audition for a school play or musical?

➤ **Sports.** Your child doesn't need to be an all-American in his sport to attract a college's attention (unless he wants a sports scholarship to one of the country's Division A College teams). Just sticking with a team indicates a dedication and discipline that colleges find appealing.

Daddy Dos and Don'ts

Though the testing agencies insist that preparing for college entrance exams will not significantly affect your child's scores, those who offer test-prep courses (which can be very expensive) generally offer up impressive numbers that they claim prove otherwise. My own opinion: Have your child—especially if she tends to do well on tests in general— shell out $15 or $20 for a book of sample tests and tips. Ask her to take some practice tests and then have your child take the actual test. When the scores come in, invest in a test-prep course only if your child did much worse than you had anticipated. Only after your teenager takes the test a second time will you have a good measure of whether the cost of the course was worth it.

➤ **Jobs.** Your teenager's experience in the working world will also carry some weight among college admissions officers. Whether he was earning money to help out the family, cover some of his own expenses, put something away for college, or save up for a trip, a car, or some other special treat, the fact that your teenager held onto a job will definitely be a plus.

This Is Only a Test. Had This Been a Real Emergency …

During her junior year, your child will begin taking college entrance exams: the Scholastic Achievement Test (SAT) or the American College Test (ACT). Most colleges require either one of these tests, but some colleges prefer one test over the other, so check a college reference guide to see which test is acceptable at the colleges your child is considering. (The PSAT, a practice test taken earlier than the entrance exams, will not count in college admissions decisions but may count for a lot in the determination of who gets scholarships and financial-aid packages and how much is offered.)

If you or your teenager is dissatisfied with the results once the scores are in, have her take the test again. College testing organizations will report only your child's best score on her college applications. So, really, she has nothing to lose by taking the test again (except the cost of the test itself).

Narrowing the Field

Where your child chooses to apply depends on a number of different considerations. These include:

➤ Geography (near or far away, ski school or beach school, that sort of thing)

➤ Size (small, medium, large, or extra large—just like T-shirts)

➤ Interests (what he wants to study)

➤ Educational philosophy (conservative or liberal, parochial or nonparochial, co-ed or single-gender, many requirements or mostly electives)

➤ Cost (whether the school is public or private)

After helping your teenager come up with his personal criteria, start doing a little research. Ask your child's guidance counselor for help. He or she may have some specific suggestions to make and probably has a dozen file drawers full of college brochures and course catalogues.

During your child's junior year in high school, take some time off to visit some of the colleges in which he has expressed the most interest. When choosing dates, call the college first to make sure it's not on a break during the time you plan to visit. (You may be able to arrange for an interview with an admissions officer at the same time.) Your child will get a much better sense of the school if he can visit some classes and meet with some students. You may even be able to arrange for your teenager to stay in one of the college dorms for a night. (Sorry, you can't stay, too.)

You will get a good idea of what the college has to offer your child if you pick up a copy of the college newspaper and a current course catalogue, check out the notices posted all across the campus, and encourage your teenager to talk to students at the school. (He may feel more comfortable, or at least less dorky, doing the latter if you conveniently disappear for a few hours.)

Daddy Dos and Don'ts

Cost should not be your number one consideration (it certainly won't be your teenager's) in choosing the schools to which your child will apply. You may qualify for financial aid (partial or full scholarships), if not from the school itself, then from a number of different sources (see Chapter 14). Loans are also available from numerous sources.

Apply to a few schools your child would like to attend even if you know you can't afford them (as well as some that, however penniless they will leave you, you can swing financially). If financial aid packages and loans still leave you short, your teenager can always decline enrollment and go to a state school instead or defer enrollment, get a job while living at home, and save his money for a year or two.

Without discouraging your teenager, try to help him to keep a level head as he narrows the field. He may be in for a major disappointment if he gets his heart set on getting into one particular school (which may be very selective), so try to help him see the good points of other schools besides his first choice. If your child chooses only super elite institutions—very selective private colleges and universities—apply to them, of course, but also encourage him to choose one or two "safety schools," colleges that are almost certain to accept your child's application, even though they might not be your teenager's first. Applying to a safety school will relieve some of the pressure on your teenager to get into his first choice of schools. (And if he gets accepted only at one of his safety schools and doesn't like it, he can always apply for a transfer after a year or two.)

Apply Yourself

After narrowing the field, obtain application forms by contacting the colleges your child has chosen. (You can considerably cut down on your child's paperwork if the schools to which she plans to apply will accept the "Common Application," a standard form accepted by many different schools.)

As you may remember from your own teenage years, most of the application will be relatively easy, requesting personal and family information and perhaps some short answers to a few questions. The college admissions office will also want to see your teenager's academic record and test scores.

In addition, the college will most likely ask for some letters of recommendation, at least one of which will need to come from one of her teachers. Encourage your child to choose a teacher who not only gave her a good grade, but who seems to know her well. Also, have her approach the teacher she has chosen early in the year, or the teacher— especially if he or she is popular—may be too swamped with requests to accept another one.

The one area of the application that gives some kids trouble is the essay section. Your child will need to write an essay, probably about one of the following:

➤ Something about herself

➤ Something about one of her special interests or ideas

➤ Something about her college aspirations and/or why she chose this specific college

➤ A hypothetical scenario that encourages your child to use her imagination

Encourage your child to write a first draft and show it to one or two people whose opinions she respects: a favorite teacher, a relative, or even you or your partner. She should then consider that person's comments and suggestions, without necessarily accepting all of them, in preparing a final draft. Your child's ability to express herself and her ideas in this essay may be the deciding factor in whether an admissions officer chooses to admit her, so help her make sure she has done the best job she possibly can.

Once your teenager has all of her applications out, it's just a waiting game to see which of the colleges she has applied to will welcome her into the fold. As long as you've applied to at least one safety school, she will almost definitely get in somewhere. Cross your fingers, hope your teenager gets into the school she wants, and get ready to say goodbye. Good luck!

The Least You Need to Know

➤ Give your teenager some space, but don't give up on him. Do whatever you can to keep the lines of communication intact, even if you can't keep them open. When your child finally decides he does want to talk, you'll want to be there for him.

➤ Ease your child into driving by having her practice first under ideal conditions. Once she has her license, insist that she obey the "car rules" if she wants to borrow the family car.

➤ The number one rule for your teenager: Don't drink and drive or ride in a car when the driver has been drinking.

➤ Since your child no doubt thinks he's immortal, appeal to his immediate self-interest rather than long-term effects in arguing against the use of alcohol, tobacco, and other drugs.

➤ Help broaden your child's horizons and not get fixated on one college that would be "perfect" for her. Try to help her see that she could be happy at any one of a number of schools.

Paterniterms: Words You May Need to Know

AFP test   See *alpha-fetoprotein test*.

afterpains   Contractions that work to shrink the uterus after childbirth.

alpha-fetoprotein test   A blood test that measures the levels of alpha-fetoprotein—a protein secreted in large amounts by a fetus with a malformed brain or spinal cord.

amniocentesis   The removal of a small amount of amniotic fluid from the womb to test for certain chromosomal defects. Amniocentesis can also determine the gender of the fetus.

axillary temperature   Body temperature obtained by placing a rectal thermometer under the axilla (armpit).

back labor   An intense backache during labor, most often caused by the position of the baby (who is facing up toward the front of the mother's pelvis, rather than facing down), which makes it more difficult for the head to flex and move through the birth canal.

bassinet   A basket—sometimes portable and sometimes attached to a stand—just big enough to hold a sleeping baby.

board certification   An indication that a pediatrician has trained for at least three years in an approved pediatrics residency training program—gaining experience not only in well-baby care, but also in treating a variety of more complicated childhood ailments—and then passed a qualifying exam.

cash value policy   Provides death-benefit insurance, as well as cash value equity at maturity of the policy.

C-section   See *cesarean section*.

Cesarean section   A surgical method of delivering a baby (and the placenta) through incisions in the abdominal wall and the uterus.

child-safety locks   Devices that make it difficult for young children—and some adults—to open drawers and cabinet doors.

colic   A pattern of intense and inconsolable crying that recurs around the same time every day (often the late afternoon or early evening). Colic begins in the early weeks of a baby's life and may continue for as long as three months. The cause of colic is unknown.

couvade syndrome   A collection of "sympathetic pregnancy" symptoms suffered by some fathers-to-be, including nausea, sleeplessness, loss of appetite, weight gain, exhaustion, and vomiting.

engorgement   1. A flow of blood that fills tissue to maximum capacity. Engorgement of genital tissue causes arousal in both males and females. 2. An excess of milk in a nursing mother's breasts, which can cause swelling, hardening, heat, or pain in the breasts.

enuresis   Habitual bedwetting, usually the result of a developmental delay.

epidural   A common method of delivering anesthetic by inserting a needle into the back during labor.

episiotomy   A controlled surgical cut of the perineum to prevent it from tearing during childbirth.

expressed milk   Breast milk—drawn either manually or with a breast pump—that is stored in a refrigerator or freezer for bottle feedings.

fontanels   Two soft spots on a baby's skull where the bones have not yet fully joined. The fontanels, which provide room for the brain to grow rapidly, are located at the back of the head and on top of the head. They close as the bones of the skull mature and join (the former by around four months, the latter by two years).

formula   Commercially manufactured liquid food for infants and toddlers, available in ready-made, liquid concentrate, and powdered forms.

grants   Money given by the federal government or private organizations for college tuition. When offered by private organizations, grants are often called *scholarships*.

inhalants   Common household products—paint thinners and airplane glue, for example—that some children inhale to get "high." Inhalants can cause brain damage, kidney failure, loss of consciousness, and even death.

lochia   The discharge of excess blood, tissue, and mucus from the uterus after childbirth. The discharge gradually lightens in color, volume, and frequency, but may last for up to six weeks after childbirth.

morning sickness   Persistent nausea, often accompanied by vomiting, caused by the hormonal changes brought on by a new pregnancy. The symptoms of morning sickness can occur at any time during the day or only in response to the smell or sight of particular foods.

object constancy   The recognition that an object can disappear from sight without ceasing to exist. Object constancy comes to most babies around the fourth or fifth month.

parallel play   The characteristic play of toddlers, who may play next to each other but seldom or never actually play *with* each other. Although one toddler may imitate the other in parallel play, the two do not interact with each other.

PCA (Patient-Controlled Anesthetic)   Anesthetic, usually morphine, administered through an intravenous line, the dosage of which a patient has some control over. A machine delivers a baseline dosage of painkiller but allows the patient to press a button that delivers more when she feels pain. An anesthesiologist programs the PCA with the maximum allowable dosage, thereby preventing any possibility of an overdose.

perineum   The area between the vagina and the anus that often gets torn or surgically cut during childbirth.

post-partum   After childbirth.

psychoprophylaxis   The Lamaze method of childbirth—a series of breathing and relaxation techniques that can help women in labor work with their contractions.

sonogram   A machine that uses ultrasound waves to produce an image of the fetus inside the womb. Sonograms are used to check the size, development, and sometimes gender of a fetus, as well as the condition of organs such as the heart.

student loans   Money lent by the federal government or private financial institutions for college tuition. Repayment is usually deferred until after graduation on loans given or guaranteed by the federal government, while repayment on personal loans begins one month after the loan is granted.

swaddling   Wrapping a baby tightly in a blanket to provide a sense of warmth and security. (Most babies don't like their arms and legs waving about free and wild.)

term insurance   A cash benefit paid upon death.

toxoplasmosis   An infection, sometimes caused by organisms in cat feces, that engender few or no symptoms in a pregnant woman but that can lead to grave consequences, ranging from blindness to stillbirth, if passed on from the mother to the fetus in the womb.

trimester   Any one of three three-month periods in a pregnancy.

tympanic temperature   Body temperature obtained by pressing a special thermometer against the tympanum (ear drum).

umbilicus   The remainder of the umbilical cord after it has been clamped, cut, and tied. The umbilicus falls off (leaving the belly button) within three weeks of birth.

vernix   A white, waxy or greasy substance that protects the skin of a fetus inside the womb. Much of this coating—which may still be present at birth, especially in skin folds, around the genitals, and under the fingernails—is absorbed by a baby's skin in the first weeks of life.

Paternal Resources

Medical Information

Listed below are organizations that might offer you information or advice on health issues that might concern you as a father.

General Medical Care

American Academy of Pediatrics
141 Northwest Point Blvd.
P.O. Box 927
Elk Grove Village, IL 60009-0927
1-800-433-9016
Fax: 847-228-1281
Online: www.aap.org
Provides information and publishes brochures on children's health issues.

American Heart Association
7272 Greenville Ave.
Dallas, TX 75231
1-800-AHA-USA1
Online: www.americanheart.org
Publishes brochures on CPR, first aid, and choking.

American Podiatric Medical Association
9312 Old Georgetown Rd.
Bethesda, MD 20814
1-800-FOOTCARE
Online: www.apma.org
Publishes brochures on caring for children's feet.

American Red Cross
431 18th St., NW
Washington, DC 20006
202-737-8300
Online: www.redcross.org
Offers courses in CPR (cardiopulmonary resuscitation) for infants and children, as well as other parenting classes.

Association for the Care of Children's Health
7910 Woodmont Ave., Suite 300
Bethesda, MD 20814
1-800-808-ACCH
Fax: 301-986-4553
Online: www.acch.org
Offers publications on children's health.

International Association for Medical Assistance to Travelers
736 Center St.
Lewiston, NY 14092
716-754-4883
A network of English-speaking doctors in more than 120 countries around the world provides health tips for international travelers.

The National Association of Children's Hospitals and Related Institutions
401 Wythe St.
Alexandria, VA 21314
703-684-1355
Fax: 703-684-1589
Online: www.nachri.org
Provides information on local children's hospitals.

Pregnancy and Childbirth

American Academy of Husband-Coached Childbirth
P.O. Box 5224
Sherman Oaks, CA 91413
818-788-6662
Offers brochures on the Bradley method of natural childbirth and provides information on childbirth classes.

Lamaze International
1200 19th St., NW, Suite 300
Washington, DC 20036-2422
202-857-1128
Online: www.lamaze-childbirth.com
Provides referrals to local Lamaze childbirth classes and instructors.

International Childbirth Education Association
P.O. Box 20048
Minneapolis, MN 55420
1-800-624-4934
Online: www.icea.org
Provides referrals to local childbirth classes and instructors.

Specific Medical Conditions

American Diabetes Association
P.O. Box 25757
1660 Duke St.
Alexandria, VA 22314
1-800-DIABETES
In Virginia and Washington, DC: 703-549-1500
Fax: 703-549-6995
Online: www.diabetes.org

Asthma and Allergy Foundation
Consumer Information Line
1125 15th St., NW, Suite 502
Washington, DC 20005
1-800-7-ASTHMA
Fax: 202-466-8940
Online: www.aafa.org

Children and Adults with Attention Deficit Disorders (CH.A.D.D.)
499 NW 70th Ave., Suite 109
Plantation, FL 33317
1-800-233-4050
Fax: 301-306-7090
Online: www.chadd.org

Cystic Fibrosis Foundation
6931 Arlington Rd. #200
Bethesda, MD 20814
1-800-FIGHT-CF
Fax: 301-951-6378
Online: www.cff.org

Epilepsy Foundation of America
4351 Garden City Dr.
Landover, MD 20785
1-800-332-1000
In Maryland: 301-459-3700
Online: www.efa.org

Juvenile Diabetes Foundation
432 Park Ave. South
New York, NY 10016
1-800-223-1138
In New York City: 212-889-7575
Online: www.jdf.org

Sickle Cell Disease Association of America
200 Corporate Point, Suite 495
Culver City, CA 90230
1-800-421-8453
Fax: 310-215-3722
Online: www.sicklecelldisease.org

Terminal Illnesses

American SIDS Institute
6065 Roswell Rd., Suite 876
Atlanta, GA 30328
1-800-232-SIDS
In Georgia: 1-800-447-SIDS
Online: www.sids.org
Provides information and referrals regarding Sudden Infant Death Syndrome.

Children's Hospice International
700 Princess St., LL
Alexandria, VA 22314
1-800-24-CHILD
Fax: 703-684-0226
Online: www.chionline.org
Provides information on hospice care and resources for terminally ill children.

The Compassionate Friends
P.O. Box 3696
Oak Brook, IL 60522
630-990-0010
Online: www.compassionatefriends.org
Offers support to families who have experienced the death of a child

The Good Grief Program
Boston Medical Center
One Boston Medical Center Pl. MAT5
Boston, MA 02118
617-414-4005
Fax: 617-414-7915
Online: www.internal.bmc.org
Offers publications and resources on children's experience of mourning.

Child Safety

Consumer Product Safety Commission
Publication Request
Washington, DC 20207
1-800-638-CPSC
In Maryland: 1-800-492-8104
Fax: 301-504-0051
Online: www.cpsc.gov
Establishes and monitors safety standards for children's products; provides safety information and lists of recalled products.

The National Highway Traffic Safety Administration
400 Seventh St., SW
Washington, DC 20590
Auto Safety Hotline: 1-800-424-9393
In Washington DC: 202-426-0123
Online: www.nhtsa.dot.gov
A nonprofit group that offers information on auto safety: seat belts, child safety restraints, and so on.

The National Safe Kids Campaign
111 Michigan Ave., NW
Washington, DC 20010
202-662-0600
Online: www.safekids.org
Provides publications on child safety and childproofing.

Telephone Hot Lines

Child Help USA (National Child Abuse Hotline)
1-800-4-A-CHILD

Provides advice and help to end child abuse.

National Institute of Child Health and Human
1-800-505-CRIB

Provides publication on prevention of Sudden Infant Death Syndrome (SIDS).

National Lead Information Center
1-800-LEADFYI

Offers pamphlets on lead and lead poisoning.

1-800-424-LEAD

Online: www.epa.gov/lead

Answers questions about lead and lead poisoning.

Window Covering Safety
1-800-506-4636

Offers repair kits for window cords to prevent accidental strangulation.

General Parental Support Groups

Consumer Information Center
Dept. 606E

Pueblo, CO 81009

1-888-8-PUEBLO

Offers catalogue of federal publications free or at a very low cost on subjects of interest to fathers.

MELD (Minnesota Early Learning Design)
123 N. Third St.

Minneapolis, MN 55401

612-332-7563

Fax: 612-344-1959

Online: members.aol.com\meldctrl\

A nationwide organization of local parental support groups.

Parents Anonymous
1-800-841-4314

Provides support and assistance to parents under stress and in danger of abusing their children.

Public Affairs Information Service
381 Park Ave. South

New York, NY 10016

212-736-6629

Publishes pamphlets on parenting, marriage, and family issues.

For Dads Only

At-Home Dad Newsletter
61 Brightwood Ave.

North Andover, MA 01845

e-mail: athomedad@aol.com

Online: www.athomedad.com

Publishes quarterly newsletter with articles and tips for the stay-at-home dad; also helps set up play groups for dads and kids across the country.

Dads and Daughters
P.O. Box 3458

Duluth, MN 55803-9911

1-888-824-DADS

Online: www.dadsanddaughters.org

Offers publications, programs, and support to fathers who want to help their daughters grow up healthy, independent, and true to themselves.

The Fatherhood Project
Bank Street College of Education
610 W. 112th St.
New York, NY 10025
212-465-2044
Online: www.familiesandwork.org
Offers books, films, seminars, and training to support fathers in their parenting roles.

Minnesota Dads at Home
2451 Simpson St.
Roseville, MN 55113
651-638-9092
Online: www.slowlane.com\mdh\
Offers support for stay-at-home dads and their kids.

National Fatherhood Initiative
One Bank St., Suite 160
Gaithersburg, MD 20878
301-948-0599
1-800-790-DADS (Orders only)
Online: www.fatherhood.org
Publishes brochures and promotes the support of involved fathers.

Child Care

Bananas
6501 Telegraph Ave.
Oakland, CA 94609
510-658-7101
A child-care information and referral service.

Child Care Aware
2116 Campus Dr., SE
Rochester, MN 55904
202-393-5501
Refers callers to local agencies that can provide lists of family day-care providers and child-care centers.

Intellectual Stimulation

The American Reading Council
45 John St., Suite 811
New York, NY 10038
Provides manuals on how to encourage your children to become readers.

National Association for Gifted Children
1155 15th St., NW, Suite 1002
Washington, DC 20005
202-785-4268
Online: www.nagc.org
Advocates appropriate education for gifted children, publishes a magazine for parents of gifted children, and offers other resources.

Mail-Order Companies

Listed below are selected mail-order companies offering products for both children and parents.

Toys

Back to Basics Toys
One Memory Lane
Ridgely, MD 21685-8783
1-800-356-5360
Online: www.backtobasicstoys.com

Constructive Playthings
13201 Arrington Rd.
Grandview, MO 64030
1-800-832-0572
Online: www.ustoyco.com

F.A.O. Schwarz
3342 Melrose Ave., NW
Roanoke, VA 24017
1-800-426-8697
Online: www.faoschwarz.

365

Toys to Grow On
P.O. Box 17
Long Beach, CA 90801
1-800-542-8338
Online: www.ttgo.com

Troll Learn & Play
100 Corporate Dr.
Mahwah, NJ 07498-1053
1-800-942-0781
Online: www.learnandplay.com

Books, Music, and Videos

Chinaberry Book Service
2780 Via Orange Way, Suite B
Spring Valley, CA 91978
1-800-776-2242

Critic's Choice Video
P.O. Box 749
Itasca, IL 60143-0749
1-800-367-7765
Online: www.ccvideo.com

Gryphon House Early Childhood Book Catalog
P.O. Box 207
Beltsville, MD 20704
1-800-638-0928
Online: www.ghbooks.com

Music for Little People
P.O. Box 1460
Redway, CA 95560-1460
1-800-409-2457
Online: www.mflp.com

The Video Catalog
P.O. Box 64267
St. Paul, MN 55164-0267
1-800-733-2232
Online: www.iloveadeal.com

Clothes

Biobottoms
P.O. Box 1607
Secaucus, NJ 07094-3613
1-800-766-1254

Hanna Andersson
1010 NW Flanders
Portland, OR 97209
1-800-222-0544
Online: www.hannaAndersson.com

Olsen's Mill Direct
1641 S. Main St.
Oshkosh, WI 54901
1-800-537-4979

Equipment, Paraphernalia, and Other Products

HearthSong
1950 Waldorf, NW
Grand Rapids, MI 49550-7100
1-800-325-2502
Online: www.hearthsong.com
Offers crafts, toys, books, and music for children.

The Natural Baby Catalog
7835 Freedom Ave., NW, Suite 2
North Canton, OH 44720-6907
1-800-388-BABY
Offers everything from clothing to toys, furniture, and baby-care items.

One Step Ahead
P.O. Box 517
Lake Bluff, IL 60044
1-800-274-8440
Online: www.onestepahead.com
Specializes in baby and toddler safety items.

Perfectly Safe
7835 Freedom Ave., NW, Suite 3
North Canton, OH 44720-6907
1-800-837-KIDS
Online: www.kidsstuff.com
Specializes in childproofing products.

Practical Parenting
Dept. MB-ID
Deephaven, MN 55391
Offers a waterproof, disposable ID
bracelet for your baby (two for a dollar).

Right Start
5388 Sterling Center Dr., Unit C
Westlake Village, CA 91361
1-800-548-8531
Online: www.rightstart.com
Offers everything from health and safety
items to toys and clothes.

The Safety Zone
340 Poplar St.
Hanover, PA 17333-0019
1-800-999-3030
Specializes in childproofing products.

Sensational Beginnings
Box 2009
987 Stewart Rd.
Monroe, MI 48162
1-800-444-2147
Online: www.sb-kids.com
Offers everything from safety items to
toys, clothes, and furniture.

Index

A

abstinence, talking about sex with children, 278-279
abuse, Child Help USA (National Child Abuse Hotline), 364
ACT (American College Test), 352
ADD, Children and Adults with Attention Deficit Disorder, 362
adolescence, 336-340. *See also* teenagers
  approaching your teens, 337-338
  colleges, 349-354
    choosing a school, 352-353
    extracurricular activities (high school), 351-352
    filling out applications, 354
    SAT and ACT, 352
    school grades (high school), 350-351
  conversing with your teens, 338-340
  driving, 340-344
    accidents, 344
    designated drivers, 343-344
    rules, 342-343
  drugs, 345-349
    alcohol use, 347-348
    educating your child, 346-347
    parents as role models, 347
    pot smoking, 349
    preventing use, 345
    tobacco use (smoking), 348-349
  talking about sex, 278-279
advice organizations
  child safety, 363-364
  medical information, 361-363
AFP test, 7
afterpains, 84
alcohol, teenage use, 347-348
allergies, Asthma and Allergy Foundation, 362
American Academy of Husband-Coached Childbirth, 33, 362
American Academy of Pediatrics, 257, 361
American Association of Poison Control Centers, 198
American College Test (ACT), 352
American Diabetes Association, 362
American Heart Association, 361
American Podiatric Medical Association, 361
American Reading Council, 365
American Red Cross, 33, 361
American SIDS Institute, 363
American Society for Psychoprophylaxis in Obstetrics, 33

amniocentesis, 7, 8
aspirin, administering to children, 122
Association for the Care of Children's Health, 361
Asthma and Allergy Foundation, 362
At-Home Dad Newsletter, 364
athletics, 329-333
  coaching, 331-333
  leagues, 330-331
Attention Deficit Disorders. *See* ADD
auditory stimulation, 136-137
authority, 284-285
  consistency, 297-299
    admitting mistakes, 298
    controlling anger, 298
    explaining the rules, 298-299
  educational values, 302-304
    household chores, 303-304
    lying, 302-303
  following the rules, 288-294
    controlling behaviors, 289-290
    role reversals and modeling, 292-293
    stating rules clearly, 291
  instilling values, 299-301
  punishments, 294-297
    loss of privileges, 297
    making amends, 296-297
    spanking, 296
    time out, 295-296
  setting the limits, 285-288
    punishments, 286-287
    redirecting behaviors, 287
    understanding good vs. bad, 285-286
  time, 284-285
axillary temperatures, 121

B

babies. *See also* newborns; children
  bonding with fathers, 133-135
    auditory and visual stimulation, 136-137
    guidelines to playing, 140-143
    how to begin, 134-135
    playing, 135-144
    reading books, 143-144
    toys, 137-140
  burping, 94
  carriages, 84
  cleanliness
    baths, 111-114
    changing diapers, 107-111

crying, 91-97
  colic, 97
  how to stop it, 93-97
  interpreting what it means, 92-93
diapers,
  changing, 94, 108-111
  rashes, 110
feedings, 93-94, 101-107
  breast-feeding, 102-103
  formula, 104-105
  middle of the night feedings, 103
  solid foods, 105-107
formula, 93
handling, 98-99
  baby's bones and head, 98-99
  sudden movements, 98
heads, fontanels, 99, 120
health fears, 7-8
homecoming, preparing, 48
medical emergencies, 126-129
object constancy, 142
pacifiers, 94-95
rocking, 95
second child
  allowing your child to view birth, 237
  battling sibling rivalry, 240-244
  contacting babysitters, 236-237
  including children in the pregnancy, 234-235
  introducing children to newborns, 237-240
  maintaining stability in routine for first child, 235-236
  preparing for the arrival, 235-237
  talking with children, 233-234
  telling children about pregnancy, 232-235
sick, 118-126
  analyzing symptoms, 118-121
  going to the doctor, 121-122
  home remedies, 124-125
  medications, 125-126
sleeping, 212-219
  establishing routines, 218-219
  games to go to bed, 216-218
  hassles, 219-227
  putting to bed, 216
  relaxing activities, 214-215
swaddling, 95-96
tubs, 113-114
walkers, 138

babysitters, 237
  contacting for birth of second
    child, 236-237
  dating after childbirth, 154-155
back labor, 30
Back to Basics Toys, 365
backup plans, delivery (labor), 49
bassinets, 52, 84. *See also* cribs
baths, babies, 111-114
  fathers role, 114
  sink or baby tub baths,
    113-114
  sponge baths, 111-112
bathing supplies, babies
  (newborns), 51-53
bedtime
  hassles, 219-227
    bed sharing, 223
    bedwetting, 225-226
    midnight snack, 219-220
    night terrors, 224-225
    showing restraint, 221-222
    sleep deprivation, 226-227
    sleepwalking, 222-223
    wake-up calls, 220-221
  relaxing activities, 214-215
  sleeping routines, 213
bedwetting, 225-226
Biobottoms, 366
birth defects, 9
blinds, childproofing, 203-204
blood tests, 7
board games, 249-250
bonding, father to child, 133-135
  auditory and visual stimulation,
    136-137
  how to begin, 134-135
  playing, 135-144
  reading books, 143-144
  toys, 137-140
bonds, 188-191
bones, babies, 99
books
  reading, 262-264
    bonding with child, 143-144
    parents reading to children,
      262-263
  role modeling, 76
bottle-feeding. *See* formula;
  feedings
bottles
  microwaves (heating), 104
  nipples, cleaning, 105
Bradley childbirth method, 362
breadwinner, fathers, 65
breast-feeding, 101-107
  expressed breast-milk, 103
  fathers role, 102-103
  middle of the night feedings,
    103
breathing difficulties, 120
brochures
  child safety, 363-364
  medical information, 361-363
  parental support groups,
    364-365
burping (baby), 94

C

C-sections (Cesarean section), 31
  childbirth classes, videos, 31-32
  heavy lifting, 84-85
  insurance paperwork, 55
  post-partum recovery, 80-82
  sex after childbirth, 146-148
car seats, 51-53
card games, 249-250
cardiopulmonary resuscitation.
  See CPR
care, medical organizations,
  361-362
care providers, professionals, 50-51
carriers (baby), 53-54
cash value policy, 184
cats, toxoplasmosis, 17
CDs (certificates of deposit), college
  planning, 188-191
cell phones, 342
certifications, professional care
  providers, 50-51
Cesarean section. *See* C-section
checkups (prenatal), 21-22
Child Care Aware, 365
Child Help USA (National Child
  Abuse Hotline), 364
childbirth
  Bradley method, 362
  classes, 30-33
    benefits, 31-32
    referrals, 362
    second trimester, 32-33
  delivery room, 25-29
    labor coaching, 30
  Lamaze method, 33
  medical information, 362
  post-partum recovery, 80-83
    baby's first nights, 82-83
    caring for your partner,
      80-82
    coming home, 83-85
    heavy lifting, 84-85
    soreness, 83-84
  second child (having)
    allowing your child to view
      birth, 237
    contacting babysitters,
      236-237
    including children in the
      pregnancy, 234-235
    introducing children to
      newborns, 237-240
    preparing for the arrival,
      235-237
    talking with children about
      babies, 233-234
    telling children about
      pregnancy, 232-235
  statistics, 9
childhood, role models, 70-76
childproofing, 195-197, 202-207
  child safety locks, 197-199
  doors, 199
  electrical outlets and cords, 206

fire evacuation plans 206-207
heat sources, 205-206
improving safety, 207-209
outdoors, 207
refinishing furniture, 204-205
removing furniture and
  decorations, 200-201
safety gates, 202-203
testing your house, 209-210
wastebaskets and garbage pails,
  201-202
windows, 203-204
children. *See also* babies; newborns
  care (child)
    information and referrals,
      365
    organizations, 365
    tax deductions, 178
  death, 279-281
    grieving, 281
    questioning and answering,
      280
  discipline
    punishments, 286-287
    redirection of behaviors, 287
    understanding good and
      bad, 285-286
  doctors, information to bring,
    121-122
  foot care, American Podiatric
    Medical Association, 361
  health issues
    American Academy of
      Pediatrics, 361
    Association for the Care of
      Children's Health, 361
  hospice care, Children's Hospice
    International, 363
  hospitals, The National
    Association of Children's
    Hospitals, 362
  illnesses, 122-126
    home remedies, 124-125
    medications, 125-126
    whining, 119
  life issues, 270-272
    avoiding, 272
    giving the facts, 271
  medical emergencies, 126-129
  mourning, The Good Grief
    Program, 363
  safety
    locks, 197, 197-199
    organizations, 363-364
  school, 319-326
    crisis management, 322-324
    homework, 324-326
    preparing, 319-320
    roles of the parents, 320-322
    safety rules, 326-329
  second child, 230-231
    age differences, 231
    allowing your child to view
      birth, 237
    battling sibling rivalry,
      240-244
    contacting babysitters,
      236-237

including children in the pregnancy, 234-235
introducing children to the baby, 237-240
maintaining stability in routine for first child, 235-236
preparing for the arrival, 235-237
talking with children about babies, 233-234
telling children about the pregnancy, 232-235
sex, 272-279
  body parts, 272-273
  dealing with sex situations, 275-277
  giving factual answers, 275
  pregnancy, 273-275
  responsibility and sex, 277
sleeping, 212-219
  bed sharing, 223
  bedwetting, 225-226
  established routines, 218-219
  games to go to bed, 216-218
  hassles, 219-227
  midnight snacks, 219-220
  night terrors, 224-225
  putting to bed, 216
  relaxing activities, 214-215
  showing restraint, 221-222
  sleep deprivation, 226-227
  sleepwalking, 222-223
  wake-up calls, 220-221
sports, 329-333
  coaching, 331-333
  leagues, 330-331
teenagers, 336-340
  approaching your teen, 337-338
  college, 349-354
  conversing with your teen, 338-340
  driving, 340-344
  drugs, 345-349
Children and Adults with Attention Deficit Disorder, 362
Children's Hospice International, 363
Chinaberry Book Service, 366
choking, American Heart Association, 361
chores, 17-18, 303-304
classes
  childbirth, 30-33
    American Academy of Husband-Coached Childbirth, 362
    benefits, 31-32
    referrals, 362
    second trimester, 32-33
  CPR (cardiopulmonary resuscitation), American Red Cross, 361
  parenting, American Red Cross, 361
cleanliness (babies)
  baths, 111-114

changing diapers, 107-111
diaper rash, 110
clothes
  baby (newborns), 51-53
  costs, 178
  mail-order companies, 366
coaching
  childbirth classes, 30-33
  labor, 26-30
  sports, 331-333
colic, 97
college, 349-354. *See also* education; schools
  choosing a school, 352-353
  filling out applications, 354
  financial planning, 185-191
    current costs, 185-186
    funding options, 187-188
    projected costs, 186-187
    saving, 188-191
  funding
    federal grants, 187-191
    federal loans, 188-191
    personal loans, 188-191
    private grants, 187-191
    work-study programs, 188
  high school grades, 350-351
  SAT and ACT, 352
communicating
  death, 279-281
    grieving, 281
    questioning and answering, 280
  encouraging discussions on sex, 272-279
    body parts, 272-273
    dealing with sex situations, 275-277
    giving factual answers, 275
    pregnancy, 273-275
    responsibility and sex, 277
  goals for parenting, 162-164
    resolving conflicting goals, 164-169
    setting goals, 163
  oldest child
    contacting babysitters, 236-237
    having a baby (new sibling), 232-235
    including children in the pregnancy, 234-235
    maintaining stability in routine for first child, 235-236
    preparing for the arrival of second child, 235-237
    talking with children about babies, 233-234
  parenting roles, 170-173
    developing skills, 170-171
    sharing duties, 172
    teamwork, 172-173
    trial-and-error process, 171-172
  pregnancy, 38-39
  sex
    after childbirth, 157
    during pregnancy, 45

teenagers, 336-340
  approaching your teen, 337-338
  college, 349-354
  conversing with your teen, 338-340
  driving, 340-344
  drugs, 345-349
companies. *See* organizations
Compassionate Friends, 363
compromise, resolving conflicting parenting goals, 165-166
computers
  monitoring technology use, 260-261
  software screening, 261-262
condoms, 151
conflicts (resolving), goals for parenting, 164-169
  compromises, 165-166
  deferential treatment, 166
  distributing authority, 167
  father authority, 166-167
  flipping a coin, 168-169
  mother authority, 167
  persuasion, 165
  trial basis solution, 168
constipation, 120
Constructive Playthings, 365
Consumer Information Center, 364
Consumer Product Safety Commission, 201, 363
consumer products, babies, 51-54
Consumer Reports, Web site, 53
Consumer Reports Guide to Baby Products, 53
contractions, sexual orgasms, 42
cords, childproofing blinds, 203-204
costs
  hospital (delivery), 55
  planning (long-term), 180-185
    college, 185-191
    life insurance, 183-185
    writing a will, 181-183
  raising a child, 175-177
    analysis, 177-180
counseling
  post-partum depression, 86
  sex and marital, 148, 158
couvade syndrome, 39
CPR (cardiopulmonary resuscitation), 208-209
  American Heart Association, 361
  American Red Cross, 361
  medical emergencies, 127-128
creativity, 253-255
  artistic activities, 253-254
  fantasy play, 254-255
cribs
  baby (newborns), 51-53
crying (babies)
  colic, 97
  how to stop it, 93-97
  interpreting what it means, 91-97
  response time, 92-93
Cystic Fibrosis Foundation, 362

D

Dads and Daughters, 364
dating (after childbirth), 154-155
day care, costs, 178
deaths
    fears, 11-12
    informing your child, 270-272
    poisoning, 198
    support groups, The Compassionate Friends, 363
    talking with your child, 279-281
        grieving, 281
        questioning and answering, 280
decorations, childproofing, 200-201
delivery room, 25-29
    labor coaching, 30
    participating, 29
        cons, 27-29
        pros, 26-27
designated drivers, 343-344
desk supplies, childproofing, 201
diabetes
    American Diabetes Association, 362
    Juvenile Diabetes Foundation, 363
diapers, 89
    baby (newborns), 51-53
    changing, 94, 107-111
    rashes, 110
diaphragms, 151
diarrhea, 120
DINKs (Double Income, No Kids), 9
discipline
    admitting mistakes, 298
    authority, 284-285
        size, 284
        time, 284-285
    bribing, 287, 290
    consistency, 297-299
    controlling anger, 298
    educational values, 302-304
        household chores, 303-304
        lying, 302-303
    following the rules, 288-294
        controlling behaviors, 289-290
        explaining, 298-299
        politeness, 291-292
        role reversals and modeling, 292-293
        sharing, 293-294
    instilling values, 299-301
        knowing right from wrong, 300
        roles of the parents, 301-302
    name-calling, 295
    punishments, 294-297
        loss of privileges, 297
        making amends, 296-297
        spanking, 296
        time out, 295-296
    setting the limits, 285-288
        punishments, 286-287
        redirection of behaviors, 287

diseases, Sickle Cell Disease Association of America, 363
disorders (attention), Children and Adults with Attention Deficit Disorder, 362
doctors
    costs, 178
    illnesses
        information for appointments, 121-122
        when to take your child, 119-121
dosages, medications, 124
Double Income, No Kids. *See* DINKS
driving teenagers, 340-344
    accidents, 344
    cars, 341-342
    designated drivers, 343-344
    parent modeling, 343
    rules, 342-343
drugs
    inhalants, 344
    teenagers, 345-349
        alcohol use, 347-348
        educating your child, 346-347
        parents as role models, 347
        pot smoking, 349
        preventing use, 345
        tobacco use (smoking), 348-349
due date, 50, 58-60

E

ear thermometers, 121
education. *See also* colleges; schools
    college, 349-354
        choosing a school, 352-353
        extracurricular activities, 351-352
        filling out applications, 354
        SAT and ACT, 352
        school grades, 350-351
    costs, 178
    drug use
        parent role models, 347
        talking with your teen, 346-347
    financial planning, 185-191
        current costs, 185-186
        funding options, 187-188
        projected costs, 186-187
        saving, 188-191
    games to play with your child, 249-250
electrical outlets and cords, childproofing, 206
emergencies
    information cards, 208-209
    medical, 126-129
        communicating with partner, 38-39
        friends, 36-37
        transformation during pregnancy, 36

engorgement, 44
enuresis, bedwetting, 225
epidural, 83, 84
Epilepsy Foundation of America, 362
episiotomy, 83
expenses
    break down of raising a child, 177-179
        tax breaks, 179-180
    planning (long-term)
        life insurance, 183-185
        writing a will, 181-183
expressed breast milk, 103

F

false labor, 58-59
families
    spending time together, 306-310
        outings, 307-308
        suggestions for entertainment, 308-310
        weekend fun, 306-307
    vacations, 310-312
        accommodation reservations, 311
        flying, 312-315
        road trips, 315-316
        where to go, 310-311
Family and Medical Leave Act, 48
family bed, 223
fantasy play, 254-255
fatherhood, 4-6
    authority, 284-285
        size, 284
        time, 284-285
    baby's crying, 91-97
        colic, 97
        how to stop it, 93-97
        interpreting what it means, 92-93
    baths, 114
    bedtime hassles, 219-227
        bed sharing, 223
        bedwetting, 225-226
        midnight snack, 219-220
        night terrors, 224-225
        showing restraint, 221-222
        sleep deprivation, 226-227
        sleepwalking, 222-223
        wake-up calls, 220-221
    bonding with child, 133-135
        auditory and visual stimulation, 136-137
        guidelines to playing, 140-143
        how to begin, 134-135
        playing, 135-144
        reading books, 143-144
        toys, 137-140
    breast-feeding, 102-103
    changes (mental, financial and emotional), 12-14
    childbirth classes, 30-33
        benefits, 31-32
        second trimester, 32-33

childproofing, 195-197, 202-207
  child safety locks, 197-199
  doors, 199
  electrical outlets and cords, 206
  fire evacuation plans, 206-207
  heat sources, 205-206
  improving safety, 207-209
  outdoors, 207
  refinishing furniture, 204-205
  removing furniture and decorations, 200-201
  safety gates, 202-203
  testing your house, 209-210
  wastebaskets and garbage pails, 201-202
  what to move or remove, 197-202
  windows, 203-204
death, 279-281
  grieving, 281
  questioning and answering, 280
delivery room, 25-29
  labor coaching, 30
  participating, 26-29
discipline
  consistency, 297-299
  educational values, 302-304
  following the rules, 288-294
  instilling values, 299-301
  punishments, 294-297
  setting the limits, 285-288
family time, 306-310
  outings, 307-308
  suggestions for entertainment, 308-310
  vacations, 310-316
  weekend fun, 306-307
fears, 7-12
  baby's health, 7-8
  being replaced by the baby, 11
  death, 11-12
  doubts, 10-11
  finances, 9
  partner's health, 8-9
feeding the baby, 104-107
financial planning, 180-185
  college, 185-191
  life insurance, 183-185
  writing a will, 181-183
handling a baby, 98-99
  baby's bones, 99
  baby's head, 98-99
  sudden movements, 98
life issues, 270-272
  avoiding the issues, 272
  giving the facts, 271
medical emergencies, 126-129
monitoring technology use, 255-262
  censoring television programs, 258-259
  computers, 260-261
  downfalls of TV, 256

roles in television use, 259-260
  software screening (computers), 261-262
parenting, 162-164
  conflicting goals, 163
  goals, 162
  resolving conflicting goals, 164-169
  roles, 170-173
paternity leave, 48-50, 236
personal health (during pregnancy), 39-41
post-partum depression, 88-89
pregnancy, 21-24
  attending prenatal checkups, 21-22
  feeling the baby move, 22-24
reading, 262-264
  choosing books, 263-264
  parents reading to children, 262-263
roles of the father, 62-70
  balancing work and fatherhood, 70
  breadwinner, 65
  full-time dad (Mr. Mom), 68-69
  shared parenting responsibilities, 66-67
  societal influences, 64
sacrifices, 13-14
schools, 319-326
  crisis management, 322-324
  homework, 324-326
  preparing children, 319-320
  roles of the parents, 320-322
  safety rules, 326-329
second child, 230-231
  age differences, 231
  allowing your child to view birth, 237
  battling sibling rivalry, 240-244
  contacting babysitters, 236-237
  including children in the pregnancy, 234-235
  informing your first child, 234
  introducing children to newborns, 237-240
  maintaining stability in routine for first child, 235-236
  preparing for the arrival, 235-237
  talking with children about babies, 233-234
  telling children about the pregnancy, 232-235
  what to expect, 230-231
sex, 272-279
  body parts, 272-273
  dealing with sex situations, 275-277
  during pregnancy, 41-45
  giving factual answers, 275

pregnancy, 273-275
  responsibility and sex, 277
sick babies, 118-126
  analyzing symptoms, 118-121
  doctors, 121-122
  home remedies, 124-125
  medications, 125-126
sleeping patterns, 212-219
  bedtime routines, 213
  established routines, 218-219
  games to go to bed, 216-218
  putting to bed, 216
  relaxing activities, 214-215
sports, 329-333
  coaching, 331-333
  leagues, 330-331
storytelling, 264
support groups, 364-365
teaching your child, 245-247
  building creativity and imagination, 253-255
  playing, 246-247
  rules of playing, 250-253
  setting the curriculum, 246
  tips on toys, 247-250
teenagers, 336-340
  approaching your teen, 337-338
  college, 349-354
  conversing with your teen, 338-340
  driving, 340-344
  drugs, 345-349
traveling with newborns, 89
Fatherhood Project, 365
fathers. *See* fatherhood
fears, 7-12
  baby's health, 7-8
  being replaced by the baby, 11
  death, 11-12
  delivery room, 25-29
  discussing with partner, 12
  fatherhood doubts, 10-11
  father's role, 36-39
    communicating with partner, 38-39
    transformation during pregnancy, 36
  finances, 9
  partner's health, 8-9
sex after childbirth, 148-153
  changed perspectives, 152-153
  interruptions, 151-152
  pain, 149
  pregnancy, 150-151
federal grants, 187-191
federal loans, 188-191
feedings, 93-94
  babies, 101-107
    breast-feeding, 102-103
    formula, 104-105
    middle of the night feedings, 103
    solid foods, 105-107
  fathers roles, 104-105
  spoon feeding, 105-107

fetuses
    movement, 22-24
    music (effects of), 23
    presence, 21-24
fever, 120
finances, 6
    baby products, 51-54
    costs of a child, 175-180
    fears, 9
    parenting roles
        breadwinning father, 65
        full-time dad, 68-69
        shared responsibilities, 66-67
        societal influences, 64
    paternity leave, 48-50
    planning (long-term), 180-185
        college, 185-191
        life insurance, 183-185
        writing a will, 181-183
fires, evacuation plans, 206-207
first aid
    American Heart Association, 361
    kits, 122-126, 208-209
        home remedies, 124-125
        stocking up, 122-123
    products needed for babies, 51-53
first trimester, morning sickness,
    18-19
flex-time scheduling, 66-67
flying, family vacations, 312-315
    entertainment for children, 315
    flight reservations, 312-313
    terrors, 314-315
fontanels, baby's head, 98-99, 120
food
    baby (newborns), 51-53
    costs, 178
foot care, American Podiatric
    Medical Association, 361
foreplay, sex after childbirth,
    156-157
formula, 93, 104-105
furniture
    childproofing, 200-201
    costs, 178

G

games, 139-140
    cards or board, 249
        winning and losing, 249-250
    observing your child play,
        250-252
    roles of the father, 252
    social play, 253
garbage pails, childproofing, 201-202
gas (car)
    preparing for delivery, 57-58
    sharing the cost with your
        teem, 343
goals
    fathers during pregnancy, 40-41
    parenting, 162, 162-164
        conflicting, 163
        resolving conflicting goals,
            164-169
        setting, 163

Good Grief Program, 363
grades (high school), 350-351
grants, 187
    federal, 187-191
    private, 187-191
grieving, death, 281
Gryphon House Early Childhood
    Book Catalog, 366

H

handling babies, 98-99
    bones, 99
    head, 98-99
    sudden movements, 98
headaches, 120
heads
    baby's, 98-99
    fontanels, 99
health
    American Academy of Pediat-
        rics, 361
    Association for the Care of
        Children's Health, 361
    babies, fears, 7-8
    father's, during pregnancy, 39-41
    medical information organiza-
        tions, 361-363
    partner, fears, 8-9
    sex during pregnancy, 41-45
    tips while traveling, Interna-
        tional Association for Medical
        Assistance, 361
heat sources, childproofing,
    205-206
hormones
    changing levels after birth, 85-87
    morning sickness, 9, 18-19
hospice care, Children's Hospice
    International, 363
hospitals
    children's, The National
        Association of Children's
        Hospitals, 362
    discharges, 48
    overnight stay
        baby's first night, 82-83
        post-partum recovery, 80-82
    visiting mom after birth, 238
hostility, sibling rivalry, 241-242
hot lines, telephone, 364
house husband, 68-69
household chores, 17-18
housing costs, 178

I

illnesses, 118-126
    analyzing symptoms, 118-121
        going to the doctor, 121-122
        whining, 119
    home remedies, 124-125
    medical emergencies, 126-129
    medications, 125-126
    terminal, 363

imagination, 253-255
infections, toxoplasmosis, 17
information
    child safety, 363-364
    mail-order companies, 365-367
    medical issues, 361-363
        general care, 361-362
        pregnancy and childbirth,
            362
        specific conditions, 362-363
        terminal illnesses, 363
    parental support groups,
        364-365
inhalants, drugs, 344
insurance
    cash value policy, 184
    life, 183-185
    paperwork and information, 55
    sports certification, 332
    term, 184
intellectual stimulation, 365
intercourse. *See also* sex
    after childbirth, 146-148
        fears, 148-153
        medical clearance, 146-147
        pressures, 147-148
        setting the mood, 153-158
    sex, 274
International Association for
    Medical Assistance, 361
International Childbirth Education
    Association, 33, 362
international travel, health tips,
    361
Internet, monitoring technology
    use, 255-262
involvement, pregnancy, 16-24
    attending prenatal checkups,
        21-22
    feeling the baby move, 22-24
    first trimester, 18-19
    household chores, 17-18
    second trimester, 19
    third trimester, 20-21
IRAs (Individual Retirement
    Account), 188-191

J-K

jealousy, siblings, 241
jobs, flex-time scheduling, 66-67
Juvenile Diabetes Foundation, 363

Keogh plan, 190

L

labor, 27-29
    coaching, 26-27, 30
    delivery room, 25-29
    false, 58-59
    sexual intercourse and orgasms,
        60
Lamaze International, 362

Lamaze method. *See* childbirth
last-minute details, 54-58
  cameras or camcorders, 56-57
  gas (car), 57-58
  packing bags, 55-56
  paperwork, 55
laws, hospital discharges, 48
lead poisoning, National Lead
  Information Center, 364
leagues (sports), 330-331
life insurance, 183-185
loans, 187
  federal, 188-191
  personal , 188-191
lochia, 147
locks
  child safety, 197, 197-199
  doors, 199

M

magazines, *Sesame Street Parents*, 71
mail-order companies, 365-367
  clothes, 366
  toys, 365-366
medical care
  CPR, 127-128
  emergencies, 126-129
  information, organizations and
    resources, 361-363
medicine,
  cabinets, 122-126
  dosages, 124
  home remedies, 124-125
  stocking up, 122-123
MELD (Minnesota Early Learning
  Design), 364
microwaves, heating bottles, 104
Minnesota Dads at Home, 365
miscarriage, 41
mobiles, 53-54
money
  analysis of spending on a child,
    177-180
    break down of costs,
      177-179
    tax breaks, 179-180
  markets, college planning,
    188-191
moon, birthing odds, 59
morning sickness, 8, 9, 18-19
mothers
  overwhelming baby responsi-
    bilities, 85-89
  post-partum
    depression, 83-87
    recovery, 80-85
mourning, The Good Grief
  Program, 363
music, effects on fetuses, 23
Music for Little People, 366
mutual funds, 188-191

N

National Association of Children's
  Hospitals, 362
National Association for Gifted
  Children, 365
National Education Association, 257
National Fatherhood Initiative, 365
National Highway Traffic Safety
  Administration, 363
National Institute of Child Health
  and Human, 364
National Lead Information Center,
  364
National Parent Teacher Associa-
  tion, 257
National Safe Kids Campaign, 363
Natural Baby Catalog, 366
nausea, morning sickness, 18-19
newborns. *See also* babies
  products, 51-54
  swaddling, 83
  traveling, 89
night terrors, 224-225
nightmares, 224

O

object constancy, 142
Olsen's Mill Direct, 366
One Step Ahead, 366
organizations
  child safety, 363-364
  intellectual stimulation, 365
  mail-order companies, 365-367
  medical information, 361-363
    general care, 361-362
    pregnancy and childbirth,
      362
    specific conditions, 362-363
    terminal illnesses, 363
  parental support groups, 364-365
orgasms, contractions, 42, 156
outings, family time fun, 307-308

P

pacifiers, 53-54, 94-95
packing hospital bags, 55-56
pagers, 57-58
parallel play, 253
Parent-Teacher Association (PTA),
  321
Parent-Teacher Organization
  (PTO), 321
parental support groups, 364-365
parenting, 62-70, 162-164
  authority, 284-285
    size, 284
    time, 284-285
  baby's crying, 91-97
    colic, 97
    how to stop it, 93-97

interpreting what it means,
  92-93
balancing work and fatherhood,
  70
breadwinner role, 65
classes, American Red Cross, 361
conflicting goals with partner,
  163
death, 279-281
  grieving, 281
  questioning and answering,
    280
discipline
  consistency, 297-299
  following the rules, 288-294
  punishments, 294-297
  setting the limits, 285-288
family time, 306-310
  outings, 307-308
  vacations, 310-316
  weekend fun, 306-307
handling a baby, 98-99
  baby's head and bones,
    98-99
  sudden movements, 98
monitoring technology use,
  255-262
  computers, 260-261
  roles in television use,
    259-260
  software screening (comput-
    ers), 261-262
  television watching, 256-257
reading, 262-264
  choosing books, 263-264
  parents reading to children,
    262-263
resolving conflicting goals,
  164-169
  compromise, 165-166
  deferential treatment, 166
  distributing authority, 167
  father authority, 166-167
  flipping a coin, 168-169
  mother authority, 167
  persuasion, 165
  trial basis solution, 168
roles, 170-173
  developing skills, 170-171
  fathers, societal influences,
    64
  sharing duties, 172
  teamwork, 172-173
  trial-and-error process,
    171-172
schools, 319-326
  crisis management, 322-324
  homework, 324-326
  preparing children, 319-320
  roles of the parents, 320-322
  safety rules, 326-329
second child, 230-231
  age differences, 231
  allowing your child to view
    birth, 237
  battling sibling rivalry,
    240-244

contacting babysitters, 236-237
including children in the pregnancy, 234-235
introducing children to the newborn, 237-240
maintaining stability in routine for first child, 235-236
talking with children about babies, 233-234
telling children about the pregnancy, 232-235
what to expect, 230-231
setting goals, 163
sex, 272-279
body parts, 272-273
dealing with sex situations, 275-277
giving factual answers, 275
pregnancy, 273-275
shared responsibilities, 66-67
sports, 329-333
coaching, 331-333
leagues, 330-331
storytelling, 264
teaching your children, 245-247
building creativity and imagination, 253-255
rules of playing, 250-253
setting the curriculum, 246
tips on toys, 247-250
teenagers, 336-340
approaching your teen, 337-338
colleges, 349-354
conversing with your teen, 338-340
driving, 340-344
drugs, 345-349
Parents Anonymous, 364
parents (in-laws), assistance after delivery, 49-50
partners
discussing fears, 12
health fears, 8-9
spending time together before the baby arrives, 59-60
supporting through pregnancy, 16-21
first trimester, 18-19
household chores, 17-18
second trimester, 19
third trimester, 20-21
paternity leave, 48-50, 236
Patient-Controlled Anesthetic. PCA, 81
pediatricians, 50-51
American Academy of Pediatrics, 361
illnesses
information for appointments, 121-122
when to take your child, 119-121
Perfectly Safe, 367
perineum, 83

planning
baby's homecoming, 48
final weeks, 54-58
calling babysitters, 236-237
cameras and camcorders, 56-57
gas (cars), 57-58
packing bags, 55-56
paperwork, 55
financial (long-term), 180-185
college, 185-191
life insurance, 183-185
writing a will, 181-183
playing
bonding, 135-144
auditory and visual stimulation, 136-137
toys, 137-140
building creativity and imagination, 253-255
guidelines, 140-143
parallel, 253
teaching your child, 245-247, 250-253
exploration, 246-247
observing their play, 250-252
roles of the father, 252
setting the curriculum, 246
social play, 253
tips on toys, 247-250
podiatrics, American Podiatric Medical Association, 361
poisons
deaths, 198
what to do if your child finds, 199
post-partum, 55
depression, 83-89
counseling, 86
fathers, contributing factors, 88-89
recovery, 80-83
baby's first night, 82-83
caring for you partner, 80-82
heavy lifting, 84-85
soreness, 83-84
sex, 146-148
pot, teenage use, 349-350
Practical Parenting, 367
pregnancy
childbirth classes, 30-33
benefits, 31-32
second trimester, 32-33
delivery room, 25-30
fathers
couvade syndrome, 39-40
goals during pregnancy, 40-41
health, 39-41
role, 36-39
sacrifices, 13-14
fears, 7-12
baby's health, 7-8
being replaced by the baby, 11
death, 11-12
fatherhood doubts, 10-11

finances, 9
partner's health, 8-9
household chores, 17-18
medical information, 362
morning sickness, 18-19
partner changes, 12-14
post-partum recovery, 80-83
baby's first nights, 82-83
caring for your partner, 80-82
coming home, 83-85
heavy lifting, 84-85
soreness (mother), 83-84
second child
allowing your child to view birth, 237
contacting babysitters, 236-237
including children in the pregnancy, 234-235
informing your first child, 234
maintaining stability in routine for first child, 235-236
preparing for the arrival of second child, 235-237
sex life, 41-45
attractiveness, 43-44
communicating with partner, 45
frequency, 43
trimester obstacles, 42-43
trimesters, 17
second trimester, 19
third trimester, 20-21
prenatal classes
benefits, 31-32
second trimester, 32-33
programs, work-study, 188
psychoprophylaxis, 33
Public Affairs Information Service, 364
punishments, discipline, 286-287, 294-297
loss of privileges, 297
making amends, 296-297
spanking, 296
time out, 295-296

R

rashes, 110, 120
reading, 262-264
books, 143-144
choosing books, 263-264
parents reading to children, 262-263
recommendations, professional care providers, 50-51
rectal thermometer, 121
referrals
childbirth classes
International Childbirth Education Association, 362
Lamaze International, 362
SIDS, American SIDS Institute, 363

resources
  child safety, 363-364
  mail-order companies, 365-367
  medical information, 361-363
    general care, 361-362
    pregnancy and childbirth, 362
    specific conditions, 362-363
    terminal illnesses, 363
  parental support groups, 364-365
responsibilities
  authority, 284-285
  baths, 111-114
    sink or baby tub, 113-114
    sponge baths, 111-112
  bonding with child, 133-135
    guidelines to playing, 140-143
    how to begin, 134-135
    playing, 135-144
    reading books, 143-144
    toys, 137-140
  caring for a sick baby, 118-126
    analyzing symptoms, 118-122
    home remedies, 124-125
    medications, 125-126
  changing diapers, 107-111
  childproofing, 195-197, 202-207
    child safety locks, 197-199
    doors, 199
    electrical outlets and cords, 206
    fire evacuation plans, 206-207
    heat sources, 205-206
    outdoors, 207
    refinishing furniture, 204-205
    removing furniture and decorations, 200-201
    safety gates, 202-203
    wastebaskets and garbage pails, 201-202
    what to move or remove, 197-202
    windows, 203-204
  death, 279-281
    grieving, 281
    questioning and answering, 280
  discipline
    consistency, 297-299
    following the rules, 288-294
    punishments, 294-297
    setting the limits, 285-288
  financial planning, 180-185
    college, 185-191
    life insurance, 183-185
    writing a will, 181-183
  medical emergencies, 126-129
  monitoring technology use, 255-262
    software screening (computers), 261-262
    television watching, 256-257
  newborns, 85-89

parenting, 162-164
  conflicting goals, 163
  resolving conflicting goals, 164-169
  roles, 170-173
post-partum recovery, 80-83
  coming home, 83-85
  heavy lifting, 84-85
  soreness (mother), 83-84
reading, 262-264
  choosing books, 263-264
  parents reading to child, 262-263
schools, 319-326
  homework, 324-326
  preparing children, 319-320
  safety rules, 326-329
second child, 230-231
  battling sibling rivalry, 240-244
  contacting babysitters, 236-237
  including children in the pregnancy, 234-235
  introducing your child to the baby, 237-240
  talking with children about babies, 233-234
  what to expect, 230-231
sex, 272-279
  dealing with sex situations, 275-277
  giving factual answers, 275
  pregnancy, 273-275
shared parenting, 66-67
sports, 329-333
  coaching, 331-333
  leagues, 330-331
teaching your child, 245-247
  building creativity and imagination, 253-255
  playing, 246-247
  rules of playing, 250-253
  setting the curriculum, 246
  tips on toys, 247-250
Reyes syndrome, 122
Right Start, 367
rocking, babies, 95
roles
  discipline, 292-293
  fatherhood, 62-70
    balancing work and fatherhood, 70
    full-time dad (Mr. Mom), 68-69
    societal influences, 64
  parenting, 170-173
    developing skills, 170-171
    sharing duties, 172
    teamwork, 172-173
    trial-and-error process, 171-172
  parents at school, 320-322
  playing, 252
rules
  discipline, 288-294
    controlling behaviors, 289-290

  role reversals and modeling, 292-293
  sharing, 293-294
playing, 250-253
  observing their play, 250-252
  social play, 253
safety, 208, 326-329

S

safety
  childproofing, 196-207
    baby gates, 202-203
    child safety locks, 197-199
    doors, 199
    electrical outlets and cords, 206
    fire evacuation plans, 206-207
    heat sources, 205-206
    outdoors, 207
    refinishing furniture, 204-205
    removing furniture and decorations, 200-201
    testing your house, 209-210
    wastebaskets and garbage pails, 201-202
    windows, 203-204
  deposit boxes, storing your will, 182
  gates, staircases, 202-203
  organizations, 363-364
  schools, 326-329
  strangers, 327
  toys, 247-250
Safety Zone, 367
Scholastic Achievement Test (SAT), 352
schools, 319-326. *See also* colleges; education
  colleges, 349-354
    choosing a school, 352-353
    extracurricular activities (high school), 351-352
    filling out applications, 354
    grades (high school), 350-351
    SAT and ACT, 352
  homework, 324-326
  preparing children, 319-320
  roles of the parents, 320-322
  safety rules, 326-329
    informing of whereabouts, 328
    talking to strangers, 327-328
second trimester
  childbirth classes, 32-33
  showing, 19
seizures, 120
Sensational Beginnings, 367
sex
  after childbirth, 146-148
  contractions, 60
  during pregnancy, 41-45

encouraging discussions, 272-279
  dealing with sex situations, 275-277
  giving factual answers, 275
  pregnancy, 273-275
  responsibility and sex, 277
intercourse, talking with your child, 274
siblings
  assistance after delivery, 49, 50
  battling the rivalry, 240-244
Sickle Cell Disease Association of America, 363
sickness, 118-126
  analyzing symptoms, 118-121
    going to the doctor, 121-122
    whining, 119
  home remedies, 124-125
  medical emergencies, 126-129
SIDS (Sudden Infants Death Syndrome)
  American SIDS Institute, 363
  National Institute of Child Health and Human, 364
sleep deprivation, 226-227
sleeping
  bedtime hassles, 219-227
    bed sharing, 223
    bedwetting, 225-226
    midnight snacks, 219-220
    night terrors, 224-225
    nightmares, 224
    relaxing activities, 214-215
    sleep deprivation, 226-227
    sleepwalking, 222-223
    wake-up calls, 220-221
  patterns, 212-219
    established routines, 218-219
    games to go to bed, 216-218
    putting to bed, 216
sleepwalking, 222-223
smoking, 41
social play, 253
solid foods, spoon-feeding the baby, 105-107
sonogram, 7, 8, 22
soreness, post-partum recovery, 83-84
spanking, discipline, 296
spoon-feeding, babies, 105-107
sports, 329-333
  certification, 332
  coaching, 331-333
  leagues, 330-331
stairs (childproofing), safety gates, 202-203
strangers, safety, 327
strangulation (accidental), Window Covering Safety, 364
strollers, 53-54
Sudden Infant Death Syndrome. *See* SIDS
supporting
  groups
    death of a child, 363
    parental, 364-365

partner, 16-21
  first trimester, 18-19
  household chores, 17-18
  second trimester, 19
  third trimester, 20-21
syrup of ipecac, 199

T

taxes, child deductions, 178-180
teaching your child, 245-247
  building creativity and imagination, 253-255
  monitoring technology use, 255-262
  playing, 246-247, 250-253
    observing their play, 250-252
    social play, 253
    tips on toys, 247-250
  reading, 262-264
    choosing books, 263-264
    parents reading to children, 262-263
  setting the curriculum, 246
teenagers, 336-340. *See also* adolescence
  approaching your teen, 337-338
  colleges, 349-354
  conversing with your teen, 338-340
  driving, 340-344
    accidents, 344
    designated drivers, 343-344
    parent modeling, 343
    rules, 342-343
  drugs, 345-349
    alcohol use, 347-348
    parents as role models, 347
    pot smoking, 349
    preventing use, 345
    tobacco use (smoking), 348-349
telephones, hotlines, 364
temperatures
  axillary, 121
  tympanic, 121
term insurance, 184
terminal illnesses, resources, 363
tests
  AFP, 7
  amniocentesis, 8
  blood, 7
  SAT and ACT, 352
thermometers
  ear, 121
  rectal, 121
third trimester, 20-21
time out, discipline, 295-296
tips, purchasing toys, 247-250
tobacco
  teenage use, 348-349
toxoplasmosis, 17
toys, 139-140
  baby (newborns), 53-54
  crib gyms, 138

mail-order companies, 365-366
  tips on selection, 247-250
    educational purposes, 249
    winning and losing, 249-250
Toys to Grow On, 366
traveling
  costs of a child, 179-180
  family vacations, 310-312
    abroad, 312
    accommodation reservations, 311
    flying, 312-315
    road trips, 315-316
  health tips, International Association for Medical Assistance, 361
trimesters
  first, morning sickness, 18-19
  second
    childbirth classes, 32-33
    showing, 19
    sex, 142-145
  third, 20-21
tubs, baby (newborns), 53-54
tympanic temperatures, 121

U

ultrasound, 8
umbilicus, 112
  baths, 113-114
  sponge baths, 111-112

V

vernix, 133
Video Catalog, 366
videos, monitoring technology use, 255-262
visiting hours, introducing your child to the baby, 238
visual stimulation, babies, 136-137
vomiting, 120
  syrup of ipecac, 199

W

waiting baby's arrival, 58-60
  false labor, 58-59
  spending time with your partner, 59-60
walkers (baby), 138
weekends, family time, 306-310
  having fun, 306-307
  outings, 307-308
whining children, illnesses, 119
wills, 181-183
Window Covering Safety, 364
windows, childproofing, 203-204
work, paternity leave, 48-50
work-study programs, 188